Paradise Past

ALSO BY ROBERT W. KIRK

Pitcairn Island, the Bounty *Mutineers and Their Descendants: A History* (McFarland, 2008)

Paradise Past

The Transformation
of the South Pacific, 1520–1920

ROBERT W. KIRK

McFarland & Company, Inc., Publishers
Jefferson, North Carolina, and London

Library of Congress Cataloguing-in-Publication Data

Kirk, Robert W., 1937–
Paradise past : the transformation of the
South Pacific, 1520–1920 / Robert W. Kirk
p.   cm.
Includes bibliographical references and index.

ISBN 978-0-7864-6978-9
softcover : acid free paper ∞

1. Oceania — Colonization — History.   2. Oceania — Colonial influence.
3. Oceania — Social conditions.   4. Social change — Oceania — History.
5. Indigenous peoples — Oceania — History.   6. Indigenous
peoples — Oceania — Social conditions.   I. Title.
DU29.K57   2012   995 — dc23   2012034746

British Library cataloguing data are available

Front cover image: an engraving from *Australia: The First Hundred Years*,
by Andrew Garran, 1886, showing natives of the Gweagal tribe
opposing the arrival of Captain James Cook in 1770.

Manufactured in the United States of America

McFarland & Company, Inc., Publishers
Box 611, Jefferson, North Carolina 28640
www.mcfarlandpub.com

For Barbara, with love

Among the islands of Polynesia, no sooner are the images overturned, the temples demolished and the idolaters converted into *nominal* Christians, than disease, vice, and premature death make their appearance.... Neat villas, trim gardens, shaven lawns, spires, and cupolas arise, while the poor savage soon finds himself an interloper in the country of his fathers, and that too on the very site where he was born.

— Herman Melville, *Typee*

Table of Contents

Preface

On September 9, 1985, I received an unexpected phone call from an official of Lindblad Cruise Lines: "You and your wife are going on a six-week cruise across the Pacific." "What?" The Lindblad official explained that my professor and mentor, Robin W. Winks of the Yale University History Department (now deceased), had been slated to give a series of talks on the small expedition ship, *World Discoverer*. He was unable to fulfill his commitment and he nominated me.

This voyage was serendipitous, a dream realized. Since childhood I had read voraciously about the world's largest — and arguably most fascinating — region, the South Pacific. I had never lectured aboard ship, nor had I been to many of the small islands we were to visit. But few other people had been to these out-of-the-way places either. I secured a leave of absence from teaching, quickly read or reread forty-three books, reviewed the lecture notes I had taken in Pacific island history courses long before, and wrote notes for a series of shipboard talks. My wife Barbara and I packed for our adventure.

In early February we were off. We flew from San Francisco to Miami, then to Santiago and finally to Punta Arenas, Chile. In six weeks we sailed from Punta Arenas at the Strait of Magellan to Port Moresby, Papua New Guinea — 12,190 kilometers (7,575 miles). We visited twenty-eight islands from Tahiti, which everyone has heard of, to an obscure atoll in the Louisade Archipelago that almost nobody had heard of and whose inhabitants had never seen white people. We met Polynesians, Melanesians, and Papuans whose ancestors may have been pagans, but who embraced Christianity; most had come to an accommodation with modern culture, and the rest were trying to.

Falling in love with the South Sea Islands and their people is no trick at all. I fell this time even harder. Robin Winks's faith in my ability to interpret the history of this vast area led to my lecturing not only on the epic voyage aboard *World Discoverer* but on sixty cruises since. These have taken me to nearly every island group in the South Pacific. Having the privilege of visiting remote Pitcairn Island twice, I wrote *Pitcairn Island, the Bounty Mutineers and Their Descendants*, which McFarland published in 2008.

Then I wrote *History of the South Pacific Since 1513: A Chronicle of Australia, New Zealand, New Guinea, Polynesia, Melanesia, and Robinson Crusoe Island* (Outskirts Press, 2011). In putting together a chronological record of more than 1,300 events, it became obvious that within 400 years of Magellan's epic voyage across the ocean, a dramatic and irreversible transformation had taken place. When the idea for this book was suggested to me, jumped at the chance. What could be more exciting to study and then explain than the hesitant — and then embracing — encounter between Stone Age people and interlopers from a rapidly industrializing civilization?

Introduction

A Traumatic Transformation

A HISTORY WITH A FOCUS

This book explains how and why transformation took place by 1920 in all of the South Pacific. It is a history of transformation in Polynesia, including Hawaii in the North Pacific. This work includes Australia, Papua New Guinea, the islands of Melanesia, and islands that are in neither Polynesia nor Melanesia: Norfolk Island and the Juan Fernández Islands. Kiribati in Micronesia is included because it was included with Polynesian Ellice Islands as part of the former Gilbert and Ellice Islands British colony. Nauru, whose inhabitants are Micronesians, is included because it was a mandate and later trust territory of Australia.

This book is history with a focus. Its twenty-one chapters seek to explain how the transformation began with Magellan's voyage in 1520, and how it progressed, slowly at first, then gathering momentum from the late eighteenth century. It seeks to explain how transformation took place unevenly, changing Polynesia and Australia profoundly, but to a lesser extent — and later — some but not all Melanesian and New Guinean communities.

DIRE PREDICTIONS

By 1920, four hundred years after Ferdinand Magellan found his way into the South Pacific, indigenous communities had undergone a profound and often traumatic transformation. Populations had fallen. Some, such as the Tasmanians, became extinct. Some reached their nadir in the 1880s and 90s, while several recorded their lowest populations in the 1920s.

Historian I.C. Campbell called attention to the "apparently universal law," widely accepted in 1920, "that in the interaction of cultures and the contact of races, one race was bound to prevail, and the other to die out. Impending extinction of 'native races' seemed to be as obviously part of the natural law as was the law of gravity."[1]

By the late eighteenth century European and American mariners were reaching the South Pacific with some frequency. Three factors enabled them to come in greater numbers: First, they established communities in Australia, and in Chile, bringing European civilization to the edges of Oceania. Second, they found that citrus juice would prevent scurvy, the debilitating disease that had made corpses of myriad mariners. And third, John Harrison's development of the marine chronometer allowed navigators to chart and read bearings with accuracy. Europeans and Americans explored, traded, copulated, infected, converted, and exploited. By the mid-nineteenth century they had found virtually all Pacific islands, a feat islanders had accomplished centuries earlier.

In Polynesia peoples lost their lands, their ancient crafts, many customs, traditional beliefs, and status. As Stephen J. Kunitz stated, New Zealand and Hawaii "were settled by Europeans and Americans who dispossessed and demographically overwhelmed the indigenous people"; whereas other islands such as Samoa and Tonga "became colonial outposts with a small European population" in relation to the "numerically superior indigenous people."[2] Penetration proceeded at an uneven pace. The potentially richest islands were those of Melanesia and New Guinea. Disease and xenophobic warriors prevented access by white people to most of those places until the last half of the nineteenth century. As a result some communities in Melanesia, Papua New Guinea, and remote Polynesian atolls have been scarcely affected.

ASPECTS OF TRANSFORMATION

The great transformation had several important aspects. The most important was the cocktail of contagions that Westerners introduced. Pacific populations had no immunity, isolated from the rest of the world as they had been for thousands of years. Their sorcerers were unable to cure imported afflictions. Even Europeans were clueless about the causes of disease until medical breakthroughs that came in the later nineteenth century. In 1844, for example, the well educated, British–born schoolmaster at Pitcairn Island, George Hunn Nobbs, wrote in the *Pitcairn Island Register Book* that disease was exacerbated by weeds that "overrun the island, worms [that] infest the potatoes and there is a comet in sight." The following year, Nobbs attributed disease to "the peculiar state of the atmosphere: whenever we have been visited by this epidemic the circumstances, as respects the weather have been invariably the same. A long drought succeeded by two or three weeks of wet, and the wind settling into the north west; in fact a north west wind is always the precursor of rheumatism, catarrh, and slight febrile affection."[3] The island was visited by perhaps two dozen ships in each of those years, and crew brought disease ashore. Even the preliterate inhabitants of the Polynesian outlier Tikopia came closer to the real cause when they attributed disease to the sound of the ship's horn that heralded the arrival of missionaries.[4]

Emotional depression that resulted from the loss of tradition and culture led to inertia, illness, and fewer pregnancies. Firearms revolutionized tribal warfare, resulting in unprecedented deaths in battle. Alcohol debilitated people, causing early death and fewer children. At the time that Abraham Lincoln freed the American slaves, kidnappers from Peru, known as blackbirders, enslaved Polynesians. Some smaller islands were depopulated by Peruvians who had come to take Polynesians away to work in guano mines and fields at home.

Christian missionaries were a powerful agent of change. They undermined traditional belief and spiritual systems. Among positive developments, infanticide, human sacrifice, cannibalism, and gratuitous cruelty in some communities were either ended or minimized. Ancient *tabus* ceased to exist and new *tabus* took their place. Missionaries insisted that adherents be clothed; as a result, a need was created and people had to work in order to earn Western clothing. Natural exuberance was frowned on: singing non-religious songs, drumming, dancing, surfing, and having fun on Sunday (or any other day). Premarital sex became a new *tabu*.

In Polynesia, traditional chiefs, and in Melanesia, "big men," lost authority to missionaries and later to colonial authorities. With the coming of colonial officials, taxes replaced or were added to traditional tribute and labor that the common people had paid to their leaders.

On many islands missionaries opened schools. People were taught what seemed to them the magic of literacy. Not only were the mysteries of Christianity opened to them, but the entire extent of developed knowledge from the rest of the world became available. Some Pacific people earned school diplomas and college degrees. Some became professionals.

Metal tools revolutionized and eased work. Islanders were eager to obtain nails and hammers and axes. Although Captain James Cook never visited Rarotonga, news of the wondrous objects aboard his ship reached its shores, and pioneer missionary John Williams attributed this prayer to a chief: "O, great Tangaroa, send your large ship to our land; let us see the Cookees. Great Tangia, send us a dead sea, send us a propitious gale, to bring the far-famed Cookees to our island, to give us nails, and iron, and axes; let us see those outriggerless canoes."[5]

Iron axes and saws replaced stone implements. Metal fishhooks improved the fisherman's luck. These implements allowed islanders more leisure at the same time that missionaries were telling them that idle hands became the devil's instruments. Had Europeans simply floated crates of tools ashore, unaccompanied by disease, alcohol, firearms and notions of cultural superiority, the coming of Europeans and Americans might have been a blessing for South Pacific people.

New crops changed agriculture and lifestyles. When Europeans brought potatoes to New Zealand, for example, Maoris were able to spend less time growing food, and they obtained more nutrients. Cows and meatier pigs supplemented traditional Pacific protein sources. Yet, nutritionists have showed that a Western diet rich in sugar, salt, and fat have led to obesity, diabetes, heart disease and other ailments of "civilization."

Intending to export tropical crops on a large scale, Westerners acquired land, hired crews of workers, and introduced plantation agriculture. Trees came down and the land was plowed. Landscapes were altered and people became landless, moving to towns or working for others. As indigenous populations declined, whites were able to buy or lease even larger tracts. As islanders did not need, or desire, to labor long hours for minimal compensation, plantation owners brought in large numbers of foreign workers, many of whom stayed at the end of their periods of indenture.

Melanesians were recruited as indentured workers on plantations in Queensland and Fiji. At best, they returned with trade goods and an increased knowledge of Western society. At worst, they were abused, shorted of wages, or failed to return at all because they died. Those who did return brought with them limited experience in another culture.

In Melanesia and New Guinea new hybrid languages were introduced by which tribes with mutually unintelligible languages were able to communicate. Pijn or Bislama are examples.

Pacific islands suffered ecological damage. In the early nineteenth century traders came to the islands for sandalwood; as a result hillsides were denuded and soil erosion resulted. Rabbits and sheep overran much of Australia, and sheep dotted New Zealand's dramatic landscape. On islands rich in guano, used as high quality fertilizer, commercial interests mined intensively; Nauru, Ocean Island (Banaba), Makatea and some smaller islands had most of their surface and plants literally scraped off, rendering all or a major part of the island uninhabitable.

With the arrival in significant numbers of Europeans to Australia, New Zealand, and

New Caledonia, and Americans to Hawaii, indigenous populations found themselves marginalized and often relocated to "native preserves" and reservations. Cities grew outward and upward where a hut or two might have been.

Caucasians brought the notion of nationalism and unifying monarchy. Chiefs in Tahiti, Hawaii, Tonga, and Fiji learned that conversion to Christianity gained the support of whites. With firearms and Western ships, chiefs were able to unify their archipelagos. Descendants of the unifying leaders built Western style palaces, were crowned in Christian ceremonies, and visited their fellow monarchs in Europe.

By 1900 nearly every isle and islet belonged to a European power, Chile, or the United States. Imperial domination had grown from ideas of cultural superiority. With Westernization the lives of women were changed, many for the better. Christianity ended polygamy and killing of widows in Polynesia and parts of Melanesia. In some cultures women could eat with men, a social occasion denied them by custom. In other places, they remain subservient and continued to perform daily tasks assigned to them. An unfortunate aspect during the early contact period was the institution of prostitution, particularly among Polynesians; sex, which had been gratuitous, was bartered for trade goods or money.

Nineteen-twenty was a watershed year for at least two reasons. First, the influenza epidemic of 1918–19 had abated, and then it was time to count the dead. Second, by 1920 the imperial race was over. No island was left unclaimed, and victorious powers in the recent Great War divided up German colonies among themselves.

But our story begins four hundred years earlier with Magellan.

Chapter 1

What Magellan
Never Found, 1520–1521

THE GLOBE'S LARGEST BLANK SPACE

For Europeans in 1520, the area of the globe that we know as the Pacific Ocean was a blank. No European had the least idea what land or people or creatures were there — or if anything at all was there. Even the size of the blank was open to question. Educated people suspected that a great southern continent, called Terra Australis Incognita in Latin, must exist in the Southern Hemisphere to balance the Eurasian landmass in the Northern. Aristotle (384–322 BCE) said the continent was there, and to educated people in the sixteenth century, it must have been — if the great Aristotle said so. Perhaps the continent contained nations with developed cultures, people eager to trade valuable products with Europe. Perhaps their armies could be enlisted to fight Moslems. If the continent did, indeed, exist, its inhabitants must be in dire need of the message of God's grace and would become Christians. The largest geographical feature of our planet constituted for people of Europe in 1520 an intriguing unknown. It was the last great place to be settled by humans and the last great place to be penetrated by European voyagers.

THE PORTUGUESE FIND THEIR WAY TO THE EAST

By the early sixteenth century Europeans were forming a clearer idea of the great unknown southern sea. In 1497 Vasco da Gama (c. 1460–1524) left Lisbon with four ships manned by 170 men. He rounded the Cape of Good Hope, sailed up the east coast of Africa, and in present-day Kenya, found a willing pilot who guided his ships to the Malabar Coast of India. There, in Calicut, he traded goods for Indian luxury products, the sale of which in Europe more than paid for the cost of the voyage. Most important, da Gama had found an alternate way to the Indies. The king of Portugal's intrepid mariners had broken northern Italy's lucrative spice monopoly and sped the decline of proud Venice. Seizing the ports of Goa in India, Hormuz on the Persian Gulf, and Malacca in Malaya, Portugal set about as early as 1511 to monopolize trade in southern Asia. It even secured the grand prize — aromatic riches to be had in the Spice Islands (the Moluccas) of present-day Indonesia.[1] Joseph Conrad recalled of these intrepid traders in his novel *Lord Jim*: "For a bag of pepper they would cut each other's throats without hesitation and would forswear their souls, ... the bizarre obstinacy of that desire made them defy death in a thousand shapes, the unknown sea, the loathsome and strange diseases, wounds, captivity, hunger, pestilence, and despair. It made them great! By heavens! it made them heroic too, and it made them pathetic."[2]

Inhabitants of the Spice Islands had long been trading with Chinese and Gujaratis from western India. The so-called Spice Islands were not large. Ambon measures 775 square kilometers, or about 300 square miles. Ternate is only 76 square kilometers—29 square miles. Others are Hamahera, Seram, Bru, Tidore, and the Banda Islands. Yet, the mountainous, wet islands were at the time among the most precious pieces of real estate in the world.

MAGELLAN FINDS A PEACEFUL OCEAN

To avoid battling each other in far-flung outposts, Spain and Portugal each marked out the areas they expected to dominate. In 1494, through the mediation of Pope Alexander VI (1431–1503, r. 1492–1502), the two Iberian powers divided all non–Christian lands and seas on the face of the planet between them. The dividing line, revised in 1506, was set at 360 leagues west of the Cape Verde Islands, a league being loosely understood at the time to be the equivalent of approximately three miles. The Treaty of Tordesillas helped the two seafaring nations avoid war. Portugal would enjoy profits from Africa's steamy slave markets and—within a few years—trade routes to the east; while Spain was to be paramount in the geographically nebulous region Columbus had reached on his four voyages, the "New World."

When in 1517 the Portuguese Fernão de Magalhães (1480–1521), the navigator we know as Ferdinand Magellan, asked his king for ships to reach the Spice Islands by sailing west through a passage he was certain he could find in the Americas, Manuel the Fortunate (1469–1521) refused. Fortunate indeed, Manuel reigned from 1495 until his death, a fabulous time to benefit from his nation's monopoly. The king had no need of opening a second route, especially through an area that may be found to have been assigned by treaty to Spain. His Lisbon warehouses were already bulging with cloves, nutmeg and pepper, and he rewarded himself with the grandiose title "Lord of Guinea and of the Conquest of the Navigation and Commerce of Ethiopia, Arabia, Persia and India."[3]

For all Europeans knew, perhaps the Spice Islands lay just beyond a narrow American continent, perhaps as narrow as the 72-kilometer (45-mile) wide Isthmus of Panama, from which on September 29, 1513, Vasco Núñez de Balboa (1475–1519) became one of the first of fifty-seven Europeans to sight the Pacific from the New World. Balboa and his companions had hacked their way through snake-infested jungles for twenty-five days. Balboa named the ocean he saw the South Sea and claimed all of it and whatever lands lay within it for the king of Spain. Ironically, the great Balboa was beheaded six years later.[4]

When King Manuel rejected his offer, Magellan went to Spain to attempt to obtain funding. If the Spice Islands lay close to the west coast of a narrow American land mass, Magellan told young King Charles I (1500–58; r. 1516–56), the fragrant pieces of East Indies real estate rightfully belonged to Spain. In that expectation, the Spanish monarch furnished Magellan with five vessels, manned by 260 men. The ships that moved slowly down the Rio Guadalquivir from Seville to the Mediterranean were *Trinidad, Concepción, Victoria, San Antonio* and *Santiago*. On September 20, 1519, Magellan saw the familiar shore of Spain receding as he embarked on the first circumnavigation of the globe.

Magellan brought with him a literate Venetian nobleman, Antonio Pigafetta (c.

1491–1534); it was Pigafetta's assignment to record the events of the voyage. We learn from Pigafetta's journal that the captain general was hampered by a lack of fluency in Spanish. From the beginning, his officers and men saw the alien commander as aloof, imperious, and uncommunicative — except when delivering abrupt orders. Far worse, they suspected him to be a foreign agent disloyal to his royal master. Magellan had always to be alert for signs of mutinous behavior.

Magellan searched for and finally found a passage through the Americas. The strait ultimately named for him lies so deep in the stormy and frigid south that it was passable only in summer months. He entered the strait on All Saints Day, November 1, 1520, and named the waterway Estrecho de Todos los Santos — Strait of All Saints. Once in the strait, Magellan found it to be a complex maze that taxed his navigation skills. When he sailed out in the ocean, Pigafetta gladly recorded: "Wednesday November 28, 1520 we debouched from that strait, engulfing ourselves in the Pacific Sea."[5] Only three ships and close to 200 men entered the ocean, one ship having been lost and one having deserted to return home. Two men had been purposely marooned, and several had died.

Magellan named the ocean Mar Pacifico because he found the waters unusually calm; since then, ship passengers and crew have marveled that an ocean so tempestuous, so boisterous, could be labeled pacific. Unlike Columbus, Magellan knew where he was, but he had no idea how far he had to sail to reach the Spice Islands. Like Columbus, Magellan had relied on the accuracy of the Greek astronomer Ptolemy (89–168 CE), who estimated the size of the Earth as approximately thirty percent smaller than it actually is. Magellan and his men would soon learn, to their acute physical distress, that the Pacific covers a third of the Earth's surface. Had Magellan known it is more than twice the area of the Atlantic Ocean and is two and a half times as large as the Indian Ocean, he probably would not have attempted to transverse it.[6]

The South Pacific measures 13,200 kilometers (8,200 miles) from Chile to Australia; the ocean as a whole measures 169.2 million square kilometers (65.3 million square miles). The Pacific is, in fact, larger than all land areas on Earth combined. A second African continent could be fit into its waters with room to spare. The equator divides the North from the South Pacific; in order to sail from his strait to Guam, Magellan and his men crossed that invisible line.

On January 24, 1521, the crew sighted a Polynesian atoll, now thought to be Puka Puka. It is considered one of the atolls in the Tuamotu Archipelago, but it lies isolated, 182 kilometers (112 miles) from its nearest neighbor. Puka Puka measures about one square kilometer, or four-tenths of a square mile. Magellan sailed around the island, named it San Pablo, and continued on his course. He reported no sign of human life and no safe place to anchor. He expected to arrive in the Spice Islands within a few days.

The estimate of a few days was wildly optimistic. The long passage across meant starvation and the agony of scurvy among Magellan's men. They subsisted at last on moldy bread, sawdust, rats, and leather. Burials at sea became routine. Pigafetta recorded of scurvy victims, "The gums of both the lower and upper teeth of some of our men swelled, so that they could not eat under any circumstances."[7] Gums that felt like sponges caused teeth to loosen. Eventually teeth fell out and gums bled continually. Scurvy was the scourge of long distance voyagers, those who ate no citrus fruits or vegetables for long periods. The affliction was a deterrent for Westerners coming in great numbers for another two and half centuries, and it saved countless South Pacific people from European diseases, alcohol, and firearms.

The Death of the Noble Captain

When the emaciated crew came at long last upon Guam on March 6, 1521, after ninety-eight days at sea, they accepted life-giving food and water from the Micronesian Chamorros. The Chamorros, like many ancient Pacific people, did not share the Portuguese insistence on property rights, and they had the effrontery to make off with the captain-general's personal dinghy, perhaps as their due for the food provided. Piggafetta recorded, "The Captain General himself went ashore with 40 armed men, who burned some 40 or 50 houses together with many boats, and killed seven men." The burning and killing would be repeated uncounted times on Pacific islands in the next three and a half centuries. Magellan named Guam and two nearby islands Islas de los Ladrones—Thieves' Islands.[8]

Pigafetta, and no doubt every other man aboard the armada, took careful note of the Chamorro women. They were naked except for a thin piece of bark strategically placed. "They are beautiful and delicate, and whiter than the men, and have hair loose and flowing, very black and long, down to earth," Pigafetta wrote.[9] The crew had last seen Spanish women a year and half earlier.

Magellan, having overcome mutineers, storms, and the physical challenge of extreme hunger and thirst, then threw away his life gratuitously. Against the advice of his officers, he participated in a cause without merit or importance to his mission. Having sailed on to Cebu in the archipelago later to be named Philippines for Felipe, the heir to the Spanish crown, Magellan saw to it that the local population were baptized as Christians. The fact that the slave he had acquired on an earlier visit to Malacca, Enrique, spoke the local language fluently helped immeasurably. Magellan then rewarded his new ally, Raja Humabon of Cebu, by offering to lead sixty armed men from his ships to overcome Humabon's arch enemies, the infidels of the nearby island of Mactan; these were infidels who obstinately refused baptism. As the battle commenced, Chief Lapu Lapu's army outnumbered Magellan's forces perhaps thirty to one, and on April 27, 1521, Magellan was shot in the right leg with a poison arrow. Mactans then hacked the noble captain to death on shore. Eight other of the crew were killed and many wounded. Then, Humabon invited officers and crew to a banquet and took the opportunity to kill twenty-six.

The Survivors Complete the Circumnavigation

One hundred and fifteen of the original 260 that started from Spain sailed away gladly from Cebu. After more adventures in the Spice Islands where one of the two surviving ships was wrecked, the new commander Juan Sebastián Elcano (1486–1526), a Basque, brought the lone surviving expedition ship, *Victoria*, into Seville on September 10, 1522.[10] The *Victoria* was stuffed with 381 sacks of cloves, valued at 7,888,864 maravedis, a handsome sum for investors and the king, and with some left over for the heroes of the voyage.[11] They had sailed some 60,000 miles.

The mariners had made it a point to keep an accurate record of the passing of the days since they had left Spain; yet, the people who greeted them insisted they had miscounted. They had lost a day. The International Date Line, which runs with some deviation down latitude 180, would not be accepted until the International Meridian Conference of 1884 in Washington, DC. The eighteen survivors puzzled over their lost day.

Eighteen Europeans, emaciated and parched, had completed the first circumnavigation of the world. Or were they the first? Magellan had acquired his personal slave Enrique in Malacca on a previous voyage to the east. Enrique was fluent in the language of the people of Cebu. He was most probably a native of the Philippines, and he returned to the Philippines, having sailed from Europe. As author Luis H. Francia strongly suggests, Enrique was the first human known to have made the first circumnavigation.[12]

WHAT MAGELLAN FAILED TO FIND

Although the captain-general circled a couple of small islands he thought uninhabited, he missed some 25,000 others, most of which are south of the equator. Some 500 in the South Pacific have permanent populations. New Guinea is the largest island, while North and South Island of New Zealand are the second and third largest. Tasmania is number four, followed by several islands of Melanesia. Tahiti, a sensuous paradise, is relatively small — only a tenth the size of the "Big Island" of Hawaii, which is the seventh largest. And Magellan missed a continent: Australia.

In Polynesia, Magellan came nowhere close to New Zealand, the Cook Islands, or Easter Island. He never saw French Polynesia — including the Society Islands, the Marquesas Islands, the Gambiers, and the Austral Islands — although he probably sighted one of seventy-eight atolls in the widespread Tuamotu chain. Magellan did not see any component of the long Hawaiian archipelago. He did not explore the cradle of Polynesian culture — the Samoas and Tonga's three island clusters. Magellan did not know about the smaller Polynesian islands — Niue; the Pitcairn Islands; Wallis, Futuna, and Alofi; the atolls of Tokelau; the scattered islands of Tuvalu; or Micronesian Nauru or Kiribati.

Nobody in Magellan's armada saw Melanesia: the Fijis — all 322 of them; New Caledonia's Grand Terre and Loyaltys and Isle of Pines; the long Solomon chain; and the islands of the New Hebrides — now Vanuatu. Magellan missed the world's second largest island, New Guinea, and its numerous nearby islands, the largest of which are New Britain, New Ireland and Bougainville.

The population in the second decade of the twenty-first century of these places that he missed is about thirty-four million, the majority residing in the largest landmasses — Australia, Papua New Guinea and New Zealand.

TYPES OF PACIFIC ISLANDS

South Pacific islands differ according to their geologic origin. Continental–type islands have rock formations and resemble continents in their geology. Some large islands such as North and South Islands in New Zealand, New Guinea and Grand Terre are examples. High islands were, in most cases, formed by volcanoes. Among these are Tahiti, Hawaii, and Rarotonga. Easter Island has three dormant volcanoes. Low islands are essentially coral beds raised by tectonic activity, often twenty-five to fifty feet. Niue is an example.

Atolls are submerged volcanic peaks with built-up coral. Coral requires water temperatures of 70 degrees Fahrenheit or more to grow reefs. Polyps secrete a substance that hardens to protect their soft, hollow bodies. When they die the limestone-like substance hardens. New polyps grow on top and die, and as a result, billions of skeletons adhere in a massive form. Polyps form on the ridges of sunken volcanic cones and build up until they form a ring of coral on the surface. Rangiroa and others in the Tuamotu chain are examples. Christmas (Kirimati) Island is the largest such coral atoll in the world, with a land surface of 322 square kilometers (124 square miles); it should not be confused with another Christmas Island in the Indian Ocean. Soil is poor on coral atolls and most support only small—if any—populations. The most spectacular display of polyp architecture is Australia's Great Barrier Reef, a concentration within 2,000 kilometers (1,200 miles) by 800 kilometers (480 miles) of some 2,600 reefs.[13]

FAUNA AND FLORA

Before people arrived, plant and animal life from Southeast Asia and New Guinea found their way to South Pacific islands. Microscopic spores were wafted by winds. Seeds floated to shore and found sustenance in island soil or rock crevices. Seeds were eaten by sea birds, digested, and deposited on islands, where some took root. Seeds adhered to birds and birds transported seeds to islands. Beyond that explanation lies a puzzle, that of the presence of the sweet potato—kumara—a South American plant. Historian K. R. Howe suggests that humans must have brought kumara from South America.[14] These humans were likely competent seafarers; Polynesians answer that description more closely than do indigenous people of South America.

The western islands are rich in fauna and flora, as they are closer to Asia. New Caledonia, for example, has 3,500 species of plant life, but Easter Island, which is in the eastern Pacific, far removed from Asia, has fewer than 50.[15]

PACIFIC ISLAND PEOPLE

Diverse indigenous cultures inhabit the South Pacific. The differences between societies in Polynesia, Melanesia, New Guinea and that of Australia's Aborigines become manifest when one examines them. Aborigines, Papuans, and Austronesians are the original people of Oceania. Papuans live in Papua New Guinea. Austronesians inhabit Polynesia, Melanesia and Micronesia; the term *Oceania* includes these three "nesias." In 1831 Pacific explorer Jules Dumont D'Urville wrote a paper for the *Bulletin de la Societé de Geographie* in Paris in which he divided Pacific islands and their indigenous inhabitants into three groups: Melanesians (black islands), Polynesians (many islands), and Micronesians (small islands), forming the designations from the Greek. He gave a speech in Paris to the Societé explaining his division. This general grouping has been broadly accepted.[16]

Melanesians populate large island groups that include New Caledonia, Vanuatu, Fiji, the Solomon Islands, and parts of Papua New Guinea. Polynesia's islands are nearly contained within an imperfect triangle whose corners are the Hawaiian Islands, New Zealand and Easter Island: some outliers such as Tikopia and Otong Java fall outside of these map lines. Micronesian islands are north of the Equator and include Guam, the Marianas, the Carolines, Palau, Kiribati, and the Marshall Islands.

Oceanic people are classified not only by physical characteristics but by language. Austronesians speak languages of the Maylayo-Polynesian language family. Maylayo-Polynesian speakers include not only those of Pacific islands, but also Indonesians, Malaya, Filipinos, indigenous Taiwanese, and even people of Madagascar off the east coast of Africa.

"Pacific People" by G. Mützel. (1) Fiji, (2) Tasmania, (3) South Australia, (4) Maori, (5) New Britain, (6) Samoa, (7) Buka, (8) Ponape, (9) Admiralty Islands, (10) Tonga, (11) New Ireland, (12) Samoa, (13 and 14) Marshall Islands. Note that the people of numbers 5–9 and 11–14 were German colonial subjects. From *Brockhaus Konversations-Lexikon* (Leipzig, 1892).

Papuan languages are not related to Austronesian languages. Papuan languages are spoken in Papua New Guinea, including the Bismarck Archipelago and some Solomon Islands; in the Indonesian provinces of Papua and West Irian Jaya; and in some Indonesian Islands. There are perhaps eight hundred Papuan languages, divided by some linguists into as many as sixty families. Aborigine languages are related to neither Papuan nor Austronesian. Nobody knows for certain how many pre-contact indigenous languages were spoken in Australia, but there may have been as many as 750 languages and dialects. Today there are probably fewer than 200.[17]

INTREPID ANCIENT MARINERS

Scientists tell us that Australia was probably settled fifty or maybe even seventy thousand years ago during the last Ice Age, when seas were lower and immigrants could cross from the East Indies across narrow bodies of water. Then, about 10,000 years ago the ice melted, the seas rose, and Australians were left by themselves to develop their Stone Age culture.

Papuans came to New Guinea thirty thousand or more years ago from Southeast Asia. Papuans were among the earliest people to develop agriculture.

Melanesians came through New Guinea and its islands and settled as far as New Caledonia 4,000 years ago. Thirty-five hundred years ago they were in Fiji.[18]

As late as 1920, learned people puzzled over origins of Pacific islanders. Writer J.P. Thompson wrote in 1921: "In the writer's view there can be no doubt that the islands of Polynesia were originally peopled by Phoenicians whose migratory influence extended to the coast of Peru. This theory is strongly supported by the presence of numerous cyclopean monuments, huge monolithic statues, paved avenues." Thompson was unimpressed by Pacific people he saw. He stated: "It is evident that none of present races could erect such immense structures as these."[19]

According to DNA and linguistic evidence, the inhabitants of the Polynesian islands originated among ancient people of Taiwan. These early Taiwanese came from southern China about 8,000 years ago. These proto–Polynesians made their way into the Pacific, settling Tonga and Fiji around 1300 BCE, or over three millennia ago, and Samoa by 1000 BCE. Polynesian voyages rank among the greatest achievements of humans. These Neolithic people reached and settled distant islands hundreds of years ago without modern navigation tools. The Polynesian "triangle" is as large as Africa, so to imagine the length of some monumental voyages, imagine sailing the distance from Capetown to Nairobi or Lagos to Zanzibar.

After a long period of undisturbed incubation, Tongans and Samoans, in frequent contact with Fijians, had developed a sophisticated society. They colonized other islands including the Marquesas by about 300 CE. Scholars continue to debate the reasons they left home on long colonizing voyages, but overpopulation on finite bits of land was probably a motive. The Marquesas may have been a jumping off point from which Polynesian navigators went to Easter Island, the Society Islands, New Zealand and Hawaii. When they desired to establish a distant colony, perhaps a small party was sent off in a canoe to find habitable islands. They would take a supply of food and water with them. When they had consumed half the food, they would return home — unless, of course, they could see an island that might sustain them. When they found an island suitable for colonization, they would return home, and colonists would set out with everything they would need for a new life. Navigating by stars, they could return. After a far distant island was located by a search party — a prodigious feat in itself ranking with the greatest accomplishments of mankind — double-hulled canoes would bring a company of colonists, seeds, chickens, pigs, rats, tools, and all of the possessions that would be needed for a brave new insular world. Females of child-bearing age, babies and children would go to assure subsequent generations in the their new world.[20] Subsequent generations in these island colonies would memorize their descent from voyagers in their tribe's founding canoe, much as Americans might establish genetic connection to people aboard the *Mayflower*, or Australians with passengers on the First Fleet.

Even the prodigious feats of memorization accomplished by Polynesians cannot give us definitive dates for settlement of their islands, for battles, for tsunamis, or births and deaths of their own towering, godlike ancestral figures. We cannot be certain about events, even the most important, before Europeans kept written records in the early sixteenth century. For purposes of this study, the statement of historian I.C. Campbell will suffice: "By about 800 A.D., all the habitable land in the eastern Pacific had been found and occupied."[21]

HIGHLY DEVELOPED CULTURES

At the time of European contact, Papuans and Austronesians (Melanesians, Polynesians and Micronesians) had traits in common. People of these cultures kept gardens for food. All of them domesticated animals such as dogs, pigs and chickens. Many built fish ponds and traps in lagoons. All had advanced to a Neolithic stage of technological development, which included grinding rather than chipping stone; using seashells as ornaments and cutting tools; and working with adz blades to produce ornaments, images, tools, and weapons from wood and stone. All used fibers and barks to produce decoration, vessels, blankets, and sails. Those in cold climates such as New Zealand produced warm clothing; other tribes wore minimal — if any — apparel.

So far as is known these cul-

Thatched hut, Vanikolo Island. Solomon Islanders for centuries had mastered construction arts using materials available to them. The inhabitants of Vanikolo are citizens of the Solomon Islands. Photograph by Robert Kirk.

tures had little or no contact with Southeast Asia after their initial migrations were completed. They eventually lost contact with distant communities in which the same language had once been spoken. Hawaiians were surprised that Marquesans existed or that very distant cousins inhabited New Zealand. Easter Islanders were surprised that they were not the only people in the world. These isolated communities developed unique cultures using the materials available to them. Oceanic people did not use the wheel or writing, nor did they enjoy the services of beasts of burden. They did not have iron, and when Europeans arrived with firearms, they were unable to resist conquest or penetration.

Most importantly, South Pacific people had never been exposed to diseases to which people in the Eurasian-African land mass had developed some immunity. It is this lack of immunity that has had the greatest impact on the people of the South Pacific in the last 500 years. Disease was the major cause of the transformation of South Pacific people and culture. Magellan's voyage proved that the Pacific was a new frontier that could be approached from the Atlantic Ocean. In their American empire Spaniards built ports on the Pacific. Yet several decades passed before Spaniards came to claim their vast watery prize.

Chapter 2

Spaniards Explore
Their Lake, 1568–1793

SPAIN BUILDS AN EMPIRE

Spain's rulers claimed the Pacific Ocean — all of it. The Spaniards based their claim on Balboa's sighting of the South Sea, on the pope's division of the world by the Treaty of Tordesillas, and of course, Magellan's crossing. Spain's efforts to make good its claim south of the equator were late, desultory and unsuccessful. Madrid had other claims, far more lucrative and more easily accessible.

Christopher Columbus (1451–1508) laid the foundation for Spain's golden age. On October 12, 1492, Columbus landed in the Bahamas after a thirty-three-day voyage from the Canary Islands. He had asked King Ferdinand (1452–1516) and Queen Isabella (1451–1504) for ships and crew to sail to Asia by proceeding west. Columbus left three months after the Moors had been pushed out of Granada, ending a western crusade that Spanish Christians had pursued since the eighth century. Their Catholic Majesties found their coffers empty at the end of the ordeal, but their people were filled with pride and crusading spirit. Adventurous young men were eager for new challenges, for glory, and for riches. Like Magellan, Columbus thought the circumference of the earth was smaller than it was; he, too, had believed the estimate of the Greek mathematician Ptolemy, who worked in Alexandria from 127 to 145 CE.

Columbus's royal sponsors had agreed to send him to Asia for three purposes: to find sources of rich trade, to form alliances against the Moslems so Spain could continue the crusade, and to convert Asians to Catholicism. Columbus accomplished none of these goals. The great man returned with meager souvenirs of his trip: parrots, hammocks, some exotic plants and frightened, shivering indigenous people he erroneously called Indians. Yet, his landfall was serendipitous for Spain. Within sixty years a huge land mass and millions of people in South, Central and North America and the Caribbean became, at least nominally, subjects of his Most Catholic Majesty Charles I, grandson and heir of Ferdinand and Isabella.

By 1521 Hernando Cortés (1485–1547) had subjugated the mighty Aztec Empire. Then, in 1533, Francisco Pizarro (1478–1541) claimed victory over the Incas of eastern South America and their nine million subjects linked to the capital by an ingenious two-thousand-mile road system. The royal coffers glittered with bullion as Spanish galleons traversed the Atlantic filled with treasures that had decorated the halls of Montezuma. After the confiscated treasures had been spent fighting Protestants, the indigenous people were put to work finding gold in streambeds. After that the Spaniards enslaved them to mine for silver in Mexico. At San Luis Potosí in Bolivia Spaniards exploited a mountain filled with silver.[1]

The Native Americans, enslaved or not, died in great numbers, having no immunity to European diseases.

THE RETURN OF SEBASTIAN ELCANO

The next Spanish voyage in the Pacific took place only four years after the *Victoria*'s circumnavigation. Having failed to lose his life on Magellan's expedition, Juan Sebastián Elcano set off again on July 24, 1525. Seven ships left Corona, Spain, bound for the Spice Islands by the Strait of Magellan. Garcia de Loaisa (1490–1526) was commander and Elcano was chief pilot. The voyage was a disaster of unremitting hardship and death. Of the seven ships, only *Santa Maria de la Victoria,* under the command of Andres de Urdaneta (1498–1568), reached the Spice Islands. Fiercely protective of the monopoly they were putting together, the Portuguese imprisoned the two dozen survivors. Urdaneta and seven others were eventually repatriated to Spain. Both Loaisa and Elcano died of scurvy during the journey.[2]

DESTINATION PHILIPPINES

In 1529 under the Treaty of Zaragoza, Spain relinquished to Portugal any claim to the Spice Islands. Spain's principal voyages after that would be in the North Pacific, with the Philippines as their destination. Instead of threading their way through the treacherous straits at the tip of South America, they would sail from ports on Mexico's west coast. The establishment of Spanish outposts on Pacific shores of the New World brought Europe with its diseases and firearms perilously close to Oceanic communities.

Alvaro de Saavedra (?–1529) headed an expedition of three ships from Mexico in 1527. He was instructed to apologize to the ruler of Cebu for Magellan's aggression and seek to free any of Magellan's crew held captive. Unable to locate Cebu, he sailed to the Spice Islands, where the irate Portuguese interned him and his men for violation of treaty terms and for transgressing in forbidden waters. When the Portuguese released the Spaniards, a single ship sailed back to Mexico. Saavedra died on the way.

Ruy López de Villalobos (c. 1500–1546) commanded the next expedition to the Philippines. Villalobos left from Navidad, in Jalisco state, 80 kilometers (48 miles) north of Manzanillo, Mexico, on November 1, 1542. The six ships and 370 men arrived at the coast of the large southern island of Mindanao. Villalobos named the archipelago for the son and heir of Spain's Charles I, Felipe. Felipe would become Phillip II (1527–98; r. 1556–98). Unable to obtain food at Mindanao, the Spaniards sailed for the Spice Islands. The Portuguese held them captive on Tidore as unwanted intruders.[3]

ORTIZ DE RETES NAMES NEW GUINEA

Villalobos sent Yñigo Ortiz de Retes back to New Spain (Mexico) on the ship *San Juan de Letran* to seek help. Ortiz left Tidore, and on June 20, 1545, reached the Mamberamo River on the world's second largest island. He named the island Nueva Guinea because the inhabitants reminded him of those of West Africa's Guinea coast. He claimed the island for Spain's king.[4] Ortiz was not the first European to find New Guinea. In 1526 Portuguese mariner Jorge de Meneses landed on the Vogelkop Peninsula. He came into contact with some of the dark-skinned inhabitants and named the island Ilhas dos Papuas from the Malay word *pupuwah*, meaning "fuzzy hair." Papua is the southeastern part of the great island.[5] In spite of these first contacts, Europeans would not seek to dominate New Guinea until the nineteenth century. Mosquitoes allied with the fierce inhabitants to protect their islands.

RIDING THE JAPAN CURRENT TO MANILA

The next transpacific expedition was launched two decades later. Miguel López de Legaspi (1510–72), commanding five ships, left Navidad on November 21, 1564, and reached Samar, Philippines, on February 13, 1565. The principal achievement of the expedition was to find an Asia-to-America crossing by sailing with the Japan Current north of Hawaii to the coast of California, and then following the coast southward to Mexico. Manila galleons used this faster route from Acapulco on their biennial voyages, ending only 1815.

The Manila galleons from Mexico had little or no effect on the people of the South Pacific. Rather, it was Spanish from South American ports who would explore that area and begin a long-term transformation. Valparaiso and Callao were the most important ports for exploration. In 1536 Spanish explorer Don Juan Saavedra (1501–72) founded the port city of Valparaiso, Chile. He named Santiago's closest port after a city in Cuenca, Spain.[6] In 1536 Spaniards founded the port city of Callao, Peru, 14 kilometers (8.7 miles) from Lima. The port was important as a shipping point for goods and treasures brought overland to be sent to Spain.[7]

MENDAÑA'S FIRST PACIFIC VOYAGE

The most important explorer to sail out from Callao was Alvaro de Mendaña (1542–95), age twenty-five, nephew of the viceroy of Peru. Mendaña was commissioned by his uncle to search for Terra Australis Incognita, believed by some in Peru to be the original homeland of the Incas. Mendaña's ships *Los Reyes*, 250 tons, and *Todos Santos*, 107 tons, held between them 150 men, including about 80 indigenous Peruvians brought along to perform labor. Mendaña was to establish a colony on the great southern continent and send a ship back for more colonists. They sailed on November 20, 1567, and somehow managed to make their way between the Tuamotu Archipelago and the Marquesas Islands without seeing any land. On February 9, 1568, they arrived at the Solomon Islands. They were famished and thirsty after sailing two and a half months. They named the large island Santa Isabel. Like Magellan and his crew, Mendaña and his men littered the shores with islanders' corpses. The Spaniards demanded food and they shot islanders when they did not deliver immediately. The islanders were reluctant to trade because they did not have surplus food. Seeking to please with a delicacy, they offered the visitors a quarter of a boy, garnished with taro; the Christians gave the body fragment a suitable burial.

At Guadalcanal, Spaniards sent a watering party ashore; islanders killed nine men, so the Spaniards burned all the villages they came across and slaughtered the inhabitants. When islanders approached the ship with a peace offering of a pig, Spaniards slaughtered

Santa Ana warriors. These ceremonial warriors are staging a traditional ceremony for visitors. Warriors on tiny Santa Ana, just off the south coast of San Cristobal in the southern Solomon Islands, had long fought a rival tribe on the island and tribes on nearby islands. War was caused by a murder, a stolen woman or pig, or an ancient grudge. Photograph by Robert Kirk.

the peace party and ate the pig. On the island of Ulawa they murdered twelve villagers of both sexes. On San Cristóbal the Christians stole food from the local tribe while they careened their ships to prepare for the return voyage to Peru. Handicapped by not being able to speak the local languages, the priests failed to convert any islanders to the Roman Catholic faith.

The two ships sailed on August 11, 1568. During six months in these malarial islands some Spaniards and Peruvians had died. It is unclear to what extent foreign contagion was spread among the Solomon Islanders. The Mendaña expedition found no South Pacific islands on the way back, but passed the Gilberts and Marshalls in Micronesia, and Wake Island. The crews underwent excruciating hunger, thirst, and scurvy. The emaciated survivors reached Callao on September 11, 1569.

When an official in the viceroy's office wrote a report for King Phillip II, he named the group the Solomon Islands, evoking the riches of the biblical ruler's fabled mines.[8] The name notwithstanding, Mendaña failed to find there the bullion or precious stones he sought.

No European located the Solomon Islands again for two centuries.

JUAN FERNÁNDEZ FINDS HIS ISLANDS

During most of the last three decades of the sixteenth century the king spent Spain's considerable riches on fighting Protestants in the Netherlands. Phillip had inherited seventeen provinces, but the ten that became the Netherlands were intent on breaking away. Due to mounting public debt, Philip was reluctant to spend money on Pacific exploration. Under the circumstances, the only significant Spanish discovery was an island group 420 kilometers (260 miles) from Valparaiso, Chile. On November 22, 1574, a sailor from Santiago, Chile, named Juan Fernández found three islands that were subsequently named for him. The islands were uninhabited and though in the eastern South Pacific are not considered part of Polynesia. The largest, Más a Tierra ("Closer to Land") is 140 square kilometers (36 square miles). Alexander Selkirk was marooned there from 1704 to 1709 and his story inspired Daniel Defoe's novel *Robinson Crusoe*. The other two islands, with no permanent settlement, are Isla Más a Fuera ("Farther from Land"), and Isla Santa Clara. The three total 182 square kilometers (70 square miles). The volcanic landscape of Más a Tierra, now called Robinson Crusoe Island, hosts 142 indigenous plants, two-thirds of which are not found elsewhere.[9]

MENDAÑA'S SECOND VOYAGE

Patiently, Mendaña waited and petitioned to be given a commission to establish a Spanish colony in the Solomons. At last, he convinced Spanish authorities to invest in a voyage that might return with significant gold and silver or spices. But now he was fifty-three years old. On April 9, 1595, Mendaña left Callao for the South Pacific a second time. This time he commanded four ships, transporting 378 crewmen and aspiring colonists. These included a hundred women and some children. One of the female passengers was his wife Doña Ysabel, accompanied by her family and servants.

On July 21, Mendaña's crew sighted Tahuata, an island in a group he named Las Islas Marquesas de Mendoza for the wife of the viceroy of Peru. The Marquesas number ten islands, totaling 1,049 square kilometers (485 square miles). They are nine degrees south of the equator and hotter than Tahiti. These high islands are protected from the sea by cliffs, and are cut into by valleys that tilt up to high ridges. Mendaña's arrival made the Marquesas the first major Polynesian group to be found by Europeans. Mendaña noted that Marquesans were tall, graceful, well built, and naked with elaborate blue tattoos. The islands look like paradise, but they were scenes of frequent terror during ongoing tribal warfare.

When Mendaña anchored, forty tribesmen came aboard with gifts of fruit and water. When a Spaniard fired a gun, they were startled and jumped overboard. Spaniards shot seven swimming in the water to maintain, as one explained, skill with firearms. The next day on Tahuata, Spaniards opened fire on canoes full of islanders who had come to greet the ship. A soldier boasted that he had killed a man and child with a single shot. A few days later the Tahuatans tried again, bringing fruit and water to the Spaniards. Spaniards shot several for trying to take glass jars. The Spaniards then raised crosses on the land and their priests celebrated mass. When Marquesans tried to bring two canoe loads of coconuts to the ships, half the people on the boats were killed and three bodies hung in the rigging as a warning.

During their two-week stay, the Spanish marksmen shot, by their own estimate, 200 Marquesans. The pilot, Pedro de Quirós (1565–1614), lamented that Marquesans and Spaniards failed to understand one another. "How often is their term savage incorrectly applied!" author Herman Melville remarked 250 years later.[10] The transformation of the Marquesas, tragic in its consequences over the centuries for the inhabitants, had begun.

Children on Vanikolo (also Vanikoro), Santa Cruz Islands. These children may well be descendants of the Vanikolo cannibals who killed crewmembers of the La Pérouse expedition in 1788. The survivors sailed off in a small boat, never to be seen. In 1826 trader Peter Dillon solved the mystery of the lost crew when he was shown artifacts from La Pérouse's ships. He was given a large pension for life by French king Charles X. Photograph Robert Kirk.

The flotilla sailed on to Melanesia. Mendaña was the first European commander to arrive in the Santa Cruz Islands, now a province of the Solomon Islands, but separated from them by 400 kilometers (240 miles) of sea. The date was September 7, 1595. He had not intended to visit these small islands. He had intended to colonize one of the principal Solomons, but he was unable to find them again.

After shooting a few Santa Cruz islanders who had approached in canoes, the Spaniards traded playing cards, cloth and beads with the survivors for food. The Spaniards tried to build a settlement at Graciosa Bay on Ndeni, which Mendaña named Santa Cruz. Ndeni (Nendo) measures 505 square kilometers (197 square miles), the largest of the Santa Cruz group. A peak rises to 517 meters (more than 1,700 feet).

At Ndeni everything went wrong for the Spaniards. The crew revolted and the commander had some of the rebels executed. Then Mendaña died of malaria. Some of the crews and passengers were ill with malaria and forty-seven died. Doña Ysabel, whom historian Ernest S. Dodge described as "an arrogant, powerful, bitchy woman of particularly unfeeling ruthlessness," assumed command of the young colony.[11] The Spainards were then attacked by islanders and had difficulty defending themselves because their powder was wet from unrelenting rain and they were weakened by disease.

Establishing a colony at the Santa Cruz group seemed a bad idea at that point. Doña Ysabel ordered all three ships to sail for Manila. The Spanish had established Manila on Luzon in 1571 as an outpost. Two of the ships sank en route due to rot. Sails of the surviving ship, the *San Jerónimo*, disintegrated. The awful voyage took 96 days, during which the starving crew ate handfuls of moldy flour with rainwater. Doña Ysabel enjoyed ample food, which she declined to share except among her relatives. She used lifesaving fresh water to wash her clothes. Women and children died of thirst, and corpses were committed to the sea each day. In desperation, crew members and passengers begged the ship's new master, the Portuguese Pedro de Quirós (1565–1614), to sink the ship and end their misery. The crew that arrived at Manila on February 11, 1596, were described as ragged, fever-ridden skeletons.

The widow Mendaña then married a Spanish official and demanded that Quirós return her and her husband to America. Quirós brought the *San Jerónimo* and its survivors across the North Pacific to Acapulco on December 11, 1596, after sailing four months. This second Spanish attempt to discover a nonexistent continent, found a colony in Melanesia, find gold, and convert islanders to Christianity was a failure. It had left yet another trail of blood in Polynesia and Melanesia.[12]

DE QUIRÓS FINDS ESPIRITU SANTO

Spain continued to explore the ocean it claimed in the early part of the seventeenth century. De Quirós was unable to convince Spanish authorities in Lima or King Philip III (1528–1621, r. 1598–1621) in Spain to fund another voyage. Obstinately, Quirós refused to take no for an answer and went over the head of his monarch. In 1601, Quirós traveled to Rome and convinced Pope Clement VIII (1636–1605, r. 1592–1605) that if he were sent back to the South Pacific, he could save souls for Christ and expand the Christian realm. Pope Clement wrote a compelling letter to the king recommending the project.

On December 21, 1605, Quirós sailed from Callao, Peru, in command of three ships, *San Pedro y Paulo, San Pedríco,* and *Los Tres Reyes.* Aboard were three hundred sailors and soldiers and ten priests. No women sailed with them this time. Intending to leave an outpost in the Solomons, he brought farm animals, seeds and farm implements.

After a voyage of over four months, on April 29, 1606, Quirós found the Melanesian island he named Espiritu Santo (Holy Ghost), one of eighty islands in what is today Vanuatu (formerly the New Hebrides). Mountainous, it measures 4,700 square kilometers (1,420 square miles). Quirós thought he had found Terra Australis Incognita. Islanders brought fruit to the Spaniards as a gift, but drew a line in the sand and made it clear no Spaniard was to advance across it. When defiant Spaniards crossed the line, they were greeted by a volley of arrows. "In payment for this audacity and evil intention," wrote a Spanish chronicler, "our people killed some of them, including the king." When a Spanish party advanced inland, islanders tried to stop them, but "the trees and leaves impeded the flight of arrows, ... but with bullets the branches made little difference."[13]

After killing a number of islanders the Spaniards celebrated a mass near the river de Quirós named the Jordan. The Spaniards seized what food they wanted, kidnapped young boys, shot indigenous people, and returned to their ships "joyful and contented at the good success of that day," as the ship's chronicler recorded.[14]

De Quirós learned he had not found a continent, and he was unable to locate either the Solomons or the Santa Cruz Islands. Having found no gold and having left behind them no converts on Espiritu Santo, the Spaniards returned to Acapulco. The journey back took four months.

Quirós then crossed Mexico and made his way to Spain. Quirós told King Philip III that the people he discovered "have not the arts, great or small, walls or forts, king nor law, nor are they but the most simple gentiles, divided into clans, and are little friends among themselves. Their arms are lances and darts of wood, clubs and bows and arrows without poison. They cover their obscene parts. They are clean, cheerful, sensible, and very grateful, as I have experienced."[15] He told the king that Espiritu Santo had abundant gold, as well as silver, pearls, and spices. Moreover, he said the "continent" was filled with riches for the taking and people eager to be converted. Convinced by this fabrication, the king financed another expedition, but Quirós died en route from Spain to Peru before he could lead it.[16]

Pedro Fernandes de Quirós's pilot, Luís Vaez de Torres (1565–1607), had separated from Quirós's ships and sailed the *San Pedrico* along the southern coast of New Guinea. In 1606 he located and was the first European commander known to have passed through Torres Strait. In 1770 geographer Alexander Dalrymple (1737–1808) named the strait, separating New Guinea from Australia, in his honor. The strait would be included in a regular European maritime route to the South Seas.[17]

Although Spanish mariners had located three groups of islands—the Marquesas, Solomons, and Vanuatu—they ceased explorations in the Pacific for a century and a half. During that time Madrid sought to defend American colonies from pirates and other European marauders.

THE VULNERABLE JUAN FERNÁNDEZ ISLANDS

Spain had to prevent enemies from using the Juan Fernández Islands as a base from which to attack her west coast ports. Food, water and wood on the uninhabited islands made them an ideal way station between the Strait of Magellan and the Polynesian islands. The islands offered life-giving sustenance to scurvy-wracked crews including English buccaneers.

In 1680 the crew of a pirate ship under command of Bartholomew Sharp had crossed the Isthmus of Panama on foot and captured Spanish ships on the Pacific coast. While in Central America they either forced or enticed a Mosquito Indian to work aboard the ship. They named him Will. The marauders raided and burned Spanish settlements in surprise attacks, sailing off aboard a captured vessel, renamed *The Trinity*, with five hundred pounds of silver. To find fresh food and water, they stopped at Más a Tierra. When three Spanish warships arrived, they made a hasty getaway, inadvertently leaving Will on the island. For three years Will was Más a Tierra's sole inhabitant.

On March 22, 1684, William Dampier (1651–1715), pirate and journalist, arrived aboard a captured ship, renamed *Bachelor's Delight*, under command of pirate John Cook. Cook died at seas shortly after leaving the island. Will was overjoyed to be rescued and was convinced the crew had sailed there with the singular purpose of bringing him away. Will was probably the inspiration for Daniel Defoe's Man Friday in his novel *Robinson Crusoe*.[18] Más a Tierra remained uninhabited and without a garrison for two decades. Then its most famous inhabitant arrived.

In February 1704, the privateer *Cinque Ports*, under Captain Thomas Stradling, and *St. George*, under William Dampier, who had initiated the expedition in England the previous year, put in at again-uninhabited Más a Tierra. There they left a lone seaman, Alexander Selkirk (1676–1721). At age 18, Selkirk had run away to sea from his home in Largo,

Fife, Scotland. During the War of the Spanish Succession (1702–13), British captains gladly attacked Spanish shipping. When they stopped at Más a Tierra, only forty-two of the original ninety men on *Cinque Ports* were alive, the others having died of scurvy and dysentery. Moreover *Cinque Ports'* timbers were dangerously invaded by worms; *Teredo navalis* ate away at the hull's planking.[19] When Stradling made ready to sail, Selkirk refused to board. He told Stradling he thought the ship would come apart. Selkirk was right. *Cinque Ports* later sank off Peru. Stradling and six others survived but spent four years as prisoners in South America.

Selkirk was the lonely inhabitant of Más a Tierra for four years and four months. Stradling had allowed him clothing, bedding, a musket, a pound of powder, bullets, tobacco, a hatchet, a knife, a kettle, a Bible and other books. Selkirk found an anchor and iron barrel hoops from which he forged an ax, blades, and fishhooks. Goats and cats had been left by earlier visitors, and Selkirk survived largely on goat meat, wild cabbage palms, turnips, and parsley. Cats were his companions. Selkirk fashioned a goatskin outfit and built a hut. When crews of two Spanish ships landed, Selkirk hid in a tree.[20]

In January 1709 Captain Woodes Rogers (1679–1732) of the *Duke*, on an around-the-world voyage from 1708 to 1711, stopped at Más a Tierra and took off Selkirk. Rodgers had to land because 130 of his 333 men were dying or had died of scurvy. Selkirk was glad to see Dampier, who was now serving as sailing master under Captain Rogers. After some thought, Selkirk decided to sail off with Rogers and Dampier. Under command of Rogers, the survivors among the *Duke*'s crew went on to capture a Manila galleon and nineteen other Spanish vessels, becoming the most successful privateers in a century. The *Duke* reached England in September 1711. Rogers sold the ship and cargo for £147,000, which was shared with the owners and the crew. Selkirk's share was £800, which made him substantially well to do. In 1712 Woodes Rogers published *A Cruising Voyage Around the World*, which included the tale of Selkirk's adventure. In 1719, inspired by Rogers' book, Daniel Defoe, age sixty, published his four hundred and twelfth and most famous work, *The Life and Strange Surprizing Adventures of Robinson Crusoe of York, Mariner.*[21]

Spanish colonial authorities were further alarmed in 1741 when a large British expedition under Commodore George Anson (1697–1772) stopped at Más a Tierra. Anson had set sail from Portsmouth commanding the man-of-war *Centurion* with five hundred men, and five other warships and two supply vessels. The crews had sailed to fight the Spanish during the War of Jenkins' Ear (1739–42), which began after a Captain Jenkins produced his ear in a box, telling Parliament that it been severed by Spaniards. By the time they reached the Juan Fernández Islands on June 9, 1741, most of Anson's crews had already died of scurvy. Only a dozen men went ashore unassisted. Ship's chaplain Richard Walter wrote of their first sight of land, "Even those amongst the diseased who were not in the last stages of the distemper, crawled up to the deck to feast them selves with this reviving prospect."[22]

Anson named the anchorage Cumberland Bay. Crewmembers found goats whose ears had been split by Selkirk. The crews remained for three months to recover their health; nevertheless, only 145 of the original complement of 961 were to return to England at the end of the 22-month circumnavigation. At Cape Espiritu Santo in the Philippines, *Centurion* captured a Manila galleon and took home 1,313,843 pieces of eight. The fifteen percent of the men who had survived received a share of the prize.[23]

In 1750, King Ferdinand VI (1713–59; r. 1746–59) sent 150 soldiers, colonists and con-

Selkirk's Lookout. High up on Más a Fuera (Robinson Crusoe Island) in the Juan Fernandez Group, Alexander Selkirk looked on the horizon for ships. Selkirk was the island's sole inhabitant from 1704 to 1709 and expected to be rescued by a British vessel. He hid when Spaniards came ashore, as they would have killed or imprisoned him as an interloper on their island. Daniel Defoe's novel *Robinson Crusoe* was inspired by Selkirk's lonely adventure. Photograph by Robert Kirk.

victs to erect a garrison and a town, San Juan Bautista on Más a Tierra. The remote island became a convict colony, and by 1793 the population was about 300. The Spanish presence prevented the island from becoming a pirate lair or a base that could be used to menace Chile. However, a second large island in the group remained with no garrison.[24]

On April 9, 1765, Captain John Byron (1723–86), grandfather of poet Lord George Byron, brought his ships *Dolphin* and *Tamar* to uninhabited Más a Fuera. His men waded through raging surf and were menaced by sharks while returning aboard with water and wood. Before entering the Pacific Byron had claimed the Falkland Islands in the South Atlantic for Britain; these islands near the Strait of Magellan would be contested by France and Spain, and more recently in 1982 by Argentina and the United Kingdom. The British Admiralty had ordered Byron to look for the fabled Northwest Passage from the Pacific to the Atlantic, but Byron ignored these instructions and sailed west to look for Mendaña's incorrectly charted Solomon Islands instead. On June 7, 1765, John Byron skirted the Tuamotus and discovered only the relatively unimportant atoll of Atafu in the Tokelau group. Byron sailed home so fast that he set a record for sailing around the world.[25]

THE LATER VOYAGES, 1770 TO 1793

After a long period of neglect of the insular world they claimed, Spanish authorities sent Don Felipe Gonzáles de Haedo (1714–92) aboard the *San Lorenzo* to continue exploring in the South Pacific. On November 20, 1770, Gonzáles' crew were the first Europeans to visit Easter Island since the Dutchman Jacob Roggeveen, forty-eight years before. The visit was, according to Gonzáles' account, without bloodshed; rather, it began when three naked males "climbed with much agility, shouting all the while and exhibiting much gayness of spirit." The visitors planted three crosses, and shot off three volleys from their muskets. The ship's cannons fired off twenty-one shots to commemorate the event. The crew shouted, "*Viva el Rey.*" "It need not be said that the islanders were terrified at the noise of the gunfire and musketry," the captain wrote.[26] Although Spain claimed the island, Spanish forces were never to occupy it.

On May 20, 1768, Captain Samuel Wallis returned to England in command of the *Dolphin*, and reported the discovery of King George's Island, known as Tahiti. Spain's ambassador to the Court of St. James bribed a member of the *Dolphin* crew for Tahiti's location. Peru's royal governor, Don Manuel de Amat y Junient (1707–82, terms 1761–76), was concerned that the British would colonize islands that he felt rightfully belonged to Spain. The governor sent expeditions to Tahiti in 1772, 1774–75, and 1775.[27]

In late 1772 the first expedition under Domingo de Boenechea (1713–75), commanding the *Aguila*, visited Tahiti to determine if Britain or France had established a military base. The ship remained for a month, and then returned to Peru, taking four male Tahitians with them. Boenechea and his crew, accompanied by priests, returned on November 27, 1774. The purpose of this mission was to convert Tahitians to Catholic Christianity. Boenechea died on January 25, 1775, and the company sailed for Peru two days later. Two priests and a sailor were left on the island to make conversions, but failed entirely. The Spanish visits to Tahiti are more fully discussed in chapter 4.

Lieutenant Commander Don Tomás Gayangos succeeded Boenechea and, commanding the *Aguila* and the *Jupiter* en route from Tahiti to Peru, stopped at Raivavae on February 5, 1775. The crewmen were the first known European visitors. Raivavae is a high island with an inner reef near shore. It measures 18 square kilometers (7 square miles). It is one of five inhabited islands in the scattered Australs, and its 347-meter (1,140-foot) peak rivals Bora Bora's peak in beauty. The population in the late eighteenth century has been estimated at 3,000. Gayagos complained that the "Indians" came aboard with the sole objective of stealing as many articles as they could, even grabbing hats off of sailors' heads. Their other avocation was war, boys being trained to use spears, clubs and slings from childhood. They created red tufa stone images of female forms, a dozen feet high. Men steered twin-hulled canoes; in these canoes they made long voyages to Tahiti.[28]

A Spanish voyage of exploration in the South Pacific was conducted in 1780–81 under the direction of Francisco Antonio Mourelle (1755–1820). On March 4, 1781, he discovered Vava'u in the Tonga Islands. After being entertained by the local high chief, he sailed to Guam.[29]

In 1793 Alessandro Malaspina (1754–1810) and the crew of the *Descubierta* spent a month on Tonga'tapu during which he buried a bottle with a message claiming the island for Spain. Malaspina was co-commander of a scientific expedition; his co-captain, José de Bustamante (1759–1825), was master of the *Atrevida*. They had sailed up the west coast of America to Alaska, been to Manila and Macau, and visited Doubtful Sound in New Zealand and Port Jackson in New South Wales. Little came of the expedition, as their reports were locked away on their return and not examined until the twentieth century. The bottle containing the claim was never found, but it hardly mattered, as Spanish ships never returned to claim Tonga'tapu. The Malaspina expedition marked the end of Spanish attempts to establish a presence in Melanesia and Polynesia.[30]

Chapter 3

The Dutch Century, 1616–1722

A New Maritime Power

In the seventeenth century the Netherlands replaced Portugal as the preeminent European maritime power. In the mid–1600s Dutch captains commanded half of the merchant ships in Europe. Motivated by profits from trade, investors sent vessels to African slave depots, Brazil, the Caribbean, New Amsterdam (New York), and the rich coasts of Asia. It would have been surprising had they not penetrated the Pacific. Although they did not establish a permanent presence there, Dutch mariners were among the most important explorers of Oceania.

The rise of the Netherlands appeared to be against all odds. Charles I of Spain (Charles V, Holy Roman Emperor) had inherited seventeen provinces, which constituted the Netherlands, Belgium, and Luxembourg. When people in the seven northern provinces embraced Calvinism, a faith which Charles and his successor Phillip II considered heretical, Spanish forces sought to repress it in their territories. In addition to attempting to wipe out Protestantism, Phillip deprived the Dutch ruling classes of their political powers, and taxed the merchants heavily. Between 1566 and 1648, the seven provinces broke away from the most powerful nation in Europe. Among the leaders of the revolt were members of a growing business class. Their unrelenting struggle is known as the Eighty Years' War.

Under the leadership of men such as William of Orange, called "The Silent" (1533–84), the provinces, though devoid of rich natural resources, refused to surrender. Phillip responded by sending an army under the Duke of Alva (1507–82; term 1567–73), arresting 12,000, and in 1584 having William assassinated.

What the Spanish derisively referred to as the "Sea Beggars" were mariners who put together an independent Dutch fleet. This fleet was the nucleus of Dutch naval power.

The Dutch had several advantages. One of these was Spain's perennial insolvency. Instead of building her own industries, trade and infrastructure, Spain spent much of her American treasure suppressing heresy and buying goods from northern Europe. Many of the products bought for consumption in Spain and in her colonies were produced in the Netherlands. The northerners accumulated capital while the Spanish monarch was burdened by debt. Second, when Spain crushed the revolt in the ten southern provinces, they harmed Antwerp's trade and financial position. Amsterdam inherited Antwerp's trade, and some of its capital. Some entrepreneurs from Antwerp relocated to Amsterdam, bringing capital and expertise with them. Third, the Dutch accessed shipbuilding materials from Scandinavia, principally timbers. Of enormous importance, Dutch banks and merchant houses developed dependable financial instruments such as credit, a stock exchange, a sound banking system, marine insurance, maritime law courts, and comparative transparency in their dealings. Thus, the Dutch accumulated capital and searched for new lucrative places to invest. Foremost, they sought to trade in spices from the Moluccas. The islands were controlled by Portugal, but from 1580 to 1640 Portugal and its trading posts fell under control of the Spanish crown by right of King Phillip II's inheritance. The Dutch were, therefore, at war with Portugal as well as with Spain because it was the king of Spain's dominion. The African slave trade, Brazil's fertile sugar fields, and East Indies spices were fair prey.

The business organization that allowed the Netherlands to dominate the Indonesian archipelago and to send explorers into the vast Pacific was founded on March 20, 1602. It was the United Netherlands Chartered East India Company. The name is often abbreviated VOC—for Vereenigde Oost-Indische Companie. Organized by investors to eliminate costly competition among rival traders, the company enjoyed a monopoly on transactions in the East. Moreover, their charter granted the board of directors—the Heeren XVII— power to mint coins, fight battles in defense of their trading privileges, and even capture rival vessels. The Dutch East Indies Company, as it is commonly known, established a commercial capital at Batavia (now Jakarta) on Java and held it for 350 years. Any Dutchman who was not a member of the company was forbidden to trade in the Spice Islands.[1]

In their explorations in the Pacific the Dutch were not animated principally by scientific curiosity, nor were they motivated to convert islanders to Calvinism. They wanted to locate areas that offered the possibility of significant financial gain.

A CONTINENT NAMED NEW HOLLAND

Dutch mariners skirted the coast of Australia from the East Indies. In 1606, navigator Willem Jansz (a.k.a. Janszoon) (1570–1630) sailed along the west coast of Queensland's York Peninsula in the ship *Duyfken*. He sighted Cape Keerweer. A landing party looking for water was killed by "these wild, cruel, black savages."[2] The "black savages" were Aborigines who peopled the continent, spread thinly, living in small groups.[3] Jansz's opinion of the north Australian coast: "There is no good to be done there," by which the captain meant he could report no way to gain a profit.[4]

On October 25, 1616, Dirk Hartog (1580–1621), a captain sailing on the *Eendracht*, landed on an island at Shark Bay off the west coast of Australia. Remaining three days, he attached a pewter plate to a post, recording his visit. He proceeded to Batam in the East Indies, trading on the company's account, and returned to the Netherlands on October 16, 1618.[5]

At a small river near Cape Duyfken in the Gulf of Carpentaria, northern Australia, on May 8, 1623, Dutch seamen clashed with 200 Aborigines. This was among the first instances when Aborigines found themselves using primitive weapons against firearms. On April 14, Captain Jan Carstenszoon had brought his ships—*Pera*, under his own command, and *Arnhem*, captained by Willem Joosten Van Colster (1570–?)—to anchor offshore. Carstenszoon reported to his superiors that he had seen neither spices nor gold; in fact, "We have not seen one fruit-bearing tree, nor anything that man can make use of." Carstenszoon named the Gulf of Carpentaria after the governor general of Dutch settlements in the East Indies, Pieter de Carpentier (1586?–1659; governor 1623–27). Carstenszoon returned to Ambon, while Van Colster found and named Arnhem Land.[6]

Dutch mariners continued to sail along Australia's west and north coast and named the shore New Holland. They perceived the coasts to be dry and forbidding. They were unsure if the areas they saw were a continent or islands, but New Holland appeared far less inviting than the islands gravid with spices that they already controlled.[7] Aborigines of Australia's western and northern shores would be relatively safe from European penetration for another two centuries.

SCHOUTEN AND LEMAIRE ROUND CAPE HORN

In 1615, Dutch shipmasters Willem Cornelis Schouten (1567–1625) and Jacob Le Maire (1565–1616) tried to break the Dutch East Indies Company monopoly in the East by reaching the Spice Islands from the west. The VOC monopoly forbade trade by nonmembers who entered the East Indies from the Indian Ocean. Neither of them belonged to the important consortium. Their two ships were the 220-ton *Endracht* with sixty-five men, and the 110-ton *Hoorn* with twenty-two men. The *Hoorn* caught fire in Patagonia and was rendered beyond repair.

In attempting to approach the East Indies from the Western Hemisphere, they found their way on January 29, 1616, through what came to be known as the Strait of Le Maire, south of the Strait of Magellan. They named the nearest land Cape Hoorn. From there they sailed to Juan Fernandez Island, where they spent three days, leaving March 3; their short stay may be explained by the fact they had taken on 25,000 lemons in Senegal, which they dried and which prevented scurvy aboard.[8]

The *Endracht* reached the Tuamotus, arriving April 10; the Dutch crew observed islanders on Takapoto to be "red folk who smeared themselves with oil." When several came aboard, one pulled out nails and tried to conceal them in his hair. When islanders tried to steal the ship, the Dutch killed several men. The Dutch navigators were fortunate not to have wrecked on what later mariners would call the Dangerous Archipelago. These atolls, today in French Polynesia, are mostly protected by treacherous reefs. The people of Takapoto, armed with clubs and slings, were fortunate that their visitors left without killing more of them.

Sailing on from the bloody scene, the *Endracht*'s crew saw a Polynesian double-hulled canoe sailing past. Not content to allow these travelers to glide by without surrendering, the Dutch forced them to halt their vessel. When the Tongans from Tafahi Island attempted to resist, the crew shot several men, killing some, wounding others and capturing two. Their curiosity satisfied after examining the terrified captives, the Dutch returned the pair to their bloodstained boat.

On April 28, 1616, Jacob Le Maire and Willem Cornelis Schouten discovered Futuna and Alofi, which they named the Hoorn Islands. They are now part of the Wallis and Futuna French possession. They remained two weeks among friendly people, and traded nails for pigs and bananas. On June 25, they fought with inhabitants of New Ireland. When these coal black people with rings through their noses rowed out to fling stones, the Dutch shot a number of them. Reaching Batavia, instead of being rewarded for their discoveries, they were arrested for breaking the VOC's monopoly. Governor General Jan Pieterszoon Coen (1587–1629; terms 1618–23, 1627–29) refused to believe that the ships had crossed the Pacific from the east. They were sent to Holland as prisoners. Le Maire died on the way. Forgiven, Schouten went on to sail for the VOC and died off the coast of Madagascar. There was no penalty to be paid, though, for leaving a series of dead islanders in their wake.[9]

TASMAN FINDS TASMANIA AND NEW ZEALAND

The most important of all Dutch explorers was Abel Janzoon Tasman (1603–59). An experienced officer, Tasman had already served as second in command on voyages to Formosa and Japan. Anthony van Diemen (1592–1645), governor of Batavia, sent Tasman into the great ocean to find Terra Australis Incognita. Van Diemen wanted new lands for trading purposes. On November 14, 1642, Tasman, commanding *Heemskerck* and *Zeehaen*, discovered the lush green island at the bottom of Australia, which he named Van Diemen's Land. What is now an Australian state was renamed in 1856 Tasmania in the discoverer's honor. Stone Age Tasmanians may have watched the Dutch from the bush, but the explorers did not record having seen them.[10]

On December 13, 1642, Tasman was the first European to find New Zealand. North and South Islands were the last large habitable landmasses in the world to be found by Europeans. All the other Polynesian islands together would fit easily into New Zealand's 209,719 square kilometers (103,738 square miles). Tasman sailed along the west coasts of North and South Island and, assuming them to be one piece of land, named them Staten Landt. Tasman drew a rough and inaccurate line showing a long coast. In 1645 a cartographer labeled it Nova Zeelandia in Latin, and later it was written Nieu Zealande in Dutch. Tasman was unaware that Maoris called their 1,200-kilometer- (745-mile-) long islands Aotearoa, or the Land of the Long White Cloud. Tasman had no idea how many people lived in the islands. Population estimates have varied from a 100,000 to 500,000, but a consensus is 115,000. About eighty percent probably lived on North Island because the plants that Polynesians had brought from their ancestral homeland, Hawai'iki, would not grow in the cold south.[11]

Tasman anchored in Golden Bay and soon two canoes approached filled with Maoris. None of these Polynesians had seen a European before. They sounded an instrument that produced a trumpet-like sound. A seaman replied by playing a trumpet tune for them. The Maoris may have interpreted the musical reply as a challenge to fight. On the following day they clubbed four Dutchmen to death. Warriors prevented Tasman from landing in the area he named Murderer's Bay.

Tasman had stumbled upon a society plagued by chronic warfare among its tribes. Thirty years was probably a normal life expectancy, and men described as "old" may have survived to forty. Victors wanted to increase their *mana* by eating the losers. News of the murderous Maoris circulated on European waterfronts. Europeans and their lethal diseases stayed away, at least until the next Western visitor arrived 127 years later.[12]

TASMAN FINDS TONGA'TAPU

On January 19, 1643, Abel Tasman and his crews were the first Europeans to visit Tonga'tapu (159 square kilometers; 99 square miles). Tonga'tapu is the largest of the 170 Tonga Islands, 42 of which are inhabited. In addition to Tonga'tapu and Eua are the Ha'apai Group and the Vava'u Group, the latter noted for elevated limestone cliffs. At the time of Tasman's visit, the islands were ruled by a supreme chief known as the Tu'i Tonga. Another chief, the Tu'i Ha'atakalaua, held the secular power. In the mid–1600s, a third semi-divine ruler, the Tu'i Kanokupolu, would wield more power than the other two. Tasman named Tonga'tapu Amsterdam. On Tonga'tapu Tasman ordered that a gun be fired into the air, and ordered a trumpet, violin, and flute to be played in order to astonish the Tongans. Tasman traded beads, nails and mirrors for hogs, fowls, yams, coconuts, fruit and water.[13]

Tasman Sails to Fiji

In February 1643, Tasman found the Fiji Islands. Fiji is composed of 322 islands totaling 18,272 square kilometers (7,126 square miles). Fiji is bigger than the land area of all Polynesian islands together except New Zealand. The two principal islands are Viti Levu and Vanua Levu; the two account for 87 percent of Fiji's area. Interrelated families of Melanesians with some Polynesian blood made up a Fijian tribe. There were seven major tribes when Europeans came; rugged mountains, swift streams and jungles kept tribal groups differentiated. Tribal members practiced *kere kere*—the sharing of goods among community members, and *lala*—mutual aid by all members of a community. They also practiced warfare and cannibalism. Tasman did not attempt to land in the Fijis because of thunderous surf, fog, and shallow reef-strewn waters.[14]

Tasman returned to Batavia on June 15, 1643. He had lost only ten men. He had found New Zealand, the Tonga Islands and Fiji Islands and named a large land area for his superior. None of that seemed to count in his favor. The VOC considered that the voyage had failed in that Tasman had not found nations with the same level of material sophistication as those of Europe.[15] He had failed to locate a southern continent and had not uncovered valuable commodities to be exploited or potential trading partners.[16]

Tasman Charts the Coast of New Holland

Tasman had been back in Batavia only half a year when he was sent off again, this time to determine the size and shape of New Holland. Tasman set sailed on January 29, 1644. On this voyage of discovery, he skirted along the north coast from Cape York to Poissonnier Point on the Indian Ocean. His three ships were *Limmen, Zeemeeuw*, and *Braek*. He was looking for a channel leading to Terra Australis Incognita, but instead found a continuous coast. By this time the Dutch had knowledge of the north and west coasts of Australia and some of the south coast, as well as Van Diemen's Land. Dutch mariners saw only a few Aborigines on what appeared to be barren shores. Tasman failed to recognize Australia as a continent and hoped the southern continent he was searching for was somewhere close. Wherever it was, it could not be as dry and forbidding as the coast of New Holland. Surely Terra Australis Incognita was full of civilized people eager to trade, people not resembling the Aborigines.

On his return Tasman was not thanked, but instead admonished for finding "nothing that could be turned to profit, but ... only naked, beach-roving wretches, destitute even of rice, miserably poor, and in many places of very bad disposition."[17] Nor would Tasman be sent into the South Seas again. Directors of the company concluded: "We cannot anticipate any great results from the continuation of such discoveries, which besides entail further expenditure for the Company." European settlement of any part of Australia would wait 144 years.[18]

Tasman is one of the great explorers of the Pacific. Tasman has been posthumously honored by having an island and several geographical features of the island named for him.

Several places in Australia bear his name, as does a ferociously ugly carnivorous marsupial, the Tasmanian devil.

THE PIRATICAL ADVENTURES OF WILLIAM DAMPIER

A remarkably literate English pirate confirmed Tasman's report of the lack of commercial possibilities on the shores of New Holland. Aboard the *Cygnet* in 1688, William Dampier went ashore in northwestern Australia. The peninsula Dampier Land near Broome is named for him. While *Cygnet*'s bottom was being scraped, Dampier had a look at plants, animals and Aborigines. He was unimpressed by the dry, barren, sandy soil devoid of edible plants or fruit.

In 1697 Dampier published *New Voyage Round the World*, which won him acclaim as the greatest expert of his time on the Pacific. In his book Dampier characterized the inhabitants of Australia as "the miserablest people in the world.... They have no sort of clothes, but a piece of the rind of tree tied like a girdle about their waists.... They have no houses but lie in the open air without any covering."[19]

On July 20, 1699, Dampier arrived at Shark Bay, midway on the west coast of Australia. He returned to Australia in command of HMS *Roebuck*, under Admiralty orders to report in some detail on New Holland. Dampier wrote the first description of the continent's fauna and flora. A crewmember drew pictures and Dampier brought back specimens, particularly of shells. After exploring much of the northwest coast, he was unable to proceed to the east coast because *Roebuck*'s timbers had become rotten. Heading home he skirted New Guinea, New Hanover, New Ireland, New Britain and proceeded through the Dampier Straits.[20]

ROGGEVEEN SAILS FOR THE WEST INDIES COMPANY

Disappointed in trade prospects in the South Seas, Dutch navigators made no more significant discoveries for nearly eight decades. Then, the Dutch West Indies Company, barred from sailing across the Indian Ocean to reach Asia and the Pacific, sent Jacob Roggeveen (1529–1629) on a westward voyage. He left the Netherlands August 1, 1721, to find the great — and presumably lucrative — southern continent. His three ships, *Arend*, *Thienhoven* and *Afrikaansche Galei*, stopped at the Juan Fernández Islands from February 24 to March 17. On April 5, 1722, Roggeveen made an astounding discovery when his ships came upon uncharted Easter Island. Roggeveen described briefly the giant *moai*, the iconic stone heads that lined the shores, but he did not think the poverty-stricken naked people capable of carving, moving, and erecting the heavy monuments.

The crew became the first Europeans to sight Bora Bora (which is in the Leeward group of the Society Islands), on June 6, 1722, but did not land on the 36-square-kilometer (14-square-mile) island with its majestic caldera. Sixteen days later, on June 22, 1722, Roggeveen charted six of the Tuamotus. Five of his men deserted at Takapoto, a Tuamotu island, becoming the first known European "beach combers" in the South Seas. At Makatea, an uplifted limestone block, Roggeveen wanted to land, but islanders prevented his men from coming ashore. The Dutch shot into the crowd to clear a landing space on the beach. Islanders stoned ten crewmembers to death.[21]

En route to Batavia in August 1722, Roggeveen and his men landed at Tutuila in what is today American Samoa to obtain fruit and water. He recorded his sighting of Rose Island and the Manua Group in the Samoas. The expedition arrived in Batavia at the end of September.[22] As an intruder from the wrong company, Roggeveen and his crews were interned by officials of the Dutch East India Company, and then sent home as prisoners. They were soon freed in the Netherlands.[23]

Roggeveen had already lost the *Afrikaansche Galei* in the Tuamotus, and the Batavia merchants sold the *Arend* and *Thienhoven*. With the end of Roggeveen's cruise came the end of significant Dutch exploration of Oceania. They had found a number of important island groups. The way was now open to British and French mariners.

Chapter 4

Disturbing the Tahitian
Arcadia, 1767–1842

PARADISE FOUND

Tahiti was discovered for Europeans in 1767 by British captain Samuel Wallis in command of the *Dolphin*. On August 6, 1766, Wallis (1728–95) received his orders from the British Admiralty:

> Whereas there is reason to believe that land or islands of great extent, hitherto unvisited by any European power may be found in the Southern Hemisphere between Cape Horn and New Zealand, in latitudes convenient for navigation, and in climates adapted to the produce of commodities useful in commerce, and whereas His Majesty ... has signified to us his pleasure that an attempt should forthwith be made to discover and obtain a complete knowledge of the land or islands.... We have caused the ship you command and the *Swallow* sloop, to be fitted ... in all respects proper for such an undertaking.

The desire of the well educated King George III (1738–1820; r. 1760–1820) "was the mainspring initiating the great activity in naval exploration." He wanted to benefit Britain and humanity in general by sending explorers to those parts of the world as yet unknown in Europe, particularly high latitudes in the Southern Hemisphere.[1]

Experts were certain the continent was there. In 1752 Moreau de Maupertuis (1698–1759), director of the Académie des sciences and first president of the Berlin Academy of Sciences, published a letter in the journal *Scientific Progress*. A noted mathematician and philosopher, he stated: "We all know there is a large unknown space in the southern hemisphere where there may well exist a continent larger than any of the other four."[2]

Wallis, commanding the twenty-four-gun frigate *Dolphin* and with Philip Carteret (1733–96) as captain of the *Swallow,* sailed out from Portsmouth, England, on August 22, 1766. Two years earlier the *Dolphin* had sailed around the world on the John Byron expedition. It became the first ship to circumnavigate the globe twice. Virginia–born master's mate John Gore (c. 1730–90) and some other crewmembers had sailed with Byron. The Admiralty's orders were to proceed through the Strait of Magellan and follow westward in high latitudes to 120 degrees west, which would have brought them south of Western Australia. If they did not find the great southern continent, they were to replenish supplies in the East Indies and return home.

By 1766 navigators were able to determine with confidence the ship's exact location at sea and to arrive at a predetermined destination. In 1759, English clock maker John Harrison (1693–1776) had perfected an accurate marine chronometer. His monumental accomplishment was in response to Parliament's Longitude Act of 1714, calling for an invention to determine exactly how far a point was east or west from Greenwich. Accuracy was essential because an hour's difference in local time from Greenwich time was fifteen degrees of longitude. An inaccurate clock would mean an error of 60 kilometers (20 miles) longitude for every minute the clock was off. It was the ability to determine longitude that allowed Pacific explorers to chart the positions of islands half way around the world and to return to the same place. The chronometer had already passed a stringent test: On January 19, 1762, the ship *Deptford* arrived in Jamaica from England with a new marine chronometer that measured longitude with only 5.1 seconds of error on the trip across the Atlantic. For his efforts Parliament awarded Harrison £8,750, less than the £20,000 it had promised.[3]

Samuel Wallis's *Dolphin* was a fine ship whose hull was sheathed with copper. *Swallow*, on the other hand, was old and her hull invaded by worms; the Admiralty planned for *Swallow* to return home from the Falkland Islands and Carteret to take command of a replacement ship that he was promised would meet them there. The replacement ship had already sailed home from the Falklands when Carteret arrived. Carteret asked to return *Swallow* to England on the grounds that the ship was not seaworthy for a circumnavigation. Wallis refused because the Admiralty's orders were for the captains to proceed together.

Swallow always trailed miles behind *Dolphin*, and when on April 11, 1767, after four months of trying to get through the tempestuous Strait of Magellan, *Dolphin* emerged in the Pacific, *Swallow* and its crew were nowhere to be seen. Carteret would make his own Pacific discoveries.[4]

On the nineteenth of June 1767 when the *Dolphin* appeared offshore, Tahiti's irrevocable transformation was assured. What change the *Dolphin* crew did not bring about, subsequent voyagers would. Captain Wallis was ill in his cabin, as were his two principal officers. The *Dolphin's* master, George Robertson, fortunately left an account of a civilization as yet unaltered. Robertson recorded that Tahiti "had the most beautiful appearance it is possible to imagine. From the shore side one two and three miles back there is a fine level country that appears to be all laid out in plantations and the regular built houses seem to be without number. All along the coast, they appeared like long farmer's barns and seemed to be all very neatly thatched, with great numbers of cocoa nut trees and several trees that we could know the name of all along the shore." We cannot know the population of the island, but to Robertson it appeared to be "the most populous country I ever saw, the whole shore side was lined with men, women and children all the way that we sailed along." Tahiti is a large island, 10,491 square kilometers (4,035 square miles), but crewmembers explored only a small part.

Completely innocent of Western firepower, Tahitians set out to show a force of overwhelming numbers to the intruders. Robertson estimated 150 canoes with 800 aboard "within pistol shot." Alongside, they made "long talks" in a language indecipherable to the British, and displayed plantain branches, symbolic of peaceful intentions. The crew was desperate for fresh food and water. They attempted to make their needs known; they grunted and crowed to indicate they wanted hogs and chickens. Tahiti had no metal, but when the people saw it and touched it aboard the *Dolphin*, they knew it was superior to stone, shell, wood, or bone. When shown ring balls and nails, the Polynesians wanted them and became "surly" when not given them. The crew fired a nine-pound shot over their heads as a warning.

As during so many initial encounters between Westerners and Pacific islanders, bloodshed was inevitable. Tahitians in a canoe threw rocks and hit some crew in the ship's cutter. "Mr. Gore ... fired at the man he saw throw the first stone and wounded him in the right shoulder, which prevented him from throwing any more stones." The man's companions all jumped into the ocean, related Robertson. Shortly after Tahitians attacked again, but Robertson "ordered the first sergeant and one of the marines to wound the two most resolute like fellows" and when the order was obeyed, "the one was killed which the sergeant fired at, and the other was wounded in the thigh," and all of their companions leaped into the water.[5]

On the fifth day of the visit, some Tahitians apparently plotted to overcome their visitors and take the ship. Robertson noted 4,000 men in a flotilla of canoes near the *Dolphin*. When the signal was given, "within a few seconds ... all of our decks were full of great and small stones and several of our men cut and bruised." The *Dolphin* crew answered the challenge by firing the "great guns and gave them a few rounds and grape shot."[6] To prevent future attacks, Wallis ordered men to go ashore and destroy canoes. The crew cut canoes in half and soon about eighty of them, which measured forty or fifty feet, had been permanently disabled. Then they fired round shot near Tahitians watching from a nearby hill.

The confrontation with stones and firearms would be the first and last serious attempt by Tahitians to deter landings by Westerners. What followed was the offering of more plantain branches. The crew became, according to Robertson, "very merry supposing all hostilities were now over and to our great joy it so happened." Islanders wanted nails to use as fish hooks, as tools, or as weapon points. Following the skirmishes, Robertson felt that "most of the natives traded very honestly," giving, for example, a hog for a twenty-penny (three-inch) nail, "but a few of them were very great rogues, and frequently attempted to defraud our men by going off with the nail or, toys, without paying for them."[7] Missionary William Ellis related in *Polynesian Researches* that he had been told the ingenuous Tahitians "divided the first parcel of nails ever received, carried part to the temple, and deposited them on the altar; the rest they actually planted in their gardens, and awaited their growth with the highest anticipation."[8]

Peace assured and stomachs full, the men could turn their attentions to Tahitian females, "some a light copper color, others a mulatto and some almost white." The Tahitian men who brought girls to the ship indicated that the crew should take those they liked best. Assuming that the British were a race entirely of males, unfamiliar with females, they tried to be helpful and by signs sought to show them how sexual intercourse is accomplished. *Dolphin's* crew did not require the lesson. Most now became "madly fond of the shore," and even those thirty who had been ill begged to go ashore to be nursed back to health by compliant girls.[9]

Tahitians saw sex as a natural need and pleasure, not as a sinful act, and gave and received sexual favors gratuitously. When sailors offered nails for sex, the natural act gradually evolved into a business transaction.

Robertson recalled that when the *Dolphin* had been in Tahiti for a month, "the carpenter came and told me every cleat in the ship was drawn and all the nails carried off. At the same time the boatswain informed me that most of the hammock nails were drawn, and two thirds of the men obliged to lie on the deck for want of nails to hang their hammocks." Inflation followed when "the young girls ... now raised their price for some days past from twenty or thirty penny nails to a forty penny, and some [were] so extravagant as to demand a seven or nine inch spike."[10] Sex became for Europeans the most astonishing and important thing about Tahiti, and the most discussed," wrote David Howarth.[11] Seamen in Europe wanted to go to Tahiti, where nails bought the favors of lovely, eager, naked girls. Many thought Wallis had located Jean-Jacques Rousseau's "noble savage."

Wallis claimed Tahiti for Britain's monarch and named it King George III's Island. On July 27, when *Dolphin* departed, Tahitians wept. Tahitians would continue to weep long after the ship was gone: Crew members, twenty of whom had been treated six months before arriving in Tahiti, infected island females with venereal disease. Sexually transmitted diseases were a European import and had not occurred in Polynesia before contact with sailors.

Unable because of the fury of the "Roaring Forties" (a prevailing wind from the west between 40 and 50 degrees south) to look for Terra Australis Incognita, Wallis decided to take the *Dolphin* home. Arriving in the Downs on May 20, 1768, Wallis was able to report that at Tahiti Europeans had found a safe and friendly port.[12] Its people proved to be "kind and gentle and astonishingly generous."[13] Beyond that, the *Dolphin* crew knew the Tahitians but knew little about them.

BOUGAINVILLE FINDS APHRODITE'S ISLE

On April 2, 1768, Louis-Antoine de Bougainville (1729–1811), commanding two French ships, *La Boudeuse* and *Etoile*, sighted Tahiti. What amazes is that it was not until two and a half centuries after Magellan opened the Pacific to Western navigators that Tahiti, crowned by Mount Orohena towering 2,236 meters (7,339 feet), visible from miles out at sea, was found by Westerners, and that it was found independently by two captains sailing for rival kings within eight months of each other. The French arrived just in time; the *Etoile's* surgeon had identified "twenty clear cases of scurvy and the crew weakened and spiritless," having lived four months on salt meat and biscuit. Fortunately for them breadfruit had ripened and fresh food was plentiful on shore. Having not learned of Wallis's visit, Bougainville thought initially he was the island's European discoverer.

Having reconciled themselves to the reality that European *mana*—or supernatural power—came from the barrel of a gun, the Tahitians did not test the French. The ten-day sojourn passed peacefully, almost, until the inevitable misunderstandings and shootings prior to sailing. Crewmembers shot one Tahitian and bayoneted three others, but despite such isolated clashes, islanders remained friendly. Friendly Tahitian males brought life-restoring food and water, as well as pliant young females. They urged the young Frenchmen to have sex with the girls. "How," puzzled the surgeon, "could such charming people be so far from Europe and how is it that in this island they are so white whereas all we have seen in the other islands since the time of our departure were different?"[14] He referred to dark people in the Tuamotus, which Bougainville named the Dangerous Archipelago. Like many Europeans at the time, Tahitians saw whiteness as a sign that the person was not low class and did not have to work in the sun to procure food. So did Tahitian aristocrats, who avoided being darkened in the sun.

Bougainville reported that his problem was how to keep 400 French sailors at their duties in the vicinity of half-clad females. In the case of a cook, he obviously failed. When the cook became excited at the sight of girls, he went ashore in an islanders' boat. There, the curious people stripped the cook bare, examined his sexual organs intently, produced a girl and demanded that he have sex with her on a pile of leaves they had arranged on the ground. Bougainville recorded that "all their persuasive arguments had no effect; they were obliged to bring the poor cook on board, who told me, that I might reprimand him as much as I pleased, but that I could never frighten him so much as he had just now been frightened on shore." Tahitians were exceedingly clean, bathing frequently; not so European crewmen such as the cook — unwashed, emaciated, and decorated with sores. Nevertheless, according to custom girls were offered to high-ranking men for sex in front of an audience in attempts to "excite and arouse the gods," and because they were white and possessed metal, the French were seen to be high ranking.[15]

The French entertained the islanders with fireworks and music. Tahitians delighted Bougainville. "These people breathe only rest and sensual pleasures. Venus is the goddess they worship. The mildness of the climate, the beauty of the scenery, the fertility of the soil everywhere watered by rivers and cascades, everything transpires sensual pleasure. And so I have named it New Cythera."[16] Bougainville called the island Nouvelle Cythere because in Greek mythology Cythera (Kyhera) was the abode of Aphrodite, goddess of love.

Diarist Charles-Felix-Pierre Fesche, sailing with Bougainville, enthused, "If happiness consists in the abundance of all things necessary to life, in living in a superb land with the finest climate, in enjoying the best of health, in breathing the purest and most salubrious air, in leading a simple, soft, quiet life, free from all passions, even from jealousy, although surrounded by women, if these women can themselves even disperse happiness, then I say there is not in the world a happier nation than the Tahitian one."[17]

Philibert Commerson (1727–73), botanist on Bougainville's voyage, explained that there are two ways to consider Tahitian morality: A prudish person "would find nothing in all of this but a breaking down of public standards, a foul prostitution, the most shameless cynicism, but he grossly deludes himself in misunderstanding the condition of natural man, ... following without suspicion as without remorse the sweet impulses of an instinct always sure, because it has still not degenerated into reason."[18] According to Commerson, these were the long-sought noble savages, uncorrupted by civilization and by the Judeo-Christian ethic. Commerson's personal view on morality may be adduced by the fact that his mistress, Jeanne Baret, sailed with him disguised as his manservant; Baret was the first female to circumnavigate the globe.[19]

Bougainville exulted that "everywhere we found hospitality, ease, innocent joy, and every appearance of happiness amongst them."[20] He was infuriated when toward the end of their stay he learned that several of his men had killed or wounded three men at the shore camp because they had refused to sell a pig for two nails. Bougainville would have ordered the offenders executed, but he did not have sufficient evidence to convict them. Tahitians expressed amazement that the French would kill their friends.

Having shown themselves to be the less civilized of the two peoples, the French claimed the island for their king and departed.

When *La Boudeuse* sailed into St. Malo harbor on March 16, 1769, Bougainville brought a Tahitian with him. Aotourou (1739?–71) became the first Pacific islander to visit Europe. Aotourou, age about twenty, was the brother and son of chiefs. Aotourou became popular among Parisians, who saw him as an uninhibited, uncorrupted noble savage. Although he learned only a few words of French during his eleven-month stay, he was able to explore much of Paris on his own.

The visit completed, Bougainville was determined to do the right thing by returning Aotourou to his people, and he spent a third of his fortune to send him to Mauritius and to have a ship hired there to return him to Tahiti. Aotourou waited on the Indian Ocean isle ten months while Marion du Fresne (1724–72), a naval officer, outfitted a ship. En route home, at Fort Dauphin in Madagascar, Aotourou died in November 1771 of smallpox.[21]

Bougainville published *Description d'un voyage autour du Monde* in two volumes, 1771–72. Bougainville is regarded as one of the principal French explorers of the Pacific, not necessarily because he made new discoveries, but because his popular book called attention to the islands, particularly Tahiti.

CHARTING THE TRANSIT OF VENUS

Britain's Admiralty had decided to commission Lieutenant James Cook (1728–79) to proceed to Tahiti to chart the transit of Venus across the face of the sun. The Admiralty

selected Tahiti after reading Wallis's report. On Friday, August 25, 1768, Cook set sail as commander of *Endeavour*. If the transit of Venus were charted from opposite sides of Earth, naval administrators thought they would be able to measure the circumference of Earth and determine the position of the stars with accuracy and thus aid navigation. Charting of the transit was performed by an international array of specialists at seventy-six points around the globe. When Cook had returned and all of the chartings had been completed, the results were disappointing because the telescopes were not powerful enough to record the transit with sufficient accuracy. Cook's secondary mission was to claim lands before France did, and to find Terra Australis Incognita. Moreover, he was "to gather specimens of minerals or gems, ores, seeds, foods and grains and to cultivate 'Friendship and Alliance' with the local populace."[22]

Captain James Cook from a 1932 Cook Islands stamp. The original painting is by Nathaniel Dance-Holland. Cook wrote of his explorations: "I, whose ambition leads me not only farther than any man has gone before me, but as far as I think it possible for man to go...."

By 1768, nearly 260 years after Magellan's circumnavigation, much of the vast Pacific remained uncharted. Questions outnumbered certainties: Where, if it existed at all, was Terra Australis Incognita? Where could mariners enter a northwest passage linking the Pacific and Atlantic? Was New Zealand one or more islands? What was New Holland — was it a continent, an island or more than one island? What island groups remained to be found? What useful species of fauna and flora might be found and exploited for profit? And, of course, Europeans wanted to learn more about the inhabitants of Oceania — their customs, religion, government, sustenance and anything else of interest.

Born the son of a Yorkshire farm laborer, Cook became enamored of the sea, learned superb navigation skills, and became a master chart maker. Cook raised himself from lower-class obscurity to the rarified pantheon of Britain's greatest notables. Cook would sail over 320,000 kilometers (200,000 miles) in the decade 1768 to 1779 and produce the most accurate map of the Pacific thus far, with all major island groups included. He would show finally and definitively that the southern continent did not exist. Scientists on his expeditions would expand the number of species known to European observers by a quarter.

Endeavour held ninety-four officers, seamen, marines, and a floating menagerie of sheep, ducks, chickens, pigs, cats, and a goat. Aboard were Sir Joseph Banks (1743–1820), age twenty-five, a rich and famous "experimental gentleman"; Dr. Daniel Solander (1733–1825), Swedish botanist; and Sydney Parkinson (1745–71), an accomplished artist, who died of dysentery on the way home from the South Seas. These men intended to learn and record all that they could about the opposite side of the world.

The crew ate ship's biscuit, salt beef, salt pork, oatmeal, and cheese—forty-five hundred calories a day per man. Banks claimed to have seen thousands of maggots shaken out of a single biscuit. Yet, none would die of the great scourge of long-distance voyages— scurvy. Cook was an enlightened commander who fed his men sauerkraut, and portable soup—a dried concoction containing some legumes. Cook insisted the men eat fresh fruit and vegetables when and where they were available. To wash down sauerkraut and ship's biscuits, *Endeavour* set sail with 1,200 gallons of beer, 1,600 gallons of brandy and rum, and 3,000 gallons of wine. Each sailor received daily a gallon of beer or a pint of rum. Cook, a product of the Age of Enlightenment, insisted on cleanliness; bedding, clothing, and hammocks were regularly laundered.[23]

Cook's crew benefited from the work of Dr. James Lind (1716–94), a Scottish physician. In 1754 Lind published *A Treatise of the Scurvy*. He identified the cause and a simple cure for the debilitating disease. Commodore Anson's voyage to the Pacific in 1741, during which he lost 816 men, pointed to the need to combat this vitamin deficiency. The disease caused debility, depression, tooth loss, and hemorrhaging, and it led to death. In 1747 Lind experimented with the diet of six groups of sailors to show that lime or lemon juice could prevent and even cure scurvy. Scientists now know that ten milligrams of vitamin C a day prevents scurvy. Nevertheless, it was not until 1795 that royal physician Sir Gilbert Blane (1749–1834) urged on the Admiralty a mandatory requirement that British sailors be given daily doses of lime juice in their grog allotment. A Scot, Blane served as a commissioner of the Admiralty's Sick and Wounded Board. Instances of scurvy were reduced but not eliminated; limes have only half the anti-scorbutic strength of lemons. Sailors in the British navy are often referred to, as a result of Blane's order, as limeys. Nevertheless, the order kept men healthier than they might have been.[24] Prevention of death by scurvy made months-long voyages in Oceania less threatening to Europeans. More Europeans and Americans were enabled to make long voyages to Oceania, often to the detriment of Pacific populations.

When *Endeavour* anchored at Matavai Bay in Tahiti on April 13, 1769, Cook set about establishing friendly relations with the islanders. Lieutenant John Gore, who had sailed there with Wallis, "observed that a very great revolution must have happened." The population had fallen within a year. Houses had been burned or demolished. Gore did not see "so much as a hog or a fowl," both of which had been much in evidence the year before.[25]

Crewmen built what Cook called Fort Venus on shore. The fort was built so the astronomer could chart the transit of Venus, but in spite of the fact that the enclosure was guarded by armed men, a Tahitian found his way in at night and stole the astronomical quadrant. What he intended to do with this complex device is anyone's guess. Without it the mission could not be completed. When the apparatus was finally retrieved, the astronomer fulfilled the primary intent of the cruise by observing the transit on June 3.[26]

Cook found Tahitians handsome, but complained, "It was a hard matter to keep them out of the ship because they climb like monkeys, but it was harder still to keep them from stealing everything that came within their reach."[27] They stole Dr. Solander's spyglass and the surgeon's snuffbox. Cook showed endless patience—except with thefts. He became enraged. When a Tahitian male grabbed a musket from a sentry, the thief was shot dead. Cook reported that he "endeavored by every means in our power to convince [the Tahitians] that the man was killed for taking away the musket and that we still would be friends with them."[28]

The younger Georg Foerster observed,

A kind of happy uniformity runs through the whole life of the Tahitians. They rise with the sun, and hasten to rivers and fountains to perform an ablution equally reviving and cleanly. They pass the morning at work, or walk about until the heat of the day increases, when they retreat to their dwelling, or repose under some tufted tree. There they amuse themselves with smoothing their hair ... or they blow the flute, and sing to it, and listen to the songs of the birds. At the hour of noon or a little later, they go to dinner. After their meals they resume their domestic amusements, during which the flame of mutual affection spreads in every heart, and unites the rising generation with new and tender ties.... Thus contented with their simple way of life, and placed in a delightful country, they are free from cares, and happy in their ignorance.[29]

Cook learned that Tahiti had no single king, but ten chiefs ruling extended families and client clans. A chief's domain was compact and a person could walk over it in a day. Europeans easily understood the hierarchy of chiefs, nobles (arii), commoners, and slaves, and they understood that a Tahitian could not rise in caste. Cook learned how privileged chiefs were when one came aboard to dine. As the chief was unaccompanied by retainers, there was nobody to feed him, and when the meal was served, "he sat in the chair like a statue without once attempting to put one morsel to his mouth and would certainly have gone without his dinner if one of the servants had not fed him."[30]

Early visitors observed no starvation. Tahitians expressed contempt for Europeans when they learned of hunger in Europe. Some must have thought Europeans came to Polynesia because they had iron but no breadfruit—or women, for that matter—in Beretani, as they pronounced Britain. To Europeans, Tahiti seemed an island of plenty. Food was easy enough to obtain that people did only minimal work in the mornings.

Cook recorded his concern about "venerial distemper." Thirty-three crew and marines reported they had contracted syphilis on the island. In June 1769 Cook noted, "Venerial distemper [on Tahiti] is as common as in any part of the world." Tahitians blamed Bougainville's crew. To Cook it appeared as if "the people bear [venereal disease] with as little concern as if they had been accustomed to it for ages past." Cook wrote that he "did all in my power to prevent its progress," but "the women were so very liberal with their favors, ... that this distemper very soon spread itself over the greatest part of the ship's company, ... and may in time spread itself over all of the islands in the South seas."[31] Cook charted Tahiti meticulously. Before leaving on July 13, he and his scientists and artists had recorded much information on Tahitian culture, plants and animals. Sidney Parkinson captured in pictures the life of the people and the setting. In July and August Cook charted Huahine, Raiatea, Moorea, Bora Bora, and Maupiti, and named them the Society Islands because they were close to one another.

Banks brought away Tupaia (c. 1725–70), an accomplished Polynesian navigator and tohunga (priest) from Raiatea, who wanted to go to England. Cook would value Tupaia's skills as an interpreter on several islands.[32]

THE DE BOENECHEA EXPEDITION

The next European expedition to arrive in Tahiti was Spanish. Having embarked in Callao, Peru, Spanish explorer Domingo de Boenechea reached Tahiti on November 13, 1772, aboard the *Aguila* with a company of 231. He brought several Peruvian Indians with the ingenuous expectation they would somehow understand the language of Tahitians. Boenechea was the first Spanish commander since Quirós 167 years earlier to attempt to claim a South Pacific island. Spanish authorities became alarmed when they learned through an article in a London newspaper of British claims to Tahiti.

The expedition had sailed on September 26, 1772, under orders from the viceroy, Manuel de Amat y Junient, to determine if Britain had established a base at either Tahiti or Easter Island from which the west coast of Spanish America could be menaced. De Boenechea was ordered also to convince the inhabitants of "the incontestable rights of our Catholic king, over all the islands adjacent to the vast dominions he owns."[33] Boenechea was ordered to make certain his crew committed no sign of "rudeness nor least sign of impropriety" onshore; in other words, they were to leave the island's females alone. Boenechea learned that Cook had been to Tahiti and was relieved that the British had left no troops.

Dwindling numbers of Tahitian traders came on board toward the end of the visit, probably because islanders were suffering from sore throats and symptoms suggesting influenza. Islanders blamed the Spaniards for bringing a disease previously unknown among them. Having established friendly relations with Tahitians, renamed Tahiti Isla de Amat (Isle of Love), and left a deadly disease on shore, de Boenechea sailed on December 20, 1772.

De Boenechea reached Peru on February 21, 1773. In his report to the governor, the commander described Tahitians as "tractable, very rational and sagacious, friends to their own interests, very astute, but likewise indolent and prone to thievishness, voracious in regard to food and wanton in sexual license." Presumably read, the report was locked away in archives.[34] The expedition brought four Tahitian males: Pautu, about 30; Tipitipia, 26; Heiao, 18; and Tetuanui, age 13 to Peru. They were taught Spanish and about Christ. Boenechea had been instructed to return a few islanders to Tahiti to spread the word of the Christian God.[35]

COOK'S SECOND EXPEDITION

On July 29, 1772, James Cook embarked on his second voyage to the South Pacific, one year after returning from his first. This time the Admiralty gave Cook two ships; Cook wanted a backup ship after his being nearly stranded on the Great Barrier Reef on the first voyage. At age forty-two, promoted to commander, Cook set out as master of *Resolution*, and of *Adventure* under Tobias Furneaux (1735–81). Furneaux had sailed to Tahiti with Wallis. Cook would sail 112,000 kilometers (70,000 miles) on this second Pacific expedition, nearly twice as far as on his first.

Cook's mandate again was to search for Terra Australis Incognita. Cook strongly doubted its existence, but agreed the matter "is too important a point to be left to conjecture, facts must determine it and these can only be had by visiting the remaining unexplored parts of this sea."[36] Sir Joseph Banks, whose reputation had gained immensely from the first voyage, planned to go with Cook, but did not; a towering superstructure he insisted be added to *Resolution* for his entourage made the ship so unsafe that the tower had to be torn off. Banks swore and stamped his feet on the wharf and took off his possessions and never visited the South Pacific again.[37]

In Tahiti, where he arrived on August 17, 1773, Cook traded for food, although he noted that pigs, previously abundant, were unavailable. He renewed acquaintances with chiefs, particularly Tu, whom he described as being *malu*, or easily frightened by loud noises or any perceived threat.[38] During his two-week stay Cook concluded that, aside from the vice of theft, "The more one is acquainted with these people, the better one likes them, to give them their due I must say they are the most obliging and benevolent people I ever met with."[39] Cook noted that during his first visit, Tahitian girls had offered his sailors sex, at least initially, without expectation of a gift. On this visit, girls demanded something in return.[40] Cook also noted the iron tools acquired by Tu's tribe had given him the ability to build large canoes faster than his warlike rivals—canoes as long as *Endeavour*—31 meters (104 feet). War preparations were ongoing during his visit. Cook declined to take sides.[41]

Cook wrote, "We were conducted to the theatre where we were entertained with a Dramatik Heava or Play in which were both Dancing and Comedy, the performers were five Men and one Woman, which was the Queen, the Musick consisted of three Drumms only, it lasted about an hour and a half ... and upon the whole was well conducted."[42]

On September 3, 1773, Cook's ships anchored at Fare Harbor on Huahine. The inhabitants were busy preparing for war with their nemeses, the aggressive warriors of Bora Bora. Crewmembers witnessed the building of a 265-meter (870-foot) war canoe capable of carrying 144 paddlers. Cook left on September 7 with fresh food, including hogs, chickens, and fruit they received in exchange for axes, nails, beads and other trade goods.[43] Captain Furneaux brought a passenger aboard *Adventure*, Mai (a.k.a. Omai, c. 1751–80), whom Cook described as "dark, ugly, and a downright blackguard," but who would be feted as an exotic celebrity in England.

Cook sailed to Raiatea. The local chief received him and his officer cordially and "desired that he might be called Cook (or Toote) and I Oreo, which was accordingly done." Thus, Cook and Oreo exchanged names and had become *tiaos*, or close friends.[44] Cook and his officers attended a "Comedy or Dramatik Heava," which consisted of drumming and appeared to star the chief's niece. Cook sailed away on September 17.[45]

On April 22, 1774, Cook returned to Tahiti after visiting other Society Islands, Tonga and New Zealand, and sailing perilously close to Antarctica. He returned to replenish food, water and wood. Tahitians wanted red parrot feathers the British had obtained in Tonga; "Not more feathers than might be got from a Tom tit," Cook wrote, "would purchase a hog of 40 or 50 pound weight."[46]

As if a pattern had formed, a Tahitian would steal an item from the ship or from a member of the ship's company. Cook would seize a hostage or property, or he would order his men to destroy canoes. In retaliation Tahitians would cut off essential trade. In one instance Cook had a Tahitian flogged before a great crowd for attempting to steal a water cask. Cook explained to a chief that the flogging "would be a means of saving the lives of some of the people by deterring them from committing crimes of this nature in which some would be killed."[47] Cook renewed his friendship with Chief Tu, a man whose descendants would become kings of Tahiti.[48] Cook sailed from Tahiti on May 14, 1774, visiting once again Huahine and Raiatea. He arrived at Huahine on May 15. On May 20, four of his men engaged in an altercation with Polynesians; the British shot several of their assailants but Cook had to take two chiefs hostage in order to retrieve his men held in captivity.[49]

On May 24, Cook reached Raiatea. Sixty canoes containing members of the Arioi sailed alongside between islands. Arioi were members of an elite society of performers of *heivas*. These elaborate entertainments were performed in honor of the god Oro. The traveling troupe practiced free love among members of their society. They insisted on abortion or infanticide so women could continue to perform as part of the troupe and the performers would remain unencumbered by children to care for.[50]

Of infanticide, demographer Jean-Louis Rallu stated that pre-contact Polynesian population growth rates had been much higher than those in Europe because there had been no sexually transmitted diseases. Without private property, inheritance was not an issue except among the *ariki*, the noble classes. Free love before matrimony also led to a high growth rate. Rallu wrote that after being settled by a few people, "Polynesians covered island landscapes to the point that new customs, such as infanticide and human sacrifice, were adopted to limit growth."[51] Cook left Raiatea on June 4.

MAI ENTERS LONDON SOCIETY

On July 12, 1774, Tobias Furneaux, commanding *Adventure*, which had separated from Cook's *Resolution* in dense fog in New Zealand, returned to England with the first Polynesian to be seen in that country, Mai. Mai was incorrectly called Omai because he answered in Tahitian, "It is Mai," when asked his name. Sir Joseph Banks introduced Mai into society and Mai set about charming London. His patrons dressed him fashionably. Painters Sir Joshua Reynolds (1723–92) and Nathaniel Dance (1735–1811) each painted his portrait. George III gave him an allowance. Mai proved an affable dinner guest at elegant homes. David Sawel, surgeon on Cook's third voyage, gave his opinion of Mai's appearance: "If Master Omaiah's Countrywomen are not handsomer than him I shall bring many of my Nails back."[52]

Mai's ingenuous remarks delighted the English public: "What do you like best about London?" Describing horses and cows, he answered: "The great hog that carries people. English hogs ver' fine. This morning Lord and Lady Sandwich show me the great hog that gives coconut milk. Ver' good. No climb tree — only put hand under hog and squeeze."[53] Banks secured for Mai an invitation to Windsor Castle: "How do King Tosh?" he inquired of George III. The king probably saved Mai's life by arranging for him to be inoculated against the dreaded smallpox. George gave Mai an allowance and a sword.[54] Mai's visit increased European interest in the South Pacific.[55]

DE BOENECHEA RETURNS

After Cook had gone, Spaniards came back. On November 27, 1774, Captain Domingo de Boenechea, sailing again from Peru, arrived in Tahiti with two padres aboard the ships *Aguila* and *Jupiter*. The viceroy of Peru wanted to establish a Spanish presence so as to prevent rival nations from stationing a garrison on Tahiti. Of the four young Tahitian males de Boenechea had transported to Peru at the end of his initial visit in 1772, two returned to be reunited with friends and family. One had died and the fourth remained in Peru.

Fathers Gerónima Clota and Narcisco Gonzales, and an interpreter named Maximo Rodriguez were rowed ashore equipped with tools, weapons, holy oil, and a portable altar. The fathers intended to rescue heathens from what they perceived to be horrendous idolatry. They proved ill-suited for their task. The crew erected a prefabricated house at Vaitepiha Bay in Tahiti-Iti, the small knob-like peninsula attached to the large part of the island. The priests sequestered themselves in it from the noisy, curious, seemingly threatening multitudes that came to observe them. Although they were under the protection of high chief Tu, and they had muskets loaded and ready, they remained terrified. Neither priest went out to learn the language or to preach with the help of interpreter Maximo Rodriguez. They blamed for their situation the two Tahitians who, returning from being schooled in Peru, went back to their families and, presumably, their old spiritual beliefs.

On January 5, 1775, the Spaniards formally claimed the island. The two Spanish ships sailed on January 7, beginning a two-week trip to inspect other of the Society Islands. The priests spent their time guarding their belongings from thieves; nevertheless, they lost various items including the sheets from their beds. Shortly after the ships returned, Captain de Bonenchea died on Tahiti on January 25, 1775. Two days later, his crews sailed for South America under command of Lieutenant Don Tomas Gayangos, leaving the hapless priests to their fears.

When the *Aguila* arrived in Tahiti on October 30, 1775, under the command of Cayetano de Langara, to bring supplies to the priests, the two demanded to be returned home. On November 12, *Aguila* sailed away with the cowed prelates. They reached Callao February 16, 1776. Spain would never again make an attempt to colonize Tahiti. The Spanish voyages to Tahiti had added to neither royal coffers, nor Spanish prestige. Maximo Rodriguez did, however, record valuable observations of life among the people. The viceroy of Peru concluded that, according to reports, the Tahitians had found the priests hilariously funny.[56]

COOK REVISITS TAHITI

James Cook anchored off of Spithead on July 30, 1775, having completed his second voyage to the South Seas. In three years he had lost only four men aboard *Resolution*, none from scurvy. His great accomplishment was to map the South Pacific, having combed the vast ocean between New Hebrides (now Vanuatu) and Easter Island, reaching close to Antarctica and proving at last that there is no great southern continent.

Cook was rewarded with a sinecure that paid £230 per annum as captain of the Royal Hospital at Greenwich. Of supervising a home for aged sailors, Cook wrote, "I must confess it is a fine retreat and a pretty income, but whether I can bring my self to like ease and retirement, time will shew."[57]

Time showed that Captain Cook was unready for semi-retirement, at least not so long as major questions of geography on the other side of the world remained unanswered. Cook sailed from England July 12, 1776, to begin his third voyage to Oceania, eight days after American revolutionary leaders signed the Declaration of Independence. He was promoted to captain. His ships were *Resolution* under his command, and *Discovery* commanded by Charles Clerke (1741–79). The Admiralty ordered Cook to search for the fabled northwest passage from the Pacific to Hudson's Bay or to sail north of Canada to Britain, or north of Siberia to Britain. A task of lesser importance was to return Mai (Omai) home to Huahine.

At forty-eight Cook was tired, having spent nearly three decades at sea.[58] Cook's crews would be gone until 1780, but Cook would not return.

On August 12, 1777, en route to North America, Cook brought horses to Tahiti. The animals astonished the inhabitants, who had never seen large beasts capable of transporting people. In Tahiti Cook put supplies aboard, trading prized red feathers from Tonga, and he renewed his acquaintance with Chief Tu. When he stopped on nearby Moorea, a goat was stolen; Cook responded by sending two large armed parties ashore and burning homes and canoes when the animal was not returned immediately.[59]

During this voyage, Cook was ill with bad digestion and rheumatism, and he may have had an intestinal obstruction due to roundworm infection. Unlike the Cook of earlier voyages, he threw temper tantrums. Cook ordered forty percent of his men flogged at different times on *Resolution*, twice as many as Charles Clerke caused to be whipped on *Endeavour*. He ordered islanders flogged—and even shot a man in Tonga for petty thievery.[60]

Cook was shown the prefabricated house of Spanish padres and the inscription written on a cross to claim the island for Charles III: "Christus vincit Carolus III imperat 1774." Cook ordered the following inscription carved on the other side: "Georgius Tertius Rex Anni 1767 69 73 74 & 77," indicating that ships sent by King George III had been there in five different years.[61]

Cook ordered his carpenters to build large chests so that Chief Tu could secure the gifts he had received from the British. "It was a sign," wrote David Howarth, "that the social system was starting to break down under European teaching." The privatization of objects led to stealing, which led to the necessity of a chest large enough for two guards to sleep on top.[62]

On October 12, 1777, Cook returned Mai to Huahine. In addition to valued red feathers, Mai returned with a suit of armor, a barrel organ, a jack-in-the box, toy soldiers, and pewter dishes, among other artifacts of English civilization. Envied, shunned, and robbed by neighbors, Mai died within two years of his return.[63]

THE *LADY PENRHYN* ARRIVES

After Cook left, no European ship came to Tahiti for eleven years. On July 10, 1788, the *Lady Penrhyn* arrived, its crew seriously ill with scurvy. She was a ship that had worked in the African slave trade, but she came to the Pacific transporting 102 female prisoners to Port Jackson, the prison colony founded at Sydney in January 1788. John Watts, who had come to Tahiti before as a midshipman under Cook, wrote a journal of the visit. Tahitians brought life-giving fruits and water to the emaciated men. This time the Tahitians were starved for iron tools, having worn out those they had used for more than a decade. The crew sold them what they could spare. The crew recovered from scurvy surprisingly quickly once they had eaten fruit and vegetables. After only two weeks the crew was able to man the ship once again and complete their planned voyage to Macao.[64]

THE *BOUNTY*'S BREADFRUIT EXPEDITION

All of these visitors, from Captain Wallis to Captain Sever of the *Lady Penrhyn,* had brought change to Tahiti. The next visitors, who arrived a week after the *Lady Penrhyn* reached Macao, would make unification of the island possible. It was the crew of HMS *Bounty*, under command of Lieutenant William Bligh (1754–1817). Bligh was as yet unaware that he would be the victim of the most notorious mutiny in history. On October 26, 1788, the *Bounty* arrived at Matavai Bay. Mutineers took the ship on April 28, 1789, off Tofua, Tonga. While Bligh and eighteen men saved themselves in the ship's launch, and mutineer Fletcher Christian took eight mutineers to isolated Pitcairn Island, sixteen of the *Bounty's* company elected to remain on Tahiti, including six who professed loyalty to Bligh.

Before they were apprehended by the crew of the *Pandora* less than a year after the mutiny, several of the sixteen had a profound effect on the ongoing power struggle among Tahitian chiefs. Several of the refugees lived with *tios* and their families. Midshipman Peter Heywood reported of his own experience at his *tio's* home, "Whilst we remained there we were used by our Friends with a Friendship, Generosity & Humanity almost unparalleled, being such as never was equaled by the People of any civilized Nations, to the Disgrace of all Christians."[65] Two mutineers, Charles Churchill and Matt Thompson, became mercenaries for Vehiatua, a chief in the southeast of the island. Both died violent deaths. Of the other fourteen, several helped chief Tu, who ruled Matavai and Pare. With their help, Tu conquered most of Tahiti. With the fear of muskets, "It was a walkover," David Howarth wrote.[66] Tu founded the Pomare dynasty, members of which were to reign until 1880.

THE LONDON MISSIONARY SOCIETY

The first missionaries in Polynesia came to Tahiti eight years after the *Bounty's* stay. These missionaries and mission workers were well intentioned and wanted to improve lives—as they saw improvement—and to enable heathen people go to heaven. They would be successful once they had mastered Tahitian and were able to bring coherency to their complex message. In doing so, they needed to convince Tahitians that their idyllic lifestyle was sinful. They faced a long and difficult task in breaking down old *tabus* and replacing them with new ones. If not always beneficial, their accomplishments were enormous. They were brave and dedicated men and women.

On September 22, 1795, hundreds of donors and wellwishers inaugurated the London Missionary Society at Spa Fields Chapel. Members were evangelicals from the Church of England as well as nonconformist Congregationalists. The London Missionary Society was founded during a period of intense spiritual and humanitarian excitement. Humanitarians wanted to liberate slaves, banish social ills, and convert the heathen not only in the Pacific but also in Africa and Asia.

The LMS collected donations to send missionaries to the South Seas. Only a year and a half after its founding, the society sent the missionary ship *Duff* on a 22,500-kilometer (14,000-mile) voyage to Tahiti. The *Duff* arrived on March 5, 1797, with thirty volunteers and their families; eighteen volunteers were to remain on Tahiti while others were to be dispersed to other islands. Four missionaries were ordained, and the mission workers were mostly artisans who had dedicated themselves to the work of proselytizing. Some of the latter had minimal formal education.[67]

From what LMS officials had learned about Tahiti, the inhabitants were in dire need of saving. However, the mission members had been unprepared for the magnitude of their task. The task consisted of preventing Tahitians from enjoying multiple sexual partners, appearing in public with inadequate clothing or none at all, practicing infanticide or abor-

Marae Titiroa, Moorea. Maraes such as this were scenes of pagan ceremonies during which offerings were made while people prayed to their gods and ancestors. Beginning in 1815 Mooreans were converted to Protestant Christianity. A number of maraes exist today in the Society Islands. Photograph Robert Kirk.

tion, sacrificing an occasional human to insure good crops, performing "lude" dances, worshipping idols, singing non–Christian songs, killing tribal enemies, flying kites, and surfing. Tahitians at first expressed curiosity about a religion centered on a god who had no parents but who sired a holy son whose mother had not lain with him. Bored with Old Testament stories and repetitious preaching, many wandered off, regarding the fantastic ideas with indifference.

In six years the missionaries received no letters from home, no directions from London.[68] In March 1798, after a trying year, eleven of the eighteen elected to leave aboard the *Nautilus*, under command of Charles Bishop. The eleven reached Sydney on May 14. Those who fled to Sydney had good reason. As the cooper John Harris wrote to LMS officials in London, the Tahitians "were greatly offended" when four missionaries went to Opare, eight miles from Matavai Bay, to ask chiefs not to trade for muskets, and "they were met by a large company, and stripped of their clothes and Mr. Puckey one of the 4 was much beat. They sent them home naked but somebody on the way after their escape gave them some Otaheitean clothes.... Report came on the back of reports that they would come in the night and put us to death." Three had lost their minds or suffered nervous breakdowns; of these, one man attempted to make love to one of Pomare's wives and to present a lesson on the intricacies of Biblical Hebrew to the chief's family and retainers.[69]

PIRATES CAUSE A MAJOR SETBACK

More trouble for the LMS occurred on the other side of the world. The *Duff* left England in December 1797, intending to return to Tahiti with thirty more volunteers and needed supplies. On February 18, 1799, French pirates aboard *La Grande Buonaparte* captured the missionary ship off Cape Frio, Brazil. The *Duff* and its passengers were taken to Montevideo, Uruguay, where the ship was purchased. Then it was captured again at sea by Portuguese pirates. The Portuguese in turn lost it to French pirates. The missionaries were returned to England on October 5, 1799, some ten months after embarking for Tahiti. The loss of the *Duff* was a financial blow to the London Missionary Society.

The LMS sent the 923-ton *Royal Admiral* under Captain William Wilson. It arrived at Tahiti on July 10, 1801, with letters, supplies and eight more LMS workers. Four among them had been prisoners of pirates aboard the *Duff*; they were James Hayward (1809–1850), William Scott, William Waters, Charles Wilson, and John Youl (1773–1827). Captain Wilson transported convicts to Sydney en route to Tahiti, and also loaded spars in New Zealand for the China market.[70]

TAHITI UNIFIED

Tahitians blamed "all the evils they suffered, to the supposed malign influence of the God of the missionaries." As a result, twenty-two years elapsed before LMS workers converted Tahitians. Their success was largely due to Henry Nott (1744–1844), a bricklayer who had arrived aboard the *Duff* and mastered Tahitian sufficiently to preach a sermon. He returned home only twice in forty-seven years. Nott was able to teach some chiefs to write in their own language.[71]

The hungry penal colony in Sydney received some relief in the form of protein in 1801 when HMS *Porpoise,* under command of Lieutenant William Scott, sent on orders of Governor Philip King, returned from Tahiti with 13,950 kilograms (31,000 pounds) of salt pork. Many of these slaughtered hogs were descendants of European pigs left on the island in 1774 by the Spaniard Boenechea; these were larger and meatier than Polynesian pigs. By 1803 private traders had purchased some 135,000 kilograms (300,000 pounds) of pork, depleting Tahiti's pig population. By the mid–1820s, approximately 1,350,000 kilograms (3 million tons) of pork had been traded. The trade continued, but at a lesser volume, until about 1825.[72] When the *Porpoise* made its first voyage for pork, it brought a variety of tools and trade goods. But Chief Pomare demanded firearms, and when the ship returned in December 1802, it brought muskets and uniforms. Muskets accelerated deaths in tribal warfare and allowed the Pomare dynasty to gain power over the island and retain it. As Colin Newbury stated, "The pork trade became for Tahiti what the sandalwood trade was about to become for Hawaii: a source of wealth and a potent catalyst for social and political change."[73]

Pomare I had ruled the Pare-Aru area. Although his powers were local, as were those of other Tahitian chiefs, Pomare had the prestige of an impeccable pedigree through his blood relationship to Raiatean royalty, and Raiatea was the sacred center of the cult of the god Oro. Because Pomare's territory included Matavai Bay, the most frequently used anchorage by European ships, he enjoyed the prestige of visits by Wallis, Cook, Bligh, fugitive *Bounty* mutineers, and Vancouver. Pomare controlled much of the pork trade with Sydney, accumulating firearms in payment.[74]

In 1803, Tahiti's would-be king Pomare I (1742–1803) died, leaving his son Pomare II (d. 1821). The advantages of prestige, firearms, and location accrued to his heir, who would consolidate power over the entire island.[75] Because Pomare II attempted to gain control over all of Tahiti, an unprecedented situation, his enemies drove him off the island and he fled to nearby Eimeo (Moorea) on December 22, 1808. His dislocation would be temporary. Missionary Henry Nott accompanied Pomare. Other LMS workers went to Huahine and then to New South Wales. A missionary wrote in a letter home: "There is no apparent desire after instruction in the blessed truth of the Gospel." Another wrote, "No success has attended our labours, so as to terminate in the conversion of any."[76]

On November 15, 1815, Pomare, professing that he fought for Jehovah, defeated his enemies at the Battle of Feipi and proclaimed himself King Pomare II of Tahiti and Eimeo. Reverend William Ellis of the LMS gave his opinion of the monarch: "His habits of life were indolent, his disposition sluggish, and his first appearance was by no means adapted to produce a favorable impression on a stranger's mind.... The habits of intemperance which Pomare was to indulge ... threw a stain on his character."[77]

Missionaries enjoyed a major breakthrough on May 16, 1819, when Pomare II was baptized in the royal chapel in Papeete. The king's baptism might have occurred much earlier, but missionaries had waited for the new king to moderate his alcohol consumption. The royal chapel was longer than Westminster Abbey and a stream ran through it. The chapel measured 217 meters (712 feet) long and 16 meters (54 feet) wide. Worshippers could enter through any one of 29 doors and look out of 133 windows. This, the largest edifice in Polynesia, could hold a congregation of 6,000 although only approximately 200 had thus far been baptized.[78] On the day of its dedication, three missionaries preached three sermons from three pulpits to three audiences—simultaneously.[79] After the king converted to Christianity, conversions of the rest of the islanders were only a matter of time. Ethnologically priceless idols were destroyed.

A CHRISTIAN KINGDOM

In 1820, King Pomare II established his administrative center at Papeete. Reverend William Crook of the LMS had started a settlement there in 1818. Pomare's problem now was how to set up an autocratic rule that would unify a small nation that had never before been united. He had no template from which to design a government. He could only ask the missionaries how it should be done. First, they explained, he needed written laws. Pomare promulgated laws that they wrote out for him to protect private property; the missionaries had substantial property and so did he. Next he adopted the Ten Commandments as the law of the land. To enforce these ancient Hebraic strictures, he needed to appoint magistrates; he appointed the missionaries and some men he trusted. Prison, unknown before the laws were written, consisted of two logs that were fixed over the miscreant's ankles to hold him in place. Those unable to pay fines in the form of pigs or cash worked to build a road reaching outward from Papeete. Every time a Tahitian was sentenced to labor, the road reached farther until eventually it encircled the island. It might have taken longer for the two ends of the road to meet had the missionaries not inspired laws against nudity and happy diversions including dancing, singing (except Christian music), wrestling, flute playing, and "unseemly levity."[80]

An observer reported of the Sabbath: "Not a fire is lighted, neither flesh nor fruit is baked, not a tree is climbed, nor a canoe seen on the water, nor a journey by land is performed, on God's holy day; religion — religion alone — is the business and delight of these simple-minded people on the Sabbath." When Russia's Antarctic voyager Baron Thaddeus

Bellinghausen (1778–1852) prepared to sail from Tahiti in 1820, girls, their heads shaved of flowing hair, came aboard his ship — not to barter sexual favors for metal products, but to sing hymns of praise to God.[81] In Papeete observers noted fashion-baffled Tahitian males dressed in European pants without jackets, jackets without pants, jackets and pants without shoes — in threadbare used clothing bought cheaply or retrieved from Sydney rag collectors by traders and sold in the island for a large profit.[82] Taught by missionary wives, Tahitian females sewed their own Mother Hubbard all-encompassing dresses to disguise their natural forms; they donned bonnets to hide whatever hair was not clean shaven.[83]

In 1823, Baltic German Otto von Kotzebue (1787–1846), sailing in the czar's service, was highly critical of the missionary endeavor: "A religion like this, which forbids every innocent pleasure and cramps or annihilates every mental power, is a libel on the divine founder of Christianity. It is true that the religion of the missionaries has, with a great deal of evil, affected some good. It has restrained the vices of theft and incontinence, but it has given birth to ignorance, hypocrisy, and a hatred of all other modes of faith, which was once foreign to the open and benevolent character of the Tahitian."[84] Kotzebue contrasted the new Tahitian with the pre-contact Tahitian, who had been "gentle, benevolent, open, gay, peaceable, and wholly devoid of envy ... who had been oppressed by no care, burdened by no toil, tormented by no passion, seldom visited by sickness, their wants easily satisfied, and the pleasures often recurring."[85]

Pomare II died at age forty on December 7, 1821, of complications brought on by overindulgence in alcohol. He was succeeded by his infant son, Pomare III (1820–27). The child's government operated under a council of regents until his own death at age seven.[86] The fact that the baby king could survive at all in an island of tribal rivalries is a tribute to the stability brought by the LMS establishment.

Fusing Chistianity with Pagan Beliefs

In 1826, the work of the LMS was undermined by a new sect in Tahiti that mixed Christian theology with Polynesian spiritual beliefs. Two men, Teao and Hue, converted a number of Tahitians and Maupitians to the Mamaia sect; these self-described prophets professed that they heard the voices of Christ and of saints, and they echoed millennial prophesies that were current among Europeans and Americans. Adherents were told they could disregard missionaries' strictures against sexual freedom, citing the biblical story of King Solomon's harem, and promised a sensual paradise. The cult spread to Raiatea, Tahaa and Bora Bora. Missionaries William Ellis (1794–1872) in his *Polynesian Researches* (1829) and John Williams (1796–1838) in *Narrative of Missionary Enterprises* (1837) expressed concern.[87] The Mamaia movement ceased to compete with Christianity after about a decade and a half, largely as result of the 1841 Tahiti smallpox outbreak. Mamaia adherents had refused inoculation and many died.[88]

Pomare IV Vahine Takes the Throne

Pomare III died on January 8, 1827, and was succeeded by his half-sister Aimata (1813–77). At age fourteen, she became Queen Pomare Vahine IV (r. 1827–77). Aimata began a half-century reign, the next to last of the house of Pomare. A visitor in 1834 heard stories concerning the queen's personal life during her early reign: "Casting aside all restraints, she shared unblushingly in the licentiousness for which this island is so notorious; nor was it until the year 1831 that she was recalled to a sense of duty."[89]

The subjects Pomare Vahine IV reigned over had diminished in number and the population continued to fall. Missionaries said people died due to their sins, but the causes of death were tuberculosis, alcoholism, smallpox, typhus, dysentery, diphtheria, pneumonia, rotted teeth and the mental depression that occurred when they were wrenched out of their ancient way of life.[90] By 1829 only 8,568 people were counted in Tahiti.[91]

KINGDOM OF CONTRASTS

Two Tahitis were in evidence by the mid–1830s. One was centered on Papeete's ribald waterfront, catering to the most prurient interests of single young mariners long separated from family and home and female companionship. A typical waterfront denizen was characterized by Alan Moorhead as "the throw-out of the west ... who simply hung about ... in a daze of drunkenness and soft sensual living until his money or his credit gave out." At least a hundred were present by the decade's end. Bars and hotel rooms with prostitutes lined the street to serve the needy crews from as many as 150 whaling and sealing vessels.[92]

Arriving in Papeete aboard the whaler *Tuscan* in March 1834, Dr. Frederick Debell Bennett noted the effects of Western contact on Tahitians in Papeete. Bennett wrote in *Narrative of a Whaling Voyage, 1833–36*: "By partaking in [debauchery] their physical no less than their moral state, and in the slovenly, haggard, and diseased inhabitants of the port, it was vain to attempt to recognize the prepossessing figure of the Tahitian as proclaimed by Cook.... The abundance and indiscriminate sale of ardent spirits," Bennett observed, "as well as the laxity of laws which permitted the sensuality of a seaport to be carried to a boundless extent caused scenes of riot and debauchery to be nightly exhibited at Papeete that would have disgraced the most profligate purlieus of London."[93]

Quaker Daniel Wheeler, in 1834, added: "There is scarcely anything so striking or pitiable in their aimless nerveless mode of spending life."[94] Visiting nearby Raiatea, the spiritual center of the Society Islands, Dr. Bennett remarked, "I know of no one spot, except within the precincts of an hospital, where I have seen so much severe disease, accumulated amongst comparatively few individuals, as upon this small island." He attributed the diminished population of Tahiti and its sister islands to disease, and to the fact that women were often sterile. When others became pregnant they often underwent abortion. Dr. Bennett noted high infant mortality.[95]

The second Tahiti was an outwardly pious hinterland. Morality police dressed in old navy or army jackets strode about on the beaches listening for the breathless sounds of illicit lovers or illegal flute notes.[96] An observer aboard the French frigate *L'Artemise* in 1839 noted "in the distance a young girl advancing timidly, her head decorated with flowers and her body enveloped in a large piece of tapa or cloth. But if a missionary spys this graceful child, he bursts out with reproaches and forces the delinquent to hasten out of the church." Monsieur Reybaud lamented, "All was harmonious in their old social organization, everything, their nudity, their freedom, their folly, their license perhaps, and it was all taken away in a day. The salvation that was to save the soul had killed the body."[97]

Morality police enforced strict sabbatarian laws. Otto von Kotzebue described Tahitian Christianity as "a religion which consists in the eternal repetition of prescribed prayers,

which forbids innocent pleasure, and which cramps or annihilates every mental power."
Girls no longer wore a flower behind an ear to signify eligibility. Women wore Mother
Hubbards from their chins to their ankles. Converts attended long Sunday services. Houses
were increasingly made of timbers and were no longer open to cool breezes. People slept
in beds.[98]

To circumvent the ban on liquor, Tahitians set up stills in the forests. To evade the
ban on prostitution and premarital sex, couples met clandestinely. Dances were performed
surreptitiously. Playing drums and nose flute was done out of earshot of the morality
police.[99]

Literacy was among the great benefits of the coming of missionaries. On December
18, 1835, Henry Nott completed his translation of the Bible into Tahitian and some islanders
were able to read it.[100]

ARRIVAL OF CATHOLIC MISSIONARIES

Tahiti had become a Protestant preserve, but Catholics vowed to contest control. On
November 20, 1836, fathers Honoré Laval and Françoise Caret, Picpusian missionaries stationed in Mangareva, arrived at Tauarabu, on the Tahiti coast far from Papeete. The two
priests made their way to Papeete by land, attempting to convert Tahitians as they proceeded. Queen Pomare, on the advice of George Pritchard (1796–1883) of the London Missionary Society, who served as British consul, evicted the priests on December 11. The two
returned to the Gambiers the last day of the year. Their expulsion would lead to a French
takeover of Tahiti within seven years.[101]

Chapter 5

In the *Bounty's* Wake, 1789–1864

SAILING TO PARADISE FOR BREADFRUIT

His Majesty's Armed Vessel *Bounty* arrived at Tahiti on October 26, 1788. Of all of the expeditions thus far to the South Seas, that of the *Bounty* should have been the most pleasant and satisfying to all aboard. Wallis, Bougainville, and Cook had reported Tahiti to be an island paradise. The *Bounty* crew's mission was simple: Proceed to Tahiti, pot breadfruit plants, take the plants to the British West Indies, and sail home.

The crew could anticipate a warm welcome from the friendly Tahitians. Because of the careful planning of the captain, a superb navigator, scurvy was not an issue. When they got back to England, the men could excite their tavern mates with tales of lovely naked girls, offering passion for the price of a nail. Having successfully completed their task, the officers would almost surely receive promotions. Britain was at peace with its neighbors. It would be as ideal an assignment as any of the world's navies could give. Instead, the voyage culminated in a notorious mutiny, reenacted in five motion pictures and examined in over two thousand books and articles. Most important, the mutineers would revolutionize warfare in Tahiti and help transform the lives of people in the Society Islands.

Wealthy sugar planters in Jamaica, St. Kitts, Barbados and other British West Indies islands were known as the plantocracy. They and their allies composed a powerful bloc in Parliament. Planters wanted cheap food for their slaves to cut costs; they had seen profits decline due to competition from French St. Domingue (Haiti), due to an oversupply of sugar, and due to lost access to easily available food from North America after the American Revolution.

A principal cause of the mutiny on April 28, 1789, was the abrasive personality of the *Bounty's* master, Lieutenant William Bligh. Bligh's temper flared continually and he vented his wrath on those around him. It is true that Bligh faced problems beyond his control. First, the 220-ton *Bounty* measured 28 meters (91 feet), and was too small for the crew of 46, a thousand plants, and stacks of wood for a stove to keep the plants warm in higher latitudes. Second, the ship was delayed at Portsmouth until December 23, waiting for written orders from the Admiralty; Bligh missed his best chance of navigating through the Strait of Magellan, as directed, and the crew tried heroically to negotiate the stormy strait for a month before Bligh had to sail for Cape Town. Third, Bligh was underpaid at seventy pounds per annum. Finally, he resented taking on responsibility for the mission with the rank of lieutenant; he felt he should have been promoted to captain or at least commander. Bligh took out his frustrations verbally on the crew, particularly on acting lieutenant Fletcher Christian (1765–94).[1]

The men aboard consisted of twenty-four able-bodied seamen, twenty officers, and

55

two gardeners. Bligh bid goodbye to his wife and daughters in London. He was robust and healthy at age thirty-three. Bligh was by all accounts an experienced navigator, and he had been to Tahiti previously with Cook. Second-in-command Christian, age twenty-four and unmarried, had already sailed with Bligh three times and should have been used to Bligh's explosive temper. With the successful completion of the breadfruit expedition, when Bligh received his promotion, Christian might look forward to command of his own ship.[2]

The notorious Captain Bligh. A superb navigator, Bligh made the mistake of accusing Fletcher Christian of stealing coconuts. His career in shambles with the accusation, Christian took the *Bounty* and set Bligh and 18 loyalists adrift off Tofua, Tonga. From William Bligh's *A Voyage to the South Seas* (London, 1792).

SIX MONTHS IN A TROPICAL ARCADIA

The crew remained on Tahiti twenty-four weeks, longer than any European visitors to that time. Bligh failed to keep his men busy; instead he bullied them unnecessarily as they spent days and nights with island females. Bligh entertained the local chief, Tu (later Pomare), and his family. These island aristocrats dined aboard at the captain's table frequently. Bligh neglected his men, but two manifestations of their dissatisfaction finally commanded his full attention. Three men deserted to Tetiaroa, 32 kilometers (20 miles) away; they apparently preferred soft balmy nights with compliant girls and plentiful fruit and pork to months at sea. The three were easily captured. Bligh also learned of a plot to cut the *Bounty* adrift so that the entire company would have to remain on the paradise isle. Finally, with 1,015 potted breadfruit plants, the *Bounty* sailed out of Matavai Bay on April 4, 1789.[3]

Tu's dominion included Matavai Bay, which gave him an inestimable advantage because Bligh treated him as a powerful ruler, although he was no more powerful than other island chiefs. By the time that the *Bounty* was ready to sail, Tu was ready to conquer his neighbors. There was no king of Tahiti, much less of the Society Islands. David Howarth stated, "That began to undermine the whole old-established structure of Tahitian society.... It made a centre of power where none had been before, and introduced jealousy."[4]

A NOTORIOUS MUTINY

On April 28, 1789, off Tofua, Tonga, Midshipman Fletcher Christian and a small group of fellow conspirators arrested the *Bounty*'s commander. Bligh wrote later: "Just before sun rising Mr. Christian with the Master at Arms, gunner's mate, and Thomas Burkitt, seaman, came into my cabin while I was asleep and seizing me, tied my hands with a cord behind my back, and threatened me with instant death, if I spoke or made the least noise. I, however, called so loud as to alarm everyone: but they had sentinels at their doors. I was hauled out of bed and forced on deck in my shirt, suffering great pains from the tightness with which they had tied my hands."[5] The previous night Bligh, in a violent outburst, had

Bligh's cave, Tofua Tonga. On April 28, 1789, Fletcher Christian and group of mutineers forced Captain William Bligh into the *Bounty*'s 23-foot launch with 18 men loyal to the captain. Tofuan tribesmen repulsed them when they tried to come ashore. One man was killed and the others saved their lives by throwing clothes into the water so they could row off while their assailants retrieved the clothes. Bligh and the survivors reached Dutch Timor, 3,618 miles away, after 41 days in their open boat. Photograph by Robert Kirk.

accused Christian of stealing some of his coconuts. An accusation of theft ended a naval career and could end a seaman's life following a court martial; theft among a seagoing community was a capital offense.[6] Fletcher Christian had invested his adult life learning seamanship under Bligh and now felt his career was over. He no longer had anything to lose, and he felt compelled to sever relations with his former mentor and to do so as soon as possible. His confederates may have been motivated by hatred for the captain, as well the desire to return to the embrace of Tahitian females.[7]

BLIGH'S EPIC SMALL-BOAT VOYAGE

The mutinous transaction was bloodless and completed in a short time. Bligh and eighteen loyalists were given the ship's twenty-three-foot launch so they could attempt, against daunting odds, to save their own lives. For his part, Bligh shouted his vow to bring justice to the mutineers. Immediately following the mutiny, the launch's company went ashore to find food and water at Tofua, a 55-square-kilometer- (21-square-mile-) volcanic island in the Ha'apai Group. Hostile Tofuans killed one of the men, so for the next forty-one days the men refused to stop at other lush islands.

Bligh was uncertain if the Botany Bay colony had been established, so he headed for Timor, the closest European settlement. They went ashore only at the Great Barrier Reef. Bligh worked out rations at two ounces of bread and a quarter pint of water a day. Bligh was a master navigator and with minimal supplies and navigational equipment, completed the arduous 6,144-kilometer (3,618-mile) voyage in an overburdened two-mast launch. After what is probably the greatest small-boat voyage of all time, the company arrived at the Dutch fort in Coupang, Timor, on June 14.

The Dutch authorities welcomed the men, who were emaciated, covered with sores, lethargic and asleep much of the time. They appeared more dead than alive. Eager to report the mutiny so revenge might be enacted, a livid Bligh returned to England on a Dutch packet. Several of the men died of malaria and other tropical diseases while waiting in the Dutch colonial port of Batavia, Java, for ships home.[8]

ABOARD THE *BOUNTY* WITHOUT BLIGH

After ridding themselves of Bligh, twenty-five men on the *Bounty* sailed to Tubuai after the mutiny, arriving May 24, 1789. They intended to make Tubuai their home. Tubuai lies 560 kilometers (350 miles) south of Tahiti. The high island in the Australs measures 140 square kilometers (54 square miles). After shooting a dozen islanders, the crew landed at a place they named appropriately Bloody Bay. Before constructing dwellings, they returned to Tahiti because, as mutineer John Adams later recalled, "We lacked women; and remembering Tahiti, where all of us had made intimate friendships, we decided to return there, so we could each obtain one."[9] They returned on June 26 to Tubuai with eleven Tahitian women and eighteen males, and with pigs, goats, chickens, dogs and a bull and a cow that Cook had left. The twenty-five consisted of true mutineers, as well as seven professed loyalists for whom no space was available aboard Bligh's launch.

The crew with native help began to build a large fort, 36 × 38 meters (120 x 125 feet) to protect themselves from islanders. They managed in a short time to offend the Tubuaians, who then tried to kill them. When a privateer, the ship *Mercury*, sailed close to the island, they realized Tubuai was a poor choice for a home, and that a British warship would arrive to deliver them for hanging. The entire company sailed for Tahiti on September 15, reaching there five days later. All but nine elected to take their chances by staying on Tahiti.[10]

MERCENARIES

The sixteen who stayed had to find their place in Tahitian society. They had two advantages. During their previous six-month stay, many had formed relationships with a *taio*, a close male friend, and were welcomed as a member of his family. Most important, the new arrivals were useful to Chief Tu. With the help of the fugitive mutineers and a beachcomber named Brown who had been ejected from a passing ship, Tu/Pomare was able to conquer Moorea and to expand his territory without fully vanquishing all of his chiefly rivals in Tahiti. Thirteen settled at Matavai Bay. Some renewed relationships with island girls and settled into monogamy; promiscuity was encouraged for experimenting teenagers, but when they matured, men were expected to settle down with wives.

Two men — Charles Churchill and Matthew Thompson — went to the southeast of the island to serve Tu's archrival Vehiatua as mercenaries. When Chief Vehiatua died, Charles Churchill, as his *taio*, claimed his throne. In a fit of jealousy and an attempt to usurp power for himself, Matthew Thompson murdered Churchill. Vehiatua's subjects killed Thompson in retaliation. Fourteen *Bounty* men were left.

Nine mutineers aboard the *Bounty* left Tahiti for the last time on September 21, 1789. While searching for a place of refuge from the law, they were probably the first Europeans to see Rarotonga, largest of the Cook Islands. In 1823 Rarotongans told the Reverend John Williams that two generations earlier a floating garden with waterfalls had arrived offshore; this seagoing garden was probably potted breadfruit, irrigated through water pumps aboard the *Bounty*.[11]

SEARCHING FOR THE PERFECT HIDEOUT

Christian looked through the books in Bligh's cabin and found reference to lonely, uninhabited Pitcairn Island in *Hawkesworth's Voyages* (1773). Pitcairn Island had been found on July 2, 1767, when Midshipman Robert Pitcairn sighted the 4½-square-kilometer (two-square-mile) volcanic island, rising to 3467 meters (1,138 feet). Carteret recorded in the *Swallow*'s log: "It is so high that we saw it at a distance of more than fifteen leagues [roughly 72 kilometers; 45 miles], and it having been discovered by a young gentleman, son to Major Pitcairn of the marines, we called it Pitcairn's Island." Carteret referred to Major John Pitcairn, who had given the order to fire on Minutemen April 19, 1775, at Lexington, Massachusetts, thus beginning the wars of the American Revolution; the major was killed shortly after at Bunker Hill.

Carteret had been unable to stop at Más a Tierra because Spaniards had erected a garrison. The *Swallow* was desperately in need of repairs, and the crew, suffering from scurvy, in need of fresh food and water. Having found and named Pitcairn Island, Carteret was unable to land there either due to raging surf "which at this season broke upon it with great violence." Significantly, Carteret represented his find as 133 degrees 21 minutes west, and 20 degrees two minutes south. Carteret's notation was wrong; it lies at 25 degrees four minutes south, 130 degrees, 5 minutes west. His mischarting made the island difficult for navigators to locate.[12]

AN ALMOST PERFECT HIDEOUT

On January 15, 1790, nine mutineers, six Polynesian men and twelve women from the Society Islands arrived at Bounty Bay, not really a bay but an indentation. Pitcairn Island was probably not only the best, but the only truly safe uninhabited hideaway in all of the Pacific. Its accurate location was not on any chart until 1808. It is isolated, 5,300 kilometers (3,300 miles) from Auckland and 6,600 kilometers (4,100 miles) from Panama. Elusive, forbidding, and difficult to access, it harbored no fierce people to attack the settlers. No disease was present. If the mutineers could not be found, they could not be hanged. The nine fugitives could look forward to long, uneventful lives unless, of course, they were victims of internal dissention. After stripping the *Bounty* of every useful article, including planking for houses, they burned the vessel on January 23 so its presence would not identify their hideout.[13]

BOXING THE ACCUSED

The Admiralty, unable and unwilling to allow mutineers to remain unpunished, sent 160 men to apprehend the mutineers and return them for courts martial. HMS *Pandora* sailed from Portsmouth, England, on November 7, 1790, under command of Captain Edward Edwards (1742–1815), an unconscionable martinet. Edwards took with him Thomas Hayward (1767–98), a loyalist aboard Bligh's launch, to identify the mutineers. Captain Edwards and the *Pandora* crew captured fourteen men from the *Bounty* on Tahiti. The *Pandora* sailed out of Matavai Bay on May 8, 1791, in search of the missing nine. Edwards put all fourteen, loyalists and mutineers together, into "Pandora's Box," an 11 × 14-foot wooden cell on deck; intense heat and pounding rain made the prisoners ill as they remained shackled in pain to the walls and floor.

Edwards searched haphazardly among the Cooks and Samoas. En route he lost a smaller ship, the *Resolution*, which mutineers had built on Tahiti. On August 28, 1791, *Pandora* struck coral on the Great Barrier Reef, and while it sank over eleven hours Edwards refused to release the prisoners from the box. Four drowned, but so did thirty-one crew members, not similarly confined. Ninety-nine survivors rowed to an island inside the Great Barrier Reef. Ten prisoners were left in the scorching sun, naked. Using ship's launches, the survivors, including prisoners, sailed four ship's boats to Coupang, a two-week, 1,100-mile journey with little food or water.[14] On September 15, 1791, they reached Coupang. Dutch authorities welcomed and fed the starving crew and their *Bounty* mutineer prisoners, just as they had welcomed Bligh and his boat company. On October 6, Edwards sailed from Coupang for Batavia, Java, on the Dutch East Indiaman *Rembang*. The *Rembang* arrived in Batavia on November 7, 1791. Edwards divided his party among several ships for passage to England.[15]

BLIGH FULFILLS HIS COMMITMENT

The *Bounty* mutiny did not end Bligh's career; instead, he was introduced to King George III, promoted to commander, and promoted to post-captain a month later. Because he had failed to complete his mission the first time, on April 9, 1792, Captain Bligh returned to Tahiti for breadfruit plants, this time in command of HMS *Providence*. This time he was protected from disgruntled crewmen by nineteen marines. In September 1793 Bligh delivered breadfruit plants to the sugar planters at St. Vincent and Jamaica. Having at last fulfilled his obligation, Bligh remained unaware that he had more mutinies and more promotions in his future. Meanwhile the Tahitian plants put out roots and grew luxuriantly on the rich soil in these islands. When breadfruit was fed to slaves, they initially found it to be insipid.[16]

THE *BOUNTY* COURTS MARTIAL

On June 19, 1792, Captain Edward Edwards brought ten *Bounty* crew members to Portsmouth for trial. He also brought eleven escapees from Sydney, the Bryant party, who had survived a perilous voyage in a long boat before having the detestable luck of encountering Edwards in Coupang, Timor.

On September 12, 1792, Admiral Samuel, First Viscount Hood (1724–1816), opened a six-day court martial aboard HMS *Duke* in Portsmouth Harbor. Four *Bounty* men accused of mutiny were acquitted. Six were condemned to death, but three of those were eventually pardoned. Three unfortunates were hanged. Thousands rode out into Portsmouth Harbour to watch the lethal proceedings take place on the deck of HMS *Brunswick*. Hangings provided free public entertainment for the masses in Georgian England.[17]

MASSACRE DAY AT PITCAIRN ISLAND

While they escaped the naval justice system, the nine mutineers who had settled Pitcairn Island could not escape each other or the Polynesian men they had brought with them. The principal causes of friction had been the shortage of three women and the British men's maltreatment of the Polynesians, whom they sought to enslave. Two of the Polynesian men were killed in December 1790 because their plot to kill the mutineers was discovered.[18]

On September 20, 1793, which came to be known as Massacre Day, Polynesian men murdered five of the *Bounty* mutineers, including Fletcher Christian, who died tending his taro patch. He was nearly twenty-nine. John Adams (a.k.a. Alexander Smith) escaped, though wounded. Three others—Edward Young, Will McCoy and Matt Quintal—hid. Still alive at the end of the bloody day were four mutineers, four Polynesian men and ten women, and by that time a number of children—all fathered by mutineers. Soon all four Polynesian men had been killed in revenge.

McCoy in 1793, suffering from delirium tremens bought on by imbibing copious quantities of ti-root which he distilled as liquor, plunged to his death into the sea with a large rock he had tied to his leg. Adams and Young killed Quintal in 1799, as Adams later explained, before Quintal could murder them.[19] On Christmas day in 1800 Edward Young died of natural causes. Now only John Adams, a.k.a. Alexander Smith (1757?–1829), remained alive of the nine fugitives. Adams had been raised in a London orphanage and was barely literate. Before he died, Midshipman Edward Young (1762?–1800), had taught him to read the Bible and other religious texts taken from the *Bounty*. According to his own account, Adams underwent a religious conversion. He formed an ardent Christian community among the women and twenty-three children.[20]

THE MISSING MUTINEERS MYSTERY SOLVED

Pitcairn Island proved a perfect hideout—for eighteen years. At last, on February 6, 1808, Captain Mahew Folger (1774–1828) of the American sealing vessel *Topaz* sighted the high island. He was the first ship commander to discover the fate of the mutineers, whose disappearance had been a matter of intense interest in Europe since they were last seen in Tahiti.

Folger was greeted by eighteen-year-old Thursday October Christian (1790–1831), son of mutineer Fletcher Christian, and the first born on the island. When told that the Pitcairn calendar was a day off due to the International Date Line, a flustered Thursday October changed his name to *Friday* October. He later reverted to Thursday and named his son Thursday October Christian II. Folger met Adams, and noted eight Tahitian women and twenty-five children, living together in apparent tranquility. The island's soil provided an abundance of food. Adams learned of the French Revolution and the rise of Napoleon Bonaparte. More important to them, the pious Pitcairners learned they had observed the Sabbath on the wrong day and began worshipping on Sunday.

Folger learned that seven of the mutineers and six Polynesian men who sailed with Christian on the *Bounty* had met violent deaths. When Folger returned home, he reported finding Adams, but the British navy was too busy defending national interests against Napoleon's French Empire to send a ship to return a single mutineer for hanging. Yet Adams continued to fear that he would be executed.

Pitcairn Island scene, 1825. Captain Frederick W. Beechey of the *Blossom*, a competent artist, sketched this scene of the last surviving Bounty mutineer, John Adams (in sailor's outfit) surrounded by Tahitian women and half-European, half-Polynesian children. From 1800 to his death in 1829, Adams led the pious inhabitants of the lonely island. From Beechey's *Narrative of Voyage to the Pacific and Around the World*, vol. I. (London, 1831).

Adams was ready to surrender on September 17, 1814, when crews aboard HMS *Briton* and HMS *Tagus* arrived. Officers expected the island to be uninhabited, as Philip Carteret had reported it be, and were unaware that Folger had rediscovered the high island. When officers came ashore through the dangerous surf, John Adams asked Captain Pipon of the *Tagus*, "Do you intend to take me with you sir?" Adams's Tahitian wife and the other Pitcairners pleaded with them not to take him. Pipon recalled: "To have forced him away in opposition to their joint and earnest entreaties would have been an outrage on humanity." As patriarch of a pious community of young people and aging Tahitian women, Adams had gotten away with taking part in stealing His Majesty's vessel, endangering the lives of Captain Bligh and the men in his long boat, and murdering a fellow mutineer as well as a number of Tubuaians.[21]

PITCAIRNERS EMIGRATE TO TAHITI

During Adams's final years three other Englishmen arrived on Pitcairn, John Buffet, John Evans and George Hunn Nobbs, expanding the restricted gene pool. Adams died of natural causes on March 5, 1829, age sixty-five. Islanders had venerated him and spoke of him as "father." Nobbs (1799–1884), who had served as schoolteacher, assumed Adams's functions of island leader.

Adams had told visiting Captain Beechey in December 1825 that he feared Pitcairn was becoming overpopulated and that his community would no longer be able to sustain themselves on the precipitous rock. Adams recalled Tahiti as a paradise and recommended the inhabitants be resettled there. The women were Tahitian and the children half Tahitian. Beechey relayed the request to authorities in London. Eighty-seven men, women and children sailed on March 7, 1831, to Tahiti on the bark *Lucy Ann*, sent by the British Admiralty. Pitcairn was not yet a British colony, so the evacuation of people was a purely altruistic act on the part of Whitehall.

The advisers of King Pomare III offered the Pitcairners land for their new permanent home. Tahiti's population had declined dramatically, resulting in unused land. The arrivals were treated well. One of the four surviving Tahitian women who had sailed with the mutineers fifty-two years earlier was reunited with her sister. But the immigrants had little immunity to the variety of lethal diseases that whites had brought to the Society Islands. First to die was Thursday October Christian. Moreover, the Pitcairn young people were enticed by the looser morals they found in Tahiti. Their more pious elders sought to prevent them from consorting with licentious sailors from whaling vessels. The Pitcairners wanted desperately to go home. The foreign community in Papeete collected $500 to send them back. All but seventeen who died on Tahiti returned to Pitcairn by September 4, 1831.[22]

"THE MUSSOLINI OF PITCAIRN ISLAND"

Stunned by the loss of loved ones on Tahiti, naive, isolated and without protection, the Pitcairn Islanders were victimized by a megalomaniacal dictator. On October 28, 1832, the bark *Maria* brought Joshua Hill, a tall and powerful Englishman, about sixty years of age. The dazed but pious islanders had had scant experience with people who lied to further their own purposes; without the leadership of their "father," John Adams, they were ripe prey for a charlatan. Hill had read or heard about the tiny Anglo-Polynesian community claimed by no nation. Calling himself Captain or Lord Hill, he presented papers, consisting of copies of letters he had addressed to officials in London requesting an appointment to govern Pitcairn. Because authorities declined or ignored his offer, he produced no replies. Nevertheless, islanders accepted these letters as his patents of office.

The first demand Hill made was that all the firearms be handed over to him. Having disarmed the people, the impostor took over the best house, that of schoolmaster George Hunn Nobbs. The tyrant next banned alcoholic beverages, which the islanders had distilled themselves. Hill declared himself President of the Commonwealth of Pitcairn. He told the Pitcairners that all gifts that had already arrived for them on passing ships had been dispatched at his orders, and that if they did not obey him, he would send for soldiers to punish them. Hill claimed to have lived in a palace and to have dined with royalty. Hill named six credulous young island men as his assistants, giving them titles of councilors and cadets; they provided muscle to enforce his rule. Hill exiled the three British immigrants, Evans, Buffett, and Nobbs, because he saw them as his competitors and most likely to see through his bombast. Novelist James Norman Hall called him "The Mussolini of Pitcairn."

After a four-year reign, Hill overreached his authority when he sought to execute twelve-year-old Charlotte Quintal (1822–83) for stealing yams. When Charlotte's father pushed the dictator to the floor and pointed a sword at him, Hill's reign was essentially over.[23] Even more damning for Hill, the British warship *Actaeon* arrived on December 6, 1837, and Hill was exposed as a charlatan. Hill had claimed to be a close cousin and intimate companion of the Duke of Bedford. Lord Edward Russell (1805–87), commander of the *Actaeon*, was the duke's son. Russell told islanders he had never heard of Hill. On December 6, 1837, HMS *Imogene* under command of Captain Henry William Bruce (1792–1863) took Hill away. Back in England Hill presented a monetary claim against the government for services rendered at Pitcairn.[24]

BRITAIN'S FIRST PACIFIC COLONY

The principal result of Joshua Hill's dictatorship was that on November 30, 1838, tiny Pitcairn Island became Britain's first colony in Polynesia. The defenseless population had been vulnerable and in need of protection from the mighty British navy. On November 29, 1838, HMS *Fly* arrived under the command of Captain Russell Elliott. Islanders told Elliott about the reign of terror imposed by Hill. Moreover, from 1823 through 1838, seventy-one ships had stopped, some sending personnel ashore. Islanders told Elliott that "half the ruffian crew of a whale ship were on shore for a fortnight, during which time, they offered every insult to the inhabitants, and threatened to violate any women whose protectors they could overcome by force, ... taunting them that they had no laws, no country, no authority that they were to respect."[25]

Captain Elliott wrote a constitution and a code of laws for the islanders. The constitution provided for a magistrate to be chosen annually by both males and females 18 and over. The captain of any Royal Navy ship that stopped could overrule the chief magistrate as representative of the London government. Compulsory education was mandated. Thus Pitcairn became the first entity in the British Empire to practice female suffrage and the first to require elementary education.[26]

EMIGRATION TO NORFOLK ISLAND

Because fewer ships stopped at Pitcairn and because the population had grown to nearly 200, British authorities decided — with their agreement — to evacuate everyone and resettle them in what authorities considered a more suitable place. On May 2, 1856, Pitcairn was abandoned again. Captain Mathers of the *Morayshire* took 194 to Norfolk Island. The British government gave the people of Pitcairn an island with an abandoned prison colony. The island served as a prison from 1788 to 1813, and then from 1825 to 1855. Prisoners had built sturdy stone buildings and good roads. Norfolk was more than four thousand miles away. At 29°05' South, Norfolk was cooler than Pitcairn. Other than the similar elevation and the tortuous boat entry, there was little resemblance between the two.[27]

A Norfolk resident of three years, Reverend F.S. Batchelor, wrote a description: "The island is about twenty miles in circumference, with an average breadth of five or six miles. It is beautifully diversified with hills and dales ...; and these low lands are exuberantly fertile. Fortunately, too, there are a number of capital stone-built houses, really large and handsome buildings, which would not disgrace our large cities, and plenty of store-houses, granaries, barns, &c., with a neat chapel capable of holding a thousand persons." All of these had been built by convict labor. "Besides tools and other implements ... there is a capital stock of cows, sheep, horses, pigs, and poultry, which would be invaluable to a new community."[28] Reverend Batchelor's description made Norfolk difficult for Pitcairners to resist, especially when offered as a gift from Queen Victoria. Just as Pitcairn had answered every need of the mutineers, Norfolk seemed to answer every need of their descendants.[29]

RETURN TO PITCAIRN ISLAND

Sixteen people returned to Pitcairn, arriving January 17, 1859. Since that day the island has been inhabited continuously. They were the families of brothers Mayhew Young (1827–77) and Moses Young (b. 1829), grandsons of *Bounty* mutineers. They returned just in time. Two boats with well-armed crews approached the landing in Bounty Bay from the French vessel *Josephine*. France had been about to occupy Pitcairn. The *Josephine*'s crews apparently had difficulty maneuvering boats between the rocks into the inner cove; so they gave up in frustration and returned to their ship.

On February 2, 1864, four more families returned on the *St. Kilda* from Norfolk Island. Both groups preferred to govern their own affairs, but they had lost autonomy on Norfolk as a community. New blood was introduced when Samuel Warren, a sailor from Providence, Rhode Island, married Agnes Christian (b. 1841), daughter of Thursday October II, the day before the *St. Kilda* sailed. When the twenty-seven eager passengers arrived in Bounty Bay after dark, they sought to arouse the attention of the Young families by firing muskets and shouting. Alarmed, the Youngs thought themselves under attack. In the light of morning after a long sleepless night the Youngs realized their long-separated relatives and neighbors had returned.

From the returned families of 1858 and 1864, the island population would grow to a peak population of 233 by 1937.[30] Pitcairn remains, in the early twenty-first century, the last British colony in the Pacific Ocean.

Chapter 6

A White Tribe
at Botany Bay, 1788–1911

COOK FINDS BOTANY BAY

Although the northwestern shores of Australia, then known as New Holland, had been skirted and visited by Dutch mariners and English pirates since the early seventeenth century, the east coast awaited European discovery until April 20, 1770. James Cook aboard the *Endeavour* arrived on that date at the southern tip of the vast area he named New South Wales. Joseph Banks said the shore reminded him of the back of a lean cow. On April 28, Cook discovered an inlet he named Botany Bay for the great quantity of plants that Banks and Dr. Solander found. The bay lies 24 kilometers (15 miles) south of Sydney, near what is today the international airport.

There, local Aborigines had their first encounter with whites. Cook saw men, women and children on the shore. When Cook and his companions approached, all but two men "who seemed resolved to oppose our landing" ran off. When one of the men threw a stone, Cook's seemingly reflexive response was to fire a musket with "small shott; and although some of the shot struck the man yet it had no effect than to make him lay hold of a Shield ... to defend himself."[1] Cook named the nearby 55-square-kilometer (21-square-mile) bay that encloses present-day Sydney Harbour Port Jackson, after Sir George Jackson (1709–98), secretary of the Admiralty. Cook meticulously mapped the coast of New South Wales and on May 3, reported finding in many places a rich black soil on which grain could be grown.[2]

Cook admitted he knew little of the Aborigines except what he could learn from observation. Even Tupaia, the Polynesian interpreter, was unable to communicate in their language. Cook noted that they "do not appear to be numerous, neither do they seem to live in large bodies, but [are] dispersed in small parties along the water side; those I saw were about as tall as Europeans, of a very dark brown color" with black hair. Men and women were naked but some "had their faces and bodies painted with a sort of white paint or pigment."[3]

CAUGHT UP ON THE GREAT BARRIER REEF

Cook sailed northward along the coast of what was later to be named Queensland. He began to chart the Great Barrier Reef, 2,000 kilometers (1,250 miles) long by 16 to 145 kilometers (10 to 90 miles) in width. It is a coral reef formed by tiny marine polyps. Yet, Cook was not the reef's European discoverer. On June 6, 1768, Bougainville and his crew had become the first Europeans to record having come upon it.[4] In spite of his superior navigational skills, Cook was no match for the treacherous coral. On June 11, *Endeavour* ran into one of the 2,900 reefs that with 900 islands compose the complex structure. To extricate the seriously leaking *Endeavour*, men unloaded fifty tons of cannons, water, firewood, ballast, even food. Then Cook had to float *Endeavour* to shore with the tide, and raise it on its side. He ordered carpenters to patch the damaged hull. Repairs and waiting for high tide to float the ship once more consumed seven weeks.[5]

While crewmembers were bathing in a river Cook had named for his ship, they confronted Aborigines. Cook noted people painted white and red, dark skinned with fine hair close cropped. Probably a third of the people in all

Aborigine warriors at Botany Bay. "The Natives of New Holland Advancing to Combat" was drawn by artist Sydney Parkinson, probably in April 1770 on Cook's first voyage. When these men saw the whites arrive, they shouted "Warra warra"—"Go away." Parkinson's figures would look quite natural on an ancient Greek vase. Original in Mitchell Library, Sydney.

of Australia lived along the coast of Queensland, a favorable environment.[6] In coastal waters Aborigines used all manner of instruments from lines and hooks to weirs to traps and spears to obtain edible fish.[7]

Cook expressed envy of the primitive people: "They may appear to be the most wretched people upon Earth, but in reality they are far more happier than we Europeans, being wholly unacquainted not only with the superfluous but the necessary Conveniences so much sought after in Europe, they are happy in not knowing the use of them. They live in Tranquility which is not disturbed by the Inequality of Condition. The Earth and sea of their own accord furnishes them with all things necessary for life, they covet not Magnificent Houses, Household-stuff &c." Cook concluded, "They set no value upon any thing we gave them, nor would they ever part with any thing of their own for one article we could offer them."[8]

The small group of indigenous people used what was probably the most effective strategy at their command to protect their territory. They set a grass fire that threatened to consume all the ship's nets and linen set out to dry. Cook claimed that he "was obliged" to shoot one of the men. He recorded that drops of the victim's blood fell on some of the linen.[9] Fire was a strategic instrument also in getting food: wallabies and possums would flee from burning fields, only to be clubbed by waiting hunters.[10] Running his ship aground was Cook's second most costly mistake. The most costly would occur on his third voyage.[11]

On August 22, 1770, *Endeavour* passed through treacherous Torres Strait. Cook ran up the union jack and took possession for King George III of "all the bays, harbors, rivers and islands"—the entire east coast. En route home Cook stopped in Batavia, Java, for supplies. Cook sent a letter to the Admiralty by a Dutch ship stating he had completed his assignment without the loss of one man; his efforts to prevent scurvy had been successful.[12]

Batavia was called Queen of the Eastern Seas, but a more appropriate name would have been "Queen of Disease." Deadly mosquitoes contributed to a death toll estimated at 50,000 a year. Only huge profits induced the Dutch to live in a place where many got sick and only the lucky survived. The entire crew of the *Endeavour* became ill, except the sail maker—who stayed drunk. Cook wrote: "We came in here with as healthy a ships company as need [go] to Sea and after a stay of not quite 3 Months left it in the condition of an Hospital Ship."[13] Cook lost twenty-three men to dysentery and malaria, called the bloody flux. Tupaia, the priest from Raiatea who interpreted for Cook, was dead as well. On July 12, 1771, Cook reached England.[14]

ENVISIONING AN OPEN AIR PRISON

In 1779 Britain was faced with finding a solution to housing convicted criminals. Overcrowding and poverty in the cities had led to increased crime. One observer estimated that 115,000 people in London—one in eight—lived off of crime. These were thieves, muggers, forgers and an estimated 50,000 harlots; but some harlots were women cohabiting with men without benefit of marriage. From 1717 until 1776, authorities had saved money and emptied cells by sending prisoners to America. When the thirteen colonies declared independence, the new sovereign states refused to accept more convicts. British jails were soon overflowing, and prisoners were housed on decaying war ships called hulks. Typhus killed many aboard these rotting ships, which looked like floating slum tenements with lines of washing slung between deteriorating masts. They were called "seminaries of vice."[15]

Sir Joseph Banks told a committee of the House of Commons that convicts could be sent to Botany Bay. Banks testified that the climate, soil, and water were sufficient to allow felons to sustain themselves within a year at no additional cost to Britain's taxpayers.

In addition to the inestimable advantage of taking miscreants so far away that they might never return, was the promise of available naval stores. The Home Secretary, Thomas Townshend, First Viscount Sydney (1733–1800), after whom a great city would be named, was eager to secure both flax and timber for the British navy vessels stationed in India and the Pacific. Strong flax, he wrote, "would be of great consequence to us as a naval power," and tall timber for masts could be cut in Norfolk Island.[16] Norfolk Island, at the time uninhabited, lies 1,678 kilometers (1,042 miles) from Sydney. Parliament agreed to fund transport to Botany Bay on eleven ships.

Convicts were exiled at hard labor for seven years, fourteen years, or life, depending on their offense. The average age was twenty-seven. The youngest was nine; he was John Hudson, who had been convicted of theft. The oldest, Dorothy Handland, was eighty-seven; as soon as she arrived at Sydney Cove, she hanged herself from a gum tree. Eighty percent had been found guilty of offenses against property. Such crimes included petty theft, burglary, cattle rustling, highway holdups and muggings. One young man was sent away for stealing a dozen cucumbers from a garden, while a fifteen-year-old boy was deported for stealing snuff.

THE FIRST FLEET ARRIVES

The First Fleet left England on May 3, 1787, and proceeded via Rio de Janeiro and Cape Town. Captain Arthur Phillip, R.N. (1738–1814), led the voyage and new colony. His grandiose title was Captain General and Governor in Chief over all of the territory that comprised the east coast of the continent. Living space aboard the eleven ships was minimal for the 548 male and 188 female hapless felons; all were bunked together in groups of four on cots the size of king-size beds, with inadequate headroom. After a 252-day voyage, on January 18, 1788, the ships, laden with convicts, arrived at Botany Bay. Sixteen had died of typhus before leaving port, and forty-eight died en route. Many survivors arrived ill. Few among them were well enough or sufficiently trained to be pioneers in an environment that was in many ways totally different from what they had known. Here at the opposite side of the world, gum trees lost bark but not leaves. January was summer and July was among the coldest months. No facilities had been prepared for their arrival. No other ship had gone to New South Wales since Cook's *Endeavour* eighteen years before.

WARRA WARRA MEANS "GO AWAY"

At their first encounter, when naked Aborigines saw whites, they brandished spears and cried, "Warra Warra!"—"Go away!" The sudden arrival of the ships proved to be a disastrous turn of events for the indigenous inhabitants. Their demand for the intruders to leave was apposite. These ancient peoples, numbering on the continent perhaps 300,000, were divided by some 500 languages. No violence took place at this first meeting; Governor Phillip had been ordered to protect Aborigines. The newcomers noted the entrails of fish frying on the heads of Aborigines in the sun, fish oil oozing down over their faces and bodies. One Aborigine scalded his hand attempting to grab a fish from boiling water; he had never seen water boiling. Their Stone Age culture did not include kings or formal councils, writing, altars or temples, domesticated farm animals, built-up shelters, or perhaps most importantly, private property. Rather their lands were communal and sacred, as they were linked to the spirit of their ancestors.[17]

On January 24, 1788, in an extraordinary coincidence, Captain Jean-François de Galaup, Compte de la Pérouse (1741–88?), brought his ships *Astrolabe* and *La Boussoule* to anchor at Botany Bay in the same week the First Fleet arrived there. La Pérouse was on a voyage of exploration. After an exchange of pleasantries, La Pérouse sailed off. He would not be heard from again. The disappearance of the 200 Frenchmen remained until 1826 one of the great mysteries of the age of Pacific exploration.[18]

RAISING THE UNION JACK AT SYDNEY COVE

Because of its poor soil and lack of adequate water, Captain Phillip and his deputy John Hunter (1737–1821) soon rejected Botany Bay as a poor place for a settlement. On

January 26, 1788, Phillip raised the union jack at Sydney Cove. The cove was in a magnificent harbor — Port Jackson — the site of modern Sydney and its suburbs. The first years at Sydney were tragic for the newcomers. The government had planned that men and women, many of whom had never been engaged in productive tasks and who were mostly unskilled except perhaps in the art of picking pockets, should pioneer a virtually unknown land, much against their will. The land looked as if it were arable, but it was sandy, swampy, and full of rocks. Prisoners built temporary housing out of palms for officers. Brick makers made bricks for a permanent town, but the soil was not suited for bricks. As a result, very little of the original settlement survives. Cholera and influenza killed a number of settlers.[19]

Sir Joseph Banks received a letter from a marine corps officer who wrote on November 18, 1788, ten months after arrival: "We have laboured incessantly since we arrived here to raise all sorts of vegetables, and even at this distant period we can barely supply our tables, his excellency [Governor Phillip] not excepted. This together with the miserable state of the natives and scarcity of animals are convincing proof of the badness of the country.... Every gentleman here, two or three excepted concerns with me in opinion, and sincerely wish that the expedition may be recalled."[20] The convicts would no doubt have agreed.

Prisoners and guards had been provisioned with six months' rations. Crops failed. Food was terribly scarce. Rations were lowered and many suffered and died from scurvy. By the end of April 1790, rations of rice and flour had been halved, along with some aged pork, largely inedible.[21]

THE WORLD OF THE ABORIGINES

Yet Aborigines had long found sustenance on the land. They had come across a land bridge at least 60,000 years before from what is now called Indonesia.[22] They used boomerangs to bring down their quarry on open grasslands. Aborigines used spears, axes, and fire sticks. They set fire to the land to flush out possums, lizards, rats, and whatever other creatures they knew to be edible. They fished and gathered shellfish. They knew all the edible plants that grew wild. They had no need to plant. They had all the necessary knowledge to survive. The lack of this knowledge nearly terminated the European settlement.[23]

The coming of Europeans nearly ended the lives of the Aborigines who lived near British settlements. The first of two smallpox epidemics raged around Sydney in 1789. Pre-contact scholars Mulvaney and Kamminga write, "How and from where the disease arrived in Australia is unknown — there were no manifestations of smallpox among the British soldiers and convicts themselves, so perhaps Indonesian trepangers introduced it in the tropics." Numerous boats came from the Indonesian island of Sulawesi to harvest beche-de-mer (trepang, or sea slugs) in Arnhem Land in the continent's far north, and they may have been responsible for transmitting the dread pox.[24]

On February 13, 1790, Governor Phillip wrote to Lord Sydney: "In the beginning of the following April numbers of the natives were found dead with the small-pox in different parts of the harbour.... It is not possible to determine the number of natives who were carried off by this fatal disorder. It must be great; and judging from the information of the native now living with us, who had recovered from the disorder before he was taken, one-half of those who inhabit this part of the country died; and as the natives always retired from where the disorder appeared, and which must have carried with them, it must have been spread to a considerable distance, as well as inland as along the coast. We have seen the traces of it wherever we have been."[25] Other diseases were probably generated from the Sydney settlers, including gonorrhea, syphilis, and tuberculosis, none of which were present before the coming of outsiders. Violent death at the hands of settlers, dislocation of clan society, sterility, loss of lands from which food was obtained — all of these led to diminishing Aboriginal populations.[26]

ESTABLISHING THE NORFOLK ISLAND COLONY

Governor Phillip's orders included establishing a colony on uninhabited Norfolk Island. James Cook came ashore there on October 11, 1774. Cook named 34-square-kilometer (13-square-mile) Norfolk to honor a patron, Mary Blount Howard (1712–73), the Duchess of Norfolk; Cook was unaware the duchess had died the previous year. He noted stout spruce, pines and flax. Flax had probably been brought from New Zealand by Polynesians sometime around the fourteenth century, but the visitors had left no trace of a permanent settlement.[27] In 1784, having read Cook's report, Sir John Call, M.P. (1731–1801), recommended settlement to secure wood for masts and flax for sails. Norfolk pines were so tall and straight that "any alert sailor could see their potential value as a source of ships' mainmasts and spars."[28]

On March 6, 1788, HMS *Supply* brought the first group of settlers. Governor Philip assigned Lieutenant Philip Gidley King (1758–1808) to take charge of nine male and six female convicts and eight free men, including guards. Lieutenant King's ship's master finally found an opening large enough in Norfolk's reef to admit the *Supply*'s boats, but not the ship itself. Once ashore, the company busied themselves building a road and a settlement. They felled trees and planted fruit and vegetables to provide food for themselves and for the Sydney colony. Their first crop failed. By 1790, a hundred and fifty prisoners and staff were working on Norfolk.[29]

THE ARRIVAL OF THE SECOND FLEET

In June and July 1790, the Second Fleet arrived at Sydney. His Majesty's government had given a contract to Camden, Calvert and King, slave transport contractors, to ship felons at seventeen pounds, seven shillings, six pence per person. According to the contract the firm was to be paid for each convict who boarded ship, whether the passenger arrived in New South Wales alive or had died en route. Convicts were bolted to bunks by ankle irons, unable to move without breaking a leg. Of 1,000 who sailed, 267 died on the voyage. Survivors arrived starving, wet, chilled, some lying in their vomit. Some died shortly after landing. In Sydney the contractors sold the food and clothing of the dead passengers to starving convicts.

Another ship, bringing food, had wrecked on an iceberg and never did arrive. As a result, in Sydney there were hundreds more people to feed, but only a small amount of additional food. Coming ashore with the prisoners were the first units of the New South Wales Corps, the military unit that would come to dominate the economy and government of the new colony.[30]

The New South Wales Corps Takes Charge

On December 11, 1792, Governor Phillip left his struggling community to return to England. Between 1792 and 1795, Major Francis Grose (c. 1758–1814) acted as governor; Grose continued to suffer from wounds incurred while fighting for the British in the American Revolution. Grose left some of his extensive powers to subordinates such as John Macarthur (1766–1834). Grose appointed Macarthur regimental paymaster and inspector of public works; these important positions gave Macarthur control of convict labor. Grose also gave hundred-acre grants to officers along with ten convicts each to work them. Grose allowed officers to buy goods from arriving ships on their own account and to sell those goods for profit. Convicts worked fifty hours a week and were allowed to sell their after-hours labor for cash, assuming they had energy for overtime work. Convicts with exemplary behavior were given a ticket of leave and allowed to be paid for work. New free settlers were encouraged to migrate from Britain; they received free passage, tools, the service of convicts, and land grants. When convicts had served their sentences, they were called emancipists and were given land and convict labor for their own use.[31] Australia had no need for African slaves; convicts served the same purpose.

The Sick Third Fleet

With ships arriving separately from July to October 1791, the Third Fleet, again under direction of Camden, Calvert and King, brought more hapless prisoners to Sydney. The *Queen* landed 222 convicts, but nine months later only fifty were alive. Governor Arthur Phillip remonstrated with the government at home, and as a result conditions aboard subsequent fleets would be healthier than those of the Second and Third fleets.[32]

George III Meets an Aborigine

Aborigines were a curiosity to the British, novel enough to amuse a monarch. On May 24, 1793, two members of the Eora tribe at Port Jackson were brought to London and introduced to King George III. Bennelong and Yenmerrawanie were the first Aborigines to visit Europe. Yenmerrawanie died in England, but Bennelong returned to Sydney in 1795. Bennelong found himself in limbo, suspended between two cultures and not accepted by either. Bennelong learned English and became functionally literate.

Governor Phillip gave him a useful tin shield and built him a brick house 12 meters (14.4 feet) square on what is now Bennelong Point, the location of Sydney's dramatic opera house. He was the first Aborigine to wear clothes, eat English food, and drink rum to excess. An officer wrote, "He had lately become so much a man of dignity and consequence, that it was not always easy to obtain his company."[33] He died at about age forty in 1813.[34] Bennelong was among the first of tens of thousands of Aborigines to attempt, with varying degrees of success, to straddle two cultures.

At War with France

On February 1, 1793, France's republican National Convention declared war on Britain. The war, with a temporary peace in 1802, was to continue until Napoleon's defeat at Waterloo, June 18, 1815. The Anglo-French struggle had three important effects on Australia: Some convicted of petty crimes in Britain were forced into the army or navy instead of being transported; those suspected of revolutionary tendencies, Irish predominantly, were transported to New South Wales; and Britain explored and settled parts of Australia such as Tasmania to preempt French fortifications.

In May 1801, a French scientific expedition led by Nicholas Baudin (1754–1803) arrived off the coast of Australia to begin mapping the south coast and to study fauna and flora. Baudin commanded *Geographe,* and Felix Emmanuel Hemein (1763–1839) commanded its sister ship *Naturaliste.* Nine zoologists and botanists were aboard these ships. British authorities became alarmed, particularly when French cartographers assigned names such as *Terre Napoleon* to Australian shores. The French, however, did not plant a colony.[35]

THE QUITE PROFITABLE "RUM CORPS"

The next problem faced by the young Sydney colony arrived from the infant United States. In 1793, the ship *Hope,* under Captain Benjamin Page (1753–1833), brought to Sydney 7,600 gallons of rum from one of Massachusetts' sixty-three distilleries, giving birth to the pernicious rum trade. Made from West Indian molasses, rum led to widespread corruption and drunkenness in the convict settlement. Lieutenant Governor Grose allowed officers to sell rum. Officers wrung as much profit from the concession as they were able. They refused to sell flour and pork to the food-deprived prisoners and free settlers unless they purchased rum as well. Convicts sought release from terror and hard work through hard liquor and often traded some of their week's flour supply for rum and tobacco. Alcohol addiction became widespread in Sydney.[36]

THE FIRST SHEEP ARRIVE

On June 26, 1796, the first merino sheep arrived in New South Wales, beginning an industry that would provide the colony's major export. En route to Sydney, Captain Henry Waterhouse, R.N. (1770–1812), master of HM *Reliance,* purchased merino sheep in Cape Town from the governor's widow. Originating in Spain, the longhaired merino is capable of producing 150 kilometers (93 miles) of wool per pound and of yielding wool superior to that of the sheep that arrived with the First Fleet. Waterhouse sold his merinos to three Sydney men, one of whom was New South Wales Corps Captain John Macarthur (1767–1834). Energetic and intelligent, Macarthur and his astute wife Elizabeth (1766–1850) experimented in methods to improve his lands, his sheep and his profits until he became the richest man in Australia. In 1806 Macarthur returned from England with two merino rams and four ewes from King George III's flock.[37]

SECURING CLAIM TO A CONTINENT

The sudden French presence during the Napoleonic period accelerated further British exploration and settlements in Australia and Tasmania. Fears led to the first circumnavigation of the continent. Matthew Flinders (1774–1814), commanding the 334-ton *Investigator,* entered Sydney Harbour on June 9, 1803, having proved Australia to be a continent.

Flinders named geographical features, including to his chagrin *Encounter Bay* where, on April 8, 1802, he confronted the French commander of *Le Geographe* and the *Naturaliste*, Captain Baudin.[38]

Flinders recorded an encounter in the far north. On February 17, 1803, at Cape Wilberforce at the Arafura Sea, he saw what he thought at first might be six pirate vessels. Rather they were wooden *praus* with palm-leaf sails and bamboo superstructures. They were from the port of Macassar (today Ujung Pandang) on the island of Sulawesi in the East Indies. Flinders learned that sixty *praus* manned by over 1,000 crew were in the waters to collect beche-de-mer for the Canton market. These Southeast Asian visitors left no permanent settlements. They may have been coming to Australia since the early 1700s, or before.[39]

On December 12, 1817, explorer Mathew Flinders proposed to the Colonial Office in London that the name *Australia* be adopted for the continent. Governor Lachlan Macquarie approved. Until the 1830s people continued to refer to the western part of the continent as New Holland, and the southeastern coast as New South Wales. By the mid-nineteenth century, the term Australia was used commonly.[40]

Alarmed that the French explorer Dumont d'Urville had been exploring unclaimed parts of Australia, the British government determined to secure the continent. On May 2, 1829, Captain Charles Fremantle (1800–69) of the Royal Navy sailed up the Swan River in Western Australia and took formal possession of the entire continent for King George IV (1762–1830; r. 1820–30). The continent was claimed four decades after the founding of the first British settlement at Sydney. Captain Fremantle was instructed by his superiors to ask Aborigines if they objected. Possibly the Aborigines failed to understand the question.[41]

Captain Bligh's Next Mutiny

In August 1806, as if the fledgling New South Wales colony did not have sufficient trouble before, Captain William Bligh, deposed master of the *Bounty*, arrived in Sydney. He had been appointed fourth governor. His orders were to accomplish what governors John Hunter (1737–1821; term 1795–1800) and Philip King (1758–1808; term 1800–06) had each tried to do without success: tame the notorious New South Wales Rum Corps. Bligh raged against officers, convicts and emancipists. He succeeded in further alienating enemies and as well as potential supporters.[42]

Bligh did not retain power for long. On January 26, 1808, the mercurial governor was arrested at Government House, Sydney, by men under the leadership of John Macarthur. It was ten years to the day after the First Fleet had arrived, and should have been an occasion for pomp, ceremony and celebration. The powerful Rum Corps obviously had more power than Bligh. The rebels accused the governor of being despotic. Bligh was quoted as saying, "Damn the law! My will is law and woe to the man that dares to disobey it!"[43] Lieutenant Governor Major George Johnston (1764–1823) held Bligh captive until arrival of the new governor, Lachlan Macquarie. Bligh was returned to England, charged as being unfit to govern. The mutineers were found guilty of conspiracy but received mild punishments. In 1811 Bligh was promoted to rear admiral, and in 1814 was promoted to vice admiral. He never returned to the South Pacific. In 1817 he died, before he could be promoted again.[44]

The Rule of Governor Macquarie

On January 1, 1810, Colonel Lachlan Macquarie (1762–1824) arrived in Sydney to assume the post of governor of New South Wales. He brought his own troops, the 73rd

Highland Regiment, which replaced the Rum Corps. Rum Corps members had the choice of either enlisting in the regiment or returning home. About half returned home. The new governor arrived with orders from the government in London: "The Great Objects of attention are to improve the Morals of the Colonists, to encourage Marriage, to provide for Education, to prohibit the Use of Spirituous Liquors, to increase the Agriculture and Stock, so as to ensure the Certainty of a full supply to the Inhabitants, under all Circumstances."[45] Macquarie would serve until February 1822, fulfilling most, if not all, of his orders.

When Macquarie arrived, the colony hovering on the coast of eastern Australia had a European population of about 11,000. Thirty percent of white Australians were convicts. Unlike black slaves, convicts could not be bought and sold, and would be emancipated when their terms expired. Under the Assignment System, convicts were assigned to free masters, but a convict's children could not be sold and convicts could not be whipped without an order from a magistrate. By 1810 emancipists outnumbered convicts; Macquarie treated emancipists as equals of free settlers, offering several of them valuable appointments. As new towns were established on the periphery of the colony, the governor required that each township establish a church and a school.[46]

LAND FOR SHEEP

The colony hovered near the coast until three intrepid explorers opened the interior. On May 31, 1813, free settler Gregory Blaxland (1778–1853), Lieutenant William Lawson (1774–1850), and William Charles Wentworth (1790–1872) discovered a path through the Blue Mountains west of Sydney. The mountains are 600 to 1,080 meters (2,000 to 2,600 feet) high. For a quarter century the range had proven to be a barrier to expansion — a protective shield for the Aborigines beyond its ridges. When the three explorers had found their way through after three weeks, they could see vast fertile lands to the west. Within two years a road traversed the mountains, built in only six months with convict labor. The discovery opened more land to white settlement; more lands of the Aborigines were taken, primarily for vast sheep runs.[47]

Wool became Australia's major industry. Unlike meat before refrigerated ships, it did not spoil during the long passage to Britain. Australia's grasslands accommodated millions of sheep. By mid-century sheep ranges of as much as 100,000 acres were not unusual. As the crow flies from Queensland to South Australia, in a great sweeping arc between the Pacific and the dry Outback, were sheep. Without the wool industry, Australia might have been confined to ports and settlements near the coast. Without sheep, the Aborigines would not have lost vast swathes of land, as much as 400 kilometers (250 miles) wide.[48]

NORFOLK ISLAND IS RESETTLED

On June 6, 1825, Norfolk Island was resettled as a prison colony. Fifty-seven convicts were put to work making existing buildings once again habitable. Norfolk represented what author Robert Hughes called "the quintessence of punishment."[49] A commandant's wife wrote of the prisoners' fate: "During the twelve months that we were on the island, 109 were shot by the sentries in self-defense and 63 bayoneted to death, while the average number of lashes administered every day was 600." Judge Roger Therry described a group of convicts sent from Norfolk to Sydney to give evidence at a trial: "Their sunken glazed eyes, deadly pale faces, hollow fleshless cheeks and once manly limbs shriveled and withered up as if by premature old age, created horror among those in court. There was not one of the six who had not undergone from time to time a thousand lashes each and more." Victims who fainted from the flogger's blows were allowed to rest for a short time until they had recovered sufficiently to continue to receive the number of lashes promised. The flesh normally split after four blows and it was not uncommon to find survivors with no flesh on their backs. Fifty lashes were laid on for smiling while on the chain gang, not walking fast enough, having a pipe, taming a bird, or singing a song. In 1834, when prisoners rebelled, many were shot and 162 locked in cells.[50] William Bernard Ullathorne (1806–89), vicar general at Sydney, visited hapless condemned prisoners on Norfolk Island in July 1834 in his capacity of Roman Catholic priest. Fifty-five convicts had been tried for a mutiny that began on January 15, 1834. Of those, thirteen were executed in July. Bishop Ullathorne wrote: "I have to record the most heart-rending scene that I ever witnessed. The turnkey unlocked the cell door and ... then came forth a yellow exhalation, the produce of the bodies of the men confined therein. I announced to them who were reprieved from death and which of them were to die. It is a literal fact that each man who heard his reprieve wept bitterly; and each man who heard his condemnation of death went down on his knees and, with dry eyes, thanked God they were to be delivered from this horrid place." Ullathorne later testified before Parliament of the evils of transportation to the prison colonies.[51]

When reformers attempted to ease the regimen and punishments, hard-liners cried out and the punishments were reinstated. Finally, in 1854, when bishops protested loudly enough, the Norfolk colony was shut down by Order in Council. The prisoners were transferred to Port Arthur in Van Diemen's Land. In 1855, the bloodied piece of imperial real estate was placed under control of the governor of New South Wales.[52]

FOUNDING QUEENSLAND

Before they were sent to Norfolk Island, many convicts had been housed at the site of the future metropolis of Brisbane. In September 1824 guards brought forty-five convicts to a site called Moreton Bay. The area had been explored the year before by John Oxley (1783–1828). It is the site of present-day Redcliffe. The forty-five prisoners were judged by New South Wales governor Sir Thomas Macdougall Brisbane (1773–1860) as the worst offenders in his charge. Soon, due to a lack of water, the colony was resettled to the present site on the Brisbane River, 21 kilometers (13 miles) west of Moreton Bay. Under its third commandant, Patrick Logan, who meted out punishments from 1826 to 1830, floggings occurred daily. As many as 900 served time in the colony. In 1839 the prison was closed and convicts were sent to Norfolk Island instead. In 1842, Brisbane was opened to free settlers. By 1846 the city had a population of 829, and by 1859, nearly 6,000.[53]

With an estimated 26,000 whites, Queensland became a British crown colony on December 10, 1859, with responsible self government. As a result of an advertising campaign the new government raised the colony's population to 110,000 in a decade.[54]

A GROWING POPULATION

In 1828, the first official census in New South Wales counted 20,870 free individuals. Many of these were former convicts who had completed their sentences and stayed, or the

"Natives of New South Wales." The lithograph by Augustus Earle contrasts the decayed appearance of Aborigines with Europeans in an urban environment, c. 1830. Note that the Aborigines are half dressed in discarded clothing. One is eating something perhaps provided by the well-dressed Europeans. Note the man with the club and particularly the discarded rum bottles. Original in Mitchell Library, Sydney.

children of convicts. These children were called currency lads and currency lasses after a slang term for script good only in the colony — an inferior form of exchange. Free English immigrants were sterling lads or lasses. The census counted 15,728 convicts still serving sentences.[55] The convict population of New South Wales in 1832 was 21,635. Of these, 13,486 were assigned to work for private individuals.[56] The year 1833 saw the most convicts arrive in Australia for any year — 6,779 aboard 36 ships. Convicts made up fifty percent of the white population.[57]

In 1849, excluding Aborigines, 265,503 people were counted in New South Wales, 70,130 in Van Diemen's Land, 63,700 in South Australia, and an estimated 4,600 in Western Australia. Victoria was still part of New South Wales.[58]

According to the census of 1871, New South Wales had grown from 197,000 in 1851 to a half million. Victoria grew nearly ten times from 77,00 in twenty years to 730,000. South Australia's twenty-year increase was from 66,500 to 189,000. Queensland had 122,000 people in 1871.[59] Aborigines were pushed away from settlements and sheep lands.

THE FOUNDING OF MELBOURNE

In May 1835 settlers from Tasmania led by John Batman (1801–39) aboard the *Rebecca*, and a second group led by John Pascoe Fawkner (1792–1869) founded Melbourne. As a representative of investors in the Port Phillip Association, Batman bought 100,000 acres of prime sheep land at the future site of Melbourne. The town was named for Britain's prime minister, William Lamb, Lord Melbourne (1779–1848; P.M. 1834, 1835–41). Batman paid 20 blankets, 30 knives, 12 tomahawks, 10 looking glasses, 12 pair of scissors, 50 handkerchiefs, 12 red shirts, 4 flannel jackets, 4 suits of clothes, and 50 pounds of flour. The aborigines failed to understand that the whites did not intend to dwell among them, but to expel them without rights to the land, the boundaries of which remained long in dispute.

Fawkner's settlers sailed up the Yarra River and arrived August 30, 1835, aboard the *Enterprize*. By 1836, 177 people were living in bark and timber huts. They plowed wheat fields in what are now Melbourne's streets. As the settlement was unauthorized by the administration in Sydney, the government ordered squatters to leave. Authorities in 1837 acquiesced to their presence and acknowledged Melbourne as part of New South Wales. Thousands of sheep were driven overland from Sydney and delivered by sea from Tasmania.[60]

TRANSPORTATION ENDS

Orders in Council, issued in London on May 22, 1840, ended the transportation of convicts to New South Wales. The orders were a result of hearings by a parliamentary commission meeting in 1837 and 1838, headed by M.P. William Molesworth (1810–55). In November 1840, the last transported convicts landed in Sydney Harbour. Convicts continued to be sent to Van Diemen's Land and to Western Australia. Transportation had been considered fiscally sound because it had saved British taxpayers the costs of maintaining prisoners; most convicts were fed by the settlers to whom they were assigned as workers. In Australia, however, free workers resented competition from convict labor and demanded that more convicts be barred from entry.[61]

After an eighty-nine-day voyage, the last convicts from Britain to arrive in Australia were taken ashore in Western Australia on January 9, 1868. The *Hougoumont*, commanded by Captain William Cozzens, had left Portsmouth October 12, 1867. *Hougoumont* was the last of thirty-seven ships to bring convicts to Western Australia. Sixty-two Fenians (Irish nationalists) were among the 279 convicts and 108 passengers. The Fenians had risen against British rule on March 5, 1867.

Transportation, which had begun in 1787, had ended previously in all other states. Over eighty-one years, 162,000 had been transported to Australia and Norfolk Island. These included 137,000 males and 24,960 females. Their mean age was twenty-six, and most had been convicted of petty theft. Sixty percent were English, thirty-four percent Irish, and five percent Scots.[62]

EXPLORER EYRE SYMPATHIZES WITH ABORIGINES

Among the most sympathetic observer of the Aborigines' plight in the face of white encroachment was Edward John Eyre (1815–1901), who explored South Australia's interior in 1839. Eyre wrote in his journal, published in London in 1840:

The character of the Australian native has been so constantly misrepresented and traduced, that by the world at large, he is looked upon as the lowest and most degraded of the human specie and generally considered as ranking little above the members of the brute creation.... [He is seen as] cruel, bloodthirsty, revengeful and treacherous.... I believe that were Europeans placed under the same circumstances, equally wronged, and equally shut off from redress, they would not exhibit half the moderation or forbearance that these poor untutored children of impulse have invariably shown.

Eyre went on to state, "By right of conquest, without pleading even the mockery of cession, or the cheatery of sale, we have unhesitatingly entered, occupied and disposed of lands, spreading forth a new population over its surface, and driving before us the original inhabitants."[63] Eyre was less sympathetic when in 1865, as governor of Jamaica, he suppressed the Morant Bay Rebellion with such brutality that he was charged with murder.

MINERS SWELL THE POPULATION

The California gold rush would lead directly to gold strikes in Australia. A gold discovery in California's Sierra Nevada foothills in January 1848 brought an estimated 6,000 Australians and 1,000 New Zealanders to the Mother Lode. These Antipodal Forty-niners arrived in San Francisco Bay, the entry to the Gold Country, on an estimated 200 sailings. In the next decade, forty percent of the gold mined in the world came from California. The *Sydney Herald* reported that one man dug up $1,200 worth of nuggets in six days and three others obtained in one day twenty-six pounds of pure metal. As a result of such reports, Australians and New Zealanders, bent on getting rich, set sail for San Francisco Bay, making the voyage in an average seventy days; they had a distinct advantage over East Coast Americans, who needed eight months to arrive in California.

Americans in California identified 279 Australians who were or had been convicts. They were called Sydney Ducks. The *San Francisco Star* declared that "Life and property are in immediate jeopardy" from the Sydney Ducks. Vigilantes, who were volunteer enforcers of law and order, cross-examined 91, hanged 4, whipped 1, deported 14, and handed 15 over to the authorities. Many Americans saw all Australians as ex-convicts. Many Australians saw Americans as uncouth pistol-packing vigilantes.[64]

On February 12, 1851, Edward Hammond Hargraves (1818–91), who had learned placer mining in California but had not done well, found gold at the Ophir Digging in the state that would become Victoria. His real achievement was triggering a population boom that made Melbourne a major city. He exclaimed to the man who accompanied him, "I shall be a baronet, you will be knighted, and my old horse will be stuffed, put into a glass case, and sent to the British Museum." Hargraves publicized the Ophir Digging because he preferred getting the reward for his discovery to actually having to dig. Hargraves found enough gold to get him the title of Finder, a ten-thousand-pound reward, an appointment as commissioner of gold mining, and an audience with Queen Victoria.[65]

The discovery of gold brought hundreds of thousands of migrants from Liverpool, Hamburg, Canton, San Francisco, and elsewhere. Emancipists flooded into the gold fields, as did Melbourne police, all of whom quit their posts and set out to seek riches. In 1852, the first full year of digging, 35,000 miners took out £16,000,000. During the 1850s Australia accounted for thirty-nine percent of the world's gold output; most came from Victoria.[66] Between 1851 and 1861, Victoria's population grew from 97,489 to 539,764. Melbourne grew faster than San Francisco during the same period.[67] As a result of population growth Victoria was separated from New South Wales on July 1, 1851, and was given its own administration.

By 1858 the gold diggings had attracted some 150,000 people to Victoria. Among them were thousands of Chinese.[68] From 1855, groups of six to seven hundred indentured laborers arrived in Melbourne from southern China, bound to pay transportation costs to a contractor by finding gold in the picked-over fields. By 1861, 24,062 Chinese were in Victoria. Six were females. White "diggers" took out their frustrations by molesting Chinese workers.[69]

Aborigines, inevitably, were overrun by hordes of miners and dislocated again. The wife of the French consul noted that Aborigines resented losing their lands: "The woods are on fire every night. The blacks set them alight in retaliation for being driven away."[70] Pawel Strzelecki (1797–1873), the Polish explorer of Victoria, Tasmania and New South Wales, wrote that Aborigines he observed were "degraded, subdued, confused, awkward and distrustful, ill, concealing emotions of anger, scorn or revenge, emaciated and covered with filthy rags." Whites set out on kangaroo hunts and were equally satisfied with having shot an Aborigine. Missionaries withdrew in some districts because Aborigines were no longer present.[71]

THE MINERS REBEL

The government of New South Wales, of which Victoria remained a part until July 1, 1851, levied a monthly license fee on all miners. Miners voiced their adamant opposition immediately. Miners wanted to work for themselves and to be left alone by authorities. Miners perceived it to be unfair that those who failed to find any gold paid the same fee as those who struck it rich.[72]

On December 3, 1854, colonial regimental forces, consisting of 276 men, and police ended a miners' rebellion centered at the makeshift Eureka Stockade in Ballarat, Victoria. In ten minutes, twenty-two miners were killed and twelve wounded, while a hundred and twenty were marched off to prison. Six soldiers were killed. Trials of thirteen miners began on February 22, 1855, and led to acquittals. Governor Sir Charles Hotham (1808–55) abolished the costly mining licenses and diminished the police presence in the fields.[73]

Including many Irish immigrants, miners had been agitating for three years for abolition of the hated mining license fee and demanding manhood suffrage. Other demands, such as the secret ballot, were inspired by Britain's Chartist Movement. In the absence of a more dramatic upheaval such as the French or American Revolution, the rebellion at the Eureka Stockade "persists as symbol of national identity," historian Donald Denoon suggested.[74]

RABBITS!

Obtaining sustenance became a still greater challenge for Aborigines after December 26, 1859, when the clipper *Lightning* landed rabbits from England. Thomas Austin of Winchelsea near Geelong, Victoria, introduced five hares and two dozen wild rabbits to his property for hunting purposes. Rabbits produce at the fastest rate of any mammal. One doe can give birth to sixty rabbits a year, and by the 1870s millions of rabbits were spreading through the continent. Grasslands that had been reserved for sheep were soon denuded by rabbits and soil erosion resulted. Land values plummeted. Aborigines lost food sources to rabbits. A farmer described rabbits in such infinite number that "the ground was scarcely to be seen for about a mile in length." The appetites of these masses of rabbits worsened the effects of the great drought of 1875–78 and sent sheep ranchers into bankruptcy. Mr. Austin, however, had no shortage of rabbits to hunt.[75]

Taking Land from Aborigines

In October 1861, the New South Wales legislature passed the Crown Lands Alienation Act, also known as the Robertson Act after Premier John Robertson (1816–91; premier 1860–61). The act allowed landless whites to select 40 to 320 acres at one pound per acre. They were to pay twenty-five percent down and the balance within three years at five percent interest. Pastoralists could lease adjoining acreage. The *Sydney Gazette* called for "particularly selected, sober, industrious men, with small families from the middling class of free people" to settle. "Selectors" pledged to cultivate at least ten percent of their land and build a house. In five years, 17,000 families settled. Australians imported American farming aids such as windmill pumps and barbed wire. Australia developed wheat strains for their dry conditions.[76]

A white citizen wrote a letter to the editor of the *Queenslander* on May 1, 1880, complaining that growth of the number of whites was a disaster for Aborigines. "On occupying new territory the aboriginal inhabitants are treated exactly in the same way as the wild beasts or birds the settlers may find there. Their lives and their property, the nets, canoes, and weapons ... are held by the Europeans as being at their absolute disposal. Their goods are taken, their children forcibly stolen, their women carried away, entirely at the caprice of the white men. The least show of resistance is answered by a rifle bullet." When Aborigines retaliated, the writer attested, "the native police have been sent to 'disperse' them," and the word *disperse* had become "a convenient euphuism for wholesale massacre."[77]

Two weeks later, on May 15, a writer for the *Illustrated Sydney News and New South Wales Agriculturalist and Grazier* stated, "The Aborigines of Australia are a doomed race." Contrasting their pre-contact condition with their state after nearly a century of European settlement, he continued: "But now their camps were scenes of abject misery. The settlers guns and the settlers dogs had harassed and destroyed their game, and semi-starvation was their lot. The poison of the grog shop had destroyed their natural acuteness, and the most horrible and loathesome diseases had spread from the vicious habits of the whites."[78]

Frozen Meat Is Exported

The first successful shipment of frozen meat from the Antipodes to Europe — 30 tons — left aboard the *Strathleven* from Darling Harbour, Sydney, in November 1879. Meat in Australia was three to four times cheaper than in England and was profitable to ship half way around the world, frozen. It arrived in London in February 1880. The ability to deliver frozen meat proved a huge advantage to the Australian economy and resulted in more land being opened to the cattle and sheep industries.[79]

Birth of the Commonwealth

In 1897 and 1898 colonial conventions had discussed federation. On July 9, 1900, Queen Victoria signed the bill approving Australian federation. New South Wales, Victoria,

Queensland, South Australia, and Western Australia joined. On the first day of 1901 the
five Australian colonies unified as the nation of Australia. The federation was headed by
Prime Minister Edmund Barton (1849–1920; P.M. 1901–03). Australians realized they would
need their own defenses against foreign attack rather than relying on the Royal Navy. Among
their principal concerns were the proximity of German and French colonies and the con-
ceivability of Japanese or Russian encroachments.[80]

TOWARD A WHITE COMMONWEALTH

In force from December 17, 1901, the Pacific Islands Labourers Act directed that all
islanders working in the Queensland fields would be returned home no later than December 31, 1906. No more South Seas island workers could enter after March 31, 1904. Australia was to be kept white and, so far as practicable, British in language, culture, and
institutions.[81] Although some Melanesians petitioned the government to be allowed to stay,
all but about 2,500 were taken home on Burns Philip ships between late 1906 and mid–1908.
By the end of 1906 Australia had repatriated 6,000 Melanesian contract laborers to their
islands. Many went reluctantly and some hid out until the deportations had ended. The
federal government offered a bounty of one to two pounds per ton of sugar for growers
who employed white labor; by 1911, ninety-five percent of Queensland sugar workers were
white.

The Act to Place Certain Restriction on Immigration to Australia received royal
approval on December 23, 1901. The act was the cornerstone of a White Australia policy.
The Barton administration gave immigration authorities the power to demand that any
applicant for admission to the country write a dictated passage in any European language.
Depending on the examiner's expectations or intentions, the test could effectively bar any
would-be immigrant. The dictation test remained in effect until 1958.[82]

In 1901 the new Australian commonwealth counted 3,773,801 people. The number in
1881 for all of the colonies that were to make up the federation had been 2,306,736; Australia experienced a 61 percent population increase in two decades.[83]

WOMEN ARE ENFRANCHISED

On June 12, 1902, Australia became the second nation to enfranchise women to vote
in Commonwealth elections. The first nation to enfranchise women was New Zealand in
1893. Only males were elected to the federal Australia legislature, however, until 1943 when
two women were seated. In state and local elections, women in South Australia voted as
early as 1894, and in Western Australia from 1899. Women could vote in state and local
elections in New South Wales in 1902, Tasmania in 1903, and Queensland in 1908.[84]

STOLEN CHILDREN

According to a Commonwealth act in 1911 any minor with an Aborigine parent or
grandparent could be placed under control of a protector and could be removed from his
or her family. Known as the Stolen Generations, at least 100,000 Aboriginal children were

taken from their families between 1911 and 1970, when the program was abolished. Many families were shattered and had little redress. In seizing children from their parents, authorities professed to believe that children could be offered a better education and opportunities among whites. They could be assimilated. Children were often told that their families had died. They were generally not released until age eighteen.

Children from unions of whites and Aborigines were a separate category, part of neither white nor Aborigine society. Taking an idea from the eugenics movement, popular in the first half of the twentieth century, officials in the states and on the federal level felt that black blood could be bred out through successive generations marrying whites. What resulted in many cases was physical and sexual abuse and the exploitation of children as workers.[85]

Knowledgeable people thought Aborigines to be dying out as a race.[86] Aborigines were not dying out, but disease had carried off tens of thousands, and thousands more were killed in a futile struggle to save their sacred, life-sustaining lands. When they lost their lands and could do nothing about it, many became apathetic and sometimes appeared as barely visible figures at the periphery of the whites' dynamic cities.

Chapter 7

The Death of the Last
Tasmanian, 1642–1876

TRUCANINI'S FUNERAL

A Tasmanian woman named Trucanini died on March 8, 1876. In Hobart, the island's largest city, townspeople had watched her walking in her red turban and cardigan sweater with her dogs. Trucanini thought she was born somewhere around 1812. Although she lived to about age sixty-four — old for an Aboriginal Tasmanian — her life had been tragic. Trucanini told her story, and it was sent by a J.W. Graves to the *Hobart Mercury* and printed shortly after her death. Her tragedies were not atypical of those of her race.

The unnamed white man who related her story prefaced it by stating that he first saw Trucanini in early 1830. "We took her, also her husband and two of his boys by a former wife, and two other woman [sic,] the remains of the tribe of Bruni Island." Bruni (or Bruny) Island is off the south coast of Tasmania. He continued, "At the time I think she was about 18 years of age, her father was chief of Bruni Island, name Mangana. She had an uncle (I don't know his native name) the white people called him Boomer. He was shot by a Soldier. I will now give you some account of what she knew."

> We was camped close to Partridge Island when I was a little girl, when a vessel came to anchor without our knowing of it. A boat came on shore, and some of the men attacked our camp. We all ran away, but one of them caught my mother and stabbed her with a knife and killed her. My father grieved much about her death.... I had a sister named Moorina, she was taken away by a sailing boat. I used to go to Birch's Bay. There was a party of men cutting timber for the Government there; the overseer was Mr. Munro. While I was there two young men of my tribe came for me, one of them was to have been my husband; his name was Paraweena. Well, two of the sawyers said they would take us in a boat to Bruni Island, which we agreed to. When we got about half way across the channel they murdered the two natives, and threw them overboard. I tried to jump overboard, but one of them held me. Their names were Watkin Lowe and Paddy Newel.

The white man who related her story continued, "This was the account she gave me. Many times her sister was in the [Bass] Straits living with a man; they called him Abbysinia Jack. She was accidentally shot by a sealer named Robert Gamble."[1]

Crowds of the curious came to Trucanini's funeral procession. Since 1803 a dramatic decrease in the population occurred of what had been estimated as anywhere from three to ten thousand Tasmanians before the arrival of white colonists. But by 1855, only three full-blooded men, two boys and eleven women were alive. In 1869 the last man died. In three-quarters of a century an ancient and vibrant Pacific island people had become virtually extinct largely as result of contact with the outside world. Disease, alcohol, white men tak-

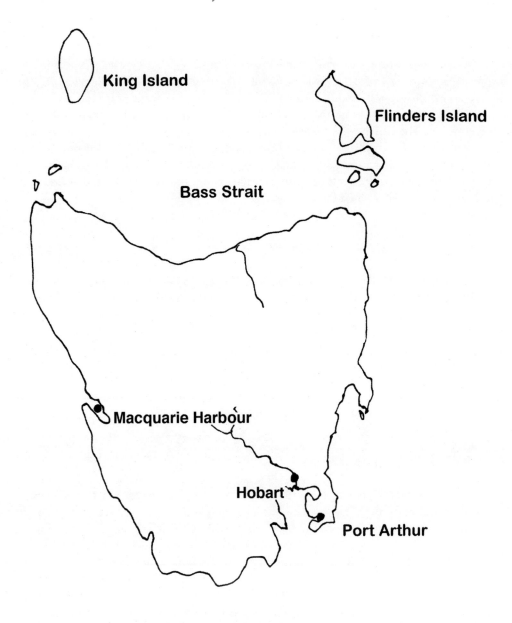

King Island

Flinders Island

Bass Strait

Macquarie Harbour

Hobart

Port Arthur

Tasmania

Map of Tasmania. Illustration by Barbara Kirk.

ing Tasmanian females, and death by firearms were the principal causes.[2] Numerous half-caste Tasmanian-Europeans flourished, the progeny of sealers, convicts and settlers and Tasmanian females. Suke, who lived in a sealer community on Kangaroo Island in Bass Strait, did not die until 1888, so she is really the last full Tasmanian, but Trucanini is her people's symbol, a survivor against daunting odds.[3]

Tasman's Discovery

Dutch navigator Abel Tasman found Tasmania on November 14, 1642, naming it Van Diemen's Land. What Tasman saw was an island measuring 68,401 square kilometers (26,410 square miles); it is mountainous, lush and green. Flowing rivers slice into the landscape. The climate is more temperate than much of Australia, with mild winters and relatively cool summers. The Dutch were traders and tropical planters, and in Tasman's view there was no profit for his company to make from his discovery. Tasman did not return. The Dutchmen did not see the aboriginal people whose progenitors had walked overland to Van Diemen's Land perhaps twenty thousand years ago and became isolated from the continent ten thousand years later when the seas rose.[4]

Nude Sailors Meet Noble Savages

On March 7, 1772, French commander Nicholas Marion du Fresne (1724–72) was the next European to arrive, 130 years after Tasman. A product of the Age of Reason, Marion sought to learn what he could about Tasmanians; perhaps they were the Noble Savages — uncorrupted by civilization — discussed in Parisian salons. To treat with the indigenes as equals, he required that two boatloads of crew and officers row into shore after stripping naked. The Tasmanian men he encountered were friendly at first, but when a third boat full of men rowed in, "The Savages rained on us a shower of spears and stones." A naked sailor fired at them, wounding several and killing at least one. After the deadly altercation, Marion had to rethink his concept of the Noble Savage.

Cook Describes the Tasmanians

On January 26, 1777, having stopped at Cape Town en route to Oceania, Captain James Cook reached the island. On this visit Cook had a good look at the inhabitants. Eight boys and a man "came out of the Woods to us without shewing the least mark of fear and with the greatest confidence imaginable." Cook said they were "quite naked & wore no ornaments except the large punctures or ridges raised on the skin."[5] They were "rather slender, their skin was black and also their hair, ... and their features were far from disagreeable" but their teeth were "very dirty."[6] Mai, the Polynesian the Cook expedition had brought at his own request from Tahiti, fired a gun, causing the group to run into the woods. Cook concluded of Van Diemen's Land, mistakenly, "I hardly need say it is the Southern point of New Holland [Australia], which if not a Continent is one of the largest islands in the World."[7]

The Tasmanians that Cook described spoke one of two languages, one northern and one southern, that differed from any on the Australian continent. They are estimated to have lived in seventy to eighty-five groups, each consisting of thirty to eighty people.[8] Nine tribes consisting of an average of nine groups numbered between 250 and 700 each.[9]

Their material possessions were exceedingly primitive. To warm themselves in their cool climate, they would bundle in a kangaroo hide or wallaby skin. Weapons were simple clubs or spears. Tools were sticks or hand-held flakes. Their culture had not developed beyond that of the Stone Age.[10]

SEAL HUNTERS AT BASS STRAIT

Only at the end of the eighteenth century was Van Diemen's Land shown to be an island. On October 7, 1798, Matthew Flinders (1774–1814), a midshipman, and George Bass (1771–1803), a surgeon, sailed from Sydney and showed that Bass Strait separates Van Diemen's Land from New South Wales. They also explored the island's Derwent River Valley.

The first white settlers in Van Diemen's Land were hunters out of Sydney who killed fur seals at Bass Strait and sold them to American traders. The Americans sold them in the Chinese market. The British pioneered the fur seal trade but two monopolies put individual British traders at a disadvantage: They needed a license from the East India Company to trade East of Cape of Good Hope, and a license from the South Sea Company to trade on the North American west coast. These disabilities allowed Americans to dominate the trade.[11] As British subjects, Australians were forbidden to trade in Canton, but Americans were not bound by the rule.[12]

Groups of ten to fifteen seal hunters remained on the island during hunting season. Some were escaped convicts. They collected kangaroo hides and sealskins to sell to visiting traders, receiving rum in exchange. Lawless characters made the "Barbary Coast of the South Seas" unsafe for whites or for Tasmanians.[13] As Abyssina Jack took or bought Trucanini's sister, they bought or captured temporary mates. Indigenous men sold women for dogs and for food. White hunters put women to work clubbing seals. In 1820, about fifty white men lived on remote islands with a hundred Aboriginal women. Hunters took an estimated 100,000 seal skins between 1800 and 1806.[14]

ARRIVAL OF SETTLERS AND CONVICTS

Forty-nine settlers, consisting of convicts and free subjects, under Lieutenant John Bowen (1780–1827), age 23, arrived in Van Diemen's Land on September 13, 1803, to found a settlement. Governor King of New South Wales ordered Bowen to sail up the Derwent Estuary. A major reason for founding the colony was that in 1802, during an interregnum in the Napoleonic Wars, a French cartographic mission aboard two ships sought to rename the south coast of Australia Terre Napoleon. Governor King feared the French would take Van Diemen's Land. From there they could menace Britain's Australian colony. The governor feared also that American whalers could settle at the mouth of the Derwent River and take over the Ireland–size island.

Bowen attempted to settle at Risdon Cove, but he noted poor soil. Meanwhile, Marine Colonel David Collins (1754–1810) attempted to found a colony at Port Phillip Bay; it is the site of Melbourne. Collins commanded three hundred convicts aboard HMS *Calcutta*. As Port Phillip Bay appeared unsuitable for cultivation, Collins obtained permission to move his charges to join the Derwent colony recently arrived in Tasmania.[15]

Collins founded Hobart Town on the Derwent River October 9, 1804. In February 1804 Lieutenant Governor Collins arrived with his convicts at Risdon Cove. Collins immediately relieved Lieutenant Bowen of his command and joined his group with Bowen's, which he moved to Sullivan's Cove, 10 kilometers (6 miles) away and on the opposite shore of the estuary. Hobart Town was named for the colonial secretary, Robert Hobart, Fourth Earl of Buckinghamshire (1760–1816). It soon became the second largest city in Australia. Hobart Town was renamed Hobart in 1875.

"Go away, you white buggers!"

Second in command Lieutenant Edward Lord wrote: "With no ships visiting us, the whole settlement was called upon to endure hardships of no ordinary kind. The governor himself, the officers, and the entire settlement for 18 months, were without bread, vegetables, tea, sugar, wine, spirits, beer, or any substitute except the precarious supply of the wild game of the country."[16] One survivor recalled eating whale blubber and boiled seaweed. The pioneers survived by killing kangaroos, which were more plentiful than in Sydney.

Before long, all kangaroos near Hobart Town had been depleted. Particularly during the hunger years 1804–08, men with dogs pursued kangaroos further into the bush; now the British were in direct competition for food with the Tasmanians. By 1808, twenty whites and a hundred Tasmanians had been killed.[17] As whites took more land, the Tasmanians were reduced to raiding settlements for sustenance. They soon learned enough English to make their demands known: "Go away, you white buggers!" Although the government advised settlers and convicts that Tasmanians were "placed in the King's Peace," whites claimed they were defending their interests—while "blacks were carrying out unspeakable atrocities."[18] Whites justified their taking Tasmanians' land and killing their prey because as uncivilized people, the indigenes had no rights. Tasmanians were considered British subjects, liable to be tried in courts of law, and without the rights of citizens.[19]

Harsh Convict Life

Aborigines were not the only victims of early white inhabitants. In January 1822, a prison was established at Macquarie Harbour on Sarah Island for the worst criminal offenders. Raging seas and miles of wilderness made escape difficult. For a decade Australia had no tougher prison. In this excruciatingly cold and wet climate, drenched by 203 centimeters (80 inches) of rain a year, guards forced prisoners to cut, saw and plane logs. Convicts worked 16 hours a day, dragging leg irons as they hobbled about. They suffered from malnutrition. At times they suffered from scurvy because the soil would not allow the growth of crops to prevent it. Most prisoners received copious lashes for infractions, perceived or real. In 1833 the prison was abandoned as being too costly to maintain.[20]

"The Lieutenant Governor of the Woods"

Until 1825 bushrangers—convicts who escaped the lash—were a greater threat to settlers than were Aborigines. Three became famous. Michael Howe (1787–1818) ran off on arrival and soon led a gang of twenty escapees. He called himself "Lieutenant Governor of the Woods." His gang terrorized the countryside for three years. It was difficult for the authorities to find him because convicts gave Howe information on the movement of troops sent to apprehend him. Howe wore kangaroo skins and a long beard, and presented "altogether a terrific appearance." On October 21, 1818, Howe was killed while hiding near the Shannon River. A soldier and a convict, both of whom wanted the reward, bashed him to death with their muskets.[21]

Alexander Pearce (1790–1824) was the second most famous figure in early nineteenth century Tasmania. He was executed on July 19, 1824, for the unspeakable crime of canni-balism. In 1819 Pearce arrived at Macquarie Harbour. He escaped twice, the only convict to accomplish that feat. After being captured the first time, he claimed to have eaten the four men who had run off with him. Authorities thought his astonishing confession was a lie to protect accomplices while they hid. When he was caught a second time, his captors discovered in Pearce's pocket some remains of a fifth convict, Thomas Cox.[22] Folk songs recall Pearce's gastronomic exploits. Movies about Pearce include *The Last Confession of Alexander Pearce* (2008), *The Dying Breed* (2008), and *Van Diemen's Land* (2009).

The third notorious individual was bushranger Matthew Brady (1799–1826), who was hanged on May 4, 1826. He had been sentenced in England for forgery. Sent to Tasmania, he escaped and became the "Gentleman Bushranger," celebrated for never robbing ladies. When Governor George Arthur (1784–1854; terms 1824–36) offered a full pardon for any convict who would bring Brady in, Brady pinned the following notice to doors: "It has caused Matthew Brady much concern that such a person known as Sir George Arthur is at large. Twenty gallons of rum will be given to any person that can deliver his person to me."[23] Brady was captured only when the governor sent men disguised as convicts in irons to apprehend him; the man credited with his capture was John Batman, a bounty hunter. John Batman would go on to found Melbourne, Victoria, in 1835.[24]

FORMING THE "BLACK LINE"

As more convicts and free settlers arrived, indigenous Tasmanians lost land and food sources. By 1830 Europeans numbered 23,500; six thousand of these were free settlers. Using vast land grants and purchases, they grazed a million sheep on the vast Midland Plains between Hobart and Launceston.[25] These settled districts comprised about thirty per-cent of the island.[26] Governor Arthur proposed to send an emissary to come to some accom-modation with the Tasmanians. People in Hobart wanted them sent to an island in the Bass Strait. Because no treaty setting out tribal boundaries with those of the European inter-lopers had been signed, Tasmanians fought back. Their method of warfare was hit-and-run — what the Europeans called depredations— actually guerrilla warfare. They maimed sheep, burned houses, and murdered isolated settlers. Fear pervaded isolated farmsteads, and settlers demanded action by the authorities.[27]

In the summer of 1829–30 Governor Arthur established the Aborigines Committee. When the committee solicited suggestions from the general public in February 1830, it received a variety of ideas, all harsh: Hire Maori warriors to capture them and take them to New Zealand as slaves; leave food laced with deadly poison for them to find and eat; organize a military campaign against them; booby-trap huts designed to capture them. One respondent called for "dogs to hunt the Aborigines as was done in Cuba and Jamaica with the negroes."[28] The idea that Governor Arthur accepted was to forcibly remove all Tas-manians to islands in the Bass Strait, thus ending the fear of raids.

In 1830 Arthur conscripted 2,200 white male civilians and gave orders to 550 soldiers to round up all Tasmanians. These men formed a human chain on the seventh of October across much of Van Diemen's Land. It is known as the Black Line. They attempted to cor-ner and remove Tasmanians to a reservation, freeing the island for their own use. They expected to capture 2,000. They carried guns with 30,000 rounds of ammunition, and 300 pairs of handcuffs. They tried to intimidate their prey by cursing, firing into the air and sounding bugles. All of this prodigious effort resulted in catching one man and a small boy.

AN INSULAR CONCENTRATION CAMP

In frustration, Arthur sent word to those few Tasmanians left at the defensible center of the island that if they came out into the open they would be well treated and given clothes and schooling. Some surrendered. They were sent from their ancestral lands to rugged Flinders Island (1,333 square kilometers; 520 square miles) in Bass Strait.[29] At their island reservation they caught new diseases, so that by 1835 there were only 150 left.[30]

White visitors and officials insisted that the removal had a positive effect on the people. In 1832 two investigators from England visited survivors at Flinders Island; James B. Walker reported:

> The tractability of the captive blacks at the settlement was remarkable. They acted like good-natured children, and were imitative as monkeys.... They showed a great desire to copy the ways of their white instructors. The men were particularly anxious to be supplied with trousers, but resented the offer of yellow trousers, the usual garb of prisoners. They also wanted to have stools to sit upon, and tables for their meals, and to be supplied with knives and forks, like Europeans.[31]

In 1839, George A. Robinson, commandant of the Flinders Island settlement mentioned in his report to the lieutenant governor that mortality had been a problem, but he insisted, "I do no consider the depopulation to be wholly attributable to their removal, for in my opinion the same causes did exist in their primeval districts. It is a pleasing reflection to know that everything has been done which ingenuity could devise or humanity suggest to alleviate their condition."[32] By 1843, their numbers had plummeted to 54. In 1847 the pitiable survivors were resettled on the Tasmanian mainland, where they were observed to drink rum and pose for cameras.[33]

THE PORT ARTHUR PRISON

In 1832, Port Arthur was opened as a penal institution 97 kilometers (60 miles) south of Hobart Town. It replaced Macquarie Harbor, which was abandoned as too expensive for the government to maintain. Tourists today see lush lawns, a romantic gothic church, and a large pink brick jail. Port Arthur's college-campus appearance belies its history as the setting for harsh punishments.

The most notable escape attempt from Port Arthur was that of convict George Hunt. Hunt attempted to disguise himself in the skin of a large kangaroo. As he hopped out the gate, he overheard hungry guards preparing to fire at him — seeing him as an ungainly marsupial they planned to share for supper. Hunt saved himself from being shot by pulling off his head covering and begging to be returned to the prison.[34]

Van Diemen's Land was, above all, a prison colony. In 1836 authorities reported that 75 percent of whites on the island were convicts, former convicts, or descendants of convicts; these numbered an estimated 17,000 males, while free men numbered 14,000. The island had all of the sinister trappings of totalitarianism for prisoners and free persons alike: passes, spies, and trade restrictions — all supervised under nine police districts.

In 1846 Van Diemen's Land became the largest prison colony in the world. The island held 29,900 prisoners. Because transportation to New South Wales had ended in 1840, new convicts—as many as 5,000 per year, including many Irish—arrived.[35] The year 1853 saw the last importation of convicts. From 1803 to 1853, 73,500 convicts had been transported to Van Diemen's Land.[36]

By Order in Council, after January 1, 1856, Van Diemen's Land, named by Abel Tasman in honor of his superior in the Dutch East India Company, became Tasmania in its discoverer's honor. The title of the chief colonial executive was raised from lieutenant governor to governor.[37]

In the 1850s and '60s, Port Arthur had seen convicts engaged in agriculture, timber cutting, and manufacturing, but by the 1870s, after long years of involuntary service, many of those who were left had become infirm or otherwise unable to work. Port Arthur was finally closed in 1877; some prisoners were freed and the rest sent to other facilities. During its 54 years of operation, Port Arthur had housed 12,500 inmates.[38]

TRUCANINI'S REMAINS

In 1878 Trucanini's remains were disinterred and exhibited in the collection of the Royal Society of Tasmania. In 1947 curators stored Trucanini's bones in the museum basement. In 1976, the centennial of her death, her remains were cremated and scattered at sea—except for her hair and skin, which were given to the Royal Society of Surgeons in the United Kingdom. The Royal College had them returned to Tasmania in 2002.[39]

Because Europeans never reached an agreement with the aboriginal Tasmanians regarding the sharing of land, Tasmanians had struck back as best they could and when they could in defense of what was theirs. The policy of the whites resulted ultimately in the genocide of full-blooded Tasmanians. Genocide was perpetrated by a people who professed to be civilized and Christian, and each action against the original inhabitants was cited as being legal. Taking into account the loneliness, nervousness, and insecurity of the white jailers and settlers, they were, in the words of Alan Moorhead, possessed by a "sadistic frenzy" not only against the indigenous people but against prisoners as well.[40]

Chapter 8

Maori Encounters, 1769–1840

What Young Nick Saw

Although it was not claimed by a European power until two centuries after Abel Tasman sighted the two great islands, New Zealand was the great Polynesian prize. It would become a populous nation dominated by *pakehas* (whites) and would attract Polynesians from smaller islands. It was Cook who brought New Zealand once more to the world's attention after it had remained unvisited by Europeans for 127 years after Tasman arrived. After three months on Tahiti during his first Pacific voyage, Captain James Cook had sailed 50 degrees south. On October 6, 1769, twelve-year-old Nicholas Young, a ship's boy aboard *Endeavour*, sighted North Island at a place Cook named Young Nick's Head.

Cook had an advantage that Tasman did not—an interpreter. He had brought the Tahitian Tupaia, who greeted Maoris in the "King George Island Language," or Tahitian, which to Cook's surprise the Maoris understood. Maoris spoke the same Polynesian tongue, but it varied by dialect. In the first confrontation between British and Maori, the coxswain feared they might seize his boats; he fired warning shots, which stopped them only momentarily, so he shot and killed a man. Later another Maori was shot dead when he tried to seize a sword, and at least three more were wounded. And so began the ongoing encounter of Maori and *pakeha*. The deaths took place at what Cook named Poverty Bay because "it afforded us no one thing we wanted." Maoris attempted to engage the visitors in traditional battle. Warriors used the *taiaha*, a long wooden sword; and *patu*, a short club. War involved small raiding parties, individual combat, or ambushes. Even in large battles only a few died. War had long been widespread and was waged to take food (including humans), to take land, to avenge insults, or to settle disagreements over control or authority. Death in battle or death imputed to witchcraft demanded revenge. The Maori name for the region of Auckland was Tamaki (Battle); Tamaki was a highly desirable region, often contested. In addition to cannibal feasts, conquests led to a lucrative trade in shrunken human heads. Shrunken heads had no economic value to a Maori; they were used in fact to ridicule the vanquished, but Europeans took them home as souvenirs, and were willing to pay muskets and rum for them, so entrepreneurial Maoris undertook to offer a sufficient supply.[1]

Warriors intimidated the interlopers with war *haka*, distorting their faces and proclaiming their prowess in battle. On the fifteenth of October Cook's crew shot "two or three more" because they tried to pull the Tahitian boy Tiata, Tupaia's servant, into their canoe. This episode took place at what Cook named Cape Kidnappers. On the following day, when Cook perceived that Maori were about to attack, the British were "obliged to fire ... and unfortunately either two or three were killed, and wounded, and three jumped overboard." The three in the water were taken aboard "and treated with all imaginable kindness."[2]

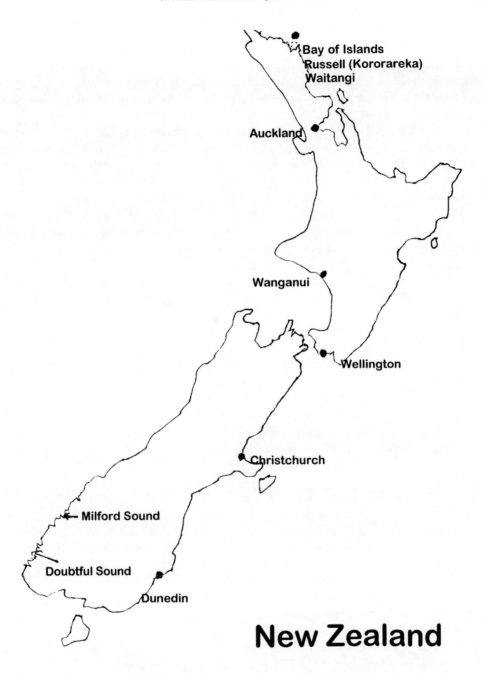

New Zealand

Map of New Zealand. Illustration by Barbara Kirk.

Cook spent six months circumnavigating New Zealand, showing it to be two major islands. He mapped over 3,800 kilometers (2,400 miles). He painstakingly described what he saw, including a stupendously large mountain Maoris called Aoraki, soaring to 3,754 meters (12,316 feet) in the Southern Alps. In 1851 it was named Mount Cook. Joseph Banks, Johann Reinhold, Georg Foerster, and Daniel Solander studied the flora and fauna. John Webber, William Hodges, and Sydney Parkinson drew pictures to capture the waning moments of a society until then undisturbed by Western influences. In fact, the Maori were the last large group of people to be disturbed by the wider world.[3]

As in other Polynesian communities, the commoners—*tutua*—were subservient to the *ariki*, or nobles. The extended family was the *whanau*, which might include three generations, aunts, uncles, and cousins. The average size was forty. Members of the *whanau* had the right to erect dwellings and to fish, hunt, and plant on family land. As sons left the *whanau* and began extended families of their own, *hapus* were created or expanded. A *hapu* was a community consisting of several *whanaus*. They lived in communities (*kainga*) that traced their common ancestry to the coming of *waka*, the first canoes according to creation myths from tropical Hawai'iki, their ancient home. In the wider region the *iwi*, a loose confederation of *hapus*, could combine for large feasts or in defense of their territory.

Maoris had developed elaborate art forms. Carvers turned out fine and lethal clubs, spears, and swords. They carved beautiful boat prows and woodwork to decorate meeting-houses. Men and women underwent painful tattooing procedures to assert their strength and celebrate individuality with elaborate designs.

When Maoris had arrived in Aotearoa, the only animals that came with them were dogs and rats. They brought tropical plants to grow, although when the plants did survive, they were often a disappointment. But there were abundant new foodstuffs to be had, including shellfish, fern roots, and large flightless moas. The Maoris killed moas until they became extinct.

As the Maori population grew and edible species became scarce or extinct, they adjusted to an ongoing competition for land and food. *Pas* (hill-top fortresses) protected them from rival tribes. In many areas warfare was ongoing. Fewer than 200 men from a single *hapu* would stage a surprise attack on a *pa*. People lived in fear of cannibal enemies. The vanquished were either killed during the battle and eaten afterwards, or they were brought back to the *hapu*, constituting a deferred delicacy to be kept alive and savored later.[4]

Maoris were obviously confounded by the arrival of white men. Tupaia's aid as an interpreter notwithstanding, misunderstandings were numerous. Because they rowed ashore facing aft, Maoris perceived the newcomers as supernatural beings able to see through the backs of their heads. The British could remove clothes and wigs, perceived by Maoris to be skin and scalp. Maoris assumed the men were homosexuals because they arrived without women; they presented Cook with a boy for his pleasure, and when he declined, they offered another. They assumed the English were omnivorous and Maoris tossed everything given them into a stew: potatoes, shoes, and candles. Some tried to drink oil from ship's lamps.

Most significantly for the transformation of the Maori world, Cook planted potatoes at an inlet he named Doubtful Sound; within fifty years potatoes had replaced fern roots in local diets. Growing potatoes provided tribes time for war, to which many were addicted. Cook left also pigs and chickens at Hawke's Bay. Pork soon became an important source of protein. Cook sailed off on April 1, 1770, at the beginning of autumn, having claimed possession of New Zealand for his king.[5]

ENTER THE FRENCH

Meanwhile, two French expeditions arrived. The first was under command of Jean-François-Marie de Surville (1717–70). On December 17, 1769, Surville passed Cook at Cape Reinga on North Island when Cook was preparing to sail south along the west coast. Because of limited visibility, neither Surville nor Cook knew that the other was nearby. Ironically, no European had come to New Zealand since 1642, and now ships from two rivals were there at the same time.

Surville had set out aboard the 650-ton *St. Jean Baptiste* from a French trading outpost in India to locate Tahiti in order to trade, but before he could find the island, he was desperate for food and water for his sick and dying men. He attempted to take on supplies in the Solomon Islands on October 7, but was driven off by hostile inhabitants. Surville knew about Tasman's discovery of New Zealand and headed there. He stayed from December 12 to 19 on North Island, obtaining food and repairing his ship. Surville was drowned the following year off the coast of Peru.[6]

The second French expedition to arrive in New Zealand was commanded by was Marc-Joseph Marion Dufresne (1724–72). Marion du Fresne had worked for the French East India Company, but when the company was dissolved in 1769, he became a Pacific explorer. Having obtained two ships, *Mascarin* and *Marquis de Castries*, from the administrator of French-dominated Mauritius, he set sail with two mandates. He was to return Aotourou to Tahiti; the first Polynesian to come to Europe had been brought to France in 1769 by Bougainville. And he was to find Terra Australis Incognita.

Marion du Fresne claimed New Zealand for France, renaming it France Australe. On July 12, 1772, while fishing at what would be named Assassin Cove on North Island, Maoris killed and ate the captain and twenty-six crewmembers. Without knowing it, the Frenchmen were fishing in an area Maoris considered *tabu*. In retaliation the crew burned a village and killed an estimated 250 Maoris. The du Fresne expedition was a total failure. Aotourou died before the ships left the Indian Ocean, the captain was killed, and there was no continent to find.[7]

CAPTAIN COOK RETURNS

From March 26 to May 18, 1773, on his second South Seas expedition, Commander James Cook replenished supplies in New Zealand. He put ashore farm animals and planted seeds. For six weeks the two ships anchored at Dusky Sound in the southwest of South Island. After that they stayed at Queen Charlotte Sound in the northeast of South Island.[8] As he prepared to sail from New Zealand to Tahiti, Cook became philosophical:

> I have observed that this second Visit of ours hath not mended the morals of the Natives of either Sex, the Women of this Country I always looked up to be more chaste than the generality of Indian [Polynesian] Women, ... but now we find the men are the chief promoters of this Vice, and for a pike nail or any other thing they value will oblige their Wives and Daughters to prostitute themselves whether they will or no ... and what is still more to our Shame as civilized Christians, we debauch their Morals already too prone to vice and we introduce among them wants and perhaps diseases which they never before knew and which serves only to disturb that happy tranquility they and their fore Fathers had injoy'd.[9]

Cook's *Resolution* was accompanied on the expedition by *Adventure*. *Adventure* had become separated in dense fog from *Resolution* in New Zealand in late October and was to return to England separately. On December 17, 1773, Lieutenant Tobias Furneaux, *Adventure*'s commander, sent a party of ten ashore to gather greens at Tolaga Bay, north of Poverty Bay. None returned. The next day a boat party found a shoe and a severed hand tattooed "TH," which they identified as belonging to missing forecastleman Thomas Hill. They found baskets of cooked and fresh human flesh. The following day they confirmed the fate of their ten shipmates. Furneaux wrote that it was "such a shocking scene of carnage and barbarity as can never be mentioned or thought of but with horror, for the heads, hearts and lungs of several of our people were seen lying on the beach, and at a little distance the dogs gnawing their entrails."[10]

Cook intended to sail below the Antarctic Circle as part of his instructions. Cook circumnavigated Antarctica three times, sailing within 160 kilometers (100 miles) of the continent but without seeing it. Cook reported they were stopped by "fog Sleet and Snow which froze to the Rigging as it fell and decorated the whole with icicles ... the cold so intense as hardly to be endured."[11] Cook was duly proud of his accomplishment, describing himself in a private letter immodestly as one "whose ambition leads me not only farther than any man has been before me, but as far as I think it possible for man to go." On January 30, 1774, at 71 degrees south, Cook reached the point from which he had to turn north.[12]

On February 12, 1777, during his third voyage to the South Pacific, Cook visited New Zealand again. Going ashore at Queen Charlotte Sound for water, Cook was unable to induce Maoris to come aboard his ship; Cook concluded they feared he would take revenge for the massacre and consumption of Captain Furneaux's boat party at Tolaga Bay thirty-eight months before. Because he had powerful weapons, chiefs asked Cook to ally with them against their enemies. Cook stated: "If I had followed the advice of all our pretended friends, I might have extirpated the whole race, for the people of each Hamlet or village by turns applied to me to destroy the other."[13] Cook confirmed that Maoris were among the most belligerent of Oceanic people he had encountered.

Frantic for Weapons

In the early 1800s, Maoris formed a symbiotic relationship with sealers, missionaries, traders, and whalers. The first Europeans to exploit New Zealand's resources were seal hunters working off the southwest coast of South Island. In 1792, the crew of the *Britannia* collected 4,500 skins at Dusky Sound. Pelts could be sold profitably in Canton, China; in 1811, fifteen American ships in Canton Harbor sold 18,000 sea otter pelts, not all from New Zealand, for a half million dollars.[14] Maoris tolerated sealers and other white interlopers because they were frantic to obtain the white man's weapons before their enemies did.

From about 1791 to 1840, the Bay of Islands was a favorite, if often lawless, site for wooding and watering, as sailors phrased the process of replenishing their provisions. Fresh vegetables, fruit, wood, flax for rope, timber to replace masts, and fresh water were abundant. Forests in the north decreased rapidly because Maori workers felled trees for Europeans. Hundreds of Maoris were employed as loggers and haulers. Maoris gained skill in dressing timber, and — with iron tools — even cabinetmaking, and constructing European-style boats. Some coastal tribes came close to starvation as they traded food for guns or neglected crops and fishing to harvest flax and timber to trade for guns.

Maoris performed several services. Some Maori women prostituted themselves to get weapons for their men. At the request of captains Maoris captured and brought back deserters, receiving a reward for their efforts. A sailor aboard the ship *Logan* in the Bay of Islands recalled: "Several of the boys tried to run away, but the Maoris caught them, tied their feet and hands together, slung them on poles, and brought them back after a reward was offered."[15] Other Maoris joined sealing and later whaling ships as paid crew. When the seals had been exterminated, sealers moved on to islands nearer to Antarctica.[16]

THE CHILLING *BOYD* MASSACRE

By 1809, the Bay of Islands was considered safe for whites from Maori attacks. In October the brigantine *Boyd* anchored in Whangaroa Harbour with seventy passengers. The *Boyd* had sailed from London to Sydney with convicts, and from Sydney to New Zealand on November 8, with passengers. Some passengers were returning to New Zealand, while others had booked passage to London. In addition to passengers, Captain John Thompson expected to load the hold with kauri wood spars to take to England. Captain Thompson had signed on a Maori, son of a local chief, as an able deckhand. Thompson named him George. When George refused to work or was falsely accused of some transgression — stories vary — Thompson had him whipped. Flogging was considered an insult by which the aristocratic George assumed himself to have been robbed of *mana*. When George reported the punishment he had received, angry members of his *hapu* stormed the ship. They massacred and ate the crew and nearly all the passengers. The four survivors were rescued by the crew of the *City of Edinburgh*. In a short time the whaling crews of five ships avenged the *Boyd*'s victims by murdering sixty Maoris; unfortunately, the sixty were from a tribe that was innocent of the crime.[17]

MISSIONARIES AND MUSKETS

From 1814 missionaries from Sydney came to New Zealand to convert Maoris. Reverend Samuel Marsden (1765–1838) of the Church Missionary Society led initial efforts during seven trips. Born in Yorkshire, he came to Australia in August 1794 as a minister of the Church of England. He accumulated large land holdings. Marsden was known appropriately in New South Wales as the "Flogging Parson," because in his other role as magistrate at Paramatta, he ordered cruel punishments. Marsden wrote: "I knew that they were cannibals — that they were a savage race, full of superstition and wholly under the Prince of Darkness — and that there was only one remedy, ... and that was the Gospel of a Crucified Savior."[18] Marsden also thought Maoris might be a lost tribe of Israel.[19]

In March 1814 Marsden made an exploratory trip to New Zealand and at the end of the year sent William Hall, John King and Thomas Kendall (1778–1832) aboard the brig *Active* on December 22, 1814, to Bay of Islands to establish the first Church of England mission in New Zealand. Marsden believed attaining the rudiments of European civilization would ready Maoris for the intricacies of Christianity, so he also brought men who were able to teach European skills such as carpentry. They built a stone mission house at Keri Keri, Bay of Islands. Marsden introduced horses and cattle to North Island. Maoris at first thought cattle were supernatural creatures and ran from them.

In 1820 teacher Thomas Kendall (1778–1832) invited Hongi Hika (c. 1772–1828), a powerful North Island chief of the Ngapuhi tribe, to sail with him to England. Hongi Hika was unimpressed with London's imposing sights, with the exception of an elephant in the zoo and the collection of muskets at the Woolrich Arsenal.[20] Kendall took the chief to Cambridge where, in collaboration with a philologist, they put together the first book in the

Maori language, *A Grammar and Vocabulary of the Language of New Zealand.*[21] King George IV (1762–1830; r. 1820–30), a rotund voluptuary, and members of London society entertained Hongi and gave him valuable gifts to take with him. But Hongi was above all a warrior and when he stopped in Sydney on the return voyage, he traded his gifts for muskets and returned home in July 1821 with a thousand. Hongi wore a suit of armor given him by the king.[22]

The mission workers and their families were often short of food. Kendall was later dismissed from his post for writing a justification of his selling guns to Maoris for food, and perhaps for leaving his wife to live with a Maori female pupil, Tungarua.[23]

Conversions came with the greatest difficulty; ten years passed before the first baptism of a Maori. Ten more years elapsed before the second baptism.

Wesleyans did no better. William White (1785–1852), arrived aboard the *St. Michael* on May 16, 1823. On June 6, White established the first Wesleyan mission station, at Kaeo, near Whangaroa. The missionaries failed to make conversions. On January 10, 1827, Maoris of the Ngati Uru tribe drove Wesleyan missionaries from Whangaroa. The following year Reverend White established a station at Mangungu, Hokianga. In 1835 White led forty or fifty British on a raid against Maoris who had attacked a man and his wife at Hokianga. White's group killed approximately 150 of the tribe's pigs and burned houses.[24]

MUSKET WARS

A series of battles on both islands between 1810 and 1839 is known as the Musket Wars. Maori tribes had long fought as a matter of course, usually in the autumn when the harvest had been put away for the winter. Muskets brought battle to a new level, the lethality of which might have been greater had muskets been more reliable and easier to load. Muskets served to strike terror in enemies who had no muskets or inferior numbers of them. Many warriors continued to use clubs and swords and used firearms to execute captives. The wars began when Hongi Hika and two thousand warriors with a thousand muskets conquered much of the northwest of North Island.

Some 400 Ngapuhi men armed with forty or fifty muskets invaded south—to the Coromandel Peninsula, Bay of Plenty, East Coast, Taranaki and central North Island. Survivors from enemy tribes in those regions were forced to acquire arms in order to defend themselves.[25] A missionary wrote: "For a musket a New Zealander will make great sacrifices, he will labour hard and fare hard for many months to obtain his musket, in fact it is an idol he values it above all he possesses, he will not only part with his slaves for one, but even prostitute his children to diseased sailors for one of these instruments of destruction."[26] When the Maoris had exhausted themselves in this series of raids, perhaps 20,000 were dead, and thousands of others had been made slaves or had fled as refugees.[27]

MISSIONARIES' SUCCESS

Missionaries were persistent, and from about 1830 began to make significant numbers of converts in the north. On December 30, 1837, William Colenso (1811–99), a British missionary sent by the Church Missionary Society, printed the first 5,000 copies of the New Testament in the Maori language. His reputation as a man of God was questioned when, as a married man, he sired a son each by two Maori women. After that he entered local politics.[28]

In 1838 Protestant missionaries were faced with competitors. On January 13, 1838, at Hokianga, Catholic Bishop Jean Baptiste Pompallier (1802–71) celebrated the first mass in New Zealand. The bishop had arrived three days earlier with Father Louis Catherin Servant (1808–60) and Brother Michel Colombon (1812–80). The arrival of the French aroused the suspicions of British authorities that France was sending priests to serve as an opening wedge in order to annex the islands; Bishop Pompallier's written orders did not confirm that suspicion. Within five years the bishop and his associates had established seventeen missions and claimed 45,000 conversions.[29]

Christianity, predominantly Protestant, spread southward, and it spread upward from common people to chiefs. Both the Church Missionary Society and the Wesleyan Missionary Society, as well as the Roman Catholics, had converted most Maoris on both North and South Islands by the late 1850s. Like many Pacific island people the converts ranged from the piously devout to adherents of heretical cults.[30]

THE BELEAGUERED MORIORIS

The Chatham Islands lie 863 kilometers (536 miles) east of New Zealand and are administered as part of New Zealand. They consist of Chatham, 902 square kilometers (347 square miles), and Pitt, 65 square kilometers (25 square miles). On November 29, 1791, Captain William R. Broughton (1762–1821), in command of the *Chatham*, charted the group of islands he named for his ship. His ship was named in honor of John Pitt, second earl of Chatham (1758–1835), first lord of the Admiralty, 1788–94. Broughton's *Chatham* was accompanying George Vancouver's *Discovery*, but the two became separated.

The Chathams were inhabited by about 2,000 Polynesians who had arrived about 1500 CE. Morioris, as the islanders were known, chased the *Chatham*'s crew away, and a crewmember killed an islander in response. Between 1809 and 1838 *pakehas* came to the Chathams to slaughter great numbers of seals. When the seals were gone so were sources of Morioris' food and clothing. Sealers brought rats, cats, and dogs, which drove off edible birds. Sealers and a few settlers brought disease, which further reduced the Moriori population. Morioris would suffer far greater depredations in the coming decades.

In 1835 an event took place that doomed and eventually extinguished the Moriori people. The population had already been reduced to 1,663. On November 14, approximately 900 Maoris arrived on the brig *Lord Rodney* from Wellington to establish permanent settlements. Members of the North Island Ngati-Mutunga, Ngati-Tana, and Ngati-Haumia tribes had sailed on October 26. These tribes had been defeated by Te Rauparaha (?–1849) of the Ngati Toa of the coastal Kawhia region of North Island. They had intended to migrate to South Island and take land from tribes there. Before they could put that plan into effect, they learned about the Chatham Islands.

Having deposited the 900 immigrants, the *Lord Rodney* left for Wellington once again on November 23, and returned to the Chathams on December 5, 1835, with another 400 Maoris. Many Maoris arrived ill from the voyage, and Morioris nursed them to health. The Morioris, who had become a distinct people from Maoris, were peaceful. They had fought among themselves earlier in their history, but their legendary chief Nunuku ordered that they stop fighting and solve differences through mediation or single-man combat. Cannibalism ended. When the Maoris had regained their health they killed or enslaved their Moriori hosts. Moriori were easy for inveterate warriors to subjugate because they were docile hunters and gatherers. A warrior explained, "We took possession ... in accordance with our customs and we caught all the people ... some ran away ... these we killed, and others we killed — but what of that? It was our custom."[31]

Maoris took all but three percent of the Morioris' land, often fighting among themselves for the best of it.[32] The Morioris were enslaved until 1863 when a New Zealand judge emancipated them, but by that time they numbered only 110. The tragedy may well have been inevitable, but it occurred decades or even centuries before it might have because *pakehas* provided vessels and muskets.

Incredibly enough, on June 16, 1870, a New Zealand land court ruled that Maoris who had seized land from the Morioris could keep it. At that time fewer than a hundred full-blooded Morioris remained alive. An estimated sixty percent of the lands had been leased to Europeans.[33] Finally, on March 18, 1933, Tame Horomona Rate, a.k.a. "Tommy Solomon," died. He was reputed to be the last full-blooded Moriori.[34]

THE ADVENTURES OF BARON DE THIERRY

Not only did missionary Thomas Kendall inadvertently accelerate the Musket Wars, he also facilitated a French attempt to colonize New Zealand. Baron Charles Philippe Hippolyte de Thierry (1793–1864) was a son of royalists who had fled the French Revolution, and godson of King Charles X (1757–1836; r. 1824–30). In 1819 de Thierry was studying law at Cambridge University. To recoup the fortune his family had lost in the revolution, he proposed to set up a settlement in Oceania. De Thierry commissioned Thomas Kendall, whom he had met at Cambridge, to purchase land for him when Kendall arrived for missionary duties. In 1820 Kendall purchased — or at least was convinced that he had purchased — 16,200 hectares (40,000 acres) from chiefs in Hokianga, North Island. De Thierry gave himself the impressive title Sovereign Chief of New Zealand. However, he was not to set foot there for seventeen years.

In 1837 in New South Wales, de Thierry recruited sixty-eight colonists for his proposed settlement. When his colonists arrived, de Thierry learned that the chiefs had subsequently sold the same land to others. The baron's recruits drifted away. Local chiefs granted de Thierry land in Tarawana on the Waikou River on North Island. He settled there, leaving in 1845. Rebuffed by the Colonial Office in London, he then proposed to the Dutch and the French governments to found a colony in New Zealand for their citizens, nominating himself as viceroy. France and the Netherlands either rejected or ignored his proposals. All of the baron's grandiose schemes, which included becoming king of Nuku Hiva (1835), and digging a canal through Panama having failed, he decided — like tens of thousands of other men — to make his fortune in the California gold fields. Like tens of thousands, he failed to find riches in streambeds, so he sailed to the Sandwich Islands, where he served briefly as French consul. In March 1853, he made his way to Auckland to try to make a living teaching music. He died there in 1864, age seventy-one.[35]

A COLONIZATION SCHEME CONCEIVED IN PRISON

In 1837 Edward Gibbon Wakefield (1796–1862) founded the New Zealand Association, seeking government approval and assistance for a profit-making colonization scheme. In

1826 Wakefield had abducted an heiress, Ellen Turner, age fifteen, from her boarding school and married her. He was imprisoned in England for three years for this romantic exploit. From prison he published *A Letter from Sydney* (1829), outlining his theory of colonization. The association would buy land cheaply from Maoris. This land would be sold at "a sufficient price" to attract settlers of substance. Some of the profit would assist the passage of indigent workers to New Zealand. These landless laborers would work for landowners until they saved enough to buy land.[36]

On September 20, 1839, the ship *Tory* arrived at Cook Straits with settlers from England to found the city of Wellington. Wakefield hastened to send settlers before the British government extended control over New Zealand and made sales of Maori land a government monopoly. Wakefield's brother William bought land in exchange for trade goods such as tools, clothing, guns, iron pots, umbrellas and red nightcaps. *Aurora*, the first of nine immigrant ships, followed on January 22. Settled in March 1840, the town was named for the Arthur Wellesley, Duke of Wellington (1769–1851), winner of the Battle of Waterloo. Wakefield set in motion colonization voyages that led to founding Wanganui (1840), New Plymouth (1841), and Nelson (1842). Investors were invited to buy unsurveyed town lots in these settlements.[37]

A Successful French Settlement

Meanwhile, in August 1838 French captain Jean François Langlois (b. 1808) purchased land at Akaroa Bay on the Banks Peninsula. He paid the Maoris some clothing and a pistol and promised a thousand francs when occupation took place. Since 1837 Langlois had been in New Zealand waters as captain of the French whaling vessel *Cachalot*. Langlois returned to France and used his connections to attract investors from Nantes and Bordeaux in what became the Nanto-Bordelaise Company. Members of his proposed colony were to engage in whaling and were intended to supply whaling vessels, returning a profit to investors.

On August 17, 1840, the ship *Compté de Paris* brought fifty-three settlers, including twelve children, to establish a French whaling colony in South Island. The *Compté de Paris* was followed by *L'Aube* under the command of Captain Charles François Lavaud. When Langlois arrived, he noted a union jack flapping above the harbor and learned to his consternation that Lieutenant Governor Hobson had only recently annexed North and South Island for Great Britain. Langlois proceeded despite that knowledge, landing his settlers at Akaroa Bay. The early days of settlement at Akaroa Bay were marred by a power struggle between Langlois and Lavaud.

On June 30, 1849, the Nanto-Bordelaise Company sold its assets to the New Zealand Company for £4,500. Langlois never returned to New Zealand, retiring from the whaling industry in 1857. The settlers achieved a measure of prosperity, numbering sixty-nine by 1843 and enjoying amenities such as a bakery, school, cafe and shops.[38]

A "Man of War Without Guns"

The governor in Sydney realized that some official British presence was essential because by the early 1830s New Zealand contained an estimated 2,000 whites—1,400 on

North Island and 600 on South Island. Most were British. Some went native and became Pakeha Maoris. In 1817 New South Wales law was extended to New Zealand, but authorities had no way to enforce it. London was not enthusiastic about annexing a large undeveloped colony in dire need of peacekeeping. Colonies were a drain on public funds. The appointment of an official without power was a compromise, if temporary, solution. New South Wales governor Richard Bourke (1777–1855; term 1831–37) appointed agriculture teacher James Busby (1801–71) British resident in New Zealand. Busby arrived at Bay of Islands on May 10, 1833, to assume his duties. He had sailed aboard HMS *Imogene* on April 21, from Sydney. Busby and his family settled at Waitangi.

Bourke gave Busby three mandates: to protect Maoris from whites; to protect well intentioned settlers and traders from Maoris and unscrupulous whites; and to facilitate the capture of escaped convicts from Australia. Because Britain did not control the islands or garrison troops there, Busby had no power except that of persuasion and reason. Maoris call him "man of war without guns." For a few months, a timber trader working in Hokianga, Thomas McDonnell (1788–1864), served as additional British resident; however, he spent much of his efforts reportedly antagonizing Busby.[39]

Without armed power or authorized government agents, events in New Zealand proved beyond Busby's control. He asked for help. In response the House of Commons commissioned Captain William Hobson (1792–1842) to investigate reports of abuses by whites and Maoris and to recommend what, if any, action Britain ought to take. On May 26, 1837 Hobson arrived at Bay of Islands aboard *HMS Rattlesnake*. When he returned to England in 1838, Hobson recommended making a treaty with the Maoris and placing all British subjects in New Zealand under British rule. If his recommendations were accepted New Zealand would be a British possession.

Meanwhile, Resident Busby convened a meeting of thirty-four Maori chiefs at Waitangi in October 1837. Busby was alarmed that French settlers seemed prepared to take over one or both islands. The chiefs reconfirmed the independence of New Zealand tribes, but requested that Britain act as "parent and protector." Later seventeen other chiefs added their names to the request. Busby had hoped the chiefs would meet annually to make laws, but his hope went unrealized.[40]

THE NEED FOR LAW AND ORDER

Making an agreement with the Maoris and bringing the force of law became essential. Whalers gathered in Bay of Islands. The commodious bay and entrepreneurial Maoris made it an excellent refreshing station. Observers counted fifty-four New England ships, fourteen British, eighteen French, and ten from Sydney. Missionary William Colenso characterized the town of Kororareka as "notorious for containing a greater number of rogues than any other spot of equal size in the universe."[41] Tribal governments and *pakeha* vigilante committees sought to enforce contradictory rules governing relations between the two races. Maori chiefs sold un-surveyed land, in some cases land that was not theirs to sell. Whites took Maori land and dispossessed the inhabitants. Numerous complaints about a lack of law and order from whites and Maoris alike indicated the need for a strong central authority. Moreover, British authorities feared, with good reason, French intentions of establishing a claim to South Island.[42]

By 1839 Maori leaders were willing to accept peace brokered by missionaries. The final battle in New Zealand's three-decade Musket Wars took place at Waikanae on October 16, 1839. Two tribes—the Te Ati Awa and the Ngti Raukawa—fought. Forty such battles had taken place in North Island. Thousands of people were slain in fighting or as captives, and some tribes were nearly extinguished. As a result of the wars, the male Maori fighting population is estimated to have declined by twenty to twenty-five percent. Children died as diseases became epidemic. Now Maoris were willing to work and trade for blankets, woolen coats, tomahawks, knives, calico, and clothing of all kinds, pipes and tobacco.[43]

CESSION AT WAITANGI

On July 30, 1839, Captain Hobson was appointed lieutenant governor by New South Wales governor Sir George Gipps (1791–1847). He arrived at Bay of Islands January 29, 1840, to assume his duties.[44] Hobson thought a treaty would solve numerous problems.

On February 6, 1840, missionaries helped convince some 400 Maori chiefs to sign the treaty of cession by telling them that it was granted as Queen Victoria's "act of love." Maoris were told the treaty, known as the Treaty of Waitangi, would enable British authorities to control troublesome *pakehas*. The chiefs debated five hours before ceding sovereignty to Britain. In the next months some 500 additional chiefs signed. Maoris were promised that the Crown would guarantee the chiefs all of their rights, lands and possessions. Only the government would buy land from Maoris and could sell it to *pakehas*.[45]

The Treaty of Waitangi proved to be detrimental to Maoris. They lost their sovereignty. Britain guaranteed their lands, but subsequently settlers took land without regard to official promises. As Claudia Orange wrote: "By 1839 the Colonial Office was no longer contemplating, as they had previously, a Maori New Zealand in which settlers had somehow to be accommodated, but a settler New Zealand in which a place had to be kept for the Maori."[46] Maoris had little opportunity for their grievances to be redressed until the Waitangi Tribunals were inaugurated in 1975.

Chapter 9

The Sandwich Islands Transformed, 1778–1874

COOK FINDS THE SANDWICH ISLANDS

On January 18, 1778, members of Captain James Cook's third Pacific expedition sighted Oahu and Kaua'i. The Hawaiian Islands were the last major island group in the Pacific to be found by Europeans. They consist of 132 islands, atolls, shoals and reefs. These are found over a length of 1,500 miles (2,400 kilometers). Cook named them the Sandwich Islands in honor of Secretary of State John Montagu, fourth earl of Sandwich (1718–92). Cook was headed for the northwest coast of North America, and Hawaii was a most welcome way station where he could replenish supplies.

Because of language and appearance, Cook knew the inhabitants to be Polynesians and marveled that the race had spread over islands within a triangle spreading out from New Zealand to Easter Island to Hawaii. Cook estimated a population of a quarter million Hawaiians, which was a pure guess, he not having explored all of the islands. Artistic people living in an advanced Stone Age culture, Hawaiians created beautiful *tapa*, feather capes and helmets, and amused themselves by surfing, swimming, and challenging waves in canoes.

When Cook arrived, Hawaiians were celebrating their Makahiki season, a time of games rather than war. *Kahunas* (priests) told Hawaiians that Cook was the god Lono. According to legend, Lono had introduced reforms centuries before; his return on a floating island during Makahiki had been long anticipated. People prostrated themselves before Cook, draped him in red *tapa*, decorated him with a cape and helmet, and put pre-chewed pork in his mouth. He was allowed to replenish his supplies, taking much of the island's food.[1] Cook recorded: "The very instant I leaped ashore, they all fell flat on their faces, and remained in that humble posture till I made signs to them to rise."[2]

Because he knew that some crewmembers on both ships had venereal disease, he sought to prevent its spread to the people he had recently discovered. He ordered men not to allow women on board and not to have intercourse on shore. Bare breasted women excited the men and, according to an officer, used "every means in their power to provoke them to do that, which ye dread of punishment would not have kept them from."[3] Cook knew, however, that "the opportunities and inducements for an intercourse between the sex, there are too many to be guarded against."[4]

Cook left the Sandwich Islands and from March to August 1778 charted the coast of North America from Oregon to the Aleutian Islands and Bering Strait. He attempted to fulfill his order to find an all-weather passage to Hudson's Bay, but failed because none existed. Cook intended to winter in the Sandwich Islands and to explore the American coast again the following summer.[5] On January 17, 1779 — one year less a day since his first arrival in Hawaii — Cook anchored in Kealakekua Bay on the Big Island, Hawai'i. By coincidence, he arrived once more in *Makahiki* season. He had come to replenish food, water, and wood, and to wait out the harsh Alaska winter before continuing his explorations. Cook found "venerial distemper" among the women, a reminder of his crew's recent recreational pursuits.

A young *ari'* — an aristocrat — named Kamehameha (1758?–1819) accompanied his uncle, Kalaniopuu, a chief of Hawai'i, on a visit aboard the *Discovery*. Lieutenant James King described the nephew as having "as savage a looking face as I ever saw, it however by no means seemed an emblem of his disposition, which was good natur'd & humorous, although his manner shewd somewhat of an overbearing spirit, & he seemed to be the principal director in this interview."[6] The powerful young man would unify the Hawaiian archipelago early in the next century and found a royal dynasty.

THE GREAT EXPLORER'S DEATH

Having filled his ships with provisions, Cook prepared to sail. Hawaiians were not sorry to see him leave because Makahiki season was over, and if Cook were indeed Lono, he would not have stayed. On February 8, the foremast on *Resolution* was damaged and the ship was unable to sail; the British returned to Kealakekua Bay to repair the mast. The ships' companies had depleted the island of food, which was acceptable to the Hawaiians so long as Cook was presumed to be the god Lono; however, eager to be rid of guests who had overstayed their welcome and harboring some doubt about Cook's divinity, chiefs asked Cook when he planned to leave.

Islanders showed their disillusion by engaging in theft. They stole the cutter from *Discovery*. In retaliation on February 14, 1779, Cook led an armed party to take Kalaniopuu hostage. A sizable crowd of excited Hawaiians ran to the shore, brandishing spears, rocks, and daggers. Outraged islanders clubbed Cook, age 51, from behind as he waded near the beach. He was stabbed in the back and clubbed again. Four marines and seventeen Hawaiians were killed in the skirmish.

An officer recalled that the crew returned to the ship and cried as though they had lost a father. The next day the crews burned 150 homes and shot many Hawaiians. Hawaiians boiled Cook's remains and returned the captain's bones to the crew; the bones were ceremoniously scattered at sea.[7]

On three voyages, 1769–79, Cook had sailed through 140 degrees of Earth's 180-degree latitudes and through all longitudes. Historian Lawrence James summarized the captain's accomplishments: "Cook towered over all. When he set sail for his first voyage in 1768, he was probably the most skilled navigator of his age.... Cook's three voyages were undertaken to add to universal enlightenment by the accumulation of geographical, scientific and anthropological observations of a hitherto secret world."[8]

Captain Charles Clerke of *Discovery* became commander of the expedition. *Resolution* and *Discovery* left Kealakekua Bay on February 23 for Kaua'i, where they took on more food and water. In mid–March they proceeded once again to look for a northwest passage, sailing to 70 degrees north. Except for being ill with tuberculosis, which he had contracted while serving a term in debtors' prison for his brother, Clerke was well qualified to lead. He had sailed with John Byron to the Pacific on *Dolphin* in 1764, and with Cook on his first two

"The Death of Cook." This painting is from a sketch by James Clevely, a carpenter on Cook's third Pacific voyage. Clevely witnessed Sandwich Islanders clubbing the great explorer to death at Kealakakua Bay, Hawai'I, on February 14, 1779. Cook had taken a chief hostage and in retaliation he was murdered and probably eaten. The original is in the National Maritime Museum, London.

Pacific voyages. Clerke died on August 22, 1779, and was buried in Kamchatka, Siberia. John Gore (d. 1790), born in Virginia, took command of *Resolution* and returned the ship to England, as did James King (1750–84), who commanded *Discovery*.[9]

The Coming of the Seal Hunters

In 1786 the fur sealing ships *King George* and *Queen Charlotte* wintered in the Hawaiian Islands, beginning a practice that would bring fur seal hunters to the islands until about

1804, when crews started wintering in North America. The fur seal trade on the northwest coast of North America flourished from the early 1780s to around 1825, when seals were depleted. Traders bartered skins with Northwest Indians and sold them for large profits in Canton, China. Hawaiians sold not only fresh food, but fire wood, excellent rope made of native vines and grasses, *tapa* to insulate ships' bottoms under copper sheathing, and artifacts to be taken home as exotic souvenirs. When crews showed respect and traded fairly, they found the Sandwich Islands an agreeable place to obtain food and water. When Hawaiians were dissatisfied with terms of trade or merely saw an opportunity, they could engage in theft, attack crewmembers, or capture essential equipment to hold for payment. With the profits chiefs bought manufactured goods, including guns.[10]

Prince Kaiana, a brother of the paramount chief of Kaua'i, asked to visit England, and in June 1787 was taken aboard the *Nootka* to the west coast of North America, the Philippines, and as far as Canton by British fur-trader John Meares (1756–1809). Meares evaded the company monopoly on trade with China by registering his ship in Macao and sailing under a Portuguese flag. During Kaiana's several months in Canton and Macau, the over-six-foot Polynesian giant dazzled the more diminutive Chinese with his size, feather cloak, helmet and spear. Kaiana was perplexed that some Chinese were without adequate food and that shopkeepers demanded coins rather than nails for purchases. Kaiana was returned to Hawaii aboard the *Iphigenia* December 6, 1788. He judiciously sided with Kamehameha the Great in his efforts to conquer the island — initially. He changed sides in 1795 and lost his life fighting against Kamehameha. Kaiana was among the first islanders to be taken abroad and the first of many to sign on to work aboard a ship.[11]

THE RISE OF KAMEHAMEHA I

So far as is known, no single person had ever governed all of the Sandwich Islands, but Western firepower and ships now made unification possible. In March 1790 Kamehameha, chief of the northern part of the island of Hawai'i, acquired the schooner *Fair American* and the ship's guns and muskets. Chief Kame'eiamoku (d. 1802) led warriors of the Kona coast of Hawai'i to capture the fur traders' vessel and slaughter four of its five crew, including the master, Thomas Humphrey Metcalfe (1771–90). They slaughtered the crew to retaliate for a whipping in January the chief suffered at the hands of Thomas Metcalfe's father, Simon (1735–94), master of the *Fair American*'s sister ship *Eleanora*. Moreover, Simon Metcalfe had killed over a hundred Maui islanders in retribution for a stolen skiff. Hawaiians called the Olowalu Massacre the Battle of Spilled Brains.[12] Kame'eiamoku was Kamehameha's great uncle and firm supporter.

Kamehameha was only one of several powerful rulers in the islands, but the capture of the *Fair American* gave him a preponderance of firepower. Of the men aboard the *Fair American*, only Isaac Davis (1758–1810) swam ashore. The *Fair American*'s muskets and cannons were taken off and Davis and a crewman of the *Eleanora*, John Young (1742–1835), were captured on shore. Instead of killing the Americans, Kamehameha employed them as technical advisors in the intricacies of operating the schooner and the weapons he had taken.[13]

In 1790 Kamehameha attempted to conquer Maui while its chief, Kahekili, was away in Oahu. Kamehameha sailed to Maui with twelve hundred men. On the third day of an epic battle against the relatively equal forces of Kahekili's son Kalanikupulu, the invaders

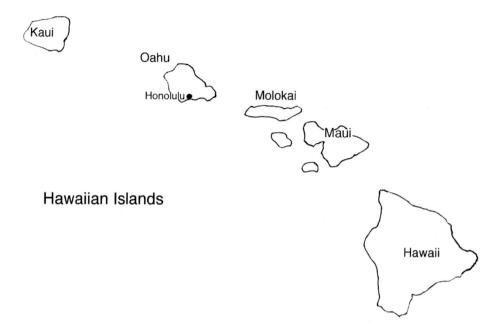

Map of Hawaii. Illustration by Barbara Kirk.

killed so many of the defenders that the stream in Iao Valley was dammed with bodies. The Battle of Kepaniwai is also known as the Damming of the Waters. Kahmehameha's victory was ephemeral. He had to return to Hawai'i to defend his rule against the encroachments of a dissident chief and his allies. Kamehameha vanquished his enemies on Hawai'i, but Kahekili resumed his independent rule of Maui.[14]

Vancouver Accepts an Island

On February 25, 1794, Chief Kamehameha asked Captain George Vancouver (1757–98), commanding the *Discovery* and the *Chatham*, for British protection for the island of Hawai'i. Vancouver gave Kamehameha a British flag; the union jack flew over his house for twenty-two years. Vancouver interpreted Kamehameha's request as the cession of the Big Island, Hawai'I, to King George III. Vancouver had been aboard Cook's voyage to the islands. Vancouver landed cattle, which Hawaiians had never seen before. The cattle proliferated over the years because killing them was *kapu* (taboo). Vancouver also introduced goats, geese, grapes, citrus and almonds, as well as various vegetables. Vancouver refused to sell or give arms to any of the competing chiefs in the islands.

Vancouver had wintered in the Sandwich Islands from 1792 through 1794. He weighed anchor on March 3, and continued to explore the west coast of North America from Monterey Bay to the fifty-second parallel. Although the British parliament never ratified the cession, the union jack forms part of the design of Hawaii's state flag.[15]

In May 1795, Kamehameha won the Battle of Pali Cliffs, also known as Nu'uanu, as 400 defenders of Oahu jumped 300 meters (1,000 feet) to their deaths rather than fall into his hands. The high chief of Hawai'i had assembled a huge army of 10,000 in 1,200 war canoes. After conquering Maui and Moloka'i, he invaded Oahu. At the conclusion of the

Battle of Nu'uanu, Kamehameha controlled all islands except Kaua'i and Lana'i. If we may assume that 10,000 died on both sides in the battle, Nu'uanu was deadliest single event in Hawaiian history.

Kamehameha had two advantages. First, a civil war had weakened two rulers, the half brothers Kalanikupule, who controlled Oahu, and Kaeokulani, who ruled Kaua'i, Maui, Lana'i and Moloka'i. Kalanikupule had been weakened by the war, however, so Kamehameha, who had taken all of the Big Island in a series of battles, sought to consolidate all the islands in the chain under his own rule. Second, Kamehameha had control of the *Fair American*, its cannons and muskets.[16]

In 1810 Kamehameha assembled a formidable fleet of thirty vessels, including Western–built ships with cannons, and Hawaiian war canoes for his projected assault on Kaua'i. American trader Captain Nathan Winship (1778–1820) of the firm Homer and Winship facilitated a meeting between Kamehameha and Kauai's chief. Chief Kaumualii (1778–1824) agreed judiciously to recognize Kamehameha's authority in return for retaining his rights on Kaua'i.

The new monarch of all he surveyed boasted seven royal wives, twenty-one "official" wives, a company of concubines and sixty recognized offspring. Except for five months in 1843 when the islands were under British sovereignty, Hawaii would remain a kingdom until 1893.[17]

THE SANDALWOOD TRADE

Chinese wanted little from Westerners in trade, but they accepted Mexican silver, Indian opium, and sandalwood. Chinese used the aromatic wood for boxes and joss sticks. A wealthy Chinese went to the temple and offered sticks three feet in length and four to six inches in diameter; a person of less means bought smaller pieces to offer. The sandalwood tree takes forty years to grow to eight feet high. Most prized is the rich oily center of the trunk, cut from close to the root. Cutters threw all else away. For thirteen centuries Asian traders had brought the aromatic wood to China by sea and overland from India and Indonesia.

In November and December 1811, three Boston ship captains, the brothers Nathan and John Winship and William Heath Davis (1822–1901), masters of *Albatross*, *O'Cain* and *Isabella*, began loading sandalwood cut in the Sandwich Islands. Chiefs conscripted commoners to cut sandalwood and carry bundles to the ships.

Kamehameha and his son Liholiho bought a dozen vessels to establish a Hawaiian navy with the money earned from selling sandalwood; the monarchs were cheated, as some vessels were inferior or unseaworthy. Chiefs also traded wood for rum, guns and manufactured goods. Chiefs slipped effortlessly into debt to Western sandalwood dealers and forced their people to cut still more wood. The sandalwood trade stripped Hawaiian hillsides bare, led to early deaths through overwork and starvation, and added European weapons to Kamehameha's arsenal.[18]

THE RUSSIANS

In 1816 representatives of the Russian American Company arrived at Kaua'i to obtain food for the company's Alaska fur traders. The Russians' arrival was well timed in that Kaumualii was intent on preserving his rule against Kamehameha the Great, as well as foreign powers such as Britain and France. On June 2, 1816, Chief Kaumualii pledged, through the Russian official Georg Anton Scheffer (1779–1836), allegiance to Czar Alexander I (1777–1825; r. 1801–25) of Russia. Kaumualii pledged to trade only with the Russian American Company. Scheffer, a German–born physician in the company service, pledged Russian protection of Kaua'i.

Scheffer built Fort Elizabeth at the mouth of the Waimea River and two forts at the entrance of the Hanalei River. Scheffer and Kaumualii planned to divide Oahu and began to build a fort there. Due to pressure from Kamehameha and American traders who had been cut out of trade with Kaua'i, Kaumualii ordered the Russians to leave Kaua'i. Scheffer and the other Russians left on May 8, 1817. By 1820 the Russian American Company had decided to obtain food from its outpost at Fort Ross in California north of San Francisco Bay, and not from the Sandwich Islands.[19]

On November 21, 1816, Otto von Kotzebue (1787–1846) visited both Kealakekua Bay on the Big Island of Hawai'i and Oahu. In both places he and his crew were welcomed and entertained lavishly. An Estonian in the service of Czar Alexander I (1777–1825; r. 1801–25), von Kotzebue was encircling the globe from 1815 to 1818 in his ship *Rurik*. He was sent by the czar to find a northwest passage in the vicinity of the Bering Straits.[20]

DESTRUCTION OF THE IDOLS

In May 1819, Liholiho (1797–1824; r. 1819–24) inherited the crown at age twenty-two when Kamehameha I died. Spoiled and immature, Liholiho shared his rule with his father's favorite wife, Kaahumanu (1768?–1832). Kaahumanu told Liholiho she wanted to end *kapus* (taboos), beginning with segregation of sexes at meals and prohibition of choice foods for women. Steven Fischer explained that depending on the island where it was declared, a *kapu* could affect "land, crops, buildings, precincts and the sanctity of individuals, but also ... speech, diet, sexual practices, beliefs and attitudes."[21] For example, commoners were not to look directly at a chief, had to keep their heads lower than his, had to have no physical contact with a chief, and had to never wear chiefly red or yellow feathers. Among the *kapus* that affected everyone was the prohibition of eating with a person of the other gender.

On May 13, 1819, Liholiho fortified himself with rum and attended his stepmother's banquet. Men and women ate together at Lailua. Women ate forbidden food. Kaahumanu's daring experiment was not based on whim; interaction with visiting seamen caused her to question the basis of *kapus*. Not only did foreigners tell Hawaiians that *kapus* were wrong, they caused her to question the validity of the ancient religion because Hawaiians were dying of diseases that did not appear to kill Christian visitors.

When a few months later participants at the forbidden feast had not been punished by gods or spirits for their infractions, Liholiho ordered *kapus* ended on November 5, 1819. Daringly, he ordered *heiaus* (temples) and idols destroyed. The hold on the people of the ancient gods began to loosen. Hawaiian was the only culture in the South Pacific in which traditional religion crumbled before the arrival of missionaries. When missionaries arrived five months later, they found their task of conversion far easier than it might otherwise have been had the old religion not been discredited.[22]

AMERICAN MISSIONARIES

Kamehameha's unification of all Hawaiian tribes and ending the *kapu* system were two catalysts for the transformation of the lives of the people of the Sandwich Islands. Then came the missionaries. Henry Obookiah (1794?–1818), a native of Napoopoo, near Kealakekua Bay, died in New Haven, Connecticut, on February 17, 1818. His short book *The Memoirs of Henry Obookiah* (1819) inspired the first American missionaries to go to the Sandwich Islands in 1820. Obookiah had come to New York in 1809 at what he esti-mated as age 15 aboard the trading ship *Triumph* captained by Caleb Britnall (1774–1850). Henry was converted and educated at Cornwall School, opened by the American Board of Commissioners for Foreign Missions. The board was composed of Presbyterians and Con-gregationalists. He spent nine years in New England. This devout young Polynesian was found weeping on the steps at Yale University; asked why he was crying, he said "My poor countrymen. They are without knowledge of the true God, and ignorant of the future world, have no Bible to read, no Sabbath." Henry died shortly after, never returning home. In 1820, justifying their journey by the Bible's admonition, "Go ye into all the world and preach the Gospel to every creature," Protestant missionaries set sail for the Sandwich Islands.[23]

On March 30, 1820, after a five-month voyage of 29,000 kilometers (18,000 miles) from New England, the brig *Thadeus*, under command of Andrew Blanchard, arrived with pious passengers in Kailua on the Kona coast of Hawai'i. The leaders of the mission were Reverend Hiram Bingham (1789–1869) and Reverend Asa Thurston (1787–1868). They and their wives were among seven couples aboard. Sailing preparations had included the neces-sity to find brides for six bachelors among them; brides were found for all six within two months. In addition to the newlyweds, the *Thadeus* carried four Hawaiians who had been brought to New England by sea captains and Christianized; they would serve as inter-preters.

Uncertain what to expect, the fearful missionaries brought cannons up on deck and rigged nets to stop islanders from boarding. Soon, they were delighted to find that the pop-ulation was not threatening. Hawaiians saw New Englanders arrive clad in layers of cloth-ing suitable for a quite different climate.[24] Hiram Bingham recorded his first impression in his journal: "The appearance of destitution, degradation, and barbarism, among the chat-tering, and almost naked savages, whose heads and feet, and much of their sunburnt swarthy skins, were bare, was appalling. Some of our number, with gushing tears, turned away from the spectacle. Others with firmer nerve continued their gaze, but were ready to exclaim, 'Can these be human beings!'"[25] Reverend Thurston and a small group remained in Kailua, while Reverend Bingham and another group went on to Honolulu, arriving April 14. A third group under Samuel Whitney (1793–1845) and Samuel Ruggles (1795–1871) and the converted Hawaiian Kaumualii went to Kaua'i, where Kaumualii's father was chief; they established a mission station at Waimea.[26]

Missionaries were unable to convert Hawaiians at first. Islanders had a hard time grap-pling with the concepts of Congregationalism, with American clothing, monogamy, and — understandably — the puzzling intricacies of literacy. Moreover, Hawaiians were told to forego pleasures that they cherished. A visitor in 1838 noted: "A change has taken place in certain customs. I allude to the variety of athletic exercises such as swimming, with or without a surfboard, dancing, wrestling, throwing the javelin, etc., all of which games, being in opposition to the strict tenets of Calvinism, have been suppressed."[27]

"Reverend Hiram Bingham Preaching at Waimea." Bingham arrived in Hawaii March 30, 1820, aboard the brig *Thadeus* with the first group of missionaries from New England. He remained until 1840. Note the Hawaiians with books. Bingham was instrumental in rendering parts of the Bible in the Hawaiian language. The sketch, probably by Bingham himself, appears in *A Residence of Twenty-one Years in the Sandwich Islands* (Hartford: H. Huntington 1847).

Shortly after the arrival of the first Protestant missionaries, officers of visiting vessels contributed some $300 to build a church in Honolulu. Hale Pule, the first Christian church to be built in the Hawaiian Islands, was dedicated on September 15, 1821. As many as 300 people were seated under its thatched roof. It was replaced in 1842 by the Kawalaha'o Church.[28]

THE BENEFITS OF LITERACY

Among the beneficial aspects of Hawaii's transformation was the ability to read. On January 7, 1822, missionary Elisha Loomis (1799–1836) printed a spelling booklet of the Hawaiian language on his secondhand Ramage press. These were the first pages to be printed in the Sandwich Islands, and the first to be printed west of the Rocky Mountains. On March 28, 1822, Reverend William Ellis arrived in Honolulu aboard the *Mermaid* from Tahiti. He remained eight months; he returned to Huahine, and came back in April 1823. Ellis reduced the alphabet to twelve letters: five vowels and seven consonants. Printers soon discovered a gaping shortage of the letters *a* and *k*, with which Hawaiian abounds; fortunately, four thousand additional *a*'s and three thousand more *k*'s arrived from New England in June 1827.[29]

Instruction began September 5, 1831, at the Lahainaluna School on Maui. The purpose of the first high school in the Sandwich Islands was to train assistant Christian ministers and teachers. Twenty-five males were enrolled under direction of Principal Lorrin Andrews (1795–1868); Andrews had arrived in 1827 with the third company sent by the American Board of Commissioners for Foreign Missions. In the same year an estimated

52,000 Hawaiians were enrolled in lower grades, up from 2,000 in 1824. The opening of a secondary school was all the more remarkable because in 1831, in all twenty-three American states, only nine high schools were functioning.

On February 14, 1834, the first issue of *Ka Lama Hawaii* (the *Hawaiian Luminary*), a newspaper in the Hawaiian language, was published at the Lahainaluna Seminary. It was the first newspaper to be published in the Sandwich Islands, and the first to be published in a future American state west of the Rocky Mountains.[30]

The Holy Bible in Hawaiian was made available to literate Hawaiians, printing having been completed May 10, 1839. Some parts had been printed on two presses in the islands and some in the United States. Translation and printing of the Bible helped secure the strong position of Protestant Christianity as the religion of the Hawaiian people. The New Testament had been printed in 1832, and the Old Testament was completed on March 25, 1839. The Bible was translated by missionaries William Richards, Asa Thurston, Hiram Bingham, Artemas Bishop, Jonathan S. Green, Lorrin Andrews, Ephraim Weston Clark and Sheldon Dibble.[31]

THE KING DIES IN LONDON

In 1824, Liholiho, styled Kamehameha II, took his consort, Queen Kamamalu, to England to visit his "good friend" King George IV. The royal party sailed on a British whaling ship, *Aigle*. Before their audience with the British king could take place, Kamamalu died of measles in London on July 8, and the king six days later. Their bodies were returned to Honolulu on May 3, 1825, by Captain George Anson, Lord Byron (1789–1868), aboard HMS *Blonde*.

Liholiho's younger brother Kauikeaouli (1813–54), age eleven, became Kamehameha III (r. 1824–54).[32] In August 1828 French trader August Duhaut-Cilley visited the king of the Sandwich Islands, at the time age 15. Duhaut-Cilley recorded that though the king had a house "built to our rules of architecture," he never lived there, but rather in a thatch house. The king slept in the thatched house "only in bad weather; when the night is fine he stays in a small hut that has to be entered on hands and knees and that is barely large enough for four people sitting or stretched out." Members of the king's court followed his example by sleeping in huts near his.[33] The picture of a boy king who slept in a grass shack, living under the rule of a dowager queen (Kaahumanu), undermined the image of confident sovereignty that Hawaii needed to present to foreign powers to maintain independence.

KAAHUMANU IS BAPTIZED

Dowager queen Kaahumanu served as regent for Kamehameha III. When Kaahumanu was baptized on December 5, 1825, missionaries realized they had achieved a major milestone. Her conversion proved the essential event that prompted Hawaiian commoners to convert. She had professed a belief in Christianity in April 1824, following an illness during which missionary spouse Sybil Bingham (1792–1848) nursed her to health. Before her conversion a missionary described the dowager queen as "haughty, filthy, lewd, tyrannical, cruel, wrathful, murderous."[34] She learned to read the Bible, and some of her negative qualities apparently dissipated.[35]

"House of Kraimoku." Drawn in 1819 by Jacques Arago aboard the *Uranie* under command of Louis de Freycinet, the sketch shows the influence of Westerners on traditional Hawaiian life. The neatly thatched cottage has a wooden door and nearby table. Note the barrel, which appears to be in motion. The woman is working on tapa, and a surfboard lies nearby. The man is identified as Kalanimoku, counselor of King Liholiho. Illustration from *Narrative of a Voyage Round the World in the Uranie* (London: Treuttel & Wurtz, 1823).

A CATHOLIC ATTEMPT

When Picpusian fathers Alexis Bachelot (1796–1837), Abraham Armand and Patrick Short, with six lay brothers, arrived in Honolulu on July 7, 1827, Protestant missionaries were horrified. Protestants feared recently converted Hawaiians might accept Catholicism and its relatively lenient strictures as opposed to those of Calvinism. As Catholics, islanders could, for example, sing, swim, or drink alcoholic beverages in moderation. Had the priests succeeded in converting large numbers, France would have been given a toehold in the Hawaiian Islands, leading perhaps to eventual annexation.

Protestant missionaries had secured the cooperation of the regent, Kaahumanu. When the queen regent ordered Captain Plassard of the *Cometé*, on which the French had arrived, to take the Frenchmen elsewhere, the captain refused. Kaahumanu ordered Catholic converts to be beaten, tortured, imprisoned, forced to perform hard labor, or exiled.[36]

On December 24, 1831, fathers Bachelot and Short were expelled. They sailed to work at San Gabriel Mission in Mexico's province of Alta California until they could see an opportunity to return to the Sandwich Islands. Their colleague, Father Abraham Armand, had sailed for France on November 1, 1829.[37]

THE CATTLE INDUSTRY

Vacqueros arrived in 1832 to train islanders to be cowboys to manage growing herds of cattle. They had been invited by a high chief who had visited Mexican California. Captain George Vancouver had left cattle in 1793–94. Because they were protected by a *kapu*, cattle proliferated. In 1812 John Parker (1790–1868) came to Hawai'i and was instrumental in starting the salt beef industry. In 1815, Parker married Kipikane, daughter of a local chief; their two sons and one daughter would continue the Parker ranching dynasty. At one time the 222,575-hectare (550,000-acre) Parker Ranch would be the largest in the United States.[38]

Salted beef, sold primarily to whalers at first, and then exported to Latin America and California, soon replaced sandalwood as the island's chief export. The cattle industry required enormous amounts of land, which led to alienation of communal lands. Before the cattle could be fenced in and managed, they did substantial damage to garden plots, reducing food availability. In 1828 horses were brought by the French to the Big Island from San Diego.[39]

Vacqueros became known as *paniolos* (a mispronunciation of "Español"). An observer noted in the 1840s that Hawaiian *paniolos* wore a *poncho*, a wide *sombrero* woven from pandanus, a silk bandana, a colorful sash around the waist, a cotton shirt, leather leggings, and slit trousers. A lasso, spurs, and saddle with a high horn completed his paraphernalia. *Paniolos* filled saddles more than three decades before the classic age of the Western cowboy.[40]

IN DEBT

Insatiable wants for manufactured goods had led chiefs to contract large debts with Americans. They had for several years ordered yachts, billiard tables, uniforms, fine china, furniture, alcohol and firearms. A female chief in Honolulu held a dinner party to honor an American captain; in what she thought was an impressive display of her wealth, she had a large chamber pot set at each diner's place. Payment for all of these items was made from sandalwood income and by signing liens on future shipments of sandalwood.

The USS *Peacock* anchored at Honolulu on October 21, 1826, under command of Thomas ap Catesby Jones (1790–1858) to collect debts to Americans. On December 27, 1826, Hawaiian chiefs agreed to pay 15,000 *pictuls* of sandalwood, worth an estimated $300,000. A *pictul* weighs 59 kilograms (133.3 pounds).[41] J.C. Furnas stated that in the 1820s and 30s, "Every year more whites settled down to exploit Hawaii in any fashion suggested by ingenuity and hope."[42]

As a result of American pressure, a Hawaiian law compelled every male to deliver a half *pictul* of sandalwood by September 1, 1827, or pay four Spanish dollars. The remaining trees were in precipitous terrain, difficult to access. Commoners had to work harder to harvest what was left. An observer, one Mr. Gulick, wrote: "Felt distressed and grieved for the people who collect sandalwood. They are often driven by hunger to eat wild and bitter herbs, moss &c. And although the winter is so cold on the hills that my winter clothes will scarcely keep me comfortable, I frequently see men with no clothing except the *maro* (loin cloth)."[43] By 1831, sandalwood trees in the Sandwich Islands were nearly depleted, the price fell in Canton, and the trade ended. The debt was finally paid in 1843.[44]

THE CATHOLICS RETURN

After having been expelled from the Sandwich Islands at the request of Protestants in 1831, fathers Bachelot and Short returned on April 13, 1837. However, by April 30 they had been forced back on board ship. Then, American and British consuls pleaded for religious tolerance and the priests disembarked once again and remained eight months. In November Father Louis Desiré Maigret (1804–82) attempted to come ashore, but authorities forbade his landing. His attempts to proselytize thwarted by authorities, Father Bachelot purchased a boat, *Notre Dame de Paix*, on which the fathers sailed from the Hawaiian Islands on November 23, 1837. Father Bachelot, ill at the time, died on December 5, en route to Ponape.[45]

As a result of the poor treatment of his fellow French, on July 9, 1839, Captain Cyrille-Pierre-Theodore Laplace (1793–1875), aboard the sixty-gun frigate *Artemise*, landed with 212 marines and sixty armed seamen. Laplace threatened to level Honolulu unless his demands were met for freedom of worship, land for a church, and the release of Catholics from prison. On July 17, 1839, Kamehameha III issued the Edict of Toleration, allowing Catholics to worship freely and to establish churches.[46] As a result of the edict, on May 15, 1840, Vicar Apostolic of the Pacific, Bishop Rouchouze (d. 1843; vicar 1833–43) arrived at Honolulu with three priests. A Catholic church was established on July 10, 1840, in Honolulu. Two hundred adherents received communion and confirmation. Soon churches were erected on other Hawaiian islands.[47]

THE PROTESTANTS STRUGGLE FOR CONVERSIONS

Catholics could hold mass and work toward conversions, but the Sandwich Islands were at least outwardly Protestant. Between 1820 and early 1838, nearly ninety Protestant mission workers had arrived. Thirty-seven ordained ministers worked at seventeen mission stations. Thousands of Hawaiians attended church, a few of them ardent Christians. Christianity was no longer blamed for disease and other catastrophes.[48]

When Dr. Frederick Debell Bennett arrived in Honolulu on April 15, 1834, he attested to the missionaries' success. Bennett wrote: "Since [1820] religion and general education have advanced so rapidly over all the islands, that idolatrous ceremonies are totally obliterated, and the rising generation now regard a ruined *morai*, or a wooden deity, with the same traditionary interest that the British attach to druidical remains."[49] Nevertheless, full membership was not automatic and followed deep, searching investigations of candidates. By 1837, after seventeen years of mission work, only 1,300 Hawaiians had been admitted to membership.[50]

On February 28, 1848, the twelfth and final shipload of Congregationalist missionaries from New England arrived aboard the *Samoser*. They were among a hundred and fifty-three Protestant missionaries who had arrived since 1820. It was not until December 21, 1849, nearly three decades after the arrival of missionaries, that James Kekela became the first indigenous Hawaiian to be ordained as a Protestant minister; he was assigned a small congregation at Kanuku, Oahu. From 1841 to 1849, nine Hawaiians had been licensed to preach, but none had been ordained. From 1850 to 1854, five more Hawaiians were ordained, three of whom were sent on missions to the Marquesas.[51] By 1853, the islands were judged to have been "Christianized."

Herman Melville saw conversion as a disaster: "Not until I visited Honolulu was I aware of the fact that the small remnant of the natives had been civilized into draught horses, and evangelized into beasts of burden. But it is so. They have been literally broken into the traces, and are harnessed to the vehicles of their spiritual instructors like so many dumb brutes!"[52]

THE WHALING ERA

Whaling was an ancient enterprise before a British ship owned by Samuel Enderby and Sons pioneered the South Pacific whaling industry. Sailing aboard the English ship *Amelia*, a boat steerer named Archelus Hammond, of Nantucket, Massachusetts, harpooned on March 3, 1789, the first sperm whale to be taken in the Pacific Ocean. The 278-ton vessel, under command of James Shields, returned to England on March 11, 1790, with 147½ tons of whale oil. The crew returned safely, except for one man, killed by a whale.[53] With the depletion of sandalwood, servicing whaling vessels became an important industry for Sandwich Islanders. In October 1819, two whaling ships, the *Balena* and the *Equator* killed a whale off Hawaii and returned home with a hundred barrels of oil.[54]

The whalers were manned by as many as 16,000 crewmen. Eighty percent of the ships flew the stars and stripes, setting out from ports such as Nantucket, New Bedford, and New London — all in New England. Yankee investors bought 300–500-ton ships for $30,000 to $60,000. By 1846 about 950 whaling vessels were estimated to exist; 722 of these were American.[55] An average sized crew was thirty-three. Melville wrote that a whaler could go no faster than "a toad through tar," and they were even slower on the voyage home, loaded down with barrels of oil. Crews could expect to be away from America for about three and a half years.[56]

Whaling was among the most dangerous of all occupations because men in a twenty to thirty-foot boat had to balance precariously on waves while trying to stick a harpoon into a 24-meter (80-foot) sperm whale. Recruiters put aboard derelicts, ex-convicts, Indians, freed blacks, Azores and Canary islanders, Polynesians, and Melanesians.[57] Among the Polynesians who had signed aboard whaling and other sailing vessels were an estimated 2,000 Hawaiians in the mid–1840s. They worked in Peru, Tahiti, the Aleutian Islands, and New England; some who were taken to Acapulco served in the Mexican navy. In Alaska and northern California, the Russian American Company employed 1,070. A demographer calculated that the diaspora of workers decreased the population of the kingdom by five percent and of working age males by twelve percent. In addition to clothes and food, some were paid ten to fifteen dollars a month.

Drunken debauchery was a consolation that whaling crews looked forward to in ports such as Lahaina. At sea for three or four years at a time, crews were crammed together in a small area — the forecastle — where each crewman had only a hammock or bunk and a chest. Their quarters reeked when whales had been killed and dissected, and the hold was filled with oil and bone.[58]

On May 31, 1823, William Richards (1793–1847) became the first Protestant missionary to come ashore in Maui. Richards arrived in the Sandwich Islands aboard the *Thames* from New Haven after 158 days at sea. He soon converted the island's governor, Hoapii, to Christianity. Richards advised Hoapii to make laws against drunkenness and debauchery. If seamen on shore disturbed the peace or exhibited riotous behavior, or engaged in so-called furious riding, they would be imprisoned in the recently completed stone fort.[59]

No towns existed in the Sandwich Islands before the coming of white people. Towns grew up as centers of trade, missionary activity, administration, and suppliers of whaling vessels. By 1846 Lahaina had become the whaling capital of the Pacific. Authorities recorded 429 whalers in Lahaina that year, and 167 in Honolulu; these were two-thirds of all whalers in the Pacific. Lahaina, Hilo, and Honolulu consisted of buildings similar to those found in the northeastern U.S. seaboard. A visitor wrote, "Could I have forgotten the circumstances of my visit, I should have fancied myself in New England."[60] Crews came ashore intent on fulfilling the needs of young men long at sea. Lahaina became, in the words of one pious visitor, "a breathing hole of hell." In October 1825, angered by a law that forbade women to visit ships, the crew of the whaling vessel *Daniel* roamed the streets of Lahaina for four days, menacing law-abiding citizens. Crewmen wanted to come ashore to get drunk and to have sex. The *Daniel*'s crew attempted to hang Reverend Richards, whom they correctly blamed for the restrictions, but Maui Christians—led by his wife, Clarissa Lyman Richards (1794–1871)—chased the crewmen back to their ship.[61]

On February 26, 1826, sailors from USS *Dolphin*, commanded by Lieutenant John "Mad Jack" Percival (1779–1862), rioted in Honolulu, menacing the Reverend Hiram Bingham. The sailors demanded that women be allowed to board their ship. Authorities finally relented.[62] In October 1827 Governor Hoapii (d. 1840) of Maui arrested Captain Elisha Clarke of the British whaler *John Palmer* for allowing island females to stay overnight on his ship. The governor refused to release the captain until the women returned to shore. The crew blamed the missionaries for their captain's arrest and shot cannon balls into the yard of Reverend and Mrs. Richards. Their captain finally released, the *John Palmer* crew sailed to Honolulu, taking the women with them.[63]

Convicts at Lahaina built Hale Paahao Prison in 1852 of stone blocks from an older fort. Posted in a cell was a list of crimes current for 1855 and the number of people who had been arrested for each: drunkenness, 330; adultery and fornication, 111; and furious riding, 89. Arrests were also made for aiding desertion of sailors or drinking the local drink *awa* [kava or kawa]. Women could be prosecuted for giving birth to "bastard" children. Fines could be ruinous: for gambling on the Sabbath, one would pay ten times the amount won or lost, or spend 60 days in jail; distilling liquor, $500 or two years' imprisonment; blasphemy, $100 or one year. "Furious riding" could cost anywhere from $5 to $500.[64]

Port regulations in Honolulu, published in the *Friend* on May 1, 1844, in Honolulu, imposed substantial fines on whalers and other crewmembers who transgressed strict rules. These included $2 for being onshore after the 9 P.M. curfew; $1 to $5 for "hallooing" on the streets at night; $6 for "striking another in a quarrel"; $5 for "swift riding"; $6 for drunkenness; $5 for fornication; $30 for adultery; and $50 for rape.[65]

Gangs of angry sailors rioted in Honolulu on the evening of November 10, 1852. The riot highlighted the weakness of the Hawaiian monarchy in maintaining civil order. Rioters stormed Honolulu's police station, broke up its furniture and set fire to the building. Several other buildings were burned. Sailors were angered because two days previously a sailor, Henry Burns from the whaler *Emerald*, had been killed by a guard in the town's fort. After his burial, sailors brandished clubs and guns. The native constabulary and 250 volunteer militiamen restored order within two days.[66]

DISEASE

Whalers brought disease as well as riotous behavior. Due to the large number of whaling ships visiting Hawaiian ports, a wave of measles, whooping cough, and influenza devastated the islanders. At least 10,000 Hawaiians were reported to have died in 1848, perhaps as many as ten percent of the indigenous population.[67] On July 15, 1853, a "Day of Humiliation, Fasting and Prayer" was proclaimed in Honolulu in order to counter a severe smallpox outbreak. The epidemic had begun in February. Ships were quarantined in Pearl Harbor. Protestant missionaries endeavored to treat the sick, while Catholic priests were kept busy administering the last rites. Not until February 1854 did new cases cease to be reported. At that time 6,405 cases were counted, resulting in 2,485 deaths.[68] The population fell to about 77,000 — perhaps a fourth of what it been when Captain Cook arrived.[69]

DECLINE OF THE WHALING INDUSTRY

In 1854 the American whaling industry furnished whalebone and oil valued at over $10,700,000, its largest total for any year during the nineteenth century. After that the industry declined steadily into the twentieth century. Whaling in the Pacific diminished due to the lower price of whale oil, depletion of schools of whales, and the discovery of petroleum at Titusville, Pennsylvania, in 1859 as a substitute for whale oil. Confederate raids on New England ships by the CSA commerce raiders during the American Civil War hastened the demise of the industry. The *Shenandoah*'s crew had sunk thirty-seven New England whalers in the North Pacific.[70] On September 14, 1872, a court of arbitration in Geneva, Switzerland, awarded $15,500,000 to the United States for ships sunk by the Confederacy. The Confederate States of America used ships built in British yards, ships that had never been to America. Britain paid the full amount for 46 ships taken or destroyed by the Confederate commerce-raiders *Alabama*, *Shenandoah*, and *Florida*.[71] Eventually Lahaina, a major whaling center, became almost a ghost town; there were far fewer whalers requiring services and it was no longer the Hawaiian capital.[72]

A CONSTITUTION

In October 8, 1840, King Kamehameha III signed into law a constitution by which he pledged to govern. Missionary influence was evident: "It is therefore our fixed decree, that no law shall be enacted which is at variance with the word of the Lord Jehovah, or at variance with the general spirit of His word." By enacting the constitution, Kamehameha hoped to convince the great powers that his kingdom was "civilized" and deserved to retain independence. The document contained a bill of rights; it prescribed rules for setting up a legislature and allowed all adult males the vote. The constitution was largely the work of Reverend William Richards, who resigned from missionary work in 1836 to become a royal advisor.[73]

Significantly, the name *Hawaii* was used three times in the document, and the name *Sandwich Islands* is entirely absent. Hawaiians preferred their islands be called by their Polynesian name rather than that of a deceased English nobleman. Americans, increasingly vocal, preferred Hawaiian to Sandwich.[74] One finds the archipelago referred to as the Sandwich Islands in the foreign press until about 1880–81, after which the islands were referred to increasingly as the Hawaiian Islands.[75]

AMERICAN AND BRITISH INTRUSIONS

In December 1842 President John Tyler (1790–1842; term, 1841–45) included Hawaii among the countries protected by the Monroe Doctrine. Representing the Hawaiian kingdom, Reverend William Richards and Timothy Haalilio told Secretary of State Daniel Webster (1782–1852) in Washington that the islands would be signed over to Britain if the U.S. did not promise protection. The so-called Tyler Doctrine, seen to be an amendment of the Monroe Doctrine, was addressed principally to Britain and France.[76]

The Tyler Doctrine notwithstanding, on February 25, 1843, King Kamehameha III signed a deed of cession, relinquishing his kingdom to Britain. Cession was demanded by Lord George Paulet (1803–79), captain of HMS *Carysfort*, which had arrived on February 10. The *Carysfort* had been sent from the San Blas Islands to press exorbitant claims of the former British consul in Honolulu, Richard Charlton. The warship bristled with cannons and the king felt he had to give in. On assuming control of the kingdom, Paulet immediately imposed new taxes on native Hawaiians, relaxed liquor laws, and repealed the laws constraining consensual sex. Hawaii's life as a British colony would be brief, only five months, but nobody in the archipelago knew that at the time. The king said to the crowd assembled to watch the proceedings at the fort in Honolulu, "I am in perplexity by reason of difficulties into which I have been brought without cause; therefore, I have given away the life of the land!"[77] The Hawaiian flag was taken down, the union jack hauled up, and the HMS *Carysfort* band played "God Save the Queen."[78]

On July 31, 1843, five months after Lord George Paulet forced cession, Admiral Sir Richard Thomas (1777–1857) arrived in Honolulu and rescinded Paulet's acceptance of the kingdom, returning sovereignty to Kamehameha III. The king told a large audience observing the lowering of the union jack, "The life of the land is preserved in righteousness" (*Ua mau ke ea o ka aina i ka pono*, in Hawaiian), which became Hawaii's official motto. Unknown to the imperialistic Paulet, the British Foreign Office had issued a policy statement in September 1842 mandating that Pacific island governments be treated with "great forbearance and courtesy."[79] Moreover, during its "Little England" period in the 1840s, the British Parliament discouraged the assumption of costly colonial acquisitions.

THE GREAT *MAHELE*

King Kamehameha III signed a document on January 27, 1848 inaugurating the Great *Mahele*. The directive expressed his intent to give up much of his crown land. In the Hawaiian feudal system commoners had been allowed to work the fields in return for a percentage of crops. Missionaries convinced the king to issue the edict; they reasoned that if Hawaiians became small farmers like landowners in New England, they would embrace frugal and pious Protestant virtues, including a compulsion for performing hard work. The Great *Mahele*, it would turn out, did little to help landless commoners. Rather, it opened opportunities for foreigners to purchase land.[80]

The *Kuleana* Act of August 6, 1850, followed the Great *Mahele*. The *Kuleana* Act allowed commoners to petition for ownership in fee simple of the land they cultivated. It was an attempt to end the ancient feudal land system. Only 14,195 claims were filed, and of those 8,421 were approved. Hawaiians received 11,463 hectares (28,658 acres), with an average of less than three acres per land holding. All of these transfers amounted to less than one percent of the land in the kingdom.[81]

A FRENCH INVASION

In 1849, France intimidated Hawaiians once more. French troops aboard the *Gassendi* and the *Poursuivante* invaded the city of Honolulu on August 25. Rear Admiral Legorant de Tromelin ordered the invasion after his demands for certain rights of the twelve French residents were not guaranteed within 24 hours. The French were looking for any excuse to assert power as part of a dramatic expansion in the South Pacific in the 1840s that had already included taking the Marquesas and Tahiti.

The excuse for using bullying tactics was the Hawaiian government's dismissal in April 1849 of French consul Guillaume Patrice Dillon. The admiral demanded that Frenchmen accused of a misdemeanor have the right to a trial by jury, the members of which must be approved by the French consul. He demanded that Protestant ministers of public instruction be held accountable for what he termed their unfair treatment of French pupils. He demanded a reduction in the tariff on French brandy.

French troops took possession of the town and seized the king's yacht, which was then sailed to Tahiti and never returned. They overran the fort and threw hundreds of kegs of gunpowder into the harbor. They ransacked the governor's house, and released all prisoners from jail. After causing damage equivalent to the kingdom's annual income, the French sailed away on September 5.[82] In 1854, out of fear of French imperialism, Kamehameha III ordered a draft treaty prepared providing for annexation of the Hawaiian Islands as a state of the United States. The draft remains undated because the king died on December 15, before he could sign it. Under the draft treaty's terms, the king, chiefs and citizens were to retain their rights, and the laws of the kingdom would remain in force. The monarch would receive an annuity of three hundred thousand dollars and a sum would be provided by the United States for higher education in the new state. The United States Senate failed to ratify the treaty. Kamehameha III's successor was his adopted son, Alexander Liholiho (r. 1854–63).[83]

POPULATION DECLINE AND FOREIGN LABOR

In January 1850, the editor of the *Polynesian* predicted that the indigenous population was declining so rapidly that by 1930 fewer than a hundred would be alive.[84] According to a census taken in 1850, the number of indigenous inhabitants of the Hawaiian Islands was 84,000; it had fallen from 142,000 in 1823.[85] One result is that foreign workers were brought in to work on the plantations. The first 300 indentured laborers from China arrived on January 3, 1852, on the British bark *Thetis* on five-year contracts. They came from Amoy and Fukien provinces. Descendants of many of these workers continue to reside in Hawaii.[86]

In 1864 the Kingdom of Hawaii's Bureau of Immigration was set up to facilitate the importation of labor. By 1900, an estimated 50,000 Chinese had been brought in. The first 150 Japanese workers arrived on June 24, 1868. They numbered approximately 100,000 by 1908.[87] Many left the islands when their indentures had been completed. From the late 1870s until 1911, some 20,000 Portuguese, largely from Madeira, arrived. By 1931, 65,000 Filipinos had come to Hawaii to work, but many also went home.[88]

THE MOLOKAʻI LEPER COLONY

On January 7, 1866, the first lepers were sent to Molokaʻi. Leprosy is thought to have been brought by Chinese field laborers. Probably 8,000 sufferers from Hansen's disease were assigned to the colony over the years On May 10, 1873, Father Damien de Veuster

(1840–89) arrived at Kalaupapa, Moloka'i. Damien had been serving the church in the Hawaiian Islands since March 19, 1864. Damien organized many of the 816 lepers to build a church, homes, and a school, and to grow food to feed themselves. In treating and ministering to lepers, Damien himself contracted Hansen's disease in 1884. He died of complications from leprosy on April 15, 1889.[89]

THE GROWTH OF THE SUGAR INDUSTRY

Because the American Civil War (1861–65) disrupted shipments of sugar from the South, planters expanded in Hawaii. By 1865 Hawaii produced ten times more sugar than she had when the war started. In 1873 more than 10 million kilograms (23 million pounds) of sugar were exported, an increase from 240,000 kilograms (555,000 pounds) in 1856. More land was acquired from indigenous Hawaiians for plantations and mills. Sugar was to replace the servicing of whaling vessels as the kingdom's most important source of foreign exchange.[90] Sugar brought more *haoles*, and they increasingly wanted to take the government into their hands.

Chapter 10

Missionaries Triumphant:
Rarotonga and Mangareva,
1818–1887

THE MISSIONARIES' ACHIEVEMENT

Protestants came to the South Seas first, making conversions in Tahiti and other Society Islands. From there they created Christian communities in the Austral Islands, Tonga, Samoa, the Cooks, and in Niue, Fiji, Tokelau, and Tuvalu. Catholic missionaries provided an opening wedge for France to take over the Marquesas, Societies, Tuamotus, Gambiers and Australs, as well as the Loyalties, New Caledonia, and Wallis and Futuna.

Successful among Polynesians, Protestants and then Catholics moved on to Melanesia and New Guinea. Proselytizing was an uneven process: island people experienced conversion at different times and under various conditions. Missionaries were successful earlier in Polynesia than in Melanesia and New Guinea.

Protestants and Catholics transformed the lives of Polynesians. They created theocracies in a number of places, but none more so than Rarotonga in the Cooks, and Mangareva in the Gambiers.

THE REVEREND JOHN WILLIAMS

Among the most energetic of South Seas missionaries was Reverend John Williams (1796–1839). Williams was instrumental in making conversions in Raiatea, the Cooks, and Samoa. His ambitions for spreading the Gospel encompassed the wide eastern Pacific. John Williams was born in 1796 in London's East End, the son of a tradesman. He apprenticed as a clerk to an ironmonger, and learned the rudiments of iron working. On the evening of January 30, 1814, Williams attended a meeting and heard a revivalist preacher ask, "What shall a man be profited if he gain the whole World and lose his own Soul?" The message led him to be ordained in September and married in October. In November he prepared to go to the South Seas to serve as a missionary. A year later he and his wife Mary arrived at Moorea in the Society Islands after a six-month voyage to Sydney, a wait of four months there for a ship, and a stop in New Zealand. From November 17, 1817, John and Mary lived in Moorea, from which they could see Tahiti easily. They stayed ten months while John mastered spoken Tahitian.[1]

On September 9, 1818, Williams arrived at Raiatea, the ancient center of pagan religion. Williams made Raiatea his home for several years, and he succeeded in converting the estimated 1,500 islanders. Adept at the use of tools, he built a seven-room house for his growing family. He taught islanders to use Western tools for carpentry, boat building, sugar boiling and iron forging. Williams organized Raiateans to produce exports they could sell in order to donate money to his ambitious proselytizing enterprises. Williams set up a clock so islanders could learn to be punctual and use their time productively for the benefit of his mission. Punctuality was an extraordinarily new departure for Polynesians, challenging if not baffling in its demands.

Perhaps it was being made to wear clothes and remain chaste or monogamous, perhaps it was being put to work at labor they deemed inessential to their needs, or maybe it was the clock, but while four islanders disrupted a church service, a drunken Rarotongan went to the missionary's home and attempted to cut Williams's throat. "He came, brandishing a large carving knife, and danced before the house, crying 'Turn out the hog, let us kill him; turn out the pig, let us cut his throat,'" Williams reported. Chiefs nearby subdued the would-be assassin. His life preserved, Williams persevered in his mission. Mary wanted to return to England; she gave birth to three babies, but lost eight in miscarriages and infant death. Stoically, Mary stayed with her husband and encouraged his work.[2]

Williams wrote laws for Raiatea and Tahaa in 1819, followed by laws for Bora Bora the following year and for Huahine in 1822. As islanders accepted Christianity they accepted new and unfamiliar rules. They attended church regularly, sang hymns, covered their bodies in European clothing, and attended school. Many islanders were intrigued by reading and writing, which they first perceived as a miraculous process.[3] The law mandated that islanders live in European–style cottages, and "the recusants had their old fashioned tenements destroyed over their heads, that they might have every incentive to commence the new and improved system."[4]

Clothing and Western housing affected the health of Raiateans. Dr. Frederick Bennett wrote after a visit in the mid–1830s, "I know of no one spot, except within the precincts of an hospital, where I have seen so much severe disease, accumulated amongst comparatively few individuals as upon this small island."[5]

CONVERTING COOK ISLANDERS

Raiatea was Williams's training ground. He had far wider ambitions for converting pagans. Williams leaped at the chance to send missionaries to the Hervey — now Cook — Islands. When a party of Cook Islanders were blown off course and their canoe delivered them to Raiatea, they expressed interest in the Christian religion and asked that Williams send teachers. On October 26, 1821, Reverend Williams dropped off two Tahitian missionaries on Aitutaki. Within a short time they converted the people of this island of low hills and triangular barrier reef. Williams then sent off more mission workers to other of the fifteen Cook Islands — Mauke and Atiu — where they were successful in making many conversions.[6] On June 20, 1823, Williams brought the Polynesian mission worker Rongomatane to 22.3-square-kilometer (8.7-square-mile) Mitiaro in the Cooks. Soon the small population, living in three inland villages, had been converted to Christianity. Rongomatane insisted they move to the coast, where a village was established near the church they constructed.[7]

RAROTONGA

Next, Williams sought to convert the people of Rarotonga. Surrounded by a lagoon and bordered by white sand beaches, Rarotonga measures 67 square kilometers (26 square miles). Te Manga, 658 meters (2,140 feet), is the highest peak. The Rarotongans were divided among three tribes under *ariki* (chiefs) and *ta'unga* (priests). Rarotongans had earlier resisted foreign encroachment. The first Europeans to land arrived aboard the sandalwood ship *Cumberland* in 1814 from Sydney. The sandalwooder's captain and crew demonstrated immediately a degree of the cultural insensitivity that led to clashes on numerous islands between whites and indigenes. The crew under Captain Philip Goodenough found no sandalwood, but they hired sixty Rarotongans to cut yellow dyewood instead. Then relations between intruders and locals deteriorated rapidly. The sailors wanted women and made the mistake of taking women who belonged to *ariki*. Whites ordered islanders to dig up dye trees growing in front of a sacred *marae*. Sailors stole coconuts from the high chief's *marae*. Islanders killed three British, including Captain Goodenough's female companion, Ann Butchers; after they cooked and ate her, they buried her bones near what is today the Rarotonga Sailing Club. For thirteen years after that whites avoided Rarotonga.

On July 26, 1823, a Raiatean missionary, Papeiha, arrived from Aitutaki at Rarotonga and stayed for the rest of his life, which ended in 1867. Williams had trained Papeiha well. Because black costumed Europeans were distrusted or misunderstood by islanders, Williams sent Polynesian preachers to smooth the way for British missionaries. Papeiha arrived at a propitious time; war and disease had killed Rarotongans and many felt the old gods had failed to help them. They were receptive to Papeiha's message. Papeiha knew the formula of conversion: that commoners would become Christians once he had converted chiefs. Four months after Papeiha arrived, a Polynesian colleague, Rio, joined him in his work of conversion. Papeiha was as successful on Rarotonga as he had been on Aitutaki.[8] When Reverends Williams and Charles Pitman arrived on Rarotonga on May 6, 1827, they were astonished by how successful Papeiha had been. Two or three thousand people lined up to shake their hands.[9] A chief had named one of his children Jehovah and another Jesus Christ.

In February 1828, Reverend Aaron Buzacott (1800–1864) of the London Missionary Society arrived. Buzacott served in Rarotonga from 1828 to 1851; Pitman from 1827 to 1854; William Wyatt Gill (1828–96) from 1846 to 1860. Williams visited several times between 1823 and 1838. Reverends Williams, Pitman and Buzacott established what they considered a model Christian village at Avarua, gathering a scattered population of islanders in one place as a community of believers. Moving to a town, when none had ever existed in Rarotonga, was a major alteration in the lifestyle of the scattered tribes people. When people lived in one place the missionaries and their workers could better monitor their actions to make certain they were obeying the missionaries' stringent new rules. Pitman noted of Papeiha and his colleague Rio, "They usurped so much authority that they were objects of fear more than love." Pitman recorded that Rio obtained compliance by use of a gun and that the two missionaries had obtained more than thirty pieces of property.[10]

Reverend Buzacott composed hymns in Rarotongan and oversaw construction of a church in Avarua made of coral blocks, a place of worship suitable for the English countryside. The earl of Pembroke called it "that vile, black and white abomination paralyzing one of the most beautiful bits of scenery in the world."[11] Buzacott encouraged his parishioners to harvest coconuts and other products to export in order to get money to support his mission. The harder a Polynesian worked, missionaries felt, the less time and energy would be available to sin. As C. Harley Gratton wrote of LMS missionaries, "They hated nudity, dancing, sex (except within monogamous marriage), drunkenness, anything savoring of *dolce far niente*, self induced penury, war (except in God's cause), heathenism in all its protean manifestations, and Roman Catholicism."[12]

With money from harvests or labor, Rarotongans were able to purchase British made clothing and shoes, and hats for women. One of every six islanders was recruited to be a *riko*—a sort of police spy who would report on his neighbors. *Rikos* reported islanders for doing work on Sunday, showing affection in public, drinking kava, or being out after 8 P.M. A man who held a woman's hand in public after dark had to hold a lit candle in the other hand, so as not to be able to embrace her. A man was subject to a fine if he wept at the grave of a woman unrelated to him. Rarotongans' right to their land was protected; according to missionary-inspired law, land could not be sold to Europeans, but could be leased.[13]

Church, Rarotonga. The Cook Island Christian Church in Avarua, Rarotonga, was built in 1853 under the direction of Christian missionaries. In 1823, the Polynesian Papeiha arrived to convert islanders and within a few years Rarotongans became ardent Protestants. Reverends John Williams and Aaron Buzacott of the London Missionary Society established a strict theocracy on Rarotonga. Photograph by Robert Kirk.

In 1828, Reverend Williams, with the help of Rarotongans, built a seagoing vessel, the 80-ton *Messenger of Peace*. The process took only three months. He constructed a forge, and from goat skin a blacksmith's bellows to shape iron, and a lathe to produce ship's planking. Islanders supplied rope from hibiscus fiber and pandanus matting for sails. Williams and his crew sailed the boat to Tahiti to buy conventional canvas sails.[14]

In 1834 the Reverend John Williams returned to London and oversaw the printing by the British and Foreign Bible Society of his translation of the New Testament into Rarotongan. Copies were returned to Rarotonga for the use of converts. Williams and his missionary colleagues had established classes to teach Rarotongans to read.[15]

In April 1837 in London John Williams published *Narrative of Missionary Enterprises in the South Sea Islands, with Remarks upon the Natural History of the Islands, Origin, Languages, Traditions, and Usages of the Inhabitants.* Williams dedicated the book to King William IV (1765–1837; r. 1830–37), and sent copies to wealthy and titled individuals. He hoped that by interesting the king and upper classes, including merchants and ship owners, in his work, his missions would gain financial and political support.[16] With sufficient financial support, Reverend John Williams was able to begin his great project — evangelization of Melanesia. It was there he was murdered in 1839.

PICPUSIANS ARRIVE IN MANGAREVA

Catholic missionaries arrived in the Gambier Islands aboard the ship *Peruvian* on July 16, 1834. It was the first organized attempt by Catholics to convert Polynesians. British Captain James Wilson (1760–1814) of the missionary ship *Duff* is credited with being the first European commander to sight Mangareva, on May 24, 1797. Wilson named them the Gambier Islands after James Gambier (1756–1833), an officer in the British Navy who later became an admiral. The largest is Mangareva, measuring 18 square kilometers (7 square miles). Four inhabited islands and ten others measure together only 31 square kilometers (12 square miles). Mount Duff looms above Mangareva at 441 meters (1,455 feet). Mangareva is partially enclosed by a barrier reef. One of five archipelagos of French Polynesia, the Gambiers look on the map as if they should be part of the Tuamotu Archipelago, but they are higher and rockier than the Tuamotu atolls and the language of the people differs from that of the Tuamotans.[17]

The missionaries were Father Louis Honoré Laval (1808–80), Father Françoise d'Assise Caret (1803–44), and Brother Columban Murphy, all of the Sacred Hearts of Jesus and Mary and of the Perpetual Adoration of the Blessed Sacrament of the Altar; the holy order was popularly known by the name of the Paris street where it was headquartered, Picpus. When they arrived they were met by schoolmaster and lay LMS preacher George Hunn Nobbs, exiled from Pitcairn Island by its dictator Joshua Hill. Nobbs witnessed the priests converting islanders before he left.

Mangarevans grew breadfruit, taro, yams, and fished in the "garden of the poor," off shore. War had been endemic among tribes, with winners destroying the food supplies of losers as a way of weakening enemies who were certain to plot revenge. As in so many other Polynesian island worlds, high chiefs had unlimited power over the people; the *ariki* controlled land, while the commoners worked it. *Ariki* ate well except in times of real famine. Commoners had to contribute food to the *ariki* for three-to-five day bouts of chiefly gorging. The small band of Picpisians saw these people as being in obvious need of serious correction, and they worked quickly. The priests congregated the Mangarevans into compact areas called reductions, where their lives could be more readily overseen.

When the fathers succeeded in converting the high chief, Maputeoa, commoners came to the mission to be converted. Laval ordered the statue of the god Tu on the sacred *marae* to be toppled, and he put an end to pagan singing and dancing. Having learned from infancy obedience to their superiors, the people of Mangareva were superb subjects for imported authoritarianism. On Mangareva, Father Laval claimed to have baptized nearly 2,000 people in four years. Converts could participate in confession and masses, and could take sacraments. The priests soon learned Mangarevan, and Father Caret wrote the Lord's Prayer in the language and taught some people to read it.[18]

On May 9, 1835, they were joined by Father Cyprien Liausu, Father Louis Maigret, and lay preachers. Liausu took charge until he left in 1855. After that Laval carried on a theocratic dictatorship until he was removed by French authorities.

Captain William Henry Anderson Morshead (1811–86) of HMS *Dido* arrived in Mangareva in November 1835 soon after an epidemic had killed several hundred inhabitants. He noted that life for the islanders had been transformed by the coming of Picpusian priests. On the side of Mount Duff, Captain Morshead visited "a convent containing one hundred nuns and sixty children, whose interval between prayers and penance is filled up by trundling a distaff, and spinning native cotton, to supply a factory with a dozen hand looms at work."[19]

On January 17, 1839, Laval laid the cornerstone for St. Michael's Cathedral in Rikitea, the only town in Mangareva. Islanders were set to work building a jail to hold people who refused to build the church. To fund the projects, parishioners dived for pearls in the lagoon. Gambier Islanders neglected their taro fields and fishing to work on the imposing edifice and to earn money to donate for its construction.

Ruined mission building at Taravai. Taravai is a small island close to Mangareva in the Gambier Islands. This decaying structure is one of 116 coral and stone buildings erected by islanders under direction of Father Laval in the 19th century. The substantial church nearby will accommodate more people than the handful that inhabits the idyllic island. Photograph by Robert Kirk.

On April 4, 1839, Bishop Etienne Jerome Rouchouze, vicar apostolic of Oriental Oceania, 1833–43, arrived and blessed the cathedral-in-progress. The largest European–style church at the time in the South Pacific, it would not be completed until 1848. It measures 487 meters (160 feet) by 183 meters (60 feet) and can seat 1,200. Its interior is decorated with mother of pearl. When an estimated 5,000 Gambier

Islanders had died of overwork, disease or starvation, Father Laval said, "True, they are all dead. But they have gone to Heaven the more quickly."[20]

By 1847, thirteen years after arrival of Picpusian fathers, the population had fallen from 9,000 to 500. Nearly 200 females became nuns, ostensibly chaste, and as a result a number of children were not born to replenish the declining population. Not to be deterred by a lack of laborers for what he saw as God's work, Father Laval organized blackbirding expeditions to the nearby Tuamotus to abduct or entice more workers to come to Mangareva to work on his grandiose construction projects or to dive for pearls to fund them.[21]

In 1854, a French sea captain who had come to trade was accused of eating meat on Friday. He was tied up and jailed. His bedclothes were burned in front of witnesses because they had enveloped the sinful man. The hut where he had slept was fumigated. Unmarried girls were locked in the convent every night so they would not have sexual intercourse. Married women were locked up on Saturday nights, the night before the holy day, so their husbands would not pollute themselves by enjoying sex with their wives when they should be concentrating on their obligations to God.[22]

St. Michael's Cathedral, Rikitea, Mangareva, was constructed by islanders from 1839 to 1848 from coral and stone. The chapel could seat 1,200 but never did because under the 37-year theocracy of Father Eugene Laval, the population fell from 9,000 to 500. Photograph by Robert Kirk.

Although Laval's tyranny was reported to Paris, he was left to run the island as he saw fit until the fall in 1870 of Napoleon III's Second Empire. The empire was soon followed in Paris by an anticlerical republican government; as a result, Bishop Monsignor Haussen ordered Laval removed to Tahiti. He sent Commandant de la Motte-Rouge and twenty gendarmes to Mangareva. When Motte-Rouge opened Laval's jail, he let out, among others, two young boys who had been incarcerated for the heinous offense of laughing during mass.

Laval was to be tried in Papeete for murder, but before the trial could take place, he was judged insane. Laval died on November 1, 1880, from infection from a cat scratch. It was not until 1887 that French annexation offered some protection to the islanders from Laval's Picpusian successors.[23]

Chapter 11

Cannibals and Crucifixes:
The Marquesas, 1774–1914

Captain Cook Arrives

James Cook aboard the *Endeavour* visited Tahuata in the Marquesas, arriving April 6, 1774. The last European visit had been by Alvaro de Mendaña, 179 years earlier. Islanders received the *Endeavour* crew with curiosity, hospitality and great excitement. The memory was erased of how Spaniards had shot their ancestors for sport, and of "the bloated putrefying corpses of relatives and friends, filling the pleasant valley with the stench of the charnel house."[1] Marquesans marveled at the odd crew, sailing without women, without fresh food, fully clothed, and speaking a language they found incomprehensible.

Cook found a stratified Polynesian society numbering an estimated 100,000 to 110,000 people.[2] Tribes were led by chiefs who descended from the founder of their valley's community. The chief would undergo tattooing over his entire face and body. The chief and his wives lived in a house erected on a *paepae*, or elevated stone platform. Commoners spent their days growing food, fishing, or working for the chief. Parents encouraged pubescent children to experiment sexually. Temples and plazas were filled with community members gathered to pay respect to gods such as Tu, Tangaroa, Tiki, and others from an extensive pantheon. The *tau'a*, or priest, interpreted to the people the wishes and commands of tribal gods; a god might demand human sacrifices. Tribes raided into neighboring valleys to obtain human sacrifices to placate the gods.

Warfare was endemic. Approaches to valleys were fortified by wooden palisades and trenches dug as a defense. Human flesh supplemented protein gained from pigs, chickens, and dogs. Captives taken in warfare were eaten for their *mana* or prowess. Eyeballs were rich in *mana*. A captive might live long enough to see one of his appendages severed and consumed.[3] With good intentions, Cook rewarded services by commoners by handing out red feathers accumulated in Brazil, and red jackets. Chiefs on Tahuata had a monopoly on the color red in the form of bird feathers, flowers, and *tapa* stained from the banyan tree.[4] Clothing commoners in the color reserved to the regal caste upset the social order within a society already balanced in power between isolated antagonistic tribes.

Cook ordered his officers to fire over the head of a thief who had stolen an iron stanchion, but "unluckily for the thief they took better aim than I ever intend and killed him the third Shott."[5] Cook sailed off and whites left the Marquesas alone for twenty-three years. At that time the population may have numbered anywhere from fifty thousand to two hundred thousand.[6]

PROTESTANT MISSIONARIES

On June 4, 1797, the missionary ship *Duff* stopped at Tahuata and left two missionaries, William Pascoe Crook (1775–1846), age twenty-two, and Reverend John Harris (1754–1819), age twenty-eight. Their piety was challenged immediately when a goat chomped off the entire costume of a young woman who had come aboard ship wearing some strategically placed leaves. Crook was to stay two years. Harris sailed away on the next ship, leaving Crook the lone white man on Tahuata.

Crook found himself on an island consisting of mountains and isolated valleys, measuring 69 square kilometers (26½ square miles). In the valleys were mutually antagonistic tribes, forming temporary alliances with neighbors, and usually at war. War could be waged because breadfruit was abundant and easily preserved, so that fighters did not have to work every day to obtain food. Each valley was ruled by a chief, the *haka'iki*, and a priest, the *tau'a*. Wars might start as raids. Success in war was guaranteed when the warrior's club could be smeared with the brains or blood of an enemy, thus transferring that person's *mana* to the victor. Wars were due to age-old enmity between valley communities.[7] Crook was handicapped at first by being unable to speak the language and in having all his possessions stolen from him. Because he had no valued skills and was not part of a local family, Crook found himself a chronically-hungry non-person. Because Crook did not fit into any apparent social hierarchy, he was considered to have no *mana*, which probably saved his life, because there was no point in eating him.

In 1798 Crook left with Captain Edmund Fanning on the *Betsy*. Fanning left Crook on Nuka Hiva, where he lived in at least more comfort until 1799 when he left aboard the *Butterworth* for London. He had failed in two years to make any conversions. His notes were compiled as a book, published in 2007, titled *An Account of the Marquesas Islands, 1797–99*.[8]

FURTHER EXPLORATION

In April 1791 Captain Joseph Ingraham (1762–1800) of Boston discovered the Leeward group of the Marquesas, and was, presumably, the first Westerner to set foot on Nuku Hiva. He named smaller islands below the equator Washington (Ua Huka), Franklin (Motuiti), Knox (Eiao), Adams (Ua Pou), and Lincoln (today's Motuoa).[9]

On June 12, 1791, the captain of *Le Solide*, Etienne Marchand (1755–93), arrived in the Marquesas June 12, 1791, and soon charted Fatu Hiva, Tahuata, Hiva Oa, Oa Pou, and Nuku Hiva. He claimed several Marquesas islands for France. French war ships would return a half-century later to confirm the claim and take over the islands. Marchand sailed on to Maui and then the northwest coast of America, to China and home. Marchand's crew completed the second circumnavigation to be performed by the French.[10]

EDWARD ROBARTS, LITERATE BEACHCOMBER

In 1798 Edward Robarts (1794–1824), a twenty-seven-year-old Welshman, deserted in Tahuata from the whaler *Euphrates*. Robarts remained seven years on Tahuata and Nuku Hiva with the same chiefs who had hosted Crook. Robarts found a female companion, built a house, and traveled from valley to valley, exchanging names with tribesmen in order to build the network of relationships that was essential for survival in Marquesan society. At times he served chiefs as a mercenary with his musket. During his stay he kept a diary that is a valuable source of information on early-contact Marquesan society.

In 1806 Robarts left Nuku Hiva with his Marquesan mate and their daughter aboard the privateer *Lucy*; he spent eighteen months in Tahiti distilling rum. Leaving Tahiti on the *General Wellesley*, he went on to New Zealand, Fiji, Malaya, Calcutta and more adventures.

Two Russian ships arrived in Nuku Hiva on May 5, 1804. Under command of Adam Johann Ritter von Krusenstern (1770–1846), a Baltic German in the czar's naval service, was *Nasheda*. *Neva* was under the command of Yuri Lisianski (1773–1837). Von Krusenstern's orders were to open trade with Japan and China and evaluate California for a possible Russian settlement. He would complete the first Russian circumnavigation of the world but fail in his mission in Japan.

On Nuku Hiva the Russians found Robarts and a Frenchman, Jean Cabri, who had "gone native" by marrying a Marquesan and participating in intertribal wars. Cabri insisted he had not been a cannibal during his stay, but had bartered human parts with cannibals for other food. Von Krusenstern took Cabri off Nuku Hiva on May 17, 1804, but Cabri found Marquesan habits hard to break. Cabri practiced sorcery aboard the ship but was unable to demonstrate results because, as he explained, there was no burial ground on the deck. He complained that he missed *les mesdames* and *les mademoiselles* of Nuku Hiva. In Russia the aristocracy considered Cabri a curiosity, displaying his Marquesan tattoos and performing island dances during parties. Back in France he performed Marquesan dances each year at an Orleans fair, while complaining about competition from the famous performing dog Munito.[11]

AN AMERICAN NAVAL BASE

On November 19, 1813, Captain David Porter, USN (1780–1814), claimed possession of Nuku Hiva for the United States. Porter was in the South Seas commanded raiding vessels, which targeted British ships during the War of 1812. He found Nuku Hiva a convenient base. Porter's ship *Essex* had rounded Cape Horn, becoming the first American naval ship to enter the South Pacific. Porter captured twelve British whaling ships off the coast of South America.

With 300 sailors and the help of Nuku Hivans, Porter built Fort Madison and the town of Madisonville at Taiohae Bay; both were named for America's fourth president, James Madison. Porter renamed the island Madison Island and Taiohae Bay, Massachusetts Bay. From October to December 1813 his men rehabilitated the *Essex*, as well as ships captured from the British. The Americans depleted Nuku Hiva's food supplies, trading manufactured products for food. Porter helped the Te'i'i tribe by sending his Marine company against rival Taipis, upsetting the balance of power on the island. In his journal Porter wrote, "The dirty smoke curls rising from burning houses and temples in Taipi Valley were further proof of the clear superiority of American arms." When Porter offered the islands to the United States, Congress refused them.[12]

Essex and *Essex Junior* were defeated in March 1814 near Valparaiso, Chile, by Royal Navy captain James Hilyer (1769–1843), commanding the *Phoebe* and *Cherub*. Porter and his crews became prisoners of war. Porter's efforts to harm the British during the War of

View from ruined Fort Madison, Nuku Hiva. In late 1813 Captain David Porter, USN, arrived with 300 sailors at Nuku Hiva. Porter built Fort Madison as a base to menace British whalers during the War of 1812. Porter sent marines inland to lay waste to the valley of the Taipis. Congress refused Porter's offer of Nuku Hiva as a colony. Photograph by Robert Kirk.

1812, however, had already been successful; in all, Porter took prize ships with cargoes valued at a quarter of a million dollars.[13]

When he sailed for Valparaiso, Porter left Lieutenant John M. Gamble (1791–1836) of the Marine Corps and twenty-two men at Nuku Hiva to defend the base and three prize ships. For Gamble everything went wrong: Thousands of hostile Taipis attacked, British prisoners revolted, and four of his men went off with Marquesan women. With a skeleton crew, Gamble made a seventeen-day voyage in one of the prize ships to the Sandwich Islands, becoming the first Marine to captain a navy vessel. In May 1814 eight of Porter's men were captured by British seamen in the Sandwich Islands. The capture of these eight and the taking by the British of two ships in Valparaiso ended Captain David Porter's strikes against British ships in the Pacific Ocean.[14]

A POPULAR DESTINATION

By 1817, at least fifty ships had visited the Marquesas. Two crews had been captured and eaten. An estimated thirty-one brave men deserted.[15] Most of these beachcombers congregated at Vaiahu on Tauata, and Taiohae and Taipivai in Nuku Hiva.[16]

Marquesan chiefs were eager to obtain muskets and traded pork and sandalwood for them. By 1817 there was minimal pork and no more sandalwood.[17] Marquesans were said to have misused muskets; they were often more injurious to the shooter than the target, and were more valued for noise than as weapons.[18]

Marquesan females aboard the *Zelée*, 1839. The sketch by A. Legrand depicts the visit of women of Nuku Hiva aboard the French exploration ship under command of Charles Hector Jacquinot, part of Dumont d'Urville's second Pacific expedition, 1837–40. The French treated the Marquesans well. Marquesan women were among the most beautiful in Oceania, which makes the seeming indifference to the scene of the French sailor second from right puzzling. The drawing first appeared in *Voyage autour du Monde* by E.J.F. Le Guillou and J.E.V. Arago (Paris: Berquet et Pétion, 1842).

Edward Robarts recalled an incident that occurred when the ship London put in at Nuku Hiva. When the ship's boat went to the shore, a Marquesan attempted to steal an object. A crewman fired a musket aimed at the thief, but "it missed the thief and shot a young lady who was sitting in the Chiefs house on the beach adjusting her turban.... The ball went through her head. She died momentarily. Here is a truly pityable case," Robarts concluded about the fate of the "very handsome" sixteen-year-old girl.[19]

When whites began arriving in greater numbers, transformation of Marquesan culture accelerated. As Greg Dening stated, "Geographical and structural fragmentation left the Marquesans ultimately defenseless in the face of western political aggression." Alcohol, opium, bullets and disease led to "genocidal assaults on their customs."[20]

CATHOLIC MISSIONARIES

Although Americans had established a fort and British missionaries had worked to save souls, it was the French who would claim the Marquesas. To begin the process of wresting control of Pacific islands, French authorities relied on Catholic priests as "pioneers of civilization"; they received free transportation to the Marquesas on French war ships. On August 4, 1838, French Picpusian priests arrived aboard the *Venus* at Vaitahu Bay, Tahuata. Other missionaries had failed in the task of conversion in these cannibal islands, but fathers Desvault and Borgella, and Brother Nil prepared well. They learned the language, learned about the customs and beliefs of the residents, and exchanged names with chiefs. On the island of Tahuata on February 6, 1839, Rouchouze celebrated the first Catholic mass.[21]

French priests set about dismantling Marquesan culture, proscribing nudity, cannibalism, infanticide, warfare, dancing, promiscuity, polygamy, tattoos, and non–Christian music. In the first decade priests claimed to have baptized 216 adults. On Nuku Hiva they crowned King Temoana with a cardboard crown, and bestowed one on King Iotete on Tahuata. Each of these puppet monarchs soon succumbed to disease and alcohol. They were, in Greg Dening's words, "kings of decay."[22]

France made the Marquesas its first Pacific possession. Rear Admiral Abel Du Petit-Thouars had recommended the Marquesas to his government in Paris because he saw the islands as "the most important military point ... on the route from Chile to China." His instructions, written in October 1841, stated that the Marquesas were "the most appropriate port to attain the goal set by the King's government in founding an establishment offering shelter and protection to our fleet in the Great Ocean."[23]

FRENCH CONQUEST

In December 1841, Du Petit-Thouars had left Brest, France, on the *Reine Blanche* in command of seven warships and a thousand men. The admiral sent 500 troops to the islands, overcoming opposition with cannon fire. The French enlisted friendly tribes as mercenaries to subdue recalcitrant tribes.[24] Chief Iotete of Tahuata signed away the southern Marquesas Islands to France on May 1, 1842; these included Tahuata, Hiva Oa, and Fatu Hiva. On May 1, 1842, Marquesan chiefs ceded Nuku Hiva, Ua Huka and Ua Pou. Having conquered a colony, bored troops—two hundred stationed on Tahuata and two hundred on Nuku Hiva—shot myriad birds.[25]

On April 28, 1843, a royal ordinance gave Captain Armand-Joseph Bruat (1796–1855) governorship of the Marquesas. To occupy the Marquesas with the least possible expense, authorities would use "draconian measures" at minimal cost.[26]

HERMAN MELVILLE AMONG THE TAIPIS

Writer Herman Melville (1819–91) arrived immediately after the French conquest. On July 9, 1842, with his shipmate Richard Tobias Greene, he jumped ship from the whaler *Acushnet*, anchored off the island of Nuku Hiva. Life aboard a cramped, unhealthy vessel could seem intolerable, and hundreds of men had jumped ship on Pacific islands and lived for varying times as beachcombers. Melville was the best known of them because his adventures on the high tropical island would lead to his writing his first novel, *Typee*; Greene became the protagonist's fictionalized companion Toby.

At age nineteen, the well-educated Melville had been unable to find work due to the financial panic of 1837 in America, so he opted to go to sea. In 1841 he shipped out with twenty Americans, three Portuguese and an Englishman aboard the *Acushnet*.

In his introduction to *Typee*, the classic tale of the Marquesas, Melville wrote: "Hurra, my lads! It's a settled thing; next week we shape our course to the Marquesas! What strange visions of outlandish things does the very name spirit up! Naked houris—cannibal banquets—groves of cocoa-nut—coral reefs—tattooed chiefs—and bamboo temples; sunny

valleys planted with bread-fruit trees—carved canoes dancing on the flashing blue waters—savage woodlands guarded by horrible idols—heathenish rites and human sacrifices!"[27] The exclamation marks were justified. Melville found all of the exotic wonders he listed and more while living among the Taipi tribe for a month — four months in his fictionalized version.

Nuku Hiva tattoo artist. This sketch is by W. Tilesius and H. Alexander Orloffsky. It depicts a scene on Nuku Hiva during the visit of Russian ships under command of Admiral Adam Johann Ritter von Krusenstern, on his expedition of 1803–06. The climate in the Marquesas is hot, and the people were well illustrated rather than well clothed. This woman is breast feeding while undergoing the painful process by a tattoo artist. The sketch appeared as plate X in *Voyages and Travels* by Georg Heinrich von Langsdorff (London, 1817).

When the *Lucy Ann*, a whaler out of Sydney, stopped at Nuku Hiva the captain offered Melville a berth; desertions created crew openings in the South Seas. Melville signed on and left for Tahiti.[28] He worked his way aboard ship to Tahiti, to Lahaina, and Honolulu. In Honolulu Melville signed aboard the *USS United States* and sailed to Boston, arriving in 1844. He was twenty-five and had been away four years. He would never see the South Seas again, but his experiences would inspire his fiction.

On February 26, 1846, Melville's novel *Typee* was published by John Murray in London. The original title was *Narrative of a Four Months' Residence among the Natives of a Valley of the Marquesas Islands*. In *Typee* Melville becomes the protagonist and his love is the dusky Polynesian beauty Fayaway. In a canoe on a nonexistent lake in the interior of Nuku Hiva, Fayaway suddenly stands up in the boat. To utilize winds to power the boat she holds up the piece of *tapa* that has covered her, spreads her arms, and—completely nude—becomes a lovely mast holding the sail. The mental picture of Fayaway would implant an exotic, erotic South Seas vision in the minds of generations of readers, a vision that continues to remind us that the South Seas are conceived of as a sensual paradise on Earth.[29]

A DIMINISHING POPULATION

Venereal disease brought by visitors debilitated increasing numbers of islanders. In 1838 Father Mathias Gracia noted after his arrival, "Because of debauchery conception is rare, and the birth of an infant is considered an exceedingly happy event in a family." Under French control, the Marquesas continued to lose population. In 1856 French authorities estimated indigenous Marquesan islanders to number 12,500; the estimate for 1838 had been 20,000.[30]

On December 21, 1862, Peruvian blackbirders aboard the *Empresa* arrived at Ua Pou. Marquesans were fortunate on several islands to be protected from blackbirders by French officials and priests. On Ua Pou, however, five islanders agreed to work in Peruvian guano mines and on plantations, obviously not understanding the terms, duration, location or conditions of servitude. Six men and boys were taken by force, as were eight women, and locked in a cabin after they had been enticed aboard. Within the next two years blackbirders had abducted thirty-three. In 1863 French authorities saved 200 from being carried off after they had boarded a Peruvian vessel to trade.[31]

In July 1864 the *Empresa* from Callao, where there had been a smallpox outbreak, returned twenty-nine Polynesian slaves to Nuku Hiva in the Marquesas; fourteen had died en route. The survivors were quarantined by the French but eager family members broke into the compound to embrace them. Contagion spread. Soon 960 died on Nuku Hiva and 600 on Ua Pou. Survivors were too few or too ill to bury the dead, and the corpses continued to spread smallpox. Most tribal leaders were dead, and anarchy ensued. Within six months 1,560 were dead. To ward off evil spirits they thought were killing their families, islanders engaged in debauchery, including orgies, drunkenness, abuse of narcotics, fighting and murder. French troops broke up bacchanalias on Hiva Oa and put people to work building roads.[32] As Robert Suggs stated, "Now with the old chiefs dead and all social control dead with them, the temples decaying, the harmless dances and music forbidden, and the children being taught to hate the ways of their parents, what reason existed for living according to any rules?"[33]

GAUGUIN

On May 8, 1903, artist Paul Gauguin died at age fifty-four in his home at Atuona on Hiva Oa. In 1895 after contracting syphilis in France, he returned to Tahiti and built a hut. He was hospitalized with a broken ankle and leg sores. By 1896, demoralized and discouraged, he was living on guava, mango and water and vomiting blood. The following year he tried to commit suicide, but having failed, took a job in the government's public works department. In and out of the hospital for various ailments, in 1901, when he was fifty-three, he recovered sufficiently to move to Hiva Oa. His grave may be visited at the cemetery above Traitors' Bay. Gauguin's exotic paintings and carvings have helped to form popular impressions of exotic life in the South Seas.[34]

APPROACHING DEMOGRAPHIC NADIR

In 1872 authorities counted 6,200 Marquesan islanders. In 1887 a census counted 5,246.[35] In 1890 there were 4,820 people and in 1897 authorities counted 4,279.[36] The nadir would be reached in 1926: 2,225.[37]

From Gauguin's gravesite, the visitor looks out across Hiva Oa toward Traitors' Bay. He looks down on a lonely verdant island against the backdrop of the azure sea. Silence pervades wooded valleys where once the thunderous cries of warriors struck fear in enemies. It is an island of graves.

Chapter 12

Vanished: Easter Island's Incredible Culture, 1722–1914

ROGGEVEEN NAMES EASTER ISLAND

On Easter Sunday, April 5, 1722, Dutch navigator Jacob Roggeveen, commanding *Arend, Thienhoven* and *Afrikaansche Galei*, came upon an astonishing sight. Giant heads, facing away from his approaching vessels, dotted the shore of a large, isolated island. He had discovered the eastern most Polynesian settlement. He named it Paasch Eyland, which translates from the Dutch as Easter Island. The Polynesians probably had no name for their 120-square-kilometer (46-square-mile) home; it was their entire world. Later islanders called it Te Pit o Te Henua (Navel of the World), and visitors from Rapa Iti in the Australs named it Rapa Nui (Big Rapa), which it is still called. Chile, which annexed it in 1888, calls it Isla de Pascua, Spanish for Easter Island. By whatever name, it is the world's most remote continuously inhabited community, 3,224 kilometers (1,240 miles) from minuscule Pitcairn Island, its closest neighbor.

Radiocarbon dating suggests that the first inhabitants arrived around 690 CE, with a possibility they came 130 years before or after. In 2011 Terry Hunt and Carl Lipo, in their book *The Statues That Walked: Unraveling the Mystery of Easter Island*, make a strong case for later settlement, about 1200. Whatever the date of arrival, the initial settlers would probably have come from Mangareva. A recreation by the crew of the *Hokule'a* in 1999 of an ancient voyage showed that the Mangareva to Easter Island trip could have been made in fewer than eighteen days. The ancient pioneers brought taro, yams, and *kumara* (sweet potatoes) to grow. They cultivated paper mulberry trees, from which they made *tapa* cloth. They brought chickens. They brought their social structure, which ranked *ariki* (nobles), *tuhunga* (skilled artisans, including priests), and *urumanu* (workers). The *ariki mao* was the paramount chief; he enjoyed the greatest prestige and authority, at least until the nineteenth century. These intrepid pioneers brought their belief system, notably the concepts of *tabu* and *mana*.[1]

The Dutch visitors marveled at one of the world's incomparable sights: stupendous *moai* (stone heads). The largest are 21 meters (69 feet) high. Many of these *moai* wore stone crowns, known as topknots. According to most studies, the *moai* were carved and moved to the coast between about 1100 and the 1600s; archaeologists estimate the height of activity to be in the 1400s, when the population, according to Jared Diamond's considered estimate, may have numbered six to eight thousand.[2] Ninety percent of the 261 *moai* which had been originally set upright paralleled the coast, and some were oriented to the equinoxes. *Ahus*, which are long altar-like structures, range from a few feet to 150 meters

(500 feet) in length. The typical *ahu* is 4.5 meters (15 feet) high and 90 meters (300 feet) long. *Ahus*, numbering about 100, held one to fifteen *moai* each. An *ahu* probably served the same purpose as a Polynesian *marae* (*heiau* in Hawaii). No two *moai* are identical. No living person knows for certain, but these mysterious stone giants are thought to have been rolled on logs to the *ahus*, which explains in part how the island was denuded of large trees. The giant heads are made of porous volcanic tuff from one of the island's three extinct volcanoes. White eyes, carved from coral, gave the *moais mana* (concentrated supernatural force).

Language was a barrier and perhaps he lacked curiosity, but Roggeveen did not find out why the statues had been erected. In fact, during the following century, no other visitor did either. Perhaps by 1722 the islanders themselves no longer knew why their ancestors made them. But Roggeveen provided our best clue when he noted that islanders "kindle fire in front of certain remarkably tall stone figures they set up; and thereafter squatting on their heels with heads bowed down, they bring the palms of their hands together and alternately raise and lower them."[3] Today's Rapanui, as the people are called, speculate that each of several tribes erected them to honor the tribe's forefathers.

Tribes probably competed in setting upright larger *moai* than their neighbors erected. El Gigante, the largest, weighs an estimated 270 tons and was too heavy to move. Over 800 *moais* survive, but the few still standing were set up again in the twentieth century under the direction of anthropologists. Some are broken. In Rano Raraku Crater, from which they were dug out and carved, 394 remain; they were left unfinished where carvers dropped their tools. Nearly 100 *moai* were crowned with red stone topknots, rolled from the quarry at Puna Pau crater to the *moai*. Some weigh ten or eleven tons. We do not know how the statues were topped with these mammoth stones.

Roggeveen estimated the population at between two and three thousand. It is possible that many people, especially women, did not emerge from their dwellings, so the population may have been significantly higher. The Dutch were amused by the appearance of some islanders with elongated ears, in contrast to those whose ears had not been stretched. The islanders were awed at the appearance of their visitors: all had skin as white as that of the whitest of their rulers, the *ariki*, who avoided being darkened by the sun.[4] Roggeveen noted that houses were made of reeds, mounted on stone foundations, looking like boats set upside down. Each was furnished with mats and headrests and might house ten to thirty people. The Dutch noted a lack of vegetation higher than three meters (ten feet).

When Polynesians arrived, the island had been studded with palms, many 24 meters (80 feet) high, but by 1400 CE islanders had cut down their trees to move *moai*, cook, and to build boats and houses, and possibly to clear land for planting. As Steven Roger Fischer explained, "At first islanders remained few. But when numbers increased exponentially, the flora and fauna crashed. Even then it took nearly a millennium to ruin Easter Island."[5] With no trees men fished off shore in leaky canoes or small boards lashed together with twine. Without large traditional Polynesian canoes, they had been unable to leave Easter Island and were trapped. Without trees, and having depleted the *Triumfetta* shrub from which they made rope, they could neither roll statues nor pull them into position. Worse, topsoil was washed away as a result of tree destruction, and hunger became prevalent. After about 1400 CE human meat became a source of protein.

During their one-day stay, the Dutch sent 137 men ashore, and 20 remained on the beach to guard the ship's boats. One or more of the guards killed twelve islanders and wounded many more, reportedly for taking guns and coats. If the officer in charge was punished, no record of it is known. In the forty-eight years between 1722 and 1770, no Europeans recorded having gone there.[6]

A Destructive Civil War

After Roggeveen sailed off and before the next European ships arrived, islanders fought a long, vicious civil war. As John Flenley and Paul Bahn stated, "The amazing peace of a thousand years—unique in Polynesia—was shattered as old rivalries were no long expressed in competitive construction but rather in raids, violence and destruction."[7] Confederations from the west fought tribal confederations in the east from about 1724 to 1750. During this period of two generations Easter Islanders destroyed much of their own culture. Gangs of thugs roamed freely. Crops were ripped out, houses demolished, and hunger ensued. Victors enslaved the vanquished. Those who escaped from their conquerors hid in caves or on rocks off the coast.[8]

The Spanish Claim Isla de San Carlos

On November 16, 1770, Don Felipe Gonzáles de Haedo (1702–92), having sailed from Callao, Peru, under orders of the viceroy Manuel de Amat y Junient, arrived. The viceroy was concerned that other European nations were colonizing islands in Spain's Pacific and sent Gonzales to investigate. Gonzales found no foreign settlements. He commanded the sixty-four-gun *San Lorenzo* and the frigate *Santa Rosalia*. On November 20, the Spaniards planted crosses at the island's three craters, shouted "*Viva el Rey*," shot off their muskets three times, and fired a twenty-one-gun salute from the ships' cannons. Gonzáles de Haedo named Easter Island Isla de San Carlos and claimed it and its people for King Carlos III.

Gonzales noted "certain huge blocks of statues in the form a human figure," but he made no mention of toppled statues, so it is possible the *moais* that had been set on *ahus* were still standing in late 1770. Gonzales estimated the population at 900 to 1,000, but estimated only seventy women among them; other females may have stayed in caves or huts and the population could have been closer to 2,000. The naked, painted men "are in hue like a quadroon with smooth hair and short beards, and they in no way resemble the Indians of the South American continent," the captain recorded.[9] Gonzales wrote that he found no tree that could be used for building. No violence was recorded during the Spaniards' visit. Rather, the captain induced three men he presumed to be chiefs to sign a document accepting Spanish sovereignty. They drew some scribbles and a geometric design, having no idea of the significance of their effort. On November 21, Gonzáles de Haedo left. Instead of sailing eastward, he took his ships home to Peru, visiting uninhabited Sala y Gomez, 420 kilometers (260 miles) from Easter Island. There the Spaniards collected eggs and birds for food.[10]

Captain Cook's Brief Encounter

On March 14, 1774, James Cook made a brief visit. His exploration of the island was limited because he suffered from an infected gall bladder. "We landed at the sandy beach,"

Moai, Easter Island. On Easter Sunday, 1722, Dutch navigator Jacob Roggeveen found and named Easter Island. His crew marveled at the 261 giant stone heads called *moai* standing on platforms. They faced inland from the coast. Some *moai* that were not brought all the way to the coast dot the denuded landscape. Islanders carved them from the 1100s to the 1600s bu nobody knows why. Photograph by Robert Kirk.

wrote Cook, "where about 100 of the natives were collected who gave us no disturbance at landing, on the contrary hardly one had so much as a stick in their hands."[11] Nevertheless, an officer shot an islander for stealing a bag of plants, which caused the captain to remark: "It is to be lamented that Europeans too often assume the power of inflicting punishments on people who are utterly unacquainted with their laws."[12]

Cook marveled at "the stupendous stone statues erected in different places along the Coast," concluding they were not places of worship, but that they may well have been erected by a "race of Giants of 12 feet high."[13] Cook saw hundreds of *moai*, some on *ahus*, some that had been toppled. It is possible that they had been toppled only recently, victims of intertribal war. In bringing down the *maoi*, vandals placed large rocks in strategic positions so that when the statue fell, the head would be severed from the torso. Cook estimated the population at seven to eight hundred, significantly less that Gonzáles de Haedo's estimate.[14]

Cook's crew may have added their genes to the population; Georg Forster (1754–94), who had accompanied his scientist father on the voyage, commented that the island women were "neither reserved nor chaste, and for the trifling consideration of a small piece of cloth, some of our sailors obtained the gratification of their desires."[15] Cook set sail after five days. Cook wrote, "There is hardly an Island in this sea which affords less refreshments and conveniences for Shipping than it does."[16]

Easter Islanders dancing. In 1838 the French under Abel du Petit-Thouars visited Easter Island. The drawing by Louis Jules Masselot portrays well-proportioned men and a woman performing on deck. Note the otherwise unclad man sporting the sailor hat. The dancers may have been aristocrats; commoners were probably not as adequately fed. Thouars annexed Tahiti but apparently saw nothing of value on Easter Island and sailed off. From *Voyage autour du Monde sur la frégate la Venus,* by A.A. du Petit-Thouars et al. (Paris: Gride 1846).

LA PÉROUSE'S VISIT

On April 9, 1786, a French expedition under command of Jean-François Galaup, compte de la Pérouse went ashore. They were greeted by four to five hundred Polynesians, some naked, many tattooed, and apparently friendly. La Pérouse noted many *moais* still standing. The French landed pigs, goats, sheep and seeds for planting, but famished islanders ate the seeds before they could bear plants. The experience of the French was similar to that of Cook's company. The Captain recorded that women "offered their favors to each who wished to give them something in exchange," while Rapanui stole what they could from the French sailors.[17]

RUSSIANS AND FRENCH NOTE FEWER STANDING *MOAI*

The log of Captain Urey Lisianski of the Russian ship *Neva* mentions in 1804 seeing twenty or more *moai* still standing on Easter Island: "The shore is encompassed by monuments very correctly described by La Pérouse," he wrote. Lisianski sailed around the island.[18] In February 1838 Thomas du Petit-Thouars of the French navy sailed around Easter Island and recorded four *moai* on one *ahu* and five still upright on another. All of the brilliant coral shell eyes were missing, presumably smashed to obliterate their *mana*. In 1840 the last *moai* was reported as having been toppled.[19]

THE CULT OF THE BIRDMAN

Because their traditional Polynesian deities had failed to protect them from famine, disease, and physical terror, Rapanui focused on a revived ancient deity, Makemake. The

Huts at Orongo, Easter Island. Every September until 1868 athletic young men stayed in these huts at Orongo waiting for the first sooty tern to deposit the first egg on Motu Nui nearby. The sponsor of the first young man to return with the egg was named Birdman of the Year. Although the competition was a good substitute for war, it encouraged the Birdman's tribe to run roughshod over other islanders. Photograph by Robert Kirk.

year the revival began is unknown, but probably after European contact. Cultists had become obsessed by a competition to anoint a new ruler. Every spring until 1868 each local chief vied for the title Birdman of the Year, and the increased *mana* that went with it. The chief chose an athletic young male to be his champion or surrogate in the contest. These athletes would go to the cliff-side village of Orongo and wait in one of the forty-eight stone houses with crawl-through doorways that had been constructed for them. They might have to wait for as long as several weeks to collect the first egg of the sooty tern deposited on Motu Nui, a large rock jutting from the sea below Orongo. The first to find an egg on Motu Nui was champion. He shouted through the surf to his master, "Shave your head; I have your egg." He swam back with the egg in his mouth or in his headband and climbed the steep cliff to present his egg to the lucky chief.

The winning chief became *tangata manu*—Birdman—until the first sooty tern deposited her first egg the following September. The egg was drained and preserved. The chief went into seclusion and, as representative of the god Makemake, did not cut his nails or hair or wash. The birdman should have ended tribal battles, but instead thugs used their leader's victory as a license to raid, rape, and burn without hindrance.[20]

THE SLAVE SHIP *NANCY*

Steven R. Fischer stated: "From 1722 to 1863 more than 1,000 islanders were gunned down or transported to their deaths by Europeans, North Americans and South Americans."[21] In addition, whalers, sealers, traders and other crews left islanders with venereal disease, further hampering population growth. In 1808 islanders suffered the first of many traumatic blows at the hands of kidnappers. The fur sealing ship *Nancy*, under command of J. Crocker of Boston, arrived. Easter Island was isolated, its population without firearms, and without protection of a large power. For Captain Crocker, the naked people were fair prey. To obtain workers for a proposed sealing station in the Juan Fernandez Islands, Crocker and crew kidnapped twelve men and eighteen women; after three days at sea all the men jumped overboard and were most certainly drowned. All the women were taken to Más a Fuera. When the crew went back to Easter Island to replace the drowned men, they were repulsed with a fusilade of stones.

When Otto von Kotzebue, on an expedition for the czar of Russia, sought to come ashore in 1816, his men were again repulsed. From a distance Kotzebue saw two *moai* on the south coast and none at Hanga Roa Bay. In 1825 Captain Frederick William Beechey of the *Blossom* was also driven off. Trading did take place with whalers and other vessels, but islanders would come to the ships in canoes with fruit and curios. Islanders amused crews by hopping on deck on one leg.[22]

A Disastrous Decade

Far worse was to come. In the 1860s Easter Island's population fell an estimated ninety-four percent. On December 22, 1862, eight blackbirder vessels from Peru arrived to recruit or capture laborers for the Chincha Islands guano mines and for work on plantations. Slavery in Peru had been outlawed and investors needed workers, willing or not. These ships were the *Rosa y Carmen, Rosa Patricia, Carolina, Guillermo, Micaela Miranda, Jose Castro, Hermosa Dolores* and *Cora*. Captain Marutani of the *Rosa y Carmen* was in overall command. On December 23, the crews came ashore and displayed trade goods. As the islanders examined the goods the crews fired shots, killing ten. They captured perhaps 200 terrified people. Most were put aboard the *Hermosa Dolores* and *Carolina* for Callao, while the other ships continued to other islands to repeat their slaving operation.[23]

Over the next few years, hundreds more were taken off Easter Island. By June 1863, 1,407 were registered as indentured laborers in Peru.[24] Peru's Chincha Island guano deposits had been created over the centuries by untold numbers of pelicans, gannets and cormorants eliminating their waste. Rain did not wash off the deposits on these arid islands. An observer recalled, "No hell has ever been conceived ... that can be equaled in the fierceness of its heat, the horror of its stink, and the damnation of those compelled to labor there to a deposit of Peruvian guano when being shoveled into ships."[25] Back on the island, survivors crawled into caves and rolled stones over the entrances. Easter Island's unique culture was irretrievably lost.[26]

At the time that Lincoln freed America's slaves, blackbirders raided not only Easter, but other small defenseless islands. For example on September 13, 1862, the *Adelante*, owned by J.C. Byrne, sailed into Callao harbor with 253 recruits from the Cook Islands. Most had agreed to work at light labor for a short period in Peru for wages, clothing and food. Without a mutual language, the Polynesians never understood the exact terms of their contract. Able–bodied men were sold in Peru for two hundred dollars, women, a hundred and fifty, and boys for a hundred.

Blackbirders caused the loss of able-bodied men and women in other of the Cook Islands—Atiu, Mangaia, Manihiki, Rakahanga and Puka-Puka. These were small communities with total populations counted in the dozens. Rakahanga lost 42 men, 20 women and 14 children. On January 27, 1863, Captain Davis of the *Jose Zhara* took 80 men and 5 men from Puka-Puka; in all, that atoll lost 145 to blackbirders. Blackbirders took away all of the chiefs. An estimated 725 people were taken from the Cook Islands. Children and parents were separated. Few—if any—were returned.[27]

In February 1863, blackbirders took 253 people from Tokelau's three atolls, about forty-seven percent of the population. Before the arrival of the blackbirders, when the missionary ship *John Williams* visited Fakaofo (207 hectares; 512 acres), Nukunono (2,125 hectares; 650 acres), and Atafu (1,255 hectares; 502 acres), they found populations of 261 on Fakaofo and about 140 each on the other two atolls. The vulnerable people left on the atolls were faced with getting food without the help of able-bodied men, few of whom were returned. Shortly after, dysentery arrived from Samoa, leaving a population of 200.[28] On May 29, 1863, the Peruvian blackbirding vessel *Dolores Carolina* and two other ships arrived at Nukulaelae in the Ellice Islands. Only two square kilometers (three-quarters of a square mile), Nukulaelae includes nineteen *motus* surrounding a lagoon. The blackbirders enticed islanders to board with the promise to teach them about God. The blackbirders trapped 250, about 79 percent of the island's population. Shortly after, the *Dolores Carolina* stopped at Funafuti and took 171, leaving 146. The first of the three barques with their human cargo reached Callao on July 27, 1863, and landed 353 slaves. Seventy-five had died en route due to a shortage of food and water. In Peru two-thirds of those landed were estimated to have died of pulmonary or intestinal diseases.[29]

An Australian became a slaver. In May 1863, Captain Thomas James McGrath of the whaler *Grecian* from Hobart captured 130 people from the Tongan island Ata. Ata is 136 kilometers (114 miles) southwest of Tonga'tapu. Seaman John Bryan, aboard the *Grecian*, recalled, "The captain there induced a large party of natives to come on board to trade, and while they were dining on the 'tween decks, closed the hatches upon them, men, women and children to the number of about 130, and sailed with them for the Peruvian coast." McGrath sold the Atans to the captain of the Peruvian slaver *General Prim*. The slave ship arrived with its prisoners at Callao on July 19, 1863.[30] King Tupou I ordered the remaining Ata islanders to settle in 'Eua, ostensibly for their own protection, and Ata remained unpopulated.[31]

In one triumphal instance, blackbirders were thwarted. Rapa-Iti islanders, with the help of three Europeans, sailed the *Cora* into Papeete Harbor on February 17, 1863. Islanders had captured the crew of the eighty-ton *Cora*. These slavers had intended to carry off much of the population of Rapa-Iti to work in Peru. Rapans took the ship by surprise. The triumph of the Rapans was the only recorded instance in Polynesia where islanders were successful in saving themselves by apprehending blackbirders. In Papeete French officials arrested the *Cora*'s officers and sentenced them to ten years' imprisonment. The *Cora* was sold in May as being unseaworthy.[32]

Blackbirders took 3,125 islanders to Peru. Of the total number, an estimated 157—five percent—survived to be returned to a Pacific island. Only an estimated 1.5 percent were returned to the island from which they had been taken; several of those died shortly after arrival. Those repatriated to their former homes were estimated to be 1.28 percent. Peruvian authorities may be blamed for not inoculating the depressed workers against smallpox, and for condoning overcrowding and starvation on the return voyage.[33]

MISSIONARIES

No Christian missionary arrived at Easter Island until 142 years after Roggeveen had found it. On the second of January 1864, Father Eugène Eyraud (1820–68) arrived aboard *La Suerte* to convert Easter Islanders to Catholicism. Shortly after he landed, islanders stripped Father Eyraud of his clothes, in fact all his belongings. Dressed in a pair of old shoes and a blanket, he gave instruction in the catechism and taught five or six islanders to read. Frustrated and threatened, he left within nine months and arrived in Chile October 11, 1864.[34]

THE CRYPTIC *RONGO RONGO* BOARDS

Father Eyraud returned on March 27, 1866, with father Hippollyte Roussel (d. 1898). Eyraud was shown the island's unique writing on *rongo rongo* boards. Steven Roger Fischer hypothesized, "Easter Island's first encounter with writing in 1770 apparently led to the elaboration of *rongo rongo* script." Fischer's theory is that when Gonzales had islanders sign a treaty giving their realm to Spain, priests and chiefs were impressed by the powerful *mana* represented by the document, and created their own form of writing, imitating what they had seen the Spaniards do. *Rongo rongo* is the only known writing by pre-contact Polynesians. Islanders claimed their progenitor, Hoto Matua, the legendary commander of the first canoe to arrive centuries earlier, had brought sixty-seven of the carved boards and that they were repositories of island tradition.

The 120-character script makes 1,500 to 2,000 compound words. Every other line is read upside down, from left to right. Experts, such as Fischer, confirm that the writing represents creation chants, a list of phenomena that begat one another; e.g., fish copulating with birds to produce the sun. These carved boards were not noted by visitors until nearly a century after the treaty signing. It was he who alerted interested Europeans to their existence. Many boards no longer existed by the 1860s; the priests either burned boards or, having lost faith in the inscriptions' *mana*, islanders used them for firewood or boat planks. The twenty-five that were not burned are found in museums.[35]

THE DUTROU-BERNIER DICTATORSHIP

Next, the unfortunate Rapanui lost their land and freedom of movement to a dictator. On November 6, 1866, two more Roman Catholic missionaries arrived. Transporting the fathers aboard the *Tampico* was a Frenchman, Jean-Baptiste Dutrou-Bornier. He had already been sentenced to death in Peru, but the French consul, a brother of Ferdinand de Lesseps who organized construction of the Suez Canal, secured his release. Less than a year after Dutrou-Bornier arrived the final paramount chief, the *ariki mau*, died of consumption. His royal line ended and the prestige of the *ariki mau* was no longer a factor in Rapa Nui affairs.[36] The following year Father Eyraud died of tuberculosis as well. As the population declined, Dutrou-Bornier was able to buy land and to negotiate a contract for his employer, John Brander of Papeete, to raise sheep on most of the island. By September 1870 Dutrou-Bornier controlled 13,237 hectares (32,695 acres) of the island's total of 16,059 hectares (39,665 acres). That left the Catholic mission and the populace slightly more than eighteen percent of Rapa Nui land.[37]

Reerected Moai, Easter Island. Of the 887 moai that were carved, 261 were set on altars facing inland. Because of intertribal rivalry, all were pulled down by 1868. Archeologists in the twentieth century had these seven reerected. Photograph by Robert Kirk.

A POPULATION IN FREE FALL

Worse was to come for the dejected Easter Islanders. In 1871, the bishop of Tahiti, Florentin-Étienne Jaussen (1815–91; bishop 1848–84), pressured authorities in Lima to return all of the Polynesians they had captured. Peruvian authorities paid owners of the *Barbara Gomez* for each returned slave as he or she boarded in Callao, so it mattered little to the captain how many were actually landed on their home islands. Eighty-five died en route. Easter was the closest Polynesian island to Callao, so fifteen survivors, ill with smallpox, were disembarked there, though they may actually have lived hundreds of miles away. Smallpox spread over the island.

The bishop of Tahiti asked John Brander to offer malnourished and terrorized Easter Islanders the opportunity to work on his plantation in Tahiti. Conditions on Rapa Nui were sufficiently harsh that nearly the entire diminished population opted to move away to work as indentured servants. On June 6, 1871, 275 would-be emigrants filled the ship *Sir John Burgoyne* to capacity. Another 230 were left on shore "weeping and wailing for their departed loved ones." Two died on board and 168 stayed at Mangareva. The rest sailed on to Tahiti, and 247 Easter Islanders were counted there in December 1872, most working as indentured laborers on plantations. Thirty-eight percent died in the first year on Tahiti.[38]

After he had ruled as a dictator for five years, driving the majority of people from Easter Island, three men murdered Dutrou-Bornier on August 6, 1872.[39] They were enraged at his kidnapping prepubescent girls for his sexual pleasure. Furthermore, Dutrou-Bornier had sent thugs to attack citizens of and destroy their crops.[40]

French writer Pierre Loti (1850–1923) arrived in 1872, and saw a few dozen people whom he wrote looked like savages, eating roots. Loti found human bones and skulls strewed about.[41] When a French expedition arrived on April 1, 1877, to assess the island for possible annexation, they were informed that the inhabitants numbered 110, only 26 of them females.[42]

148

With Dutrou-Bornier's death, the island then fell under the control, for a decade, of Alexander Salmon, Jr. (1855–?), a partner of Brander. Wars and terror ceased. Ten thousand sheep dominated the stark landscape. By 1882 wool exports amounted to 20 tonnes (44,000 pounds) a year. The surviving islanders did not share in the profit other than their meager wages. They earned a little money carving curios to sell to visiting crews.[43]

During a twelve-day visit to Easter Island beginning December 19, 1886, William Thompson, an American aboard the *Mohican*, noted human bones scattered at the *ahus*, in caves, and elsewhere. He counted 155 inhabitants. All the *moai* lay on the ground, many heads having been broken off.[44]

A CHILEAN COLONY

On September 9, 1888, Chilean naval officer Policarpo Toro (1856–1921) claimed what he called Isla de Pascua in the name of Chile. The nation of people of largely European origin gained the prestige of possessing overseas colonies when it annexed Easter Island and the Juan Fernandez Islands. The Chilean government then bought out lands belonging to the Catholic mission, and they leased the lands of Maison Brander. The new government confined the 178 Polynesians to 2,000 hectares (5,000 acres) around the sole village of Hanga Roa.[45]

In September 1895 all of the lands under government control were sold to a Valparaiso merchant, Enrique Merlet. The vast majority of the island was given over to livestock. Merlet sent a manager and a few workers and employed fifty Rapanui in his sheep operations. The people were put to work building a wall to sequester themselves within the village. In 1900, when some of the 213 islanders demonstrated against the company, the leaders were put on a ship for exile in Chile. No record indicates that they actually arrived in South America. Again in 1903, six dissidents being transported to Chile never arrived.[46]

In March 1914 amateur archaeologist Katherine Scoresby-Routledge (1866–1935) arrived to catalog artifacts at Easter Island. At her own and her husband's expense, Mrs. Scoresby-Routledge commissioned a ninety-foot schooner, *Mana*, and set sail from England. She spent seventeen months from March 1914 to August 1915 cataloging *moai* and other artifacts and preserving oral history. In 1920 Mrs. Scoresby-Routledge published the record of her findings, *The Mystery of Easter Island*. She suffered, particularly in later life, from delusional paranoia. In 1929 her husband had her kidnapped and assigned to a mental facility. She died there in 1935.[47]

THE ISLAND AS COMPANY PROPERTY

When Enrique Merlet was unable to pay loans to a Scottish firm, Williamson, Balfour and Company, Merlet transferred his right to Easter Island to his creditor. Little changed for the Rapa Nui people; they remained confined to Hanga Roa, their interests supposedly overseen by the Chilean government.

Leprosy had been introduced to the island when three workers returned from Tahiti with the affliction, and a leper colony was duly established three kilometers (two miles) north of Hanga Roa. Some of the healthy islanders left Hanga Roa to relocate there, away from foreign influence. Steven R. Fischer wrote: "So it came about that, in the second decade of the twentieth century, old Rapa Nui society silently passed away at two ramshackle shacks for lepers in the quiet countryside."[48]

Chapter 13

Bayonets and Baguettes:
French Polynesia, 1842–1914

The French Pacific Imperium

By 1900, France controlled a Polynesian and Melanesian Pacific empire. Nations recognized the republic's sovereignty over five archipelagoes, which she designated Établissements Française d'Oceanie, or EFO. These are the Society Islands, including the principal island, Tahiti; the Tuamotus; the Marquesas; the Gambiers, principally Mangareva; and the widely spread Australs. France dominated New Caledonia and Wallis and Futuna as well. The total area of France's Pacific possessions was 24,000 square kilometers (9,360 square miles).

Beginning in 1838, French naval personnel set out to accomplish the goal clarified by France's foreign minister François Guizot (1787–1874; foreign minister 1840–47). Guizot told the Chamber of Deputies on March 31, 1843: "What is advantageous to France and indispensable for her is to possess points on the globe destined to become great commercial centres of trade and navigation, which will prove secure and strong maritime stations" so that French ships would not have to rely on foreign ports.[1] Profit did not appear to be a motive in France's Pacific imperialism, although New Caledonia would prove later to have rich mineral deposits. France wanted ports where she could obtain food, wood, and water — and later as a depository for coal for steam ships. France also wanted the prestige which empire brought, prestige lost in 1815 on the field at Waterloo.

Catholic missionaries came to islands first, often paving the way for French occupation. Two missionary societies brought the faith to islanders. The Vicariate Apostolic of Eastern Oceania was assigned to the Picpusian order; Picpusians converted Polynesians in what became French Oceania — the EFO. Marists (Society of Mary) took the lead in New Caledonia and Wallis and Futuna and New Hebrides. Marists also competed against strong Protestant influence in New Zealand, Australia, Tonga, Samoa and Fiji.[2] In March 1842, thirty-seven months after priests celebrated the first mass, France claimed several of the Marquesas as a protectorate. They stationed troops and appointed administrators. Tahiti's turn was next.

Tahiti Subjected

On August 27, 1838, Captain Abel du Petit-Thouars (1793–1864) arrived in Papeete. Britain had never claimed Tahiti, but British Protestant missionaries had converted large

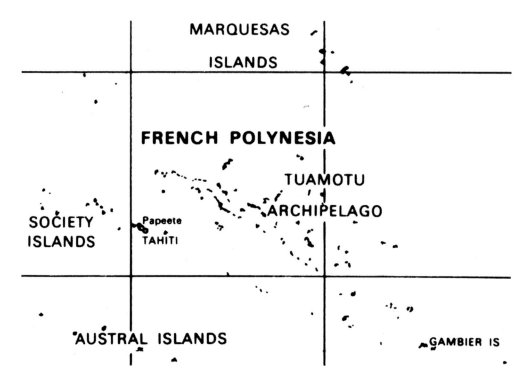

Map of French Polynesia. By permission of the Office of Planning, State of Hawaii.

numbers of the people, and these Protestants advised the queen and government. In December 1836 the priests had been expelled at the request of entrenched Protestant missionaries and British representative Reverend George Prichard (1825–95).

On August 30, 1838, during an audience with Queen Pomare IV, du Petit-Thouars delivered a letter in which he demanded a written apology to the king of the French, reparations in the amount of two thousand Spanish dollars within twenty-four hours as compensation for the expulsion of fathers Claret and Maigret, as well as that of fathers Laval and Caret.

Du Petit-Thouars threatened that if the reparations were not paid in time, "I shall see myself under the obligation to declare war, and to commence hostilities immediately against all the places of your Majesty's dominions, and which shall be continued by all the French vessels of war which shall successively call here, and shall continue to the time when France shall have obtained satisfaction." Incongruously, after threatening utter devastation, he signed the message, "I am, of your Majesty, the most respectful Servant."

The admiral sent marines ashore, blockaded the port, and according to Prichard's son, William, "he even invited Prichard and other Europeans to come aboard his vessel as a refugee while he bombarded the town. It became apparent that they were dealing with a military madman and they had no resources whatever to protect themselves from complete destruction."[3] Foreign residents paid the reparations and the queen signed an apology. Du Petit-Thouars left in mid–September after eliciting the queen's promise that in the future French priests would be welcome.

The young monarch was virtually illiterate, knew some English and no French, so she relied on for Reverend Prichard's advice. She and Prichard reasoned that only British intervention could rescue the island from the French. On September 18, 1838, Queen Pomare addressed a letter to Queen Victoria (1818–1901; r. 1837–1901). Probably written by Prichard, the plaintive letter stated: "We have nobody to assist us in our helplessness except you, who implanted in our hearts, through your people, the love of Jehovah, the love of order and industry. Do not let these good seeds perish; do not leave unfinished what you have begun, and what is progressing so well. Lend us your powerful hand, take us under your protection, let your flag cover us, and your lion defend us."[4] Although British Protestants had been active in Tahiti for four decades, Queen Victoria's ministers did not come to Pomare's aid. Britain was content that France did not annex South island, New Zealand or all the other Society Islands.[5]

On September 7, 1842, du Petit-Thouars, promoted to the rank of rear admiral the previous year, summoned four Tahitian chiefs aboard the war ship *Reine Blanche* to sign an agreement by which Tahiti became a French protectorate. The cession had far-reaching ramifications in that Tahiti and the Society Islands remain in the early twenty-first century a French possession. The previous month du Petit-Thouars had brought French armed vessels from the Marquesas to Tahiti to demand ten thousand Spanish dollars as compensation for perceived injustices perpetrated against French citizens. The admiral privately admitted that the bulk of these were merely "grudges of drink-dealers." Queen Pomare IV was unable to pay, or at this time to lead any attempt at resistance; she was in Moorea preparing to give birth. To protect the island from invasion, four chiefs signed the note asking for French protection.

When the occupation was executed, an observer, the trader Lucett, wrote, "600 men with 4 howitzers march to the *Marseillaise* toward the royal palace.... Mare, the Queen's orator protests. He is drowned out by drums. Captain d'Aubigny makes a proclamation, 'Hear ye, hear ye, officers, soldiers and sailors of France, and you inhabitants of these islands! I take possession of this country in the name of His Majesty Louis-Philippe, King of the French.' We are ready to die if it must be, to make respected our flag of three colors." The tricolor was hoisted and troops shouted "*Vive la France, Vive le Roi!*" three times.[6]

Entrepreneur Jacques Antoine Moehrenhout (1797–1879) was named French commissioner for the new colony. Born in Belgium, Moehrenhout had served as United States consul for the South Pacific from 1836 to 1839 and French consul from 1838. A merchant with interests in the Gambier Islands pearl beds, he lived in Tahiti about twenty-five years. He is author of *Voyages aux iles du Grand Ocean* (1837).[7] With the coming of Catholic priests, Protestant missionaries lost their monopoly on promoting the Christian faith among Tahitians. Representatives of the London Missionary Society had labored there four decades, frustrated for years before making conversions.[8]

HERMAN MELVILLE, A LITERATE WITNESS

Seaman Herman Melville was a witness to the beginning of French dominance. Melville arrived in Tahiti on September 23, 1842, from Nuku Hiva, Marquesas, and was promptly jailed in the loosely run *Calabooza*, or jail, in Papeete. The twenty-two-year-old had taken part in a mutiny aboard the whaler *Lucy Ann*. Melville learned that the captain of the *Lucy Ann*, which had brought him to Papeete, was more of a tyrant than the skipper of the *Acushnet*, from which he had deserted in Nuku Hiva. Melville found the *Calabooza* to be uncom-

fortable, but it provided him free lodging. Because it was not locked, it proved a good location from which to wander about during the day and observe momentous events.

In 1847, John Murray of London published Melville's *Omoo, A Narrative of Adventures
in the South Seas*, recalling his stay in Papeete.[9] The young author offered readers verbal
snapshots. Of Papeete as seen from offshore, he wrote: "Lying in a semicircle around the
bay, the tasteful mansions of the chiefs and foreign residents impart an air of tropical ele-
gance, heightened by the palm-trees waving here and there, and the deep-green groves of
the Bread-Fruit, in the background. The squalid huts of the common people are out of sight,
and there is nothing to mar the prospect."[10]

Melville felt excitement in the air as the French were in the process of taking control.
When Melville decided to leave jail, he walked away and signed aboard another whaler,
Charles and Henry, bound for Lahaina, Maui. From there he reached Honolulu on Febru-
ary 2, 1843.[11]

POMARE IV: LADY IN DISTRESS

Although she had not received a reply to her letter written in September 1838, Queen
Pomare IV sent another plaintive letter dated January 23, 1843, to her "dear Friend and Sister Queen," Victoria. Pomare begged: "Commiserate me in my affliction, in my helplessness in which my nation is involved with France.... Do not cast me away, my Friend; I run
to you for refuge ... my only hope of being restored is you.... My friend, send quickly a large
ship of war to assist me."[12] Victoria referred the note to her foreign office, which wanted
to prevent war with Louis Philippe's France, and allowed the French to proceed with the
annexation.[13]

On March 13, 1844, French authorities took British consul George Prichard (1796–1883)
out of a prison cell and deported him to Valparaiso, Chile. Ten days earlier, as Prichard's
son William recalled, "In the afternoon of the 3rd of March, he was seized by a party of
gendarmes and, without ceremony, led through mud and rain to a blockhouse, hastily prepared for his reception."[14] Prichard's expulsion for having Catholic missionaries expelled
seven years earlier and for influencing the queen against the French marked the end of significant British influence in the island.

Britain, whose seamen discovered Tahiti and whose missionaries pioneered spreading the gospel, promised not to fight for Tahitian independence when France agreed not
to take over the Leeward Islands of Raiatea, Bora Bora and Huahine. Nevertheless, the
French minister of marine, Admiral Roussin, wrote: "To gradually join the whole of the
Polynesian group to the French establishments, missionary influence will be our principal
means of success."[15]

THE FAILED WAR OF LIBERATION

The French tried to prevent rebellion and in so doing precipitated it. When Governor
Armand Joseph Bruat (1796–1855; term 1843–47) arrived from the Marquesas to take
charge in Papeete, he demanded that all chiefs come to his headquarters. Most did not obey,
and when soldiers apprehended them, Bruat had them chained on board French ships in
the port. Those he was unable to catch lost their property.[16] Melville noted, "In several

interviews with the poor queen, the unfeeling governor sought to terrify her into compliance with his demands; clapping his hand upon his sword, shaking his fist in her face, and swearing violently. 'Oh king of a great nation,' Pomare pleaded in her letter to Louis Philippe, King of the French [1773–1850; r. 1830–48], 'fetch away this man; I and my people can not endure his evil doings. He is a shameless man.'"[17]

On March 13, 1844, armed opposition commenced on Tahiti against the French occupation. Led initially by a chief named Fanave, Tahitians fortified mountain valleys in the island's center. Lacking sufficient muskets and powder, rebels executed night raids, wielding clubs and spears. French troops shot many down.[18] On April 17, 1844, French forces won the Battle of Mahaena against Tahitian guerrilla fighters; France suffered 15 dead, while Tahitians lost 102. The guerrilla war would continue to 1846.[19] Melville predicted for the Tahitians, "These disorders must accelerate the final extinction of their race."[20]

In July 1844 Queen Pomare IV fled from her capital to neighboring Raiatea, as French forces occupied Tahiti. She had

Queen Pomare IV of Tahiti reigned from 1827, when her seven-year-old half brother King Pomare IV died, until her own death in 1877. When she was 21 a Western visitor observed, "Casting aside all restraints, she shared unblushingly in the licentiousness for which this island is so notorious." When the French annexed her kingdom in 1842 she was forced to come to an accommodation with them in order to keep her throne. The engraving is from *Le Tour du Monde* by Auguste Bertrand.

not agreed to France's declaration of a protectorate over her nation.[21]

Operating from Tahiti in January 1846, Captain Louis Antoine Bonnard attempted to conquer Huahine. When he tried to land at Maeva, his forces were repulsed by warriors under the island's queen, Teri'itaria. The French lost eighteen killed and forty-three wounded.[22] British observer Captain Henry Byam Martin, R.N., added, "They had burnt the settlement, destroyed the bread fruit and coco nut trees and caused as much sorrow and suffering as their means permitted."[23]

A Tahitian guerrilla fort at Fautaua fell to French forces on December 17, 1846. In May 1846 French troops won the Battle of Punaruu. These victories ended Tahiti's guerrilla war, an attempt by indigenous people to remain independent of French control.[24]

THE QUEEN CEDES TAHITI

Queen Pomare IV left exile in Raiatea and signed a document in Moorea on February 7, 1847, accepting a French protectorate over Tahiti. When she stepped ashore at Papeete on February 9, according to Captain Henry Byam Martin of HMS *Gampus*, "A vast concourse of natives crowded the beach.... There was no sound of joy — no demonstration of pleasure — no expression of satisfaction at her return. A solemn deathlike silence prevailed; not a whisper was uttered.... As she stepped from the pier, she looked as though she were stepping on the scaffold.... As she passed within 10 feet of me I observed she was in tears."[25] She was restored to her throne, but without many of the powers she had enjoyed before the French takeover.[26]

If the queen lost powers, she gained material possessions: Queen Victoria sent her a carriage and horses, a crown, and some of the objects Melville saw when he visited her palace: "Superb writing desks of rose-wood, inlaid with silver and mother-of-pearl; decanters and goblets of cut glass; embossed volumes of plates; gilded candelabras; sets of globes and mathematical instruments; the finest porcelain; richly mounted sabres and fowling-pieces; laced hats and sumptuous garments of all sorts, with numerous other matters of European manufacture...." These were placed haphazardly among Tahitian-made fish spears, *tapa*, coconut shells, and unwashed calabashes.[27]

Captain Martin described the monarch in 1846: "Queen Pomare is a thick made, sepia coloured woman, with a profusion of very black hair.... She stands revealed as a fat oily woman without a particle of clothing but a cotton shirt."[28]

Defeated in battle, the docile people lived under French rule and, as historian Edward Dodd states, "Now there was no action to be taken, no feelings to be aroused, simply the carrying on of everyday living. The French demanded very little from them." Because no taxes were collected, they had little incentive to earn money. With the population reduced, food could be easily had. "So the early years of foreign rule were stable, orderly and peaceful" under the Code Napoleon.[29]

Britain and France signed the Declaration of London on June 19, 1847. It is also known as the Jarnac Convention. It was understood that Britain controlled New Zealand, and France controlled Tahiti, Moorea, the Tuamotus and Tubuai. The Leeward Islands — Bora Bora, Huahine, and Raiatea — were to remain independent of either power.[30]

THE LMS MISSION ENDS

French authorities obviously wanted LMS missionaries out of Tahiti, and in 1851 passed a law that only a single missionary could serve each district. In 1852 a law provided for the election and removal of missionaries by district notables. Soon all ten Protestant missionaries had either left or become government employees.[31] On September 17, 1866, French Protestant missionary Charles Vienot (c. 1840–1903) reopened a Protestant school, closed since the French takeover of the island. He had arrived in Tahiti on February 25, 1866. A member of the Societé des Missions Évangéliques, Vientot took over responsibility for Protestant churches, missions and schools.[32]

Because French officials appointed Protestant church pastors who were French, the London Missionary Society left Tahiti in 1886, and in 1890 left the other Society Islands. Their work had begun there eighty-nine years earlier. Doctrinal differences played little part in the evacuation; rather, British clerics simply acquiesced in the dominance of French culture, language and educational institutions over their own.[33]

SHIPS AND DISEASE

Missionaries and French colonial administration had brought European institutions and provided law and order, particularly to Papeete. When mutineers took the American vessel *Auckland* in Papeete Harbor in 1854, for example, French police apprehended all the culprits. Ship captains knew they could reprovision with fresh water and food and crews could find willing female companions in Papeete.[34] In the years leading to 1840, some 150 whaling ships— mostly Americans— with 3,000 thirsty, sex-starved crew came ashore and, fueled with drink, demonstrated how rowdy single young men can be. Twenty-three whaling vessels operated in the vicinity of Tahiti in the single year 1852.[35]

Frequent visitors brought frequent epidemics, further reducing the population. By 1848 only 8,082 Tahitians were counted along with 475 foreigners.[36] There were 1,372 Polynesians on Moorea. Papeete was estimated to have over a thousand inhabitants.[37] Tahiti's population continued to decline due to diseases. The more notable outbreaks included influenza (1772–74), tuberculosis (1775), influenza (1820), whooping cough (1840), smallpox (1841), and scarlet fever (1847). Eleven epidemics were recorded between 1843 and 1858.[38] A measles outbreak in 1854 killed seventy out of every thousand Society Islanders. Contrasting the 1854 rate to that of seven-tenths of a percent during a measles outbreak in 1951, Jean-Louis Rallu noted that in 1951 "medical facilities existed and the population was more immunized."[39]

Other agents of death for Tahitians were infanticide, sterility from sexually transmitted diseases, firearms, and alcohol. A brandy bottle that crowns the tomb of Pomare V at Point Venus is a clue to how the final king died in 1891. During epidemics, when able-bodied people became ill, starvation ensued because there were few healthy people to obtain food for their families. In Tahiti, as in many Polynesian islands, wholesale death caused people to doubt their old religions and to question the basis on which their own culture rested.

While indigenous people were diminishing in number, the French population was not increasing fast enough to take their place, or even to justify French sovereignty. In 1863, except for government and military personnel, only 210 French lived in Tahiti and Moorea. Other Europeans numbered 231.[40]

COTTON AND CHINESE LABORERS

As a consequence of the lack of available cotton for English mills from the U.S. South during the American Civil War (1861–65), Scottish entrepreneur William Stewart (1820–73) established a cotton plantation at Atimaono on Tahiti. Because Stewart needed laborers, 320 Chinese arrived from Hong Kong so on February 28, 1865, aboard the Prussian ship *Ferdinand Brunn.* Before the Chinese arrived Stewart had brought in ninety-six Cook Islanders to clear fields and plant. On December 8, 1865, 342 more Chinese arrived aboard the *Spray of the Ocean,* followed by 339 on January 6, 1866, on the *Albertine.* Stewart was able to fill three schooners to ship cotton to England from his 7,868 hectares (17,000 acres). Workers were paid 78 centimes for a 12-hour day, 26 days a month. Those who worked twenty-six days a month for seven years and spent nothing would take home a few hundred dollars.[41] They received in addition to their minuscule pay eight ounces of meat or fish, and four pounds of fruit or vegetables.

On September 24, 1873, Steward declared bankruptcy. He owed a reported £13,000 because he could no longer compete with reviving cotton production in the American South after the Civil War. He died that night.[42]

Forced to leave the cotton fields, many of the thousand Chinese workers he had brought

Otemanu Peak, Bora Bora. Rising 727 meters (nearly 2,400 feet), the collapsed volcano wall makes the entrance to Bora Bora one of the most dramatic sights in the South Seas. In 1722 Jacob Roggeveen was the first European commander to come upon the island. Cook visited twice. Bora Borans were feared as implacable enemies by people of nearby islands. France annexed the Society island in the late nineteenth century. Photograph by Robert Kirk.

to Tahiti became market gardeners or street merchants. The descendants of Chinese who remained in Tahiti were granted French citizenship only in 1964, though ethnic Tahitians became French citizens as early as 1946.[43] Descendants of the Chinese that Stewart imported continue to live in the Society Islands in the early twenty-first century.

THE END OF THE TAHITIAN MONARCHY

In 1872, French writer Pierre Loti met the queen, "an old woman [who] filled the whole width of her chair with the disgraceful mass of her person.... In this old face, lined, bronzed, square, hard, there still was a grandeur: there was above all an immense sadness."[44] Five years later, after a fifty-year reign, on September 24, 1877, Queen Pomare IV died. Her son Ariane, titled Pomare V (1839–91; r. 1877–80), was to reign only three years. As queen, she had maintained a semblance of Polynesian autonomy, but on June 29, 1880, Pomare V abdicated, effective December 30, 1880. The king received a pension of five thousand francs a month. France had ruled the island for thirty-eight years as a protectorate already, so the change had little immediate impact on Tahitians, except that the Civil Law Code of 1881 provided for land registration so that land could be more easily bought and sold.[45]

On March 16, 1888, France took formal possession of three Society Islands she had not annexed previously: Raiatea, Tahaa, and Huahine. Three days later France added Bora Bora to its "establishments" in Oceania. Britain acquiesced in the annexation because France renounced any intention of taking sole possession of the New Hebrides as a colony. These acquisitions completed France's Society Islands colony.[46]

GAUGUIN SEARCHES FOR PARADISE

In great anticipation of confronting an earthly paradise, artist Paul Gauguin (1848–1903) arrived in Papeete on June 8, 1891, after a sixty-nine-day voyage from Bordeaux, France. Only 446 other French people lived in Tahiti and Moorea at the time, as well as 410 other Europeans.[47] Tahiti disappointed Gauguin. Civilization had preceded his arrival; yet attracted by easy sex, cheap living, exotic faces and passionate colors, he was able to work there and to add a sensational tropical dimension to French impressionist painting. Gauguin hoped to execute enough paintings to stage an exhibit in Paris and establish his reputation as an artist. Gavan Daws wrote, "Everything about Gauguin broadcast the insistent message that he did not need people."[48] He did not appear to need family, as he had left behind a wife and five children in Europe and — later — more than one child in the islands. Gauguin lived in Mataiea, 16 kilometers (25 miles) from Papeete, surrounded by Tahitians and with his mistress, Titi.[49]

On November 9, 1893, badly in need of money, Gauguin returned to France and exhibited forty-one paintings and twelve sculptures at the Durand-Ruel Gallery in Paris. All were executed in Tahiti. Eleven items sold.[50] When he returned to the Pacific, Gauguin would settle in the Marquesas and die there.

RAIATEA: THE LAST HOLDOUTS

On February 16, 1897, French troops captured the chief of Raiatea, Teraupoo, at the Battle of the Avera Valley. Of all the people eventually included in French Oceania, the people of Raiatea fought longest and hardest to maintain independence. French warships arrived January 4 with approximately 200 soldiers from New Caledonia and 50 Tahitian volunteers; they marched inland and bayoneted or shot 17 Raiatean insurgents fighting from a trench; some 63 insurgents fled, many of whom were captured.[51] French officials deported Teraupoo, the insurgent leader, to New Caledonia on February 28, with his wife and approximately 150 followers. French officials sent the queen of Raiatea and 136 others to exile in the Marquesas. Men not deported were formed into three road gangs to improve public thoroughfares.[52]

AUSTRAL ISLANDS

By 1901, France had annexed each of the Austral Islands: Tubuai, Rimitara, Rururu, Rapa Iti, and Raivavae. They are the southernmost island group of French Polynesia. The first white people in the Australs had been mutineers aboard the *Bounty* in 1789; they had tried to settle on Tubuai, but had been repulsed.

In July 1821, Rurutu in the Austral Islands welcomed two Tahitian deacons who accompanied Reverend John Williams. Williams did not stay, and when he returned after a trip to Sydney, he saw islanders in bonnets and hats producing coconut oil and arrowroot for sale to benefit missionary enterprises. The entire island had been converted.[53]

On December 22, 1791, Captain George Vancouver (1758–98) aboard HMS Discovery charted 24-square-kilometer (15-square-mile) Rapa Iti. Rapa Iti means Little Rapa, whereas Easter Island is Rapa Nui or Big Rapa. Rapa Iti is distinguished by twenty-two *pas* (forts) perched on spectacular ridges that crown a volcanic cone. Its temperature is moderate, dropping to as low as 52 Fahrenheit (11.5 Celsius) in September and October. Ahurei Bay, one of fifteen bays, is a drowned volcano, six million years old.[54]

In 1826 John Davies of the London Missionary Society led the conversion of the Rapa Iti islanders, who were estimated to have numbered two to three thousand. By the time Caucasians arrived, Rapans formed a highly stratified society with *ariki* ruling over commoners. Davies was successful because in July 1825 the LMS schooner *Snapper* enticed two Rapans, Paparua and Aitareru, aboard and took them to Tahiti. When the two were returned in September 1826 with tales of white people's wealth, chiefs invited missionaries to visit. Davies brought four Tahitians and their wives as teachers. He also brought seeds, tools, Bibles in Tahitian, and lumber for a chapel. Davies learned that disease had killed the chief and others since the *Snapper*'s previous visit. Missionaries attributed the plague to the worship of pagan gods. Islanders said it was caused by the firing of muskets at ducks.

Between 1824, when foreigners began stopping at Rapa Iti, and 1830, three-quarters of the population died, mostly of disease. Davies returned to Rapa Iti in 1831 and estimated the population at 600. In those five years sandalwood traders, pearl fishers, whalers, and beachcombers brought disease and taught Rapans how to distill liquor. An indeterminate number of able men left with the visitors to work as seamen, divers and whale ship hands; some failed to return.[55] In 1836 only 453 Polynesians remained alive on Rapa Iti. Historian F. Allan Hanson stated: "Nearly every visitor during these fatal years describes the Rapans as a wretched lot, diseased and dying in bewilderment and despair."[56]

The next event of note in Rapa was tragic. The ship *Barbara Gomez*, entrusted with returning 470 indentured or kidnapped slaves from Peru to their home islands, set sail from Callao on August 18, 1864. En route to Rapa Iti the crew threw 439 ill or dead passengers overboard. When the *Barbara Gomez* arrived at Rapa Iti, crews told the Rapans that if they did not accept the remaining sixteen, none of whom were Rapans, all sixteen would be thrown overboard. The sick slaves were from Tokelau, Niuaf'ou, Tongareva, Manhiki, Rakahanga, Atiu and other small islands in the Cooks. Compassionate Rapans accepted the ill passengers. One or more of them introduced smallpox among Rapans, and by 1867 the population had fallen to 120, down from an estimated 2,000 in 1825.[57]

On March 6, 1867, France annexed Rapa Iti, the first of the Australs she claimed. A major reason France coveted Rapa's secure harbors was that the Panama-New Zealand and Australian Mail Company started regular service, sending one ship a month between Panama and New Zealand; however, when the Panama Canal opened in 1914, Papeete, Tahiti, became the logical port en route to New Zealand, and ships bypassed Rapa Iti. France did little to develop the protectorate other than to send a French resident in 1868 to administer the island, and later *gendarmes*. On June 18, 1887, France abolished the hereditary position of *ariki* (chiefs). Because the climate is not conducive to growing coconuts, no merchant ship came for copra, or for any other marketable product. Rapa Iti became a backwater.[58]

Once Pomare II had secured power in Tahiti he was eager to expand his realm. In 1819

Pomare arrived in Raivavae with his queen and several chiefs aboard the three-masted ship *Arab*. The scenic volcanic island measures 16 square kilometers (6.2 square miles), with an elevation of 437 meters (1,434 feet). Pomare announced he would rule over the tribes on Raivavae by right of inheritance. He determined to extend his kingdom and the Christian religion to the Austral Islands. The new subjects had no concept or need for a political organization larger than their tribes. Nevertheless, the king was able to obtain oaths of loyalty to him from chiefs. Pomare left a native Tahitian missionary to convert the inhabitants. A year and a half later an American trading ship captain reported seeing eighty-eight islanders assembled in church. Idols had been brought down from *maraes*. In 1824 a new chapel was opened with a crowd of a thousand in attendance.[59]

In 1826 an epidemic arrived at Raivavae from Tubuai and carried off ten to fifteen islanders each day. The population, estimated to have been around 3,000, plunged to 120. Teachers of oral tradition were dead and the island's history was irretrievably lost.[60]

France annexed Raivavae in 1880, Tubuai in 1881, and Rimitara in 1901.

GAMBIERS AND TUAMOTUS

On November 2, 1881, France took formal possession of the Gambier Islands and the Tuamotus. They were to be administered as part of French Oceania. The inhabitants of remote Tuamotu atolls were scarcely affected and continued to conduct local affairs; a gendarme performed any essential administrative functions. In the Gambiers, the population gained a measure of official protection.[61]

THE FRENCH ADMINISTRATION

Government functions on outer islands in French Polynesia were assigned to bureaucrats on some islands, and to gendarmes assisted by native police on others. In addition to law enforcement duties, gendarmes were to collect taxes, supervise road maintenance, record vital statistics, and in some cases operate postal services. Local law enforcers had little training for these assignments, but the governor's office in Papeete was able to save money by not requiring additional officials to fulfill those functions. Island populations were affected by having to work on road maintenance and to pay taxes.[62]

These small, neglected pieces of the French Empire contained surprisingly few French people. Ninety-two percent of those in the EFO lived in Tahiti. Including government and military personnel, eleven were in the Gambiers, seven in the Tuamotus, only five in all of the Australs and three in Moorea. Thirteen French lived in the several Leeward Islands in the Societies. In these outer islands in 1907 were 254 Germans, British, and other colonists. An observer wrote, "The ordinary colonist in Tahiti lives from day to day, getting drunk on gin, indulging in all sort of debaucheries, his excesses and laziness rapidly leading him to a state of wretchedness."[63]

The chief source of income for many of these outer islands was *copra*, dried meat from the coconut palm. A healthy mature tree could produce 250 to 300 coconuts a year. Traders would take away the *copra* and pay islanders in imported goods.[64]

Établissements Française de d'Oceanie remained a backwater well into the twentieth century. Except for exploiting valuable phosphate deposits at Makatea, France ruled the colony loosely. Twenty-four governors served between 1882 and 1914.[65]

Church at Raroia, Tuamotus. This Catholic church was probably funded by pearl fishing and built at the request of priests by the small atoll's inhabitants. Today the church serves fewer than 100 inhabitants. In 1947 Thor Heyerdahl and the *Kon Tiki* crew landed on Raroia after their raft voyage from South America. Heyerdahl tried to show that South Americans colonized the Polynesian islands. Photograph by Robert Kirk.

WALLIS AND FUTUNA

On August 16, 1767, Captain Samuel Wallis, commanding the *Dolphin*, sighted 77.5-square-kilometer (30-square-mile) Uvea, a Polynesian island his officers named Wallis in his honor.[66]

On November 1, 1837, the chartered schooner *Raiatea* dropped off Father Pierre Bataillon (1810–77) and Brother Joseph Xavier Lugy on Wallis Island to convert the islanders to Catholicism. On November 8, the *Raiatea* dropped Father Pierre Louis Chanel (1803–41) and lay brother Marie-Nazier Delorme at Futuna for the same purpose. In each place, the fathers were successful in converting the people.

In 1870 Queen Amelia Tokagahahau of Uvea (r. 1889–95) announced a new legal code for her people. She approved the code written by the missionary Pierre Bataillion. Fines were imposed for theft, prostitution, staying home from Sunday mass, or harming women and animals. Land was not to be alienated to foreigners.[67]

On April 5, 1887, the queen of Wallis Island signed a document asking for French protection. The kings of nearby Futuna and Alofi placed their people under French protection on February 16, 1888. Wallis and Futuna were united as a single unit as a French protectorate on March 5, 1889. The chiefs who agreed in 1887 to French protection had little choice in the face of French naval power. These islands remain a French *collectivite*.[68]

Chapter 14

French Melanesia
Subdued, 1774–1914

Cook Names New Caledonia

With Tahiti at last under control, France decided to take control over New Caledonia and its smaller neighbors, the Loyalty Islands and the Isle of Pines. On September 5, 1774, crew member James Colnett on Cook's second expedition was the first European to sight Grande Terre, which Cook would name New Caledonia; Caledonia had been the Roman name for Scotland. Cook's crew remained one week. "No people could behave with more civility than they did," wrote Cook of the indigenous *Kanakas* (or Kanaks) he encountered.[1] At Balade in the northeast, naturalist Georg Foerster (1754–94) set up a makeshift observatory to chart the eclipse of the sun.

Of Kanak men, Lieutenant Charles Clerke wrote: "When we found them they were totally naked to the penis, which was wrapped up in leaves, and whatever you gave them, or they by any means obtained, was immediately applied there.... I gave one of them a stocking—and he very deliberately pulled it on there—I then gave him a string of beads; with it he tied the stocking up—I then presented him with a medal which he immediately hung to it." Clerke concluded, when "that noble part be well decorated and fine, they're perfectly happy and totally indifferent about the state of the rest of the body."[2]

Grande Terre, which measures 16,648 square kilometers (6,467 square miles), is the sixth largest island in the South Pacific and is exceeded in size by New Guinea; both North and South Island, New Zealand; Tasmania; and New Britain. It consists of a mountainous central range between two long coasts; Mount Humboldt, the highest peak, is 1,500 meters, or 5,308 feet. Half of Grande Terre consists of mountains; about a fifth of the island is good agricultural land. A barrier reef 10 kilometers (6.2 miles) off both coasts is second in size only to the Great Barrier Reef. New Caledonia is rich in mineral resources; between 25 and 42 percent of Earth's nickel, tungsten, cobalt, copper, manganese, iron, and chromium exist there. The only indigenous animals are the flying fox and rat. The population at the time has been estimated at 70,000. Cook named the nearby Isle of Pines for its *Araucaria* trees, but was unable to land due to fringing reefs.[3]

French Expeditions

In April 1793 Bruni d'Entrecasteaux and Huon de Kermadec, aboard *L'Espérance* and *La Recherche*, stopped at Balade in Grande Terre and at the Isle of Pines. The mariners

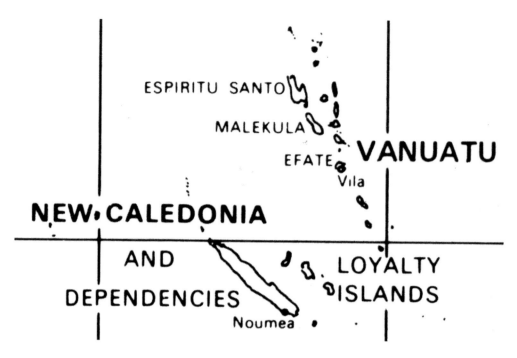

Map of New Caledonia and Vanuatu. By permission of the Office of Planning, State of Hawaii.

charted both the Belep Archipelago, 69.5 square kilometers (26.8 square miles), and the Huon Islands, 65 hectares (160 acres), both coral groups lying to the immediate north of Grand Terre. France would later cite this visit to justify her claim to the islands.[4]

France further justified its claim to the islands on the explorations of Jules Sébastien César Dumont d'Urville (1790–1842). The French scientific expedition left Toulon on September 7, 1837. Dumont d'Urville commanded the corvette *Astrolabe*, while Captain Charles Hector Jacquinot (1796–1879) commanded the *Zelee*. The expedition collected more scientific information than any prior single Pacific expedition; it resulted in the publication of twenty-three volumes of data, drawings, and description, and five atlases. Passing through the Strait of Magellan, Dumont d'Urville reached Mangareva on July 31, 1838. The crews anchored days later at Nuku Hiva in the Marquesas, and at Tahiti just over a year after leaving France. They stopped at other Society Islands and in Samoa and Tonga — both the Vava'u and Ha'apai groups. Leaving Fiji October 29, 1838, they passed the New Hebrides, the Solomons and the Admiralty Islands.[5]

Loyalty Islands

In 1790, Captain Jethro Dagget named the Loyalty Islands after his ship, *Loyalty*. The Loyalties lie 100 kilometers (62 miles) from Grande Terre. Lifou is by far the largest, 1,196 square kilometers (466 square miles); it is larger than Tahiti. Maré measures 642 square kilometers (250 square miles). Ouvea, the smallest, is almost exactly the size of Moorea, and offers long stretches of white sand beaches; it measures 132 square kilometers (51 square miles). People on each island speak their own Melanesian language, but a Polynesian dialect is also spoken by immigrants from Wallis who settled on Uvea in the eighteenth century.

Foreign penetration of New Caledonia began not in Grande Terre itself but in the Loyalty Islands and on Isle of Pines. Sandalwood traders and missionaries played the major role. Sandalwooders were the first white men to arrive at Lifu. In August 1842, Andrew Cheyne wrote that while purchasing sandalwood, about thirty-five Lifouans came on deck, "stealing every thing they could pick up, and flourishing their clubs and Tomahawks over my head. No threats or entreaties of mine, would make them go into their canoes, and at last we were obliged to charge them with the Bayonets to clear the deck."[6]

On April 8, 1841, the London Missionary Society vessel *Camden* brought two Samoan Christian teachers to Marè. They were fortunate to encounter a small group of Tongans who had somehow drifted to Mare "a long time ago." As they were able to communicate with the Tongans, they were introduced to the local chief, Yeiw. Yeiw promised to protect the two Samoans. Although he found the people of Maré naked and "without the slightest sense of shame," the Reverend Archibald Wright Murray was glad that they were "in a remarkably prepared state for the reception of the Gospel, so peaceable and apparently so little attached to any system of false religion."

The fate of the crew of the sandalwood ship *Martha* disproved Murray's sanguine prediction. On April 10, 1842, Captain Nichols and four men went ashore at Maré to trade for sandalwood. According to an islander questioned later, the five were eaten, and the surviving crew were menaced by two or three hundred club-wielding islanders; the informant attributed the attacks to Captain Nichols having struck a chief for trying to take his handkerchief.[7]

On September 6, 1842, having heard that the bark *Juno* had located sandalwood at Uvea, Andrew Cheyne found his way in through the island's reef. Cheyne received a friendly reception from a chief named Hwenegei, who said the *Juno* crew and Cheyne's crew from the *Bull* were first white people to come to Uvea. Cheyne quoted the chief as stating that he wanted friendly trade with the whites, that they were glad to sell sandalwood, and that "all his natives would cut a sufficiency to fill both vessels."[8]

In the 1840s more Samoan and Rarotongan Christian teachers were landed in Maré, Lifou and Uvea. The population of all three islands embraced Christianity, the first Melanesian communities to do so. When LMS bishop George Augustus Selwyn visited in the early 1850s, he noted that the islands had "probably more Christians than anywhere in these seas."[9] Chiefs and missionaries built stone houses and churches. Island chiefs used the new religion to enhance their own powers and possessions. Chiefs enacted laws imposing penalties for theft, adultery, and failure to attend church. K.R. Howe stated: "There was a genuine and even aggressive enthusiasm for wearing clothes, church going, singing hymns, reciting catechisms, learning to read and write."[10] Because the French found little of value to exploit, Kanakas of the Loyalty Islands were secure in their customs and native governance, as modified by Christianity. In 1899 French authorities in New Caledonia designated the Loyalty Islands an indigenous reserve, which helped preserve the land and culture.[11]

ISLE OF PINES

The first sustained contact between Kunies—Isle of Pines inhabitants—and Westerners came in 1840 when the LMS vessel *Camden* arrived on May 13. All went well at first as chief Touru (a.k.a. Matuku) dined on board and welcomed two Samoan Christian teachers to remain on the island. Kunies knelt with the Samoans while the teachers prayed.

Touru offered a loan of some of his estimated fifty wives to the Samoans, an offer apparently rejected.[12] Had the Protestant missionaries been successful in converting the islanders, New Caledonia might have become British, rather than a French, possession.[13]

When the *Camden* returned to Sydney on April 28, 1841, a member of the crew disclosed that he had seen sandalwood on the Isle of Pines, and in the following twelve months at least two dozen ships left Sydney for sandalwood in the Isle of Pines and the Loyalties. Kunies and Kanaks could not understand the passion of Europeans for sandalwood, and could only conclude that they made the unpalatable ship's biscuits from sawdust.[14] In August 1841 the *Orwell* and *Diana* arrived. Supercargo Andrew Cheyne (1817–66) recorded that the ships took on three or four boatloads of wood a day. Crewmen cut the wood, and local men and women carried bundles to the beach and loaded the ships' boats. Chief Touru received hoop iron in return. "He visits the ships very frequently," Cheyne wrote, "and seldom comes on shore without his small bag full of Iron Hoop." Cheyne described the Kunies as "truly wretched in every sense of the Word, degraded beyond the power of conception." Its hold full, the *Orwell* sailed to China on September 11, leaving the *Diana* crew to continue to cut wood. Captain Watson of the *Diana* was mortally threatened by an angry group of Kunies after he struck one for stealing a piece of wood. "He did very wrong in striking the native," Cheyne observed, "as we were completely in their power." Watson returned to the ship and did not set foot ashore again. The ship weighed anchor for Sydney on October 30, 1841.[15]

Thirteen sandalwood vessels arrived within three months of the *Diana's* departure, and Touru complained about the abuse of Kunies by crew members. In July 1842, the *Camden* returned. Reverend Thomas Slayter noted that Touru was mostly angered by the visit of an epidemic that had killed many islanders, alleging that the scourge "sprung from the deities of Samoa and Britain — that Jehovah has caused it." The Samoan teachers had unwisely threatened Kunies with plague and pestilence if they did not accept the Christian God. Incensed by the intrusion of white men, Kunies were ready to slaughter the crew of the next ship to arrive. On November 1, 1842, Captain Thomas Ebril of the *Star of Tahiti* arrived for sandalwood. Thirty Kunies came aboard and, with permission, sharpened their axes on the ship's grinder. They split Captain Ebril's head. They killed nine Europeans, the Samoan teachers, and seventeen Polynesian crewmembers. The ship was stripped and burned and all of the victims were eaten.[16]

Before news of the *Star* massacre reached Sydney, the *Catherine* sailed to the Isle of Pines in early 1843. When Kunies attempted to take the ship and slaughter the crew, the mate blew up the powder casks, killing the attackers and two sailors, but saving the severely crippled ship. After the *Catherine* returned to Sydney on May 3, 1843, and its story got out, no ships went to the Isle of Pines for eighteen months.

On September 28, 1853, four days after claiming Grande Terre, Rear Admiral Febvrier Despoints (1796–1855) claimed the Isle of Pines in the name of Napoleon III (1808–73; r.1852–70).[17]

The largest number of whites settled on the Isle of Pines were prisoners. On September 29, 1872, the first of 4,166 Communards arrived as convicts in New Caledonia on the *Danae*. After Napoleon III lost the disastrous Franco-Prussian War, Communards had seized the government of Paris from March 26 to May 30, 1871, and attempted to erect a socialist state. During "Bloody Week" in late May, an estimated 50,000 had been killed by French troops. The commune ended.[18] These convicts were housed on the Isle of Pines and contributed to its development through their manual skills. By 1873 they outnumbered Kunies

"Nouvelle-Caledonie/Vue de Port de France" is a view from the late 1850s of the city that was named Nouméa in 1866. The French founded Port de France in 1854, after claiming Grand Terre, New Caledonia, the year before. The settlement was founded as a penal colony. The engraving is from *Le Tour du Monde: Nouvelle Journal des Voyages*, edited by Eduard Charton (Paris: Hachette, 1863).

two to one. To accommodate the new prisoners, 200 Melanesians lost lands, and 700 Maré islanders, who had been refugees, were taken away.[19] On March 3, 1879, those still held prisoner of the more than four thousand Communards who had been brought to New Caledonia were amnestied and allowed to return to France. One hundred and forty chose not to return.[20]

As the island had little to exploit, the governor of New Caledonia declared the Isle of Pines a native reserve on April 1, 1913. Kunie life and lands were to remain undisturbed so far as possible. As a result, Kunies were able to maintain their culture, as altered by missionaries and the presence of a prison.[21]

FRENCH ANNEXATION OF GRANDE TERRE

A monument erected in 1913 at Balade reads in translation: "Here, on 24th September 1853, Rear Admiral Febvrier Despointes has taken over New Caledonia in the name of France." As the imperial flag was hoisted, 150 Christianized Kanaks were permitted in the stockade to witness the dramatic moment, while thousands of presumably hostile Kanaks watched from a distance. Because they were fighting at the time on the same side in the Crimean War, France's emperor guessed correctly that Britain would not jeopardize the alliance by interfering in his imperialistic aggrandizement.[22]

Napoleon III intended to transport his political opponents as well as convicted criminals to Grande Terre. The island was to be a French Botany Bay. The emperor ordered his naval ships at the time in Lima, Peru, to proceed to New Caledonia. The emperor was able to justify his act of aggression because of a massacre of fourteen crewmembers of the French survey ship *Alemène* in 1850. Members of the Paaba and Yenghiebane tribes had, reportedly, eaten them.[23] On June 25, 1854, Louis-Marie-François Tardy de Montravel (1811–64) founded Port-de-France, as administrative center of Grande Terre.[24] In 1866 the settlement was renamed Nouméa. In 1890, visitor Robert Louis Stevenson quipped: "It looks as if were made of vermouth cases."[25]

On May 9, 1864, the ship *Ephigénie*, from France, landed 248 prisoners at Ile Nou in Nouméa. The *Ephigénie* was the first ship of 75 convoys over 33 years to bring prisoners. The journey could last anywhere from 80 to 140 days, while prisoners were housed in crowded cages and allowed only minimal exercise.[26]

LOSS OF KANAK LAND

The French found these Melanesians physically unattractive, at least in contrast with Tahitians, and unreliable as workers. The Europeans denigrated their customs, belief systems, economic activities, and social organization. Moreover, Kanak populations continued to decline and Europeans thought — and some no doubt hoped — they would "quite literally, become an extinct species."[27]

Under French domination, Kanaks began to lose substantial amounts of land. Although they allowed some lands to lie fallow, Kanaks grew taro, yams, bananas, and coconuts, and they fished. Their meat consisted of birds and bats. Land was vital to Kanaks not only for producing food, but for their cultural identity, which was tied to ancestral lands. When they lost their clan's homelands, they lost a link to the past and their ancestors.[28]

In 1855, the governor decreed the government would sell Kanak lands declared vacant. In Paris the minister of the navy pronounced: "The uncivilised inhabitants of a country have over that country only a limited right of domination, a sort of right of occupation.... A civilised power, on establishing a colony in such a country, acquires a decisive power over the soil, or, in other terms, she acquires the right to extinguish the primitive title." Because Kanaks were considered to be primitive, their uncultivated lands were termed *terra nullis*, or land without owners and free to take.[29]

In the twenty years after 1860, when they claimed a thousand acres, settlers acquired 230,000 hectares (575,000 acres), the southern third of Grande Terre. Kanak land went to the Roman Catholic Church as well, which soon had extensive holdings. Kanaks protested their loss of land, and protested against settlers foraging cattle in taro patches, a practice which led to famine.[30] According to a French government decree of May 16, 1867, the appointed governor was given extraordinary power over the colony's indigenous tribes. He could, with approval of the colonial minister, exile or imprison Kanaks without a trial, and even dissolve and disperse a tribe. The governor's power to seize land was confirmed.[31]

In 1868, Kanaks were allocated 320,000 hectares (800,000 acres) as native reserves. From 1869 authorities had granted freed convicts four to five hectares (10 to 12½ acres) of land to till, and from 1878, convicts still serving sentences were given land to grow their own food.[32] Kanaks lost their taro fields, which caused clans to fight with neighboring clans for diminishing available land. Article 4 of the Decree of May 27, 1884, granted to French immigrants a plot in a town, grazing land and crop land. In 1897 the government decreed that they could take reserves lands and relocate Kanaks. By 1902, Kanak land area fell from 320,000 hectares to 120,000 hectares (300,000 acres).[33]

GARNIER FINDS NICKEL

In 1864 French geologist Jules Garnier (1839–1894) discovered a rich nickel deposit at Diahot, Grande Terre. In 1873, additional deposits were found at Bourail, Canala, Thio, and Hoailu. Most Kanaks refused to work underground. From 1878 French mining supervisors used prisoners from France, Loyalty Islanders, and New Hebrideans for the work.[34]

In 1880 Garnier and Scottish-born John Higginson (1839–1904) formed the Societé le Nickel (SLN), which became the world's largest nickel producer. Within ten years New Caledonia was the world's biggest producer not only of nickel but of cobalt, chromium, and manganese. Mining was a disaster for Kanaks, as they saw their croplands stripped for minerals.[35]

ARRIVAL OF INDENTURED LABORERS

In 1866 Rear Admiral Charles Guillain (term 1862–70), governor of New Caledonia, assigned convicts to work for free settlers. In addition, he abolished corporal punishment. Looser control of convicts contributed to increased criminal activity. One result was the importation of laborers from the New Hebrides; by 1870, they numbered 720.[36] Workers from other islands or colonies were unlikely to simply walk away from a job. They worked on three-year contracts, at the end of which they were paid. Pay was minimal. In the next several decades Japanese, Chinese, Javanese and Indo-Chinese were brought to work in New Caledonia.[37]

ATAI'S REBELLION

On June 25, 1878, High Chief Atai of La Foa, Grande Terre, launched a seven-month guerrilla war of liberation. The rebellion was the best chance that the Kanaks had to stem the advance of settlers' land acquisitions. Nickel and copper mining and stock grazing had taken all but eleven percent of the land from Kanaks. Cattle ranching led to the land being concentrated within a few European families.

By some accounts the uprising and necessary accumulation of weapons had been ongoing for a decade. On the first day, four gendarmes at La Foa were killed, as were forty *caldoches* (settlers) in surrounding areas. In the next few weeks, more farms were raided and the European inhabitants killed. In September ten French in a supply boat were killed and eaten. The governor, Admiral Jean Olry (1832–90; term 1879–80), called out the 2,600 troops in the colony as well as free settlers; even some convicts were armed for the fight.

When Chief Galina of Canala sided with French forces, the tide of rebellion turned. On September 1, a Canala Kanak threw a spear through Atai at a place called Fontimoulou. Atai's head was severed from his torso and sent to Paris as a trophy. In a series of battles and skirmishes that continued to December 1878, an estimated 1,000 Kanaks and 200 Europeans were killed. The rebellion was declared to have ended on June 3, 1879, nearly a year after it began. The Kanak population was estimated in 1878 to be 60,000. Although the Kanaks were to lose the fight, the ferocity of the conflict was such as to retard economic growth of the colony for two decades. Settlers were fearful of Kanaka reprisals and wanted them gone. One demanded "the extermination in mass by every means of the indigenous race" and could see "no other remedy than the annihilation of the *Canaque* race without distinction of friends or enemies."[38]

PRISON ISLAND

By 1879 free colonists numbered 1,700; soldiers, 700; prison administration employees, 450; and prisoners, about 1,000.[39] Three hundred North Africans lived on Grande Terre;

the first seventy-two arrived in 1872, Kabyls from Algeria, who were exiled after an aborted revolt against French rule of their country.[40] An estimated 80,000 head of cattle roamed the countryside, often destroying Kanak gardens.[41] In 1887, some 6,000 freed prisoners remained on New Caledonia. The number of free settlers was 9,000. Many former convicts preferred to return to France but a law of 1854 stipulated that, once freed, convicts with sentences of eight years or more had to remain on New Caledonia for the number of years of their original sentences.[42]

The *Indigénat* Code

From 1887, under the Indigénat system imposed by France, Kanaks were treated as prisoners in their own land. This indigene or native code classified tribes as subjects rather than citizens and imposed severe restrictions on them. Authorities could arrest them without probable cause and impose punishment without trial. Their property could be taken and fines could be imposed on entire communities. Kanaks could be punished for cutting wood without authorization; failing to tell authorities about births, deaths, or illnesses; even littering. Kanaks could not leave reservations except to work, and they were subject to curfews.[43] From 1894 to 1946 French authorities imposed a head tax on Kanak males, age twenty-nine to fifty-five. This tax, to be paid in money, caused most to abandon taro fields and work for French settlers and as miners.[44] The *Indigénat* Code was imposed on subject peoples in most other French colonies as well.

Transportation of Prisoners Ends

In 1897 Governor General Paul Feillet (1857–1903; terms 1894–1902) vowed to "Turn off the tap of dirty water"— the arrival of French prisoners. From 1864 to 1897, some 21,630 had arrived in 75 convoys following four-month sailings from France. In 1901 there were 10,500 prisoners, and in 1911, still 5,700.[45] Only 1,700 were to stay in the colony. From 1864 to 1896 authorities guillotined eighty prisoners. The condemned were first administered a cigarette and a shot of brandy.[46]

Kanaks Are Further Victimized

Some settlers, soldiers, convicts and officials victimized Kanaks. Females were kidnapped, raped and forced into unpaid labor. Kanaks were beaten or killed. European employers did not always pay Kanaks the full amount agreed on for work, or did not paid them at all. Some merchants cheated them. Whites encouraged tribal disputes. Purveyors of alcohol encouraged dependence.[47]

Priests complained about the influence not only of prisoners and emancipationists, but of settlers as well. A Father Testory bemoaned "the whites who flock here, with an unknown past, greedy, violent and debauched. It is obvious that the bad example shown by such a population is hardly appropriate to give the indigenes an elevated notion of Christian and civilised life." Father Nicholas wrote to his superior, "Sunday work is the rule everywhere. Foul language, swearing and blasphemy are not hushed; drunkenness is frequent; you can guess the rest." Father Rougeyron wrote, "I have a great deal to do in this colony where there are two races to convert: the black and white: the latter, save several exceptions, has as much need of it as the former."[48]

In an attempt to bring administrative order to the governance of New Caledonia's Kanaks, Governor Paul Feillet ordained that they be organized in 150 villages as "tribes." The order of October 27, 1897, decreed that officials called *syndics des affaires indigenes* were to govern fifty native districts; thirty-seven were on Grande Terre and thirteen in the Loyalty Islands. Kanak chiefs were given the task of collecting the

Kanak chief. This tall and powerful Kanak of New Caledonia can be distinguished from his fellows by his textile clothing, European hat and umbrella. The two hats and umbrella and staff indicate he is straddling two cultures. Lithograph from *Isles of the Pacific; Sketches of the South Seas,* by B. Francis (London: Cassell and Co., 1882).

head tax, of which they were allowed to retain five percent for their own use. Tribes lost traditional lands, chiefs were deprived of traditional roles, and Kanak culture suffered a degree of disintegration as a result of the governor's reorganization of tribes.[49]

New Caledonia was the most important French possession in the Pacific. At the end of the nineteenth century, 22,450 French citizens lived in the colony. They numbered 46 times as many as the 487 who lived in French Polynesia.[50] They constituted the largest white population in any South Pacific island group except New Zealand.[51]

While the white population grew, indigenous populations declined. New Caledonia had an estimated 100,000 Kanaks at the beginning of the century and 34,218 in 1900.[52] It would be difficult to make a case, after looking at the demographic trauma, that the coming of Europeans to Tahiti, New Caledonia and other islands in the French emporium was beneficial to the indigenous people.

Chapter 15

Rocking the Cradle:
Tonga and Samoa, 1773–1914

THE CRADLE OF POLYNESIAN CULTURE

Tonga and Samoa have been called the cradle of Polynesian culture. Sustained contact with the Western world rocked the cradle, but it did not fall. To a greater degree than Hawaiians, Tahitians or Maoris, Tongans and Samoans have retained much of their ancient culture, land and governance. They were not inundated with foreign settlers and indentured workers. Neither Apia nor Tonga'tapu became a major port. Foreign entrepreneurs did not find outstanding profit-making opportunities in either island group. Tonga retained at least a semblance of sovereignty. Samoa was not only taken over, but divided; the United States took Tutuila because Pago Pago Harbor was one of the best in the Pacific, and Germany took Upolu and Savai'I because it had commercial interests there and was attempting to assemble an overseas empire.

The island groups were settled around 3,000 years ago. The proto–Polynesians probably came via Fiji, bringing their navigational abilities and their skill in creating decorated Lapita pottery. Lapita takes its name from a site in New Caledonia where remnants were first found. Pottery making for some reason died out in the first centuries of the Common Era, but when shards are found archaeologists are able to better trace settlement patterns. Polynesian culture developed in Tonga and Samoa during a centuries-long incubation period. Around 300 CE during a golden age of intrepid mariners, Tongans and Samoans settled islands such as the Marquesas and the Societies. From there they later spread throughout the Polynesian triangle.[1]

COOK NAMES THE FRIENDLY ISLANDS

On his second voyage to the Pacific, James Cook visited Tonga and pronounced the people to be friendly. Arriving at 87-square-kilometer (54-square-mile) 'Eua, third largest of the Tonga Islands, on October 2, 1773, Commander Cook marveled at the neat gardens and houses. No European ship had come to Tonga since Abel Tasman found Tonga'tapu on January 19, 1643. The people of 'Eua marveled at their white visitors, the first they had ever seen. Because Eua islanders did not want to trade their food, Cook sailed the following day to nearby Tonga'tapu (259 square kilometers; 160 square miles), the largest island. Cook traded for food, was hosted by and hosted chiefs, and visited a large *marae*. During three days Cook was much impressed by the islanders' agriculture. Entering a "plantation," he marveled: "I thought I was transported into one of the most fertile plains in Europe, here was not an inch of waste ground." Cook stayed five days.[2] His supplies replenished, Cook sailed south.

On June 27, 1774, Cook arrived at Nomuka, 7 square kilometers (4.3 square miles). Nomuka is one of the Ha'apai group. Cook stayed until the end of June. Tasman had come ashore on January 24, 1643, and named it Rotterdam Island. As the men landed in small boats, Nomukans stole two guns. When Cook had their boats seized, the guns were returned and trade of food for trinkets and tools began. Cook wrote that he had named Nomuka, Tonga'tapu and 'Eua, now all part of Tonga, the Friendly Archipelago because "a lasting friendship seems to subsist among the inhabitants and their Courtesy to Strangers intitles them to that Name."[3]

On April 29, 1777, during his third voyage, Cook returned to Nomuka to trade for food. Cook and his officers were entertained with a feast and by wrestling matches, featuring female as well as male contestants. As was true almost everywhere Cook went, "The people very frequently took oppertunities to shew us what expert thieves they were."[4] In retaliation Cook would flog islanders and even take several hostage, but his measures did little to stop thievery.

Chief Finau, who had brought Cook to Lifuka from Nomuka, plotted with local chiefs. Chiefs of what Cook called the Friendly Archipelago planned to murder Cook and his crew in order to plunder *Resolution* and *Discovery*. They invited Cook and his men to a feast. An attack was not perpetrated because, according to one report disclosed long after the event, the chiefs argued whether to kill them during daylight or wait for night. During the eleven weeks Cook stayed in the "Friendly Isles," he remained unaware he was in mortal danger. The crews remained a month in Tonga'tapu, enduring grand and repetitive entertainments of dancing and drumming. Before sailing on July 17, Cook left several horses and cows on Tonga'tapu, and his interpreter Mai (a.k.a. Omai) instructed people how to care for them.[5]

Spanish and French Expeditions

A Spanish voyage of exploration was conducted in 1780–81 under the command of Francisco Antonio Mourelle (1755–1820). On March 4, 1781, he discovered Vava'u in the Tonga Islands. After being entertained by the local high chief, he sailed to Guam.

On March 24, 1793, Bruni d'Entrecasteaux landed in Tonga. When he demonstrated firearms, Tongans failed initially to see a connection between a loud noise and a dead bird at thirty yards, but they soon caught on that these implements could provide victory in battle and wanted firearms desperately. They learned eventually that wet powder is useless, that a dirty or overloaded musket could kill or maim a rifleman, and not to place powder close to open flames. The expedition naturalist Jacques Julian de Labillardière (1755–1834) took extensive notes on Tongan life and customs. In 1799 Labillardière shared his findings in his publication *Relation du Voyage à la Recherche de la Péruse*.[6]

A Failed Mission

On March 26, 1797, after dropping workers off at Tahiti, the London Missionary Society ship *Duff* arrived at Tonga'tapu with nine volunteers to convert the population to Christianity. The Christian workers could tell that Tongans were a heartless people desperately in need of divine salvation. The LMS party noted, for instance, that a chief's boat knocked over commoners' smaller boats to reach the *Duff*, dumping passengers into the sea. One mission worker left immediately. Tongans killed three of the nine mission workers who landed.

The mission workers, unable to communicate with Tongans, were further undermined by escapees who had arrived the previous year from Sydney on the *Otter*, and seven more who arrived October 6, 1797, on the *Mercury*. The convicts encouraged the Tongans to menace the missionaries and to take their iron tools. The survivors who elected to stay, except George Vason (1772–1838), who adapted to Tongan life, were hungry and at the mercy of the Tongans, who were at the time having an intertribal war.[7]

THE ADVENTURES OF WILL MARINER

Neither British, Spanish or French explorers, nor missionaries stayed long enough to learn the language and observe customs carefully over a period of time. Will Mariner (1790–1853) was the first European to achieve fluency in Tongan. Will arrived at age fifteen, a decade after the LMS landing. Mariner reached Lifuka, Ha'apai on December 1, 1806, from London on the English privateer *Port-au-Prince*. The crew had preyed on Spanish shipping. The son of a sea captain, Will had served as cabin boy since age thirteen. The captain of the *Port-au-Prince* anchored to make repairs. The crew was doomed when some 300 club-wielding Tongans climbed aboard. When the warriors killed and ate half the crew, they made Will their prisoner. A local chief, Finau, liked Will and adopted him. Young Will stayed four years at Lifuka, December 1806 to November 1810, and "went native," living with Tongan families. When a passing ship picked him up, he returned home to England. Will's recollections were published as *An Account of the Natives of the Tonga Islands in the South Pacific Ocean*, written with the assistance of amateur anthropologist John Martin and published in 1817. The book is a principal account of Tongan life in the early nineteenth century. Back at home, Will married, sired a dozen children, and went to work as a stock broker. In 1853 he drowned in an English canal.[8]

The literature introducing Tonga to the reading public was further enriched by George Vason, the missionary who stayed. In 1810 Vason, an LMS volunteer who had arrived in 1797 aboard the *Duff*, published in London *An Authentic Narrative of Four Years Residence at Tongataboo, One of the Friendly Islands*. Vason survived and thrived in his new environment. He married a Tongan woman and was given land to work. He had his body tattooed and abandoned his English clothing. In 1801 he left on a passing ship.[9]

THE COMING OF THE WESLEYANS

A quarter century after the failure of the London Missionary Society to convert the Tongans, Methodist missionaries arrived. Reverend Walter Lawry (1793–1859) came ashore on August 16, 1822, at Mu'a on Tonga'tapu aboard the *St. Michael*. He was aided by an interpreter, William Singleton, a survivor of the 1806 *Port-au-Prince* massacre. In addition to Lawry's wife and baby, Charles Tyndall, a blacksmith; George Lilley, a carpenter; and Thomas Wright, a farmer, accompanied Lawry.

Two Tongan youths were sent to Sydney aboard the *St. Michael* as hostages for the safety of the Lawrys and their companions; they were Tahtah and Footahcava. Tahtah and Footahcava entertained people in Sydney with Tongan dances, returning home in April 1823.

Unsuccessful at making conversions during twelve months, Lawry left with his wife and child on October 3, 1823, claiming their lives were in danger. Lawry claimed that an escaped Botany Bay convict named Morgan had undermined his relations with the Tongans. Lawry left two English artisans, Lilley and Tyndall, to guard the supplies that were to be held for future mission workers.[10]

It was not until April 1826 that the first Tongans were converted. Two Pacific islanders, sent by the London Missionary Society in Tahiti, stopped at Tonga'tapu on their way to Fiji. They were Hape and Tafeta. These men laid solid groundwork in Tonga for the institution of Christianity. A high chief, Aleamotu'a of Nuku'alofa, sponsored their work as they set up a school and conducted worship services. Lawry had already taken another converted Tongan, Tamma, to England with him. Tamma would be instrumental in teaching Tongan to the next Wesleyan missionaries to arrive.[11]

The next Wesleyan missionaries arrived at Tonga'tapu from London on June 28, 1826. They were the reverends John Thomas (1786–1875) and John Hutchinson and their families. Thomas and Hutchinson were greeted by Tyndall. John Hutchinson would work in Tonga until 1828. John Thomas remained until 1850, and then returned from 1855–59.[12]

Wesleyan missionaries Nathaniel Turner and William Cross opened a school in Nuku'alofa, Tonga, on March 17, 1828. Missionaries had created writing in Tongan and taught students in the vernacular. By September 150 were enrolled. Schools were opened in three more locations, because unraveling the mystery of the reading process brought prestige to the successful student.[13] Literacy among the indigenous population accelerated their conversions. Former blacksmith John Thomas translated parts of the Bible into Tongan, and in 1844 selections from the Bible had been printed in Tongan by Wesleyan missionary John Hunt. In 1849 the New Testament was made available and in 1852 the entire Bible was printed.[14]

THE RISE OF KING GEORGE TUPOU

Taufa'ahau (1797–1893; r. 1845–93), who had become chief in 1820 of the Ha'apai Islands on the death of his father, requested a Wesleyan European missionary to reside near him, but had to be satisfied with a Christian Tongan teacher. Taufa'ahau was baptised in 1831. Taufa'ahau took the name George in honor of Britain's George III, pronounced in Tongan *Siaosi*. His wife became Charlotte, named after George III's consort, but pronounced *Salote*. When the chief converted, his subjects soon did so as well.

In 1833, the principal chief of Vav'au, Finau, died, and the chief of Ha'apai, Taufa'ahau (George) became chief of Vav'au as well. Taufa'ahau now controlled two of the three principal Tongan island groups. Because Taufa'ahau had become a Christian, the populations of both island groups accepted Christianity, at least nominally. A missionary witnessed Taufa'ahau preaching and noted the chief's apparent sincerity: "His action was dignified and proper, his delivery fluent, graceful and without majesty. He evidently engaged the attention of his hearers, who hung upon his lips with earnest and increasing interest."

When Taufa'ahau's rivals resisted his control, he proclaimed he was fighting for Christianity. Wesleyan missionaries encouraged his holy wars. As a Protestant Christian he could request help from the Royal Navy. In 1852 Taufa'ahau had to besiege the fort at Pea. This time his enemies had become Roman Catholics. Catholics missionaries had been in residence since 1852, but it was not until the Tui Tonga accepted the faith, probably to emphasize his independence from Taufa'ahau, that Catholics enjoyed a measure of success. HMS *Calliope* under command of Sir Everard Home arrived on August 9 and compelled the besieged fort to surrender to Taufa'ahau.[15]

TAUFA'AHAU BECOMES TONGA'S KING

Taufa'ahau controlled Ha'apai and Vava'u island groups. When chief Ale'amotu'a of Tonga'tapu died, Taufa'ahau — or George — assumed the powers of chief of Tonga'tapu on November 18, 1845, completing his control over all three island groups, and proclaimed himself king. Ale'amotu'a had taken the Christian name Josiah Tupou when he was baptized, so Taufa'ahau adopted the designation Tupou I. The Tongan Islands had never had an autocrat, so his action was a new departure in governmental organization.

Tupou I was the most successful nineteenth century Polynesian ruler: The Pomares of Tahiti and Kamehamehas of Hawaii also united their islands, but their families are no longer in power, yet Tupou I's descendants continue to rule Tonga in the early twenty-first century. The king based his power not only on firearms, but also on hereditary rank and position, performing prodigious feats of memorization to recite genealogy, tracing his ancestry back to the first Tu'i Tonga.[16]

KING TUPOU AND REVEREND BAKER

King George Tupou I transformed the centuries-old social order by proclaiming in the Code of 1850 that the monarch — and not the chiefs— was clearly in charge: "Article 3. Whatever is written in these laws, no chief is at liberty to act in opposition, but to obey them together with his people. Article 4. The King is the Chief Judge; and anything the judge may not be able to decide upon, shall be referred to the King, and whatever his decision may be, it shall be final."[17]

Tupou I came to rely on the advice of an unlicensed medical practitioner, Wesleyan missionary Reverend Shirley Waldemar Baker (1830–1903). Baker had arrived in Tonga in 1860 and, incredibly enough, learned in only a month to preach in the Tongan language. The missionary soon ingratiated himself with the king, with whom he would share seventeen years of collaboration. Baker had studied some law and medicine and acted as physician to the aging monarch. The only man on Tonga with a claim to medical knowledge, he wrote "M.D." after his name. Baker also designed a coat of arms for the kingdom. Baker wrote Tonga's national anthem. These laws, the coat of arms, and the anthem remain in use in the early twenty-first century.[18]

With Baker's advice, the old social order that saw hereditary chiefs controlling their tribal lands was replaced by the king's appointment of local governors and other officials. Working with Baker, he emancipated commoners from their ancient feudal obligation of having to work for chiefs. The liberal decree of June 4, 1862, read: "All chiefs and people are set at liberty ... and it shall not be lawful for any chief or person to take or seize by force or beg authoritatively in Tongan–fashion anything from anyone."[19] Tongans were freed

Royal Palace, Tonga. In 1867 Reverend Shirley Baker inspired King Tupou I of Tonga to erect a Victorian–style palace from materials sent from New Zealand. The palace chapel has been the scene of four royal coronations. Baker and the king collaborated for 17 years. The palace remains a major landmark in Nuku'alofa, the capital of Tonga. Photograph by Robert Kirk.

seven months before Abraham Lincoln's Emancipation Proclamation promised freedom to American slaves. In addition, the monarch decreed that each Tongan receive a town lot and 3.34 hectares (8.3 acres) of arable land for a token rent. The sale of land to foreigners was forbidden. Weeks of feasting followed the proclamation, during which a reported 8,000 pigs were consumed.[20]

By the mid–1860s Tonga's king assumed the ancient powers and prestige formerly enjoyed by the Tu'i Tonga. On December 8, 1865, Laufilitonga, thirty-ninth and final Tu'i Tonga, died and was duly entombed at *langi* Tu'ofefafai at Mu'a with his predecessors. A Catholic, his tomb is crowned by a cross. Around 900 CE Tongans developed the concept of a spiritual and temporal leader called the Tu'i Tonga, and enthroned Aho'eitu, the first Tu'i Tonga. The Tu'i Tonga's residence for six hundred years (c. 1200s to 1865) was at Mu'a, 9.6 kilometers (6 miles) east of Nukua'lofa. Mu'a has the richest archaeological structures in all of Polynesia other than on Easter Island. Among the monuments are twenty-eight *langi*. These burial monuments are great limestone stepped platforms as high as 61 meters (20 feet). Wooden houses were placed on top for corpses.[21]

In 1867 King Tupou I and Baker ordered opulent Victorian homes prefabricated in New Zealand. Both mansions were erected in Nuku'alofa. The king, who enjoyed immense wealth from land holdings and taxes, wanted to present himself as a modern Westernized monarch, and felt the palace would contribute to that image. Baker, for his part, wanted a nice European–style house. The palace chapel has been the scene of four coronations.[22] Both dwellings are standing today, the king's serving as the royal palace, and Baker's as the house of the president of the Wesleyan Church.

By 1872, Baker increased significantly contributions by members of the Wesleyan Church. Baker instituted a method of contributing called *sivi* by which worshipers lined up and dropped coins into the collection one at a time; the last person who still had a coin to drop received applause and adulation. *Sivi* was a variation of the game musical chairs that apparently appealed to Tongans' competitive spirit. In 1870 contributions amounted to £3,200; in 1871, £4,500; and in 1872, nearly £7,000. In order for parishioners to earn coins to contribute, Baker arranged for them to sell copra to Godeffroy und Sohns of Hamburg, Germany, traders established in Tonga in 1867. If the copra crop was not ready in time for the church contribution, Godeffroy accepted crop liens and provided the money. Many Tongans found themselves in debt due to their church contributions.[23]

The King Grants a Constitution

On November 4, 1875, Tupou I granted a constitution to his subjects. Baker was the principal author of the document. The constitution established a privy council appointed by the king. Tonga was to be administered by the king's relatives, while the king would listen to the advice of a legislative assembly. In the assembly, seven nobles represented thirty-three nobles; commoners shared seven elected representatives. Thus each noble vote counted for 2,000 commoner votes. The constitution states, "The Sabbath Day shall be sacred in Tonga forever, and it shall not be lawful to do work or play games or trade. Any agreement made or documents witnessed on this day shall be counted void and not recognized by the government."[24]

Baker inaugurated compulsory education as well. Laws prohibited adultery, dancing and wrestling. Wearing *tapa* was prohibited because Tupou wanted his subjects to wear European clothing. Thus, the king made a small attempt to modernize his administration, but he relinquished few of his considerable powers.[25] When his laws had been promulgated and his control tightened, Tupou I controlled a bureaucratic structure that gave him supreme authority.[26]

Balancing Two Great Powers

Tonga and Germany signed a treaty in Nuku'alofa on November 1, 1876, guaranteeing reciprocal rights and trade privileges to their citizens. The German ship *Hertha* had arrived shortly before. Germany obtained the right to establish a coaling station at Vava'u, and Tongans gained the right to refuel their warships—in the event they were ever to obtain any—in German ports. Fearing that Germany would soon dominate Tonga, Britain agreed to a treaty of "perpetual peace" with Tonga. Tonga had signed a similar treaty with Germany, and by balancing these great powers one against the other, she maintained her independence. Tonga is the only island group in Polynesia not to lose her independence and become a colony.

Prime Minister Baker

Reverend Baker returned to Tonga from temporary exile, and the king made him his chief minister on July 24, 1880. In addition, Tupou made Baker minister of foreign affairs, president of the court of appeal, auditor general, minister of lands, minister of education, and more. Baker was nearly a one-man administration. Baker soon found himself arraigned before a Wesleyan missionary commission of inquiry on charges of embezzlement and being a foreign agent. The king testified in Baker's favor, and he was found innocent and continued in his offices.[27]

On January 4, 1885, King Tupou I broke with the Wesleyan Church and established the Free Church of Tonga with himself as head. Prime Minister Baker persuaded the king to make the startling move on grounds that too much money was leaving Tonga to finance Wesleyan foreign missions. Although the king ordered all of his subjects to join the Free Church of Tonga, some insisted on remaining in the Wesleyan Church. Doctrinal differences were minimal. Those who resisted were reported to have been beaten by chiefs and to have lost property. Many fled to Fiji. The schism would not be partially healed until 1924.[28]

Following an assassination attempt on Baker's life on January 12, 1887, during which his son and daughter were shot, the prime minister started to try his enemies in secret and had six executed. British High Commissioner for the Western Pacific Sir John Bates Thurston (1836–97) arrived and forced Baker to stop the secret trials. Baker was expelled again from Tonga on June 17, 1889. When Tongans staged a tax revolt, the British high commissioner returned and declared him "a person dangerous to the peace and safety of the Western Pacific." Baker left for New Zealand aboard the *Wainui*. Baker had accumulated extraordinary power but had made enemies among traders, some Tongans, other missionaries, and powerful British officials. Baker was sent away because he made two decisions that the British found inimical to their interests. First, Baker gave Germany exclusive rights to use Vav'au Harbor as a coaling station, and as a result the British accused him of being a German agent or sympathizer. Second, he encouraged Tongans to borrow in advance on their copra crop to donate to the church; this led to a judge declaring some Tongans in default and their property being forfeited.

For all of his faults, Baker had helped Tonga remain independent. By helping to Westernize the monarchy through a constitution, abolition of feudal labor, land redistribution, and establishment of a state church, Baker helped Tonga remain unique among South Pacific islands in keeping a degree of independence. In May 1898 Baker returned to Ha'apai and built a small house. He would never again be a major influence in island affairs. In 1903, Baker died in Tonga.[29]

"LONG LIVE TUPOU II"

On February 18, 1893, Taufa'ahau Tupou I, the founder of the Tongan monarchy, died and was succeeded by his great grandson, Taufa'ahau Tupou II (1874–1918; r. 1893–1918). The monarchy was strong enough and chiefs sufficiently subdued that succession was not contested.

On May 16, 1900, Tonga's King Tupou II (r. 1893–1918) signed a Treaty of Friendship and Protection with Great Britain. The treaty enabled Tonga to avoid actual colonial status and to continue its monarchical form of government. Germany had shown interest in dominating Tonga, but the two colonial powers agreed that Germany would have a free hand in Western Samoa, and Britain in Tonga. According to the treaty with Tupou II, Britain was to control defense, banking, currency, and foreign relations.[30]

Although Tonga did not lose its independence, it did lose population due largely to disease and warfare. According to estimates, Tonga had perhaps 40,000 people at the time of contact. In 1911 Tonga's first census report indicated a population of 23,017.[31]

King Tupou II died on April 5, 1918, having reigned in Tonga since 1893, and his daughter Salote I (1900–65; r. 1918–65) ascended the throne. The previous year Salote had married Viliami Topouahi Tungi (1887–1941), a descendant of the Tu'i Ha'atakalaua, one of the highest titles in the Tonga Islands.[32]

While change swept Polynesia, the Tongan social order remained in place. Queen Salote enjoyed political supremacy so long as Britain approved of her actions. Nobles and their families enjoyed local and bureaucratic power so long as the monarch approved their actions. Under queen and nobles were the mass of the Tongan people. K.R. Howe described a landscape with "many signs of English inspired civilisation — the neat villages with white picket fences, cobbled streets, village church spires, well clothed congregations, the choirs at evensong." Yet, Nuku'alofa never became a raucous whaling port full of beachcombers, sailors, and prostitutes. The country's land was never taken over by white plantation owners. Without minerals or large guano deposits, the islands were not stripped bare of natural vegetation. Large numbers of Asian workers were not imported to live among the Tongans. Tonga remained "a socially and economically stagnant backwater."[33] Unlike Tonga, Samoa would undergo civil wars beyond mid-century and then be divided by the great powers. Western Samoa did not become unified until the great imperial powers decreed it be unified.

FIERCELY INDEPENDENT SAMOANS

Jacob Roggeveen in 1722 and Louis-Antoine Bougainville in 1768 helped put Samoa on nautical charts. Bougainville named Samoa the Navigator Islands, which they were called during much of the nineteenth century. Samoans demonstrated their fierce independence and xenophobia on December 26, 1787, when the La Pérouse expedition entered Samoan waters. On the northwest coast of Tutuila Samoans killed a boat party of twelve and wounded twenty. A monument, erected in 1883, near the village of Aasu overlooking Massacre Bay honors the victims. La Pérouse praised the natural beauty of the islands, but condemned the inhabitants for their savagery.[34]

ARRIVAL OF THE LMS

In 1832, Reverend John Williams of the London Missionary Society arrived at Leone Bay in Tutuila, where a monument in his honor was later erected. Among the teachers brought to Samoa was the Rarotongan chief Makea, who told Samoans they should adopt Christianity so they could enjoy literacy, peace and eternal salvation. When Samoans did convert, it was often because they were impressed with the material possessions of white people.[35]

In 1836, LMS missionary Reverend Archibald Wright Murray (1811–92) arrived at Tutuila. Murray and George Barnden, who drowned two years later, established a mission at Leone and soon converted most of the islanders. In 1854 Murray moved to Upolu. In 1876 Murray published *Forty Years' Mission Work in the Western Pacific*, a record of his successes.[36]

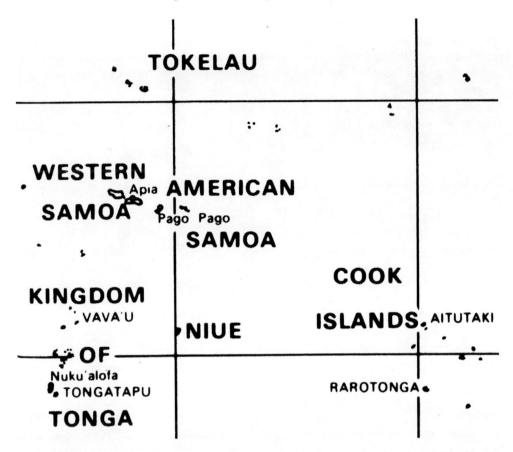

Map of Tonga, Samoa and the Cook Islands. By permission of the Office of Planning, State of Hawaii.

On August 24, 1839, Reverend John Williams and ten mission workers arrived aboard the ship *Camden*. On Upolu Williams built a spacious house for his family. Reverend Williams established his headquarters at Upolu because it was closer to Melanesia than his former homes in Raiatea and Rarotonga. With success in Samoa, Williams looked for new conversions to make.

CHRISTIAN ISLANDS

The London Missionary Society pursued its strategy of sending Polynesian Christian teachers into islands in advance of white missionaries. On September 24, 1844, Malua Theological College opened on Upolu with twenty-five male pupils, age twelve to twenty-four, embarked on four years of study. They were training to become teachers and pastors. Reverends Charles Hardie and Dr. George Turner (1818–91) of the LMS had purchased 120 hectares (300 acres) situated 19 kilometers (12 miles) from Apia. The first students helped clear the site for their school. After a quarter century, 1,143 graduates had been sent on proselytizing missions in the South Pacific.[37]

Commodore Charles Wilkes of the American Exploring Expedition visited Samoa in 1839. When officers spent the night of October 11 in the hamlet of Leone on Tutuila, Midshipman William Reynolds was much impressed by the civility of the Samoans. He wrote, "I noticed in the men a fondness & care displayed towards their children, which I had not expected to find. While on the beach many huge fellows had infants and babbling youngsters in their arms." In the village "there was a deep quiet & the little scene around me, in the grove of Magnificent Bread Fruits, was so simply innocent that my soul was touched. My pride as a white man melted away & I thought in my heart, these people have more claim to be good than me.... I could not help thinking, what would be the reception of these people in our Land?"[38]

THE GREAT POWERS INTERFERE

By mid-century the internally-divided Samoans suffered interference from foreign powers. Whaling crews came increasingly to Apia; seventy-two ships arrived in 1846. A town grew where none had previously existed. Missionaries urged local chiefs to agree to port regulations. Regulations included the mandated service of pilots, payment of harbor dues, and rules for crew conduct. Rules specified that no liquor was to be landed, that no seaman could stay on shore at night, and that deserters were to be apprehended. Washington and London appointed consuls.[39]

Samoa was weakened by internal divisions. Samoan aristocrats vied through military or personal prowess, or the oratory of their talking chiefs, for four titles: Tui Atua, Tui A'ana, Catoatele, and Tamasoali'i. None of these titles actually guaranteed control of the archipelago. Even when one man attained all four with the paramount of title Tafa'ifa, he was still not the king, but had instead the most prestige possible for any Samoan to achieve. From 1841, when Malietoa Vai'inupo, who had held the titles that constitute being Tafa'ifa since 1836, died, civil wars for the supreme title continued until 1873.[40] With interference from missionaries who backed candidates for high titles and with eager suppliers of arms in Apia, wars were ruinous to the Samoan people.

British missionaries were in residence, but Britain made no attempt to rule Samoa or to exclude citizens of other nations from establishing residence. In 1857 the firm Cesar Godeffroy und Sohns of Hamburg established a plantation on Upolu. By the late 1860s the German traders were shipping out copra, coconut oil, cocoa and coffee. The Godeffroy firm would provide a unified Germany a plausible claim to control Samoa.[41]

COLONEL STEINBERGER

From the mid–1870s the Samoan Islands became of interest to Britain, Germany and the United States. Unlike Tongans, Samoans were appalled at the amount of land they had alienated to buy weapons in their civil wars. By 1873 Godeffroy und Sohns had purchased some 10,000 hectares (4,000 acres). The Central Polynesian Land and Commercial Company of San Francisco held claims to 120,000 hectares (48,000 acres), as much as half of the all the islands' land. Other Europeans claimed to have bought vast acreage. Thousands of Samoans found themselves landless.[42] In 1873 Samoan chiefs appointed seven of their number to draft laws and write a constitution that would limit the alienation of land. Their key adviser was Colonel Albert Barnes Steinberger (1840–94), sent by U.S. president Ulysses S. Grant (1822–85; terms 1869–77). Grant instructed Steinberger that he had no diplomatic function but was only to furnish reports.[43]

On May 18, 1875, the Samoan Faipule Council approved Steinberger's new constitution, by which leaders of the Malietoa and Tupua tribal units would avoid armed conflict by alternating in power every four years. Malietoa Laupepa (1841–98) was first to reign.[44] In 1874 Steinberger had traveled to Hamburg and made an agreement with Godeffroy's managers that he would help the firm in return for a share of profits. Steinberger had himself appointed prime minister on the fourth of July 1875. He had clearly disregarded Grant's instructions.[45]

On January 24, 1876, Samoan and German officials signed a treaty by which Germany obtained a naval station in Upolu.[46] Due to his pro–German policies, Britain's high commissioner ordered Prime Minister Steinberger arrested and taken to Levuka, Fiji, aboard HMS *Barracouta*. From there he went to New Zealand and to the United States, never to see Samoa again.[47] Although Britain was not prepared to annex Samoa, London wanted to prevent Berlin from doing so.

AMERICANS IN PAGO PAGO

Because the United States needed a coaling port between San Francisco and Sydney, Commander Richard W. Meade (1837–97) of the USS *Narragansett* made an agreement on January 17, 1878, with the chief of Tutuila to use Pago Pago Harbor. When the six-foot four-inch "Tattooed Prince" Le Mamea came to Washington, DC in 1878, Congress ratified the treaty.[48]

SAMOANS LOSE CONTROL

Deutsche Handels und Plantagen Gesellschaft des Sudsee zu Hamburg, known as the Long Handle Firm, succeeded Godeffroy und Sohns and controlled most of Apia's imports and exports. Copra was the most important export. On March 21, 1887, the Long Handle Firm forced Samoa's king Malietoa Laupepa to relinquish power and appointed in his place rival chief Tupua Tamasese Titimaea. The Samoan people clearly had lost control over not only land but their own affairs.[49]

In early 1889 American and British national interests were compromised since Samoans had protested against high taxes imposed by the Germans and in retaliation Germans had removed their king. When a rival chief, Mata'afa, led a rebellion, German gunboats shelled the shore. It had appeared to American officials that the Germans were determined to subjugate the Samoans. The United States Congress voted $500,000 to protect U.S. lives and property on Upolu and another $100,000 to develop Pago Pago Harbor.[50] American, German and British ships at Apia guarded the interests of their nationals.

SAVED BY A HURRICANE

Two or all three of the powers might have gone to war over the copra islands, but a hurricane hit poorly protected Apia's harbor on March 16, 1889. A British vessel escaped in time. Three German and three American ships were sunk or driven onto the beach by the hurricane with 146 men killed — 54 Americans and 92 Germans. The *New York World* pronounced: "Men and nations must bow before the decrees of nature. Surely the awful devastation wrought in the harbor of Apia makes our recent quarrel with Germany appear petty and unnatural."[51]

Fortunately, Britain, Germany and the United States signed the Tripartite Pact in Berlin on June 14, 1889; the signatories agreed that Chief Malietoa Laupepa (1841–98) would form a government for Samoa and that the consuls representing the three signatory powers would administer Apia, the commercial center. The treaty was a temporary compromise because the three powers wanted to prevent war over the islands, having come close to clashing at Apia three months earlier. The treaty postponed for a decade the question of which power would dominate Samoa.[52]

The Act of Berlin mandated an International Land Commission to adjudicate land claims. Foreigners claimed two and a half times the amount of land existing in the islands. The commission confirmed foreign rights to about one fifth of the land. Further alienation of land was forbidden. Samoan autonomy was saved, temporarily.[53]

THE TELLER OF TALES

Later that year on December 7, 1889, Robert Louis Stevenson (1850–94), author of *Treasure Island, Kidnapped* and other popular works, arrived at Upolu aboard the yacht *Casco*. Stevenson could see the wreckage of the German warship *Adler* on the reef, and of the American ships *Trenton* and *Vandalia*, casualties of the great storm in March of that year. Stevenson soon interested himself in the local politics, which pitted Samoan indigenous factions, as well as Germany, Britain and the United States, against one another for control of the islands. Stevenson wrote *A Footnote to History: Eight Years of Trouble in Samoa*, in which he blamed Samoa's chronic instability on the successor to the German firm of Godeffroy und Sohns, Deutsche Handels und Plantagen Geselschaft fur Sud-See Inseln zu Hamburg. He wrote: "But the true centre of trouble, the head of the boil of which Samoa languishes, is the firm." He blamed the "Long Handled Firm" for alienating native lands and for bringing in Melanesian laborers, some of whom escaped and became fearsome marauders in the interior.

Chronically ill, the Scotsman found that the climate of Samoa helped him to feel better. His Samoan friends called him Tusitala, "Teller of Tales." Stevenson, his wife, mother, and other family members settled into Valima, a home on 125 hectares (314 acres) on the slopes of Mount Vaea, purchased from a Scottish blacksmith. With additions by 1893, Valima became the largest residence in Samoa, a comfortable showplace to which a stream of visitors such as American writer Henry Adams (1838–1918) came to meet the great man. Valima was furnished with seventy-two tons of furniture and housewares shipped from Britain. Stevenson spent a pleasant five years on Upolu before being felled suddenly in his kitchen in December 1894 by a cerebral hemorrhage.[54]

CARVING UP THE SPOILS

On December 2, 1899, Germany, Britain and the United States disposed of the independence of the Samoans. The opinions and welfare of the Samoan people were not under consideration; the division was an imperialistic compromise to avoid future conflict among the signatories. Germany and Great Britain renounced "in favour of the United States" Tutuila and other islands east of longitude 171 degrees. Britain and the U.S. renounced "in favor of Germany" Upolu, Savai'i and other islands that were to compromise Western Samoa. In return, Germany recognized Britain's interests in Tonga and the southern Solomons. Thus, a long-festering international rivalry was ended — at least for the next fifteen years, until the outbreak of the First World War.[55]

On April 17, 1900, the high chiefs of Tutuila and Aunu'u ceded their islands to the United States. Tutuila is a volcanic island, crowned by Matafao peak, 700 meters (2,300 feet). It is bordered by coral reefs and a shallow lagoon. Pago Pago Harbor, one of the best in the Pacific, is a submerged volcanic crater. Following the ratification on February 19, 1900, of the tripartite treaty, President William McKinley signed an executive order instructing the navy to take over Tutuila and its 6,000 Polynesians.[56]

On July 14, 1904, the chief of the Manua Group — the Tui Manu'a — ceded Ta'u, Ofu, and Olosega to the United States. At his request, Tu'i Manu'a Elisara's title was not passed on when he died on July 2, 1909. The Manu'a group is 110 kilometers (70 miles) from Tutuila. America's dependency totals 512 square kilometers (197 square miles), about the size of Andorra.[57]

The Samoans could do little to prevent their takeover. To its credit, the U.S. Navy prohibited alienation of native lands and provided some medical care, but left education to missionaries as part of a policy of benign neglect. One advantage American Samoans have had since the takeover is that they are U.S. nationals, and as such have the right to enter the United States.

THE GERMAN COLONY

Germany set about governing Samoa by promising to help preserve Samoan culture. Samoan became the language of culture for indigenous children, while German children were urged to learn Samoan. Samoans were not forced or coerced to work on plantations; Chinese were brought in as laborers. Immigration from Germany was not encouraged. German governors tolerated Samoan customs and allowed chiefs to govern their areas so long as they did not defy authority. As Hermann Joseph Hiery stated: "Germany's claim to hegemony and the right to formulate the overall rules for the colony had to be accepted. Opposition was not tolerated, whether it came from Samoans or German settlers."[58]

On January 18, 1909, a Samoan orator from Savai'i, Lauati Namulau'ulu Mamoe, brought a large group of warriors to Vaiusu near Apia to demand a share of power with Germany's Governor Wilhelm Solf (1862–1936). They were members of the Mau a Pule movement. Solf was sufficiently diplomatic to avoid a physical confrontation. Frustrated, the warriors returned home. Within a short time three German war ships arrived. Lauati and other leaders were deported to German–held Saipan in the northern Marianas.[59] Increased opposition to German rule may well have materialized, but in 1914 such events were preempted by war and New Zealand's conquest of the islands.

THE POPULATION IN 1914

In 1839 the missionaries carefully estimated the population of each island and declared it to be 56,600. In 1853, fourteen years later, census estimates put it at 33,901. By 1914, the population had not declined, but increased slightly to an estimated 35,000. At that time 373 Germans, 140 British and 2,100 Chinese lived in the islands.[60] As a result of the First World War, Western Samoa would fall under control of an entirely new imperial power — New Zealand.

Chapter 16

King Cakobau's Dilemma: Fiji, 1803–1914

"Take My Kingdom ... Please"

Like Kamehameha of the Sandwich Islands, who tried to give the nation he had formed to the United Kingdom, Ratu Sera Epenisa Cakobau (1815–83) of Fiji tried desperately to give away the kingdom he had painstakingly created. At last he succeeded and ceased to be a king.

King Cakobau's dilemma was the decision of whether to give up the throne he had fought hard to attain, or to try to retain it while facing down rival chiefs and a vengeful adolescent nation — the United States. Finally in 1874 the British permitted him to sign over rule of his rich island nation. For the next ninety-six years Fiji was ruled by a governor appointed from London. King Cakobau had reigned a little more three years. The transformation of Fiji, before and after King Cakobau, began in the early years of the nineteenth century. Until then Westerners avoided Fiji.

From the 1640s the Fiji islands were known in vague outline to European navigators, having been found by Abel Tasman. Coral outcroppings dug into ships' hulls, and no reliable charts showed where they were. Word spread among Pacific voyagers that Fijians were man-eaters who salivated over the stray mariner who arrived on their shores. On his open boat voyage from Tonga to Timor in 1789, for example, Captain Bligh, formerly of the *Bounty*, sailed through the islands, and as hungry and thirsty as his men had become, were afraid to go ashore. Fijians continued to fight among themselves, but were spared the scourges of imported germs and firearms.

Weapons for Wood

Profit-hungry Europeans and Americans risked their lives from 1803 onward by coming to Fiji for aromatic sandalwood, and later beche-de-mer (sea slugs). Both commanded attractive prices in Canton. In 1803 the *Marcia* sailed from Fiji to Sydney and then to China filled with aromatic sandalwood. The *Marcia*'s owner was emancipist Simon Lord (1771–1840), a wealthy Sydney trader and merchant. The voyage marked the beginning of intense denuding of forests in the Fiji Islands. The sandalwood trade flourished in Fiji from about 1804 to 1810.

Sandalwooders had to deal with one or more of seven powerful chiefs who ruled separate *vanuas* (tribes). On Viti Levu were the Rewa, Verata, and Bau. In the Lau Group of islands the predominant tribe was the Lakeba. Vanua Levu was divided among the Cakau-drove, Macata, and Bua. When chiefs learned they could gain Western goods by delivering sandalwood, they ordered commoners to perform the task. Commoners neglected farming and fishing as men devoted themselves to cutting down trees at a chief's order.[1]

Peter Dillon fighting off Fijians. Third mate Peter Dillon arrived on a sandalwood expedition to Fiji in 1813. Attacked by cannibals, Dillon related in *Narrative and Successful Result of a Voyage in the South Seas* (London, 1829) how he and four others held off an attack. This picture is the frontispiece of Dillon's book.

Having obtained firearms for delivering sandalwood, chiefs required instructors to show them how to load a musket and to shoot effectively. The appropriately named Charlie Savage was a Swedish sailor who arrived in Fiji in 1808 aboard the brig *Eliza*. The *Eliza*, under command of Captain E.H. Corey, was wrecked on a reef off Vanua Levu; Fijians were quick to seize the firearms on board. Charlie's shipmates hurried to Sandalwood Bay and were eventually rescued by other ships, but Charlie knew a few Fijian words and was convinced to stay. He became a mercenary for Tanoa, chief of the island of Bau, training Bau men in the use and care of muskets. One result was that Bau was enabled to conquer part of the major island Viti Levu. In order to retain Savage's services, the chief gave him thirty wives. After helping Tanoa for five years, Savage was captured by a rival tribe, cooked and consumed.[2]

The acquisition of firearms accelerated warfare and cannibalism. Evidence in Fiji suggests that cannibalism was practiced as early as 500 BCE. Fijians ate prisoners taken in battle and shipwrecked sailors. Custom required that "long pig," or *bokolo* (man meat), be eaten on the day the victim was caught. Some tribes, however, fattened captives over time before killing them; they then tied them in bundles and roasted them. Some human parts were considered gastronomic delicacies. Chiefs and aristocrats ate first. They used wooden forks to avoid touching eyes and heart, both of which were thought to radiate *mana* so powerful as to be injurious to the recipient. The expected abject greeting of a commoner to his chief was reported to be "Please eat me."[3]

The champion cannibal was Chief Udre Udre. In 1849 Reverend Richard Lyth (1810–87), a Wesleyan missionary in Viti Levu, found 872 stones neatly arranged. He learned that each stone represented a person eaten by Chief Udre Udre. Udre Udre's son, Ravatu, told Reverend Lyth that his father had consumed nothing other than human flesh, keeping a supply always at hand in a box. Udre Udre's macabre tomb is off Kings Road, 12 kilometers (7½ miles) before reaching the village of Valieka.[4]

The lucrative Fijian sandalwood trade reached a peak in 1809. By 1816, all of the sandalwood trees had been cut down and the wood shipped to China.[5]

PROFITS FROM SEA SLUGS

As sandalwood was diminished, the trade in beche-de-mer began. In 1828 Captain Benjamin Vanderford (1788–1842) of Salem, Massachusetts, and his mate William Driver (1803–86) arrived at Fiji to obtain the first cargo of beche-de-mer for trade with China.[6] Sea slugs abounded in Fiji's coastal waters. In Canton the dried slug was sold as a delicacy. Wealthy Chinese enjoyed it as a soup enhancement or flavoring. An islander would take sea slugs from about twelve meters (forty feet) of water to the shore. The slug would be slit and the entrails removed before being washed. It would then be boiled, buried for four hours, and boiled again. Beche-de-mer was then dried and shipped.

Chiefs conscripted commoners to dive as deep as three fathoms to bring up the most valuable slugs. Large numbers of men learned to store, clean, slit, boil and cure the beche-de-mer in smokehouses. Commoners worked hard to process the delicacy, but failed to benefit from their work; rather, their chiefs received muskets, alcohol, knives and tools. Time devoted to the industry necessitated the neglect of agriculture and fishing. Commoners suffered from malnutrition. For a decade the trade was dominated by traders from Salem, Massachusetts.[7] Selling sea slugs was quite profitable. Captain J.H. Eagleston collected 4,437 pictuls of sea slugs on five voyages to Fiji from 1830 to 1841. A pictul weighs 133½ pounds. The cargos sold for $80,241, and expenses were only $10,397.[8]

The trade accelerated war between tribes during the years of rich harvests: 1828–35 and 1842–50.[9] From 1828 to 1850 entrepreneurs, chiefly American, gave an estimated 5,000 firearms to chiefs. Firearms revolutionized warfare and intertribal politics; chiefs formed new confederations of coastal tribes. Modern weapons enabled the rise of Cakobau, nephew of Naulivou, chief of the Mbau tribe in Bau and western Viti Levu. Cakobau was the most powerful tribal leader but definitely not all-powerful. The other reason for Cakobau's rise was marriages with daughters of chiefs of other vanua (tribes) such as Rewa and Cakaudrove. He also had access to huge war canoes built in the Lau Islands.[10]

THE COMING OF THE MISSIONARIES

Christian missionaries arrived to reform the bellicose cannibals four decades after the London Missionary Society had arrived in Tahiti. In all, the missionary effort brought positive reforms to Fijian culture. Missionaries tried to end customary cruelty such as burying people alive in post holes during construction or using them as human rollers. Superstition and abject submission to chiefs could end the life of a commoner in a ghastly manner comparable to being eaten. Missionary Walter Lawry observed in the 1840s: "No eastern tyrants can rule with more absolute terror than the Chiefs do here; and few people are more thoroughly enslaved and trampled than are these islanders."[11] A commoner explained to beachcomber William Diaper: "If the canoe was not hauled over men as rollers, she would not be expected to float long, and in like manner the palace could not stand long if people were not to sit down and continually hold the posts up.... They said, if they sacrificed their lives endeavouring to hold the posts in the right position ... that the virtue of the sacrifice would instigate the gods to uphold the palace after they were dead, and that they were honoured by being considered adequate to such a noble task." Diaper added, "When the canoe hauling song became less clamourous one could distinctly hear the piercing shrieks of the poor fellows for half a mile."[12]

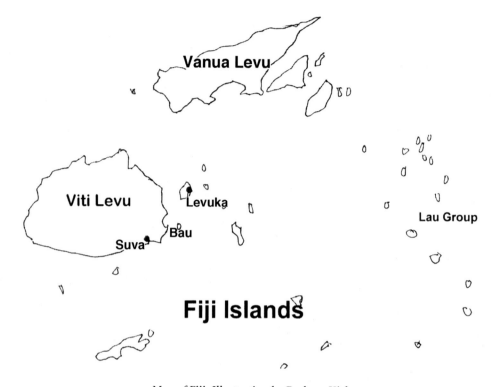

Map of Fiji. Illustration by Barbara Kirk.

In 1830 the LMS sent three Tahitians—Tahaara, Arue, and Htai—as Christian teachers to Lakeba in the Lau Group. The hundred Lau Islands, consisting of a total 487 square kilometers (188 square miles), are the frontier between Melanesian Fiji and Polynesian Tonga. The three came at the behest of Takai, a Lakeba native who had arrived in Tahiti by way of Sydney. Finding Takai obstructive of their efforts, they moved on in 1832 to Oneata Island, nearby. Having some success in conversions, they built a church, the first Christian church to be erected in Fiji.[13]

On October 18, 1835, Methodist missionaries David Cargill (1809–43) and William Cross (1797–1842) arrived at Lakeba from Vava'u, Tonga. Lakeba is also in the southern Lau group, and it neighbors Oneata. The LMS teachers had already paved the way for them by gaining the trust of southern Lau Fijians and introducing Christian concepts. The converts they made were mostly resident Tongans.

Cross and Cargill had to learn Fijian to be effective, and they devised an alphabet for the local Fijian dialect. Later when it became apparent that the dialect of the island of Bau would gain ascendancy throughout the Fiji Islands, they revised their work to reflect Bauan pronunciation. As there were no exact letters for Fijian sounds, Cross and Cargill compromised, thus confounding generations of readers: b = mb, c=th, d=nd, g=ng and q=ngg. Cakobau is pronounced Thak-om-bou and Bequa becomes Mbenga.[14] A printing press having arrived in 1838, the missionaries were able to print a thousand copies in Fijian of the New Testament by 1847. John Hunt (1812–48), who served as a missionary in Fiji from 1838 until his death from dysentery, printed the Testament at the island of Viwa, near Bau. Conversions did not come easily or quickly. By 1851, only 2,322 Fijians had been admitted to the Wesleyan church, while another 535 were candidates.[15]

AMERICA FLEXES ITS MUSCLES

As though Fijian warriors were not busy enough defending against each other, in July 1840, the United States Exploring Expedition (1838–42) under Charles Wilkes arrived and demonstrated the power of the half-century-old American nation. Six ships of the expedition had set sail from Hampton Roads, Virginia, on August 18, 1838, bound for the Pacific Ocean. They were USS *Vincennes, Peacock, Porpoise, Relief, Flying Fish*, and *Sea Gull*, weighing from 96 tons to 780 tons. The expedition commander, Lieutenant Charles Wilkes (1798–1877), was ordered to explore, to chart new discoveries, and to improve charts of known islands and other lands. Nine scientists, including naturalists, philologists, mineralogists and botanists, sailed with the naval personnel. The ships came through the Strait of Magellan, and after stopping in Chile and Peru they made for the Tuamotu Archipelago. From there they visited Samoa, Tonga, Tahiti, New South Wales, Antarctica, and then Fiji.[16]

Members of the so-called Wilkes Expedition massacred several dozen residents of Malolo Island off the east coast of Viti Levu because while they bartered ashore for food, Maloloans killed two officers, one of whom was Wilkes' nephew. The Americans may not have felt much pity for their prey. William Reynolds, an officer with the expedition, reported that in Fiji elderly people were strangled and buried. When a chief died, all of his wives were killed. When a chief launched a war canoe, the decks were washed with human blood and human bodies were used as rollers to move the canoe to the water. Reynolds described Fijians as being larger than Polynesians, but repulsive rather than attractive. They were "begrimed with dirt, daubed with red paint & soot, the ear slit & hanging down to the shoulder, with a bone or shell thrust in the hole, hair frizzled out to a most grotesque extent from the head, dyed of various hues & teeming with life; naked, save a girdle of Tappa around the loins, they presented a spectacle of hideousness & ferocity that well becomes the character they have earned for themselves."[17]

When Wilkes ordered retaliation, his men marched inland. They set Sualib village on fire and fired as people fled the flames. George Sinclair, commander of the *Flying Fish*, reported, "The scene was grand, and beautiful and at the same time horrible, what with the volleys of musketry, the crackling of the flames, the squealing of the Pigs..., the shouting of men and women and the crying of children. The noise was deafening, above which you could hear rising now and then, the loud cheers of our men with 'There they go,' 'Down with them,' 'Shoot that fellow,' etc., etc."[18] The retribution force then marched on to another village, Aro. Sinclair wrote: "We continued as we had commenced to destroy every house and plantation that we came across, and as we marched in three lines, I do not think that one escaped us." With great satisfaction he continued, "Thank God we have taught these villains a lesson." Wilkes' crew killed, by various estimates, as few as fifty-seven and as many as eighty Fijians. Wilkes proudly described a scene in which forty subdued Fijians came to him on their hands and knees moaning and wailing. The forty men, according to Wilkes, "acknowledged themselves conquered and that the island belonged to us; that they were our slaves, and would do whatever I desired; that they had lost every thing; that the two great chiefs of the island, and all their best warriors had been killed, all their provisions destroyed, and their houses burned."[19] Wilkes justified the massacre as a necessity to uphold the honor of the American flag. "On taking our final departure from these islands," Wilkes recalled, "all of us felt great pleasure."[20]

Wilkes returned to New York in the summer of 1842. Of 435 men who began the voyage, 23 died, 127 deserted, and 88 were signed off sick to return home before the expedition had concluded. In Washington Wilkes was court martialed and reprimanded for his frequent uses of the whip; witnesses said Wilkes displayed paranoid tendencies.[21] Wilkes was acquitted and later promoted to the rank of commodore.

Primus Inter Pares

Cakobau considered himself, as the Romans expressed it, *primus inter pares*, first among his peers—forty chiefs, many who contested his claim. Because of his claim of being the man to deal with in Fiji, Cakobau would be menaced by the United States for a quarter century. On July 4, 1849, the U.S. consul in Fiji, John Brown Williams (1810–60; consul 1846–60), ordered a cannon fired to commemorate the seventy-third anniversary of the signing of the American Declaration of Independence. The cannon exploded and the consul's two-story wooden house on the island of Nukulau caught fire. Onlookers set about with great enthusiasm looting what they could; their logic suggested that a dwelling fire was an invitation to help oneself to items that might be destroyed if left for the flames. Williams billed Cakobau for damages totaling $5,001.38. Williams obtained his government's backing, and the U.S. inflated his demand to an exhorbitant $38,531. Cakobau professed himself not only Tui Viti — paramount chief of Fiji — but also unable to pay.[22]

The American debt was one of several of Cakobau's concerns. He was alternately menaced and aided by Tongans who controlled much of eastern Fiji. In 1848, the nominally Christian Tongan chief Ma'afu Ma'afotu'toga (1826–81), nephew of King Tupou (a.k.a. George) I of Tonga, invaded Fiji at Lau, contesting control with the chief of Bau, who had claimed control over the Lau Group. Ma'afu offered support to Wesleyan missionaries, who had been working in the Lau Group since 1835. Cakobau was angry that his subjects were becoming Christians and that a Tongan held what he claimed as his domain. Cakobau held back from war. He was also struggling for supremacy with the neighboring chiefdom of Rewa. Had he gone to war with Ma'afu, Cakobau might well have been defeated and Fiji might have become a colony of Tonga.[23]

In order to achieve his ambition of becoming the first king of all Fiji, Cakobau accepted the advice of Taufa'ahau George I of Tonga, who wrote to him on February 28, 1854, telling him to be baptised. Taufa'ahu knew that John Brown Williams had published a letter in a Sydney paper advising, "Bau ought to be destroyed, and the people swept from the face of the earth."[24] In addition to claims against him by the United States, in 1853 Europeans had held him responsible for the destruction by fire of the commercial town of Levuka, and they blockaded his island of Bau. If Bau were Christian, its people might earn missionary support and avoid that disaster. On April 30, 1854, Cakobau was converted to Christianity by Wesleyan missionaries, whom he had admitted to Bau in 1853. Conversion was a diplomatic ploy, and it brought in its wake the conversion of Fijian commoners who changed their personal religion because their leader did so.[25]

In February 1855 with 2,000 Tongan warriors and 1,000 Fijian warriors, transported in forty canoes, Cakobau defeated his rivals from Rewa at the Battle of Kaba. Rewa leader Ratu Mara was hanged at Levuka, Fiji, but not eaten. As Christians, Cakobau and his followers gave up cannibalism. Having won the battle, Cakobau was able to claim to be leader of all Fiji, although several other chiefs still held considerable authority over their own areas and disputed his claim. Cakobau's principal remaining rival was Taufa'ahu's nephew Ma'afu, ruler of much of eastern Fiji.[26]

Cakobau's Debt Crisis

Americans calculated that Chief Cakobau, as self-proclaimed head of Fiji, owed American citizens $43,686, and on September 12, 1855, a naval detachment sailed in to collect it. Commander E.B. Boutwell of the U.S. warship *John Adams* demanded payment for damages incurred by the looting of consul John Brown Williams's burning house, and for purported losses by other Americans during the ongoing tribal wars. One third was to be paid in each of three installments in twelve, eighteen, and twenty-four months. On September 22, Cakobau signed a promise to pay.[27] To hasten payment, on October 28, 1855, the Americans returned and a landing party under Lieutenant Louis C. Sartori burned three villages. One American was killed and three were wounded. The troops returned to their ship by October 31.[28]

Cakobau's intractable problems seemed to pile one on another. On October 12, 1858, on the advice of British consul W.T. Prichard, Cakobau offered Fiji to Britain as a protectorate with the stipulation that Britain pay the debt to Americans, and that Cakobau rule as Tui Viti (paramount ruler). Cakobau was forced to wait four years. The London government sent Colonel W.T. Smythe to investigate the local situation and make a recommendation. Smythe arrived at Levuka on July 5, 1860, and sent his report to London on May 1, 1861. Smythe related that he had interviewed all of the paramount chiefs and concluded that Cakobau's claim to be the national leader was self-proclaimed and had little basis in fact; therefore, Fiji was not Cakobau's to offer. Britain did not accept the offer.[29]

The dreaded Americans returned. The USS *Vandalia* landed forty sailors and ten marines on October 9, 1859, at Waya in Fiji to revenge the murder and consumption by cannibals of two Americans. After a five-hour march the company confronted hundreds of Fijian warriors. Singing "The Red, White, and Blue," the Americans set fire to the village and left dozens of Fijians dead and wounded. Six Americans were wounded in the action.[30]

The Fijian Confederacy

Fijian chiefs realized that if Britain would not offer protection, they would have to take responsibility for protecting their islands. In 1865 the Confederacy of Independent Kingdoms of Viti attempted government by consensus, linking loosely the chiefs of Bau, Lakeba, Rewa, Bua, Cakaudrove, Macuata and Naduri. The chiefs attempted to bring an end to the wars among them, which had been made more lethal due to the importation of muskets. Cakobau was elected chairman for two one-year terms. Ma'afu, the Tongan leader of the Lau Group and southern Vanua Levu, withdrew when he was denied the chairmanship during the third year. The experiment soon ended.[31]

The Last Missionary Consumed

Efforts to show the world that Fiji was now a civilized country suffered a severe setback in 1867. Several Fijians at Nubutautauon, Viti Levu, clubbed to death and ate parts of Reverend Thomas Baker (1833–67). A chief had taken Reverend Baker's comb and put it in his hair; the missionary compulsively grabbed back his comb, committing the unpardonable sin of touching a chief's head. The monumental indiscretion proved to be Baker's death sentence. Jack London's short story "The Whale Tooth" was inspired by the incident. Baker was the last missionary known to have been eaten in Fiji.[32]

LAND FOR DEBT PAYMENTS

With no help coming from Britain, Cakobau bartered other people's land to gain some protection from the American navy. Officers of the Polynesian Company, owned by Australian investors, paid the first installment on Cakobau's long-standing debt to Americans. In return, on the same day, July 13, 1869, Cakobau and other chiefs signed over 10,800 hectares (27,000 acres) to the company, and granted them a banking monopoly and tax-free status. The remainder of the debt was paid November 19, 1870. Because the chiefs signed over land that did not belong to them, the company was able to use about half of the acreage promised. Payment of the debt relieved Cakobau of the threat from American warships that had begun two decades earlier.[33]

A ROWDY PORT TOWN

In 1870–71, about 1,500 Caucasians arrived in Fiji, many aboard the 158 ships anchored in the islands in 1870. In 1870 approximately 3,000 non–Fijians were living in the island group. A correspondent of the *Melbourne Argus* predicted that as more whites settled, Fijians would die off and it would become a white nation.[34] A thousand whites were estimated to live in Levuka, the principal town. Levuka catered to sailors in fifty-two bars that lined the waterfront. A visiting barrister from Sydney wrote that the whites in Levuka "spent a great deal of the day and the night too, tippling in the public house bars, and of the row of houses that make Levuka, half are hotels or public houses. Swilling gin and brawling are the principal amusements." The barrister alleged "roguery and scheming at every hand," and that the town was governed by "a set of adventurers from Sydney and Melbourne, who would most certainly be sent to the treadmill in their home cities."[35]

KING CAKOBAU

In 1870 the *Fiji Times* noted: "The Fijians control themselves better than the European settlers. It is not for the natives that we want a strong government for, but ourselves." In response to Fijian defense of their own lands, settler John Hall Davis wrote in 1871, "We rushed in and shot all we saw. We then plundered and burnt everything, destroying all else we could. We then sat down and had a smoke."[36]

Although he was marginally the most powerful among other Fiji chiefs, caucasians appointed Chief Cakobau of Bau king of Fiji on June 5, 1871. White traders and plantation owners needed personal safety, security of land tenure, and legal armed force to end the frequent tribal wars. The editor of the *Fiji Times* wrote six weeks after the proclamation, "In all other respects the Europeans will rule: the power of education and civilisation must come to the front, and if the prominent figure be a native, whether in the form of a king or a president, it is only a puppet, the strings of which are pulled by a white man."[37] Honorary British consul John Bates Thurston (1836–97) was instrumental in getting whites and chiefs to agree to a constitutional monarchy. In return for £800 per annum and the lieutenant governorship of Lau, Ma'afu, the Tongan ruler of much of eastern Tonga, supported the nomination.[38]

Cakobau's cabinet consisted of whites. On August 1, 1871, Fiji's House of Representatives met for the first time and set up agencies of governance and public service. This supposedly democratic body was instituted to further the economic interests of non–Fijians. Cakobau's first premier, Sydney Charles Burt (d. 1905), was, in the words of Philip Snow, "an absconding bankrupt Australian auctioneer."[39] Not surprisingly, the new government quickly accumulated an unmanageable debt, left largely to be repaid by Fijians. The legislature established a postal system, ordered the printing of currency, wrote bank regulations, and set up a committee to sort out land claims.

Nevertheless, the unpopular regime could do little to bring law and order to the island nation. Cakobau spoke in March 1872 to about sixty whites in Levuka's town square: "We Fijians understand revenge

Ratu Epenisa Seru Cakobau became chief of the powerful island of Bau in 1852 and was recognized as king of the Fiji Islands in 1871. The United States menaced Cakobau, demanding money for losses real and invented. Cakobau surrendered his kingdom to Britain in October 1874 and lived on a British pension until his own death in 1883. The painting by P. Spence is from a photograph by the studio of Francis Herbert Dufty II and William Buchanan Dufty in Levuka, Fiji.

and the law of the club. You white people said such things were cruel and savage. You brought us civilization, and you brought us law ... [but] When a native does wrong, there is no rest until he is punished, yet three natives have been killed lately and nothing has been done.... Perhaps you think laws are to protect one race only."[40]

Tribal chiefs continued to oppose one another in lethal confrontations, and to threaten Cakobau's throne as well. Meanwhile, as historian I.C. Campbell stated: "The Cakobau government staggered impotently from crisis to crisis in a climate of no-confidence on a path of near-bankruptcy and increasing racial violence."[41]

THE SWEET INDUSTRY

The sugar industry was started in Fiji in 1872, when the firm Brewer and Joske planted 260 hectares (640 acres) of cane and erected a mill. The industry came to be dominated by big Australian corporations such as Colonial Sugar Refining Company, which controlled production from 1881 to 1973. Colonial Sugar Refining by 1900 produced all but twelve and a half percent of the unrefined sugar in Fiji. The company brought in 65 percent of Fiji's export income.[42]

Queen Victoria Accepts

On March 21, 1874, Cakobau had once again offered Fiji to Queen Victoria. The British accepted this time because authorities sought to end blackbirding and to protect Fijians from Europeans and to protect investments. On September 23, the future governor, Sir Hercules Robinson (1824–97), arrived aboard HMS *Dido* and greeted Cakobau with a twenty-one-gun salute, designated to honor royalty. Cakobau signed the deed of session on September 30, and then sailed around the islands aboard HMS *Pearl* to obtain the signatures of other chiefs.[43] At last, on October 10, 1874, Britain annexed Fiji and pensioned King Cakobau with a magnificent £1,500 per annum. Cakobau agreed to renounce his title of Tui Viti. Cakobau, Ma'afu and several senior chiefs signed two copies of the Deed of Cession.[44]

Disease and Death

The following year catastrophe struck. In 1875 retired King Cakabau and two of his sons had visited Australia and returned in January 1875 aboard HMS *Dido*. One royal son and several crewmembers disembarked, having been stricken with measles. The steamer *Wentworth* arrived about the same time from Sydney, again with measles aboard. No official would accept the responsibility to quarantine the former king and his sons, and the disease spread. The epidemic killed an estimated 40,000 people out of 150,000. Some people in the hills concluded that their old gods were punishing them for accepting Christianity, and reverted to paganism. The chief medical officer, Sir William McGregor, estimated that indigenous Fijian mortality in 1875 was 540 per thousand, compared to immigrant Indian mortality of 20 per thousand.[45]

Some 62,000 Melanesians came to Fiji to work in the sugar fields. Between 1877 and 1911, when indentures ended, approximately 23,000 died of dysentery. Many of those that survived died later of tuberculosis. Most who survived those illnesses, eventually returned home.[46]

Governor Gordon

On September 1, 1875, Sir Arthur Charles Hamilton-Gordon (1829–1912; term 1875–80), later first baron Stanmore, arrived to take up his duties as second governor of Fiji. Gordon worked to end blackbirding. Melanesians were repatriated to New Hebrides and the Solomon Islands. He tried to end human sacrifice, cannibalism, and warfare. Gordon protected the rights of chiefs. He promised to protect Fijian rights to lands; ten percent of the land was already owned by foreigners, but he was able to help Fijians retain eighty-two percent. Fijians could not be forced to work on plantations owned by Europeans.[47]

On August 13, 1877, the Colonial Office established the office of High Commissioner for the Western Pacific. The commissioner had jurisdiction over British subjects and affairs in the New Hebrides, Pitcairn Island, the Cook Islands, Niue (to 1901), the Union Islands—or Tokelau (to 1926), the Phoenix Islands (to 1939), Tonga (to 1952), Gilbert and Ellice Islands (to 1971) and the Solomons Islands (to 1974).[48]

INDENTURED INDIANS ARRIVE

On May 14, 1879, the ship *Leonidas,* sailing from Calcutta, brought the first group of 481 indentured Indian workers to Fiji.[49] Fijians did not need or want to do the work, and labor recruiting from Melanesian islands was strictly controlled by colonial officials. Fiji's second governor, Arthur Gordon, had been governor of Trinidad and of Mauritius; Indians had been found to be productive and cost effective working in plantations on both islands, and Gordon recommended they be brought to Fiji on five-year contracts. The name for the contract was *girmit,* a Hindu pronunciation of agreement. Most of the Indians were from Uttar Pradesh, Bihar and Madras. Eighty-five percent were Hindu and fifteen percent Muslims.

By 1884 more Indian indentured workers arrived aboard eighty-seven ships; they were guaranteed assisted repatriation after ten years, or they could return to India after five years at their own expense. Many worked in the sugar fields fifty hours a week for no more than a shilling a day. Indians later brought wives, and their population grew. The number of Indians in Fiji had risen by 1901 to 17,105, or 14.2 percent of the population. Fijian numbers had declined to 94,397 from 105,800 a decade earlier.[50]

Indians by 1911 numbered 40,286. Fijians numbered 87,096, a decrease of 7,200 in a decade. In 1911, Indians constituted 28.87 percent of the population and Fijians 62.42 percent. In 1912, about sixty percent of Indians who had come to Fiji from India since 1879 elected to remain in the islands. Between 1888 and 1912, some 12,000 were returned at no cost to themselves after ten years of work. They brought back to India a reported £62,073 in money and another £117,962 in jewelry and other items.[51]

SUVA AS ADMINISTRATIVE CENTER

Because Fiji's principal town — Levuka — had little room to grow, colonial authorities moved the administrative center to Viti Levu. On August 30, 1882, the ship *Ocean Queen* took the governor and other colonial officials to the new capital, Suva. According to the *Fiji Times,* an eighth of Suva's site was "fetid and pestiferous mangrove swamps."[52] Suva has remained Fiji's capital.

MELANESIANS DEPART

In 1911, Melanesian contract laborer traffic ended in Fiji. Melanesians had been replaced by Indians.[53] Most Melanesians who were not carried off by dysentery or tuberculosis returned to their home islands, and the few who remained blended into Fijian society.[54]

With their numbers in obvious decline, native Fijians realized they were sharing their island with more worldly Indians, whose numbers were obviously in the ascendant. Indians would eventually count for half of Fiji's population, would come to dominate much the colony's business and professions, and would contest indigenous Fijians for political control.

Chapter 17

Maoris Marginalized,
1840–1914

SETTLERS V. WARRIORS

Both British and Maori hoped in the early 1840s that the Treaty of Waitangi of February 6, 1840, would solve the problem of allocation of land between their people. It did not. Pakeha encroachments on Maori land would lead to a series of wars.

Optimistically, on November 1, 1841, London declared that New Zealand was to be governed as a separate colony and was no longer under the jurisdiction of New South Wales.

Over the next twenty years more settlers arrived seeking land, and Maoris fought to retain land. On February 5, 1842, the *Whitby*, with a small advance company under direction of Arthur Wakefield, brother of colony promoter Edward Gibbon Wakefield, arrived to survey the north shore of South Island. Wakefield selected a site on Tasman Bay, South Island, to establish a city. Thirteen months later, 500 immigrants were living in the new city named for the hero of the Battle of Trafalgar in 1805, Lord Horatio Nelson (1758–1805).

On May 30, 1842, Anglican bishop George Augustus Selwyn (1809–78) arrived at Auckland to establish a New Zealand diocese. Selwyn appointed clergy to serve in Wellington, Nelson, and New Plymouth and made plans to convert Maoris to Christianity. Having been tutored by a Maori aboard ship, he began preaching in the Maroi tongue. Selwyn served as bishop of New Zealand from 1841 to 1858, and primate of New Zealand from 1858 to 1868.[2]

The Treaty of Waitangi convinced the British that they had gained a colony, but did little to convince Maoris that land issues were finally settled. Maoris resented settlers spreading out from Nelson across the Richmond Range and taking land in the fertile Wairu Valley. On June 17, 1843, settlers and Maoris of the Ngati Toa tribe clashed. When Maoris pulled up survey stakes, a local magistrate wrote out an arrest warrant for their leaders, Te Rauparaha and his son-in-law, Te Rangihaeata (1805?–1855). A settler shot and killed Te Rangihaeata's wife, the daughter of Te Rangaraha. Maoris massacred twenty-two settlers at Wairau. Five Maoris were killed. Twenty-seven settlers retreated to Nelson. Governor Robert Fitzroy (1805–65, term 1843–45) refused to allow reprisals. This was the only major war on South Island between settlers and Maoris, but would be followed by wars on North Island.[3]

Sheep grazing resulted in massive losses of Maori land. In 1843 Charles Robert Bidwell (1820–84) brought 400 sheep from New South Wales and landed them at Wellington. Although a hundred sheep were present as early as 1834, Bidwell's flock was the real beginning of New Zealand's thriving sheep industry. By 1871, an estimated ten million sheep dotted the landscape, requiring vast amounts of land.[4]

SHOWDOWN AT KORORAREKA

Ships that visited New Zealand normally came to the Bay of Islands. Kororareka had been New Zealand's largest white settlement, and was known as the "Hell Hole of the Pacific" because of riotous whale ship crews on shore leave. Governor William Hobson renamed it Russell in honor of the secretary of state for the colonies, Lord John Russell (1792–1878).

The next war began when on July 8, 1844, Maori chief Hone (also Honi) Heke (1807?– 50) made a profound statement about sovereignty by chopping down the flagpole from which the union jack fluttered at Russell. Hone Heke had several festering grievances: When the British laid tariffs and port charges at Bay of Islands, fewer ships came, which meant far fewer trades and less income for Maoris from agricultural products, timber, and flax. Instead, American whalers and traders obtained wood and water in Hobart Town, Lahaina, or Honolulu.[5] The chief also resented the fact that if Maoris wanted to sell land, they had to do so through the government, often for less than they might have been paid had they negotiated the sale themselves. Hone Heke was reacting against these regulations as much as against his own perceived loss of *mana* and his tribe's loss of sovereignty.

The flagpole was reerected. On January 10, 1845, Hone Heke cut it down again. Governor Robert Fitzroy (1805–65; term 1843–45), formerly captain of Charles Darwin's *Beagle*, offered a £100 reward for the chief. Hone Heke posted an award in the same amount for the head of the governor.[6] On March 10, 1845, Hone Heke, leading 600 warriors, attacked 250 defenders at Russell. During the fighting a powder magazine exploded and ignited several buildings. Flames traveled through the streets and the town was virtually destroyed. Maoris killed thirteen defenders.[7]

On January 10, 1846, some 1,100 white and Maori troops assaulted Hone Heke's *pa* at Raupekapeka on North Island. The attackers lost forty men and took the fortress, ending the war. During the war, British officers came to respect the strong earth fortifications dug to protect Maori *pas*; in fact, some military historians believe that admiration for Maori defenses led the British army to construct underground defenses in the Crimean War less than a decade later, and then trenches on the Western Front in World War I. Hone Heke got away, and died four years later.[8]

WAR AT HUTT RIVER AND WANGHANUI

In 1846 British army units engaged the Ngati Toa tribe, led by Te Rangihaeata, over land claims in the Hutt River Valley near Wellington. The Ngati Toa sought refuge by escaping toward the north.

On April 18, 1847, a British sailor killed a Maori, and his action set off a brief war on the west coast of North Island. Maori chief Topine Te Mamaku (1790?–1887) attacked the settler town of Wanganui. Wanganui had been founded in 1841 and, isolated, had no more than 200 Europeans. Governor George Grey (1812–98) sued for peace. The truce lasted twelve years.[9]

SCOTS FOUND DUNEDIN

On March 23, 1848, the ship *John Wycliffe*, sailing from Gravesend, England, arrived at Port Chalmers on South Island, bringing ninety-seven passengers. These settlers founded the city of Dunedin. Dunedin and the Otago Peninsula were settled by members of the Scottish Free Church Association. The *John Wycliffe* was under command of Captain William Cargill (1784–1860), who became the community's leader. The next ship, *Philip Laing*, arrived on April 15, carrying 247 passengers from Greenock, Scotland; the leader of its 239 settlers was Reverend Thomas Burns (1796–1871), nephew of poet Robert Burns. They named their city Dunedin from the Scottish name for Edinburgh, Dun Eideann or Eden on a Hill.[10]

Failure of Wakefield's Company

On July 4, 1850, the New Zealand Company, founded by Edward Gibbon Wakefield, declared it was unable to pay £268,000 it owed to creditors. The debt, later reduced to £200,000, was imposed on New Zealand colonists and finally satisfied in 1856 by proceeds from the sale of a public bond. The company surrendered 1,092,000 acres to the government. The problem lay in Edward Gibbon Wakefield's initial business plan, which envisioned buying land cheaply from Maoris and selling it at a "sufficient" price to well-to-do British émigrés. That part of the profit not going to stockholders would be devoted to financing transportation for indigent workers. Many indigent people envisioned a better life in New Zealand and were willing to have their passage subsidized, but the more comfortable classes remained at home. Finally, in May 1858 the company was dissolved. It had been responsible for founding several cities and towns.[11]

Christchurch Founded

Four shiploads of passengers arrived December 16, 1850, at Lyttleton, South Island, to found the city of Christchurch. The four ships were *Randolph, Cressy, Sir George Seynour* and the *Charlotte-Jane*. John Robert Godley (1814–61) wanted to create a planned city for adherents of the Church of England, and to make it an approximation of an English town in the South Seas. Godley set up the Canterbury Association. Among its members were two archbishops, seven bishops, fourteen peers and sixteen members of Parliament. Migrants were carefully selected and required to furnish a certificate from their vicar vouching that the applicant was "sober, industrious and honest," and that "he and all his family are amongst the most respectable in the parish." By 1855, thirty-five hundred migrants had arrived. The new city was laid out on a grid pattern. No building was to be higher than the Anglican cathedral, which dominated the center — until February 22, 2011, when it was toppled by an earthquake.[12]

Democracy Begins

On June 30, 1852, the New Zealand Constitution Act gave British males twenty-one or older the vote if they owned property valued at fifty pounds, or leased or rented property at ten pounds per annum or more. Maori males were granted the same right. Only about 100 out of 5,849 eligible males qualified, because most Maori land was owned communally. According to the constitution, New Zealand was divided into six provinces or separate colonies. An appointed governor and a nominated council and an elected house of representatives controlled each colony. The London Colonial Office regulated Maori affairs. New Zealand would not be a united colony until 1875.[13]

HAU HAU AND THE KING MOVEMENT

In December 1854, North Island Maoris proclaimed the Hau Hau Movement. Hau Hau was a spiritual and political movement that blended Maori traditional beliefs with Christianity. Belief centered on the angel Gabriel. Adherents believed they would not be harmed by bullets and set out to exterminate all whites. Some pagan customs, including cannibalism, were practiced. Missionaries despaired that their work was being perverted. By 1870 the rebellion had been largely suppressed.

Frustrated over extensive land alienation, in 1856 North Island Maori chiefs met at Pukawa, Lake Taupo, and voted against selling any more land in a specified wide area of North Island to the white government or to individual *pakeha*.[14] Then in April 1857, at Pukawa, paramount chiefs selected Potatau Te Wherowhero (1800?–1860) of the Waikato tribe for the entirely new honor of Maori king. Leaders of twenty-three North Island tribes pledged allegiance to King Potatau I. Members of the movement, known as Kingitanga, hoped that their symbolic monarch would have the regal authority to deal with Queen Victoria on a basis of equality. Potatau I claimed to be in a line of descent from all canoes, or founding Maori settlers. The Foreign Office in London urged New Zealand authorities not to recognize Potatau as king, because by the Treaty of Waitangi Maoris had relinquished sovereignty to the Crown and therefore could not have their own king.[15]

GOLD!

On May 20, 1861, Gabriel Read (1824–94), an Australian who had prospected in California and Victoria, found gold on the banks of the Tuapeka River near Lawrence, west of the new city of Dunedin. News of riches to be picked out of a stream soon spread and by 1864, ten thousand argonauts had arrived. Dunedin became a miners' service center with assay offices, saloons, brothels, gambling dens, and boarding houses. Dunedin became for a short period the most populous city in New Zealand. Smaller gold strikes followed and as a result, for the rest of the century South Island could boast a larger population than North Island. Miners enriched Dunedin, which soon boasted New Zealand's first university and medical school, first electric trams, first cable car outside San Francisco, and the country's first daily newspaper. By the 1880s gold was less economical to mine and the rush subsided.[16]

WAR AND MAORI POPULATION DECLINE

After a decade of relative peace, on March 17, 1860, a war broke out between the British army and Maori at Northern Taranaki, near New Plymouth. Members of the Te Atiawa tribe refused to sell a block of land to the crown, and under the leadership of Wiremu Kingi built a *pa*. Soldiers fired on the *pa*. A truce was signed at Te Arei Pa in 1861. Nevertheless, fighting would continue on North island during much of the decade.[17]

On July 12, 1863, General Duncan Cameron (1808–88) led his troops across the Mangatawhiri River into the Waikato region, the domain of Maatutaera, Maori king since 1860 when his father King Potatau I had died. Fifteen of North Island's twenty-seven tribes participated in the defense of King Country against as many as 12,000 Pakeha troops. The British achieved a final victory at Orakau ("Rewi's Last Stand"), and the Maoris fled into the bush. The Waikato War was substantially over by April 5, 1864. Maoris lost good land as a result of the invasion, and were relegated to less productive land.

In 1872 Maori Chief Te Kooti (1832–91?) of the Ngati Maru finally accepted a truce, bringing an end to the long war. Chief Te Kooti had escaped from the Chatham Islands in 1869 and led a series of raids in central North Island. The truce marked an end not only of significant fighting, but to any real Maori hope of stemming the advance of white settlers. By 1872 Europeans numbered a quarter million, and Maoris were only one fifth of the population. According to historian Ernest S. Dodge, the "catastrophic" defeat left them "dispirited, debt-ridden, drunken, and landless." Depopulation followed demoralization.[18]

Maoris Lose More Land

In December 1863, the New Zealand Settlements Act authorized Governor George Grey (1812–98; terms 1841–45; 1845–54) to take land for *pakeha* settlement from vanquished tribes. In the Waikato area, the government took 480,000 hectares (1,202,172 acres), and in Taranaki, 510,000 hectares (1,275,000 acres). Tribes in Tauranga lost 116,000 hectares (290,000 acres), and in Bay of Plenty, 180,000 acres (448,000 hectares).[19]

On October 30, 1865, New Zealand authorities established a native land court. The court investigated and made judgments on land titles. Maori communal lands were assigned to individuals. This development facilitated the sale of Maori lands to whites and the alienation of even more lands.

On October 2, 1873, New Zealand's parliament passed the Native Land Act. Drafted by Native and Defense Minister Donald McLean (1820–76), the law mandated that all owners of Maori land must agree before the land could be alienated. Prior to 1873, ten owners were listed on the title deed. Written to prevent Maoris from losing their land, the law led instead to further sales; an individual could sell his interest in the land without obtaining the permission of other title deed holders.[20]

In 1877, the Ngati Toa tribe sued in the Supreme Court for the return of land that had been issued to the bishop of Wellington but not used. Chief Justice Sir James Prendergast (1826–1921) wrote that the Treaty of Waitangi (1840), which set parameters for alienation of native lands, was "a simple nullity." Judge Prendergast argued that Maoris had not constituted a body politic and were incapable of entering into a treaty obligation. He labeled Maoris "primitive barbarians." The judgment had minimal effect because the government had not regularly complied with the strictures or spirit of the treaty.[21]

Maori Representation

On October 10, 1867, the Maori Representation Act became law. All Maori males age twenty-one and over could vote for four representatives out of a total of seventy in the New Zealand Parliament. Although some conservatives opposed votes for Maoris, others saw an advantage in *pakeha* candidates not having to address Maori concerns when contesting for seats. New Zealand thus became the first colonial nation to allow indigenous males to vote before all European males and before any females were enfranchised. After July 26, 1865, parliament met in Wellington. The capital had been moved from Auckland, largely because of Maori threats in the north. According to the Qualifications of Electors Act, 1879, all males, twenty-one or older, who were British subjects, resident in New Zealand for twelve months, were granted the vote.[22]

SUBSIDIZING IMMIGRANTS

At the urging of treasurer Julius Vogel (1835–99; P.M. 1873–75, 1876), New Zealand borrowed ten million pounds in 1870 from the Bank of England for public improvements. The loan, used to build roads, railways, and communications, was a measure to create jobs during an economic downturn brought on by the end of the South Island gold rush and by the ongoing Maori land wars on North Island. Over

"Maori." This handsome New Zealander was drawn in 1827 near Whangarei by Louis Auguste de Sainson on Dumont d'Urville's visit aboard *l'Astrolabe*. The picture appears in Dumont d'Urville's *Voyage de la Corvette l'Astrolabe* (Paris: J. Tasto, 1830). Note the lack of tattooing on the young man's face.

the decade the government borrowed twenty-two million pounds.[23] Loans enabled the government to subsidize the passage of 32,118 immigrants who arrived in New Zealand during 1874. It was the largest number of arrivals in any single year. In all, the government would subsidize the migration of some 350,000 people. The Immigration Restriction Act of 1899 stipulated that immigrants who were not British and who were unable to complete an application form in a European language would not be admitted as permanent residents.[24]

The application form was one further impediment to the entry of Asians. Chinese had come to work in the South Island gold fields, and an estimated 4,000 were in the colony in 1876, most in Otago province. An act passed by New Zealand's legislature in 1881 prohibited most residents of the Celestial Empire from entering the islands.[25] According to the legislation, one Chinese immigrant was allowed for every ten tons of his transporting vessel's weight, as well as payment of a "poll tax" of ten pounds. By 1896 the entry of Chinese was virtually prohibited when only one Chinese could arrive on a ship for every 200 tons of the vessel's weight plus a poll tax of one hundred pounds.[26]

BIRTH OF A MODERN COLONY

On November 1, 1875, six provincial governments were abolished and New Zealand was administered as a single colony.

From December 1876, the colony was connected with Sydney and London by cable. An undersea telegraph cable was completed by Eastern Extension, China and Australasia Telegraph Company, between Australia and New Zealand. The cable, between Sydney and Wakapauka, a suburb of Nelson on Tasman Bay, South Island, was some 1,900 kilometers (1,200 miles) long and linked New Zealand indirectly through Australia to London and much of the rest of the world.[27]

Meat and Dairy Exports

From the 1880s onward the sheep industry became central to the economy. On February 15, 1882, the 1455-ton *Dunedin* left Port Chalmers near Dunedin, New Zealand, and for the first time brought refrigerated mutton and dairy products to Britain. Entrepreneur William Sotau Davidson (1846–1924) had commissioned the fitting of the *Dunedin* with a compression refrigeration unit. The steam-powered Bell-Coleman unit required three tons of coal a day and kept food 40 degrees below air temperature. Aboard were 3,350 mutton carcasses, 490 lamb carcasses, pigs, hams, turkeys, rabbits and 245 kegs of butter — all preserved in a freezing chamber.

The vessel arrived in three and half months, but not without problems: sparks from the refrigeration machinery set fire to sails, and the captain nearly froze to death while repairing the freezer air duct. Nevertheless, the meat arrived safely, and as a direct result, sheep in New Zealand were raised for meat as well as wool. In the next five years, 172 shipments were sent to Britain. Shipments of frozen food proved to be quite profitable and led to the increase of small dairy farming. Until 1973, when it joined the European Union, Britain would be New Zealand's primary customer.[28]

The Liberal Party Takes Control

The parliamentary election of 1890 in New Zealand brought John Ballance (1839–93; P.M. 1891–93) to office on December 5, 1890, and ushered in two decades of Liberal Party government. Beginning May 1, 1893, English–born Richard Seddon (1827–1906) commenced New Zealand's longest lasting tenure as prime minister, holding office from 1893 to 1906. Reform legislation was passed during his terms that put the colony at the forefront of progressivism. These reforms included stringent factory laws, a progressive income tax, pensions for aged poor, industrial arbitration, and the eight-hour day for workers. The Seddon administration also oversaw a growth of trade unionism. A principal reason Seddon was elected as a reformer is that the price of wool and grain had dropped; New Zealanders were dependent on income from these commodities and a depression ensued.[29]

The New Zealand Electoral Act, which came into effect on September 19, 1893, was the most celebrated of the liberal legislation. On that day New Zealand became the first nation to grant women the right to vote. A quarter of the females twenty-one and over — 32,000 women — had signed a petition asking for the franchise.[30]

On August 31, 1894, New Zealand mandated a minimum wage, varying by occupation and industry. Wage stipulations were included in the Industrial Conciliation and Arbitration Act. The bill was drawn up by Minister of Labour William Pember Reeves (1857–1932). It was the first national minimum wage legislation in the world. Using arbitration and conciliation courts, New Zealand suffered no strikes for eleven years, while wages and workers' living conditions improved.[31]

On November 1, 1898, an act to offer pensions to white citizens 65 or over, sponsored by Seddon, was approved in parliament. If an applicant qualified by having a low income and low property accumulation, and if he or she had resided in New Zealand for twenty-five years, the applicant could collect a pension of eighteen pounds per annum. Asians, Maoris, and aliens were excluded.[32]

AIDING THE MOTHER COUNTRY

After only two weeks' training, the first New Zealand contingent sailed on October 21, 1899, on the *Waiwera* for South Africa. They would participate with other imperial forces in the Boer War (1899–1902). Participation in an imperial war against an array of ethnic Dutch farmers to wrest away precious minerals on a distant continent was not something New Zealand soldiers had to do; the remote islands could have remained neutral. However, as historian Michael King wrote: "Patriots were keen to show their mettle in a scrap; they wanted to demonstrate the country's unswerving loyalty to Mother Britain." Nine more contingents sailed to South Africa, a total of over 6,400 men. When Maoris offered to form a contingent, they were dissuaded by the argument that "blacks should not be employed against whites." New Zealanders counted 59 killed in action, 160 from other causes.[33]

THE MARGINALIZED MAORIS

By the end of the nineteenth century, through disease and warfare, New Zealand's Maori population had fallen to an estimated 40,000, its lowest point in historic times.[34] When chiefs signed the Treaty of Waitangi, Europeans sought to carve out a place in a Maori world. By 1914, except for those few who had availed themselves of Western education, Maoris had been pushed to the outer margin in a land dominated by *pakehas*.

Chapter 18

Holding Out: New Hebrides, the Solomons and New Guinea, 1767–1914

CHARTING DARK ISLANDS

Melanesia and New Guinea were saved from the detrimental effects of Western contact until the last half of the nineteenth century. Their multiple languages, cannibalistic fierceness, dense jungles, torrential downpours, enervating humidity, and their ally — the malarial mosquito — held off interlopers for decades. By the mid–1880s whites were able to penetrate some coastal areas. Three factors were helpful in establishing settlements. Whites used firearms to neutralize resistance. Melanesians and Papuans became increasingly desirous of obtaining manufactured goods and tolerated intruders. Scientists found the cause of malaria and increased the production of quinine. All these islands would be claimed by a European power by the early twentieth century.

Portuguese traders had skirted and named New Guinea in 1545. In 1568 Mendaña had visited large, long islands that Spaniards named the Solomons. More extensive charting of Melanesia and New Guinea was conducted in the eighteenth century. On August 12, 1767, six weeks after discovering Pitcairn Island, and desperate for a landfall to repair the leaking *Swallow* and to find fresh food for his scurvy-wracked crew, Captain Philip Carteret came upon the Santa Cruz Islands. One hundred and seventy-two years earlier, Mendaña's crew had attempted to found a colony there. Carteret named them the Queen Charlotte Islands in honor of King George III's wife. He described the "Indians" in his journal as being black with "wooly" hair and naked, while the jungle appeared to be impenetrable. When Carteret sent a watering party ashore, islanders attacked them by shooting arrows, killing crewmembers. The British shot islanders. The British left because, as Carteret stated, "like Heroick defenders of their country the islanders boldly pursued the invaders of their property, as far into the water as they could wade, the boat having got clear of those was pursued by the Canoes, but after a few shots they return'd to the shore."[2]

Melanesians such as those who chased off Carteret fought as a matter of custom. They battled against neighboring tribes to retaliate for a wrong, as a form of competition, and even to elevate status. Because all deaths, diseases, or misfortunes were thought to be caused by sorcery, accusations of sorcery could start a war. Combat enhanced and confirmed masculinity. The war might last for only a few hours while opponents went through elaborate gyrations to frighten tribal enemies. Casualties were light before the arrival of European technology. The war might end as soon as the first wound was inflicted, and certainly if a

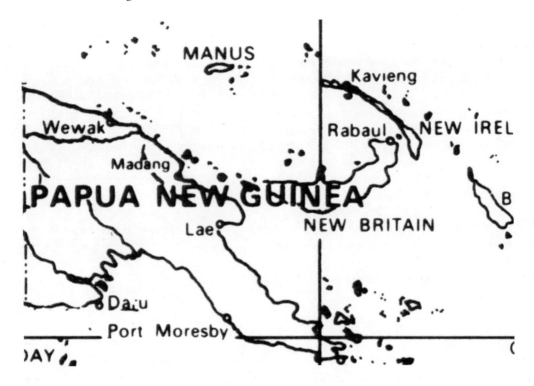

Map of Papua New Guinea. By permission of the Office of Planning, State of Hawaii.

tribal leader were killed. That wound or death would be avenged, but sometimes only years later. Melanesians had to remain vigilant. A man defeated might be enslaved. Being a slave in a cannibal tribe was an outcome to be avoided at all costs.

On August 26, 1767, Carteret brought his badly leaking ship *Swallow* to anchor at New Ireland in the Bismarck Archipelago. Tribal groups on the 8,650-square-kilometer (3,374-square-mile) island spoke twenty languages and forty-five dialects and sub-dialects. Carteret was able to take on some food and water. He and his crew sailed around the island to prove that, contrary to the report of Schouten and Le Maire a century and a half earlier, New Ireland is separate from New Britain.

Still desperate to repair *Swallow*'s worm-infested hull and to take on sufficient food and water to get home, Carteret pressed on, coming to Batavia in May 1768. Finally, thirty-one months after setting out with Wallis's *Dolphin, Swallow* anchored in the Thames. Carteret's greatest achievement had been to circumnavigate the globe in a vessel that should never have left port.[3]

On May 22, 1768, Louis-Antoine de Bougainville and his crew were the first Europeans since Quirós to report seeing the New Hebrides. He named them Les Grandes Cyclades, evoking the name of an island group in Greece. Encountering hostile islanders when he landed on Ambae (a.k.a. Aoba), the French shot a few men and gathered fruit and firewood. Bougainville mistook tattoo markings on the people for leprosy, and named the place Ambae, or Lepers' Island.[4] Ambae is 405 square kilometers (158 square miles) and is crowned by an active volcano 1,500 meters (4,920 feet) high.

On July 2, 1768, Bougainville and his crew sailed between two of the Solomons: Choiseul, where landing was thwarted by hostile islanders, and Bougainville Island, named for the navigator. The strait that separates the two is also named for him.[5] Bougainville Island is 200 kilometers (125 miles) long. Its highest peak, Mount Balbi, is an active volcano; it erupted between 1972 and 1993. Nearly joined to Bougainville Island is the smaller (492 square kilometers; 190 square miles) island he named Buka because people in canoes answered "*buka*" when asked the name of their home. "*Buka*," in the indigenous language, is the question who or what, as in "Who or what are these weird-looking creatures?"

On July 6, en route home on his circumnavigation, Bougainville stopped at a place he named Port Praslin on New Ireland. There they found Carteret's camp, abandoned eleven months earlier. Bougainville claimed New Ireland for his king and departed on July 24, 1768.[6]

On August 5, 1774, in need of fresh food and water, Cook anchored *Adventure* and *Resolution* on 212-square-mile (550-square-kilometer) Tanna Island in the archipelago he named New Hebrides. The crews were the first white people to arrive there. Unable to converse in any one of the five languages of the Tanna islanders, Cook and his crew had difficulty trading. In fact, "some [islanders] more daring than the others were for carrying off every thing they could lay their hands upon," Cook wrote.[7] Musket shots fired over their heads served to disperse the thieves.

SOLVING THE LA PÉROUSE DISAPPEARANCE

One of the great Pacific puzzles was the fate of the La Perouse expedition. On August 1, 1785, on orders from King Louis XVI (1754–93; r. 1774–91), Jean-François de Galaup, compte de la Pérouse (1741–88?) set off from Brest, France, to complete Cook's unfinished mapping of the Pacific. He was also to recommend trade and whaling opportunities for France, and to pursue scientific investigations. Among the 220 men aboard *Astrolabe* and *La Boussoule* were ten scientists and illustrators.[8]

An ambitious and energetic Corsican lad named Napoleon Bonaparte (1769–1821) had offered to use his precocious mathematical ability to further La Pérouse's objectives. For unknown reasons, La Pérouse rejected the application of the sixteen-year-old to sail with him. Turned down, young Bonaparte became an army officer. Had he vanished in the Pacific with La Pérouse, Europe might have been spared sixteen years of brutal warfare and hundreds of thousands of deaths.[9]

La Pérouse visited Easter Island on April 6, 1786, and then sailed to Maui. He investigated the west coast of North America from Alaska to California, sold furs in Macau, went to Manila and to Sakhalin Island, and explored the Kuriles. At the Russian settlement of Petropavlovsk on the Kamchatka Peninsula, Barthélemy de Lesseps (1768–1834) disembarked from the expedition, and La Pérouse sent reports home with him. De Lesseps saved his own life by returning to Paris and was the sole survivor of the *Astrolabe* and *La Boussoule*.[10] De Lesseps' nephew, Ferdinand, would be responsible for construction of the Suez Canal.

On January 24, 1788, the prisoners and troops of the First Fleet, having arrived at the opposite side of the globe less than a week before, were astonished when La Pérouse's *La Boussoule* and *Astrolabe* appeared at Botany Bay. One of the count's orders from Paris was to ascertain if the British were actually establishing a colony in New South Wales. As 1788 was one of those exceptional years when Britain and France were at peace, Governor Phillip magnanimously offered the French any help at all — except food, stores, sails, ammunition, or any item La Pérouse might actually need. Following their cordial meeting La Pérouse sailed on, but not before sending letters and reports back to France on a British vessel.[11] No European saw the two ships or the expedition members again.

In May 1793 Antoine de Bruni d'Entrecasteaux (1737–93) came close to discovering the fate of La Pérouse. He was in command of *Recherche*, while Jean-Michel Huon de Kermadec (1748–92) commanded *Esperance*. On a French exploring expedition, which was also charged with finding and rescuing La Pérouse, they arrived in May at Vanikoro in the Santa Cruz Islands. They saw smoke but failed to investigate because they were unable to get through the surrounding reefs. After that, the expedition underwent trying experiences. Huon de Kermadec died and was buried in New Caledonia. D'Entrecasteaux died of scurvy en route back to France. When his successor as expedition commander learned that France had fallen under control of the radical Convention during the ongoing French Revolution, he handed over his ships to the Dutch in Batavia. D'Entrecasteaux's thirty-nine carefully plotted charts of Pacific islands were later published and used by mariners.[12]

It was not until May 13, 1826, that Irish–born trader Peter Dillon solved the La Pérouse mystery. In 1813 Dillon had survived a massacre in Fiji while supervising the cutting of sandalwood. He agreed to take another survivor, the Prussian Martin Bushart, to his next landfall, which happened to be Tikopia, in the Santa Cruz Islands. Thirteen years later Dillon stopped again at Tikopia and encountered Bushart, who had remained there with his Fijian wife. Bushart and a lascar (Indian seaman) named Achowlia showed Dillon a sword hilt and other French–produced artifacts thought to be from the *Astrolabe* and *La Boussoule*. Tikopians, they explained, had brought the artifacts from nearby Vanikoro.

Dillon sailed away and sent the news to Europe from Bengal. On his return to Europe he was invited to Paris. De Lesseps, the survivor, provided positive identification of the objects as having been taken from La Pérouse's ships. French officials introduced Dillon to King Charles X (1757–1836; r. 1824–30). Charles created him a chevalier of the Legion of Honor, reimbursed his travel expenses, and gave him a pension of 40,000 francs for life. In 1828 Dumont d'Urville found other items on Vanikoro from the La Pérouse expedition; islanders told him the two ships had been wrecked on the reef and the crews killed and—presumably—eaten.[13]

THE RISKY SANDALWOOD BUSINESS

Traders came to the New Hebrides first for sandalwood. The problem was in getting it. Dorothy Shineberg, chronicler of the sandalwood trade, wrote: "Sandalwood traders pioneered this area, mapping the coasts, noting winds, currents and reefs, in many cases the first Europeans to land on some shores, and certainly the first class of Europeans to appear in numbers and at regular intervals."[14] In 1825 Peter Dillon discovered forests of sandalwood on 688-square-kilometer 265-square-mile) Eromanga. But he and his crew were chased away. Nearly-naked Eromangans were baffled by Europeans. Because of their clothing and hats, Eromangans may have assumed Europeans to be evil spirits with removable pale skins and odd-shaped heads. Eromangans sought to protect ancestral lands by driving these evil spirits away. The islanders could only satisfy themselves that the Europeans were humans when they had killed one or more and inspected their corpses. As a result, although Dillon identified a profitable sandalwood source for future traders, he left with an empty hold and obtained wood in Fiji instead.[15]

On August 10, 1829, the *Sophia* under Captain Samuel P. Henry anchored in Dillon's

Bay, Eromanga. Henry sent 113 Tongans ashore to cut wood. During their twenty-three-day stay, the expendable Tongans warded off attacks by Eromangans, but beyond that were unable to make close contact, even to distribute gifts.[16]

On December 2, 1829, Prince Boki (c.1774–1829), governor of Oahu, left Honolulu commanding two ships and five hundred men. The Hawaiian Islands had been nearly denuded of sandalwood, and Boki was intent on harvesting large amounts to pay Oahu's share of the $48,000 that Americans alleged was owed to their citizens. The *Kamehameha* and its sister ship *Becker* reached Rotuma, now part of Fiji. From there Boki sailed the *Kamehameha* to Eromanga. The *Becker* left ten days later. The *Becker* crew never saw the *Kamehameha* again. A few survivors of the Becker returned to Honolulu on August 30, 1830. They were unable to account for the disappearance of Prince Boki and some 300 others aboard the *Kamehameha*. They described their six-week stay at Eromanga as marked by malaria and hostility.[17] Smaller vessels out of Sydney and Hobart continued to bring Polynesians to cut wood at some of the other islands such as Aneitym and Aniwa. Many were felled by fever.[18]

In September and October 1842, Captain Samuel P. Henry, son of an LMS missionary, brought sixty-seven Tongan workers under command of Christian chief Ma'afu; they filled the holds of two ships. Eromangans learned that by cutting, hauling, and loading wood, they could obtain tools, cloth, tobacco, alcohol, guns and other trade goods without risking their lives by attempting to slaughter crewmen.[19] At the New Hebridean island of Efate, Henry and Ma'afu loaded more sandalwood, but fighting broke out between Efatese and Tongans. The Tongans herded sixty or seventy Efatese into caves and suffocated their victims with smoke.[20]

In 1844, trader James Paddon bought the tiny island of Inyeug off the south coast of Aneityum (also Anatom) Island in the New Hebrides. Paddon paid a rug, axe, and a string of beads for an island that Aneityumese were convinced was haunted by evil spirits. Paddon bought sandalwood and traded with whalers and other vessels. Within the next two decades European trading posts had been established also on Eromanga and Espiritu Santo.[21] Not every transaction between traders and islanders ended in violence. K.R. Howe estimated there had been thirty to forty publicized incidents out of thousands of satisfactory negotiations.[22]

When trades were successfully completed, Iron Age tools replaced crude tools from the Stone Age. Brush could be cleared, trees felled, canoes built, houses erected, land plowed, and enemies slain all the more efficiently. Tribal leaders called *big men*, with access to Western goods, aggrandized their power. Tribesmen who could accumulate pigs or trade goods could rise up to take their place as big men.[23]

SOULS IN NEED OF SAVING

The conversion of Melanesians to Christianity was achieved, where it was achieved at all, several decades after the conversion of Polynesians. Even when quinine was available, malaria was a deterrent to missionaries to stay long enough to convert people. Many islands had several mutually incomprehensible languages, which hindered communication between missionary and Melanesian; Polynesian languages, on the other hand, were often at least vaguely similar, so when a missionary learned one, he could more easily learn another. Unlike Polynesian tribes, Melanesian tribes did not have a hereditary chief whose conversion would lead to the conversion of his community. Melanesians were, with exceptions, more warlike than Polynesians and more wary of inscrutable Westerners. Like Polynesians, though, they coveted fishhooks, metal tools, tobacco, alcohol, cloth, firearms, and other trade goods; only because they did so, and because Christian missionaries were willing to defy death in their determination to make conversions, could they hope to live on these inhospitable islands.

Reverend John Williams of the London Missionary Society went to Eromanga in late 1839. Williams had done much to convert Polynesians and now intended to convert Melanesians. He wrote, "What an extensive field opens as we proceed Westward to the Fijis—New Hebrides, New Caledonia, Solomons Archipelago—with many other isolated Islands scattered thickly over the Pacific ocean so that the Ocean is teeming with hundreds of thousands still who have never heard of the Gospel of Salvation."[24]

Williams was unable to communicate in the language of the Eromangans to tell them of his peaceful intentions. As they waded ashore on November 20, 1839, islanders first killed James Harris, a young man who had trained to be a missionary and who had accompanied Williams. Then two men clubbed Williams and riddled his torso with arrows. They pulverized his body with stones, stripped his corpse, and carried it off into the bush. Stunned, the company aboard the vessel *Camden* sailed to Sydney to report the tragedy.[25] Because of the bellicose culture of these tribesmen, it would have been surprising had Williams not been killed on the beach at Eromanga.

In 1839 LMS missionaries Aaron Buzacott and Charles Pittman established the Takamoa Theological College in Rarotonga to train Polynesian Protestants to proselytize in Melanesia. Between 1839 and 1893, nearly 500 male pupils were educated and encouraged to take their message to the Loyalty Islands, New Guinea, New Hebrides, and other locations.[26]

In 1840 the LMS placed two Samoan workers on Tanna. They were ill with malaria and were reported to be "very uneasy and unhappy and painfully anxious to return to their native land." Two years later the LMS sent missionaries George Turner (1818–91) and Henry Nisbit (1818–76). They arrived June 30, 1842. They made no permanent conversions, and when an epidemic of dysentery arrived in 1843, they were blamed. The two escaped aboard a whaler, arriving in Upolu, Samoa, February 18, 1843. Again in 1845 the LMS sent seven teachers to Tanna, but again they were blamed for an epidemic and after one was killed, escaped on a passing vessel.[27] It would have been surprising if LMS workers had not failed on Tanna as well.

Catholic as well as Protestant missionaries had ambitious plans for converting Melanesians. Catholics were already producing converts in the Loyalties, Isle of Pines, and New Caledonia. Protestants had taken the lead in Tonga, Samoa, New Zealand, and Fiji, but the Solomon Islands—where Mendaña's priests had sought converts nearly three centuries earlier—were wide open. Jean-Baptiste Épalle (1808–45) went to Santa Isabel, a major Solomon Island measuring 4,136 square kilometers (1,600 square miles). Épalle had been accompanied by seven Marist priests and six lay brothers; he had been appointed vicar apostolic and first bishop of Melanesia. December 16, 1845, Épalle, three priests and several sailors went ashore at Astrolabe Harbor. Santa Isabel tribesmen killed a priest and a sailor and slammed an axe five times into the bishop's head. The others fled in terror to the ship. Épalle died three days later. Next, at San Cristobol nine Marists built a house in a malarial area and all became ill. One died and three were murdered. They withdrew in 1847.[28] The Society of Mary waited until 1898, a half century, before returning to the Solomons.

"The Massacre of the Lamented Missionary the Rev. J. Williams and Mr. Harris," by George Baxter. On November 20, 1839, two Eromanga Islanders in the New Hebrides (Vanuatu) clubbed the missionary to death and then pulverized his body with stones. Williams and the mission worker Harris were unable to speak the local language and to make their peaceful intentions known. Even if they had, the xenophobic Melanesians would probably have killed them anyway. The picture was published by the artist in 1841 and is in the National Library of Australia, Canberra.

On December 23, 1847, the Anglican bishop of New Zealand, George A. Selwyn (1809–78), sailed to Melanesia. Selwyn noted an error in his Anglican Church commission; it defined his territory as 34 degrees 30 minutes north rather than south; 34 degrees south is the northern limit of New Zealand, which is what his superiors had intended to be his jurisdiction, while at 34 degrees north is Osaka, Japan. Selwyn decided that the error gave him the authority to convert Melanesians, whose islands lay within the unintended but generous latitudes. The bishop sailed on the *Undine* and later the *Southern Cross*.

Bishop Selwyn thought Melanesians would have a good chance of converting their own people and brought back boys and young men to educate at St. John's College in Auckland, a biracial school. The volunteers learned to read the Bible and to sing Christian music. They were returned within a few months to their islands of origin.[29] In the next decade, 152 graduated at St. John's. Unfortunately, most of the youths came to Auckland for "excitement and material goods" and had little enthusiasm to convert their fellow tribe members on their return.[30]

From 1847 to 1859, Selwyn made eleven voyages to Melanesia. With his colleague Bishop Patteson, Selwyn would eventually visit eighty-one islands, mostly in the New Hebrides and Solomons. His second through eleventh voyages commenced from New Zealand on August 1, 1849; May 1850; July 8, 1851; June 19, 1852; July 1853; November 8, 1853; May 1, 1856; July 22, 1857; April 21, 1858; and August 1859.[31]

Among the most successful at making conversions was John Geddie (1815–72), a Presbyterian missionary from Nova Scotia, who arrived in July 1848 with his wife at Aneitum, the southernmost inhabited island of the New Hebrides. Two Samoan Christian teachers, Simeona and Pita, were already established there but had made no converts. Geddie was helped by the fact there was a single language, Aneityumese, which he finally mastered, for the entire island of 3,500. By the late 1850s Geddie reported "The church members number 297, and the candidates for admission to the church 110. The island is enriched by fifty-six school houses, eleven chapels, and sixty native teachers and assistants."[32]

Before Geddie's arrival Aneityumese had not congregated indoors, but as professed Christians they spent several hours a week together inside a church. Moreover, without fear of enemies lying in wait along paths, islanders traveled among settlements, so if one were infected, others in distant communities would be as well. When in early 1861 a sandalwood trading ship, *Hirondelle*, brought crew members with measles, the disease spread quickly. Over a thousand Aneityumese died. Some islanders burned Geddie's chapel in retaliation. Nevertheless, when the epidemic had passed survivors moved to the coast to be closer to mission headquarters. More disease arrived: influenza and tuberculosis in 1863, diphtheria and whooping cough in the mid–1860s. Three cyclones wrecked homes and plants. People went hungry. When all of these catastrophes had taken their toll, the population of Aneityum had fallen to half that of 1860.[33] To his credit, Geddie was able to limit the use of firearms and alcohol. He directed people to build roads, schools, chapels, and new villages. He tried to put an end to sorcery and even warfare.[34]

A Presbyterian missionary who suffered resolutely for his work was Scottish born Reverend John Gibson Paton (1824–1907). Paton and his wife arrived at Tanna on November 5, 1858, and built a house at Port Resolution, which had been Cook's landing place. Their son was born in February 1859 and his wife Mary died nineteen days later. Baby Peter died after living 36 days. In 1865, Julius Louis Brenchley (1816–73), a traveler and naturalist aboard HMS *Curacoa*, marveled at what Paton had endured for his mission to convert the islanders:

> Though he had fever and ague 24 times in one year and has buried his wife there; though he has had his house and church destroyed, his own life several times attempted and only saved by interposition of a friendly chief, and though he had to watch gun in hand by his wife's grave ten consecutive nights until her body was completely decomposed to prevent cannibals from exhuming it for food, he still wished to return and resume his labours.[35]

Paton never lost his desire to convert the people.[36]

With his second wife, Margaret Whitcross, Paton settled on the small island of Aniwa, near Tanna. Aniwa, a raised coral atoll, is a Polynesian outlier, and the people spoke a Polynesian dialect, which Paton was able to master. Aniwa measures a mere eight square kilometers (three square miles). Paton converted the people of Aniwa and made frequent voyages to Tanna and other islands. Paton left in 1881 but continued to raise funds for missionary work in the New Hebrides.[37]

On May 20, 1861, Canadian missionary George N. Gordon (1822–61) and his wife Ellen were killed by Melanesians on Eromanga, known justly as the Martyrs' Isle. The Gordons had arrived in June 1857 from Prince Edward Island, British North America, and established a mission at Dillon's Bay. Gordon learned the local language and served islanders as a physician. In four years the Gordons had converted forty islanders to Christianity. In 1861 measles was brought ashore by sandalwood traders. Among those who died were two children of a chief. The chief thought Gordon had put a curse on his family and ordered him killed. In August 1865 the British navy took revenge when guns from HMS *Curacao* bombarded the area where the murders had taken place. After several hours of shelling villages, 170 crewmen were landed "to commit such devastation as was in their power."[38]

K.R. Howe wrote that fewer died on Eromanga and Tanna because there were fewer Christians to congregate in enclosed spaces, and because missionaries had not stopped warfare, so people's travel was restricted as was their ability to infect one another.[39] Assuming Howe is correct, in the New Hebrides peace proved more lethal than war.

On March 7, 1872, James D. Gordon (1832–72), brother of George N. Gordon, was also murdered on Eromanga. James had arrived on June 5, 1864, aboard the *Dayspring*, a two-masted brigantine built by contributions of Prince Edward Island Presbyterian parishioners. James also spent six months on Espiritu Santo, establishing a mission there.[40] Bishop George Augustus Selwyn had consecrated John Coleridge Patteson (1827–71) as first Anglican bishop of Melanesia on February 24, 1861, at St. Paul's Church, Auckland. Melanesia as yet had few Christians, so the consecration may be viewed as an act of optimism. Selwyn, who had been Patteson's tutor at Eton, was instrumental in bringing Patteson to the Pacific.[41]

Bishop Patteson founded the Melanesian Mission on Norfolk Island in October 1866 to train Melanesian islanders as Christian proselytizers and to return them home as ambassadors for the faith. The church purchased 378 hectares (933 acres) for four dollars an acre and was granted 40 more hectares (99 acres) at no charge. A large home, Bishopscourt, was built for Patteson, and soon approximately two hundred boys and girls from thirty different islands were being educated. Patteson argued that whites should change the life and customs of the islanders as little as possible, except to persuade Melanesians to stop cannibalism, placating spirits, polygamy, dancing, and sipping kava.[42]

On September 20, 1871, John Coleridge Patteson and two others were murdered at Nukapu in the Santa Cruz Islands. Patteson had held his high office for nearly a decade. The murders were in revenge for blackbirders having taken off five men to work in Fiji.[43]

On July 1, 1871, Reverend Samuel Macfarlane (1837–1911) arrived aboard the *Sapphire* and came ashore at Erub Island in Torres Strait to convert islanders to Christianity. Macfarlane met resounding success in his mission, known to the islanders as "The Coming of the Light." Macfarlane would establish twelve mission stations in the Torres Islands and in Papua. A Scottish–born member of the London Missionary Society, Macfarlane had arrived from Lifou, Loyalty Islands, with native teachers on what was to become the first of his twenty-three proselytizing missions to the Torres Strait Islanders. Populated by Melanesians, the islands span 150 kilometers (93 miles) between Queensland and New Guinea. Every July 1st, inhabitants of various Torres Islands celebrate the anniversary of Macfarlane's arrival with hymns and feasts.[44]

Prelates were not the only victims of xenophobic warriors. On August 12, 1875, hostile islanders at Carlisle Bay, Santa Cruz Island, shot poison arrows into the back of Commodore James Graham Goodenough (1830–75), commander of the Royal Navy's Australia Station. Islanders had invited the visitors to their village, but on the way Goodenough realized they were trying to divide the British party, so he ordered his men back to the ship's boats. During their attempt to return to the ship, they were shot. Five others were wounded. Three died, including Goodenough, who succumbed on August 20. Before he died, Goodenough ordered the village burned but told his men not to kill in retaliation. An island and bay in Papua New Guinea are named for the commodore. Goodenough had come to assess the islanders' level of hostility.[45]

By 1900, six decades after missionary efforts had begun in the New Hebrides, the

Solomon Islands, Papua, and New Guinea, results had been disappointing. While Fiji and New Caledonia were Christian colonies, these others were not, except in some island communities.[46]

INDENTURED LABOR—WILLING OR COERCED

While missionaries were being martyred on Melanesian islands and in New Guinea, ambitious ships' captains and businessmen found more productive activities for the islanders. By the 1840s Tannese and Eromangans joined men from the Loyalty Islands and Isle of Pines as sailors aboard ships from Europe. Their sense of adventure led them to foreign ports such as Sydney or San Francisco. During the period of the California and Victoria gold rushes there was a shortage of regular sailors, and more islanders signed on. Other New Hebrideans worked at cutting sandalwood and at trading stations in their own archipelago. So long as they were taken from their home village to another place or another island, they were considered reliable workers.[47]

Robert Town 1794–1873), who had engaged in the sandalwood trade in the New Hebrides in the 1840s, brought sixty Melanesians to Queensland in 1863 aboard the ship *Don Juan*. These workers were from the New Hebrides, the Solomons, and New Caledonia. Town began a labor trade that continued four decades. An estimated 62,000 Melanesians and New Guineans were to participate in plantation labor in Queensland by 1904, ninety-five percent of them males. They included 18,000 from the Solomon Islands, 40,000 from New Hebrides, and 2,800 from New Guinea.[48] Most signed contracts willingly. In other cases, chiefs sold tribe members to blackbirders. Others were kidnapped. Blackbirders were observed to sink canoes and bring the struggling survivors aboard only to take them away for plantation labor.

When some workers were returned after three years, they told of horrible experiences that led islanders, in self-defense, to attack any whites they saw, including legitimate traders and missionaries. Some were returned to other islands at the end of three years because it was more convenient for the ship's captain; in a few instances, these unwanted arrivals were massacred. In Queensland many died of diseases such as tuberculosis; some died from depression or physical exhaustion.

In the best of circumstances, workers returned home with clothes, trinkets, and guns, becoming the envy of tribe members. Minimal pay in Queensland was five pounds a year, less debts accumulated at the plantation store. Some plantation owners paid workers at the end of their contract in truck, which was trade goods, or script to be used in the store. The employer would enjoy a large markup of truck when selling to the worker. Whether the worker returned with a gift box bought with truck or bought with his five pounds, he could trade tools for pigs and host feasts and become the tribe's big man, or in some cases pass the goods to the village big man who had contracted him out, so the big man could retain or enhance his status.[49]

BRUTALITY ABOARD THE *DAPHNE*

Several cases involving slavery and brutality shocked the Australian and British public. Authorities had difficulty apprehending offending blackbirders because ships changed their names and owners and flew various flags to avoid detection.[50] On September 24, 1869, Judge Sir Alfred Stephen in Australia dismissed a case against two men for operating the slave schooner *Daphne*. Owner Thomas Prichard and Captain John Daggett were tried for the transportation of 108 Tanna, Loyalty, and Banks islanders to Fiji as indentured laborers, although the ship's lessor, Russ Lewin, was licensed to bring no more than 58, and to bring them instead to Queensland. Captain George Palmer of HMS *Rosario* had apprehended Lewin in Leveuka, Fiji. Palmer found a hundred prisoners lying on shelves, "stark naked, and had not even a mat to lie upon." By the time of the trial, Lewin had absented himself. Lewin explained to Palmer that Fiji planters would pay five pounds each for 108 workers, whereas he could get three pounds in Queensland, but for only 58, as mandated by Queensland's Polynesian Labourer's Act. Although sympathetic to the antislavery cause, Stephen dismissed the case, stating that Britain's Slave Trade Act of 1839, under which the case was prosecuted, pertained to Africa, not Melanesia. At the same time, Stephen appealed to the British government to pass a law under which similar cases could be successfully prosecuted. His appeal led to the Pacific Islander Protection Act of 1872.[51]

MASSACRE ABOARD THE *CARL*

The brig *Carl* sailed out of Levuka, Fiji, on July 4, 1871. The crew kidnapped islanders in the New Hebrides and the Solomons. On September 12, captives from Buka Island rioted in the hold, broke open the hatch and came on deck. Crewmembers shot them and then shot into the hold, and killed fifty, while wounding sixteen. Five emerged from the hold in the morning alive after being shot at for eight hours. All were thrown overboard, dead or alive. The hold was cleaned and whitewashed. Because the ship's owner, Dr. James Patrick Murray, told about the incident in Fiji, two crew members were sentenced to death. As a witness for the prosecution, Murray was not prosecuted.[52]

THE PACIFIC ISLANDER PROTECTION ACT

On June 27, 1872, Britain's Parliament passed the Pacific Islander Protection Act. The act's purpose was to protect islanders from blackbirding, from mistreatment as indentured laborers, and from being cheated by labor recruiters or shipmasters. Shipmasters transporting laborers had to obtain a license and post a £500 bond against the mistreatment and abduction of workers. Parliament acted at the request of Australians who were outraged at the dismissal of blackbirding cases such as that of the slave ships *Daphne* and *Carl*. The full title of the law is An Act for the Prevention and Punishment of Criminal Outrages upon Natives of the Islands of the Pacific Ocean.[53]

THE CASE OF THE *HOPEFUL* SLAVERS

Yet atrocities continued. The ship *Hopeful* sailed from Townsville, Queensland, on May 3, 1884, to bring back laborers from New Guinea and its islands. The demand for workers for Queensland's fields exceeded the supply. The ship's company burned village homes and forcibly took men on board. Several Papuans were killed in the process. Thirty who had boarded to trade for tobacco at Waraol on the coast were kept aboard the *Hopeful* by force. After a royal commission investigated allegations of murder and kidnapping, two were indicted for murder, while the captain, Lewis Shaw, the government agent Henry Schofield, the mate, and two seamen were charged with kidnapping. Sixty members of the Queensland legislature asked for mercy, and the executive council commuted the murderers' death sentences to life in prison. All of those convicted were released in 1889, none having completed his sentence.[54]

Indentured in Queensland

By 1891 the highest number of Melanesians, called Kanakas, to work as laborers in Queensland at any one time numbered 10,037, consisting of 9,116 males and 921 females. They had been recruited in the New Hebrides, the Solomon Islands and later New Guinea. As many as a quarter of all Kanakas to work in Queensland had been forced or tricked into leaving home. Workers returned from Queensland or Fiji with trade goods and, even if they had been kidnapped, spoke favorably of their experience abroad and the material awards. Others were so eager to contract as workers that they lit fires on shore to advertise their availability to captains of passing ships. Many of the "time expired boys" signed on for a second or even third three-year term. In 1869 a royal commission investigated contract labor and reported: "the strongest desire is manifested by the natives ... to leave their homes, either to serve on board English ships, or to labour on the plantations of Queensland; and that any attempt to kidnap them would be not only unnecessary, but most impolitic and even dangerous."[55] The return of indentured workers contributed to the transformation of Melanesia and New Guinea. As Harley Grattan explained, "Since it took individuals out of the context of their society, breaking up patterns of family life, labor, and warfare, it contributed to the disintegration of native life. Returned laborers were, in effect, deracinated men let loose in tightly organized societies."[56]

Indentured labor was not ended by Melanesians, most of whom saw it as a young man's rite of passage, but by the Australian and Fijian governments. When Australia became a federal union in 1901, parliament enacted a law to end Pacific island immigration by 1904. The law furthered the new government's white-only policy. In 1906 or before, nearly all Melanesians and New Guineans had been returned. Fiji ended its own influx of Melanesian and New Guinean workers in 1911; there were sufficient Indians present to perform tasks on plantations.[57]

Whalers in the Solomons

Until mid-century the first contact Solomon Islanders had with Westerners was with whaling crews who came to barter for water, food and wood. Judith A. Bennett wrote that the "iron, infection, and ideas they left behind set in motion changes not only in the basic technology but also in the economy and wider society of the Solomons." Whalers saw islanders as black, naked, savage cannibals, and in turn were perceived as ghosts without islands of their own, given to roaming the seas in search of yams and women. Like Polynesian adolescents, Solomon females were free to experiment sexually. Islanders who had little else to trade sent their females onboard to spend the night among twenty-five or thirty

Houses, Utupua. These seaside structures in the Santa Cruz Group of the Solomon Islands are built without monetary cost and effectively shield families from rain. They must be re-thatched from time to time or rebuilt after a hurricane. Life for Utupans has been changed by Western cultures in that the people profess to be Christians and wear clothes — at least when visitors arrive. Photograph by Robert Kirk.

men, and received trade goods in exchange. Syphilis, gonorrhea, and other sexually transmitted diseases brought by whalers affected fertility.[58]

The trade goods most coveted were iron tools for felling trees, planning planks, hollowing out canoes, or severing enemies' heads. Tools saved men and women a third of their work time. Their use as weapons took fighting to a new level. Some tribes were wiped out or forced to flee.[59] Communities that lost population required less food but had more available land for growing coconuts; they sold their surplus to white coastal traders.[60]

GERMANY AND BRITAIN DIVIDE THE SOLOMONS

Germany had claimed Bougainville and Buka in the northern Solomon Islands. On March 15, 1893, to counter further German encroachment, Britain declared a protectorate over the islands of New Georgia, Guadalcanal, Makira, Santa Cruz, Rennel, Ballona, and Malaita. An additional reason was to control blackbirding; islanders often retaliated with violence following a blackbirding raid, sometimes punishing innocent mariners.[61] Islanders living near the coasts— known as "saltwater people"— were to experience increased foreign control and economic domination, while those in some inland areas—"bush people"— scarcely realized they had become subjects of Her Britannic Majesty. Yet, iron tools and weapons obtained in trade or by fighting altered their lives, and germs ended many.

Missionaries expanded their scope under British administration in spite of having to

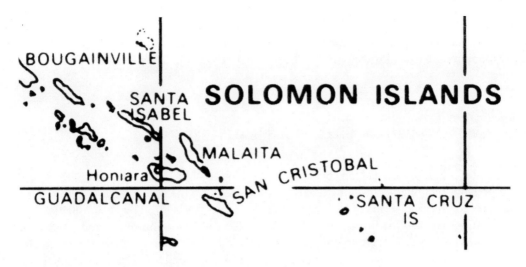

Map of the Solomon Islands. By permission of the Office of Planning, State of Hawaii.

learn one or more of eighty different languages to make their case to Solomon Islanders. One of the tasks of both administrators and missionaries was to end cannibalism. When author Michael Krieger asked a former cannibal on Malaita why islanders had eaten humans, he answered, "What happened is that we eat flesh, human flesh, not because of anything, but because it has already been practiced long ago and that we just feel like eating human flesh."[62]

In 1896, High Commissioner for the Western Pacific John Bates Thurston (1836–97) appointed Charles Morris Woodford (1852–1927) deputy resident commissioner in the Solomon Islands. Woodford, who had visited the Solomons as a naturalist on three occasions between 1886 and 1889, retained the position until January 1914. Woodford set up his headquarters at Tulagi Island, off Florida Island; on September 29, 1896, he paid local chiefs forty-two ounces of gold for the use of Tulagi as the Britain's administrative center. Tulagi would remain the administrative center until the Second World War.

The Colonial Office stipulated that the colony's administration must cover its own operating expenses, so Woodford's bare-bones administration consisted of himself and eight Fijian police officers with the help of an occasional British warship that might visit. His tiny staff was charged with overseeing 150,000 to 200,000 islanders and a few hundred Europeans. Woodford assumed that islanders would eventually become extinct due to disease, and if the administration were to pay for itself without subsidies from London, it was necessary to lease plantation lands. Plantations were soon established by Burns Philp, Levers, and Fairymead.[63]

In 1898 Woodford acquired the assistance at Gizo of Resident A.W. Manaffy and twenty-five indigenous Solomon Islands police. Eventually government officials were posted to the Shortlands (1907), Malaita (1909), and Guadalcanal (1914). For the most part, plantation managers needed to defend their own operations.[64]

New Georgia and Guadalcanal were the first islands to be pacified. The new regime ended the practice of head hunting and the selling of slaves. The white man's law replaced age-old tradition and declared practices handed down from past generations to be crimes. Judith Bennett wrote that with those sudden changes, "Solomon islanders began to doubt the wisdom of generations. The young lost respect for elders and big men who give no answers to the questions of the time."[65] On November 14, 1899, Britain claimed the Santa Cruz Islands, Rennel, Ontong Java, and the Bellona Islands, adding them to the British Solomon Islands Protectorate.[66] They were pretty much all that was left for the taking.

FRANCE AND BRITAIN SHARE THE NEW HEBRIDES

France and Britain had long been rivals in taking colonies, annexing areas of the world to preempt the other from doing so. In the New Hebrides the two powers agreed to joint control to preempt Germany from annexing the archipelago. Both French and British had plantations and trading firms in the islands, but French citizens outnumbered the British three to one. The largest enterprise was owned by John Higginson, a Scot with French citizenship. The New Caledonian nickel magnate formed the Societé française des Nouvellles Hebrides (SFNH) in 1882, and with his partners eventually bought half the land in the archipelago. Higginson purchased unsurveyed land that had never been registered, and he bought it from men whose title to it was dubious. Moreover, he failed to attract many French colonists or to make a significant profit. However, he established France's strong stake in the islands and received the Legion of Honor for his efforts.[67]

Britain and France agreed that their respective interests would be best protected by a joint naval commission. Joint control began November 16, 1887. The commanders of two French and two British warships would be charged with protecting life and property of their nationals, and with controlling the trade in contract laborers to protect Melanesians. Most of the islands' Melanesian residents were not directly affected, unless they worked for Europeans as laborers.[68]

In 1906, officials in Paris and London decided to set up a rare form of government, a condominium, established on October 20, 1907. The two powers would rule jointly, but dual sovereignty required expensive duplication of administration, judiciary and police. Islanders dressed in British or French police uniforms patrolled in pairs. The British and French established separate hospitals and missionary schools, and each power issued its own stamps. The indigenous inhabitants gained neither French nor British citizenship and were considered stateless; in order to travel they required documents from both British and French island administrators.[69] Some characterized condominium as pandemonium.

To fund the expensive condominium administration, authorities leased land to planters. In 1907 a commission composed of French and British declared that all land not directly occupied by tribesmen became government property and could be leased. Much of the land had been tribal hunting areas for centuries. Other lands were purchased from tribes, though indigenous people had little concept of ownership or permanent alienation of tribal lands.[70]

Traffic rules are an example of the problems that bi-nation rule created. In 1919, condominium officials were faced with the question of whether newly imported motor vehicles should drive on the right, as was the practice in France, or on the left as in Britain. Authorities left the decision pending until the next vehicle arrived; if it were delivered to a French person, drivers would stay on the right, if to a British customer, on the left. The next automobile arrived for a French clergyman and the rule of driving on the right came into force.[71]

Construction, Laughlin Islands. Without the need of building permits or subcontractors the inhabitants of the remote Laughlin Islands build their own houses from native materials. Located in the Solomon Sea Islands, the Laughlin Islanders are rarely visited and, although they profess to be Christians, have been little changed by Western culture. Photograph by Robert Kirk.

New Guinea: The Last Great Place

New Guinea was the last great land area in the Pacific to be explored. In 1849 British naval officers Owen Stanley (1811–50), aboard the *Rattlesnake*, and Charles Bamfield Yule (1806–78), commanding the *Bramble*, identified the Owen Stanley Mountain Range, previously unknown to outsiders. Stanley's mission was to chart the northern part of the Great Barrier Reef and the Torres Strait in order to make navigation in those areas safer. The Owen Stanley Range is approximately 300 kilometers (190 miles) long, and 40 to 115 kilometers (25 to 70 miles) wide. The highest peak is Mount Victoria, 4,040 meters (13,240 feet) high. The best pass through the range is the 100-kilometer (60-mile) Kodoka Track, from Buna to Port Moresby; defense of the track would be vital for Australians in the Second World War.[72]

The 1870s and 80s saw the establishment of western settlements. In 1873 Captain John Moresby (1830–1922) sailed aboard HMS *Basilisk* through a reef to a fishing village called Hanubada on the southern coast. He named the settlement that he founded Port Moresby for his father, Admiral Sir Fairfax Moresby (1786–1877), commander of the Royal Navy's Pacific Station at Valparaiso, 1850–53. Port Moresby was situated on a fine harbor, but had no land connection to the rest of the island.[73]

On November 21, 1874, Reverend George Lawes (1839–1907) arrived at Port Moresby to establish a center for the London Missionary Society. Three years later James Chalmers joined Lawes. Lawes stayed thirty-three years. In 1901, a Fly River tribe ate Reverend Chalmers.[74]

On August 15, 1875, Methodist missionary George Brown (1835–1917) brought six Fijian Christian teachers to the Duke of York Islands, today part of Papua New Guinea. The thirteen islands, totaling 60 square kilometers (23 square miles), are in St. George's Channel near New Britain. Brown studied the local languages and cultures. Brown spent approximately a year at his mission, departing on August 31, 1876. Five of the Fijians were killed and in 1878 Brown led a punitive expedition in retaliation. Brown left for Sydney in 1881.[75]

For eight weeks in 1876 Italian naturalist Luigi d'Albertis (1841–1901) aboard the launch *Neva* explored far up New Guinea's Fly River, one of eastern New Guinea's two principal rivers; the Sepik is the other. He was the first European to go as far as 900 kilometers (580 miles). Using dynamite and rockets to deter possibly hostile tribesmen, d'Albertis found specimens and artifacts in villages from which inhabitants fled immediately prior to his arrival. The specimens of birds, plants and insects that he collected are in the Museum Giacomo Doria in Genoa, Italy.[76]

THE PRICE OF GULLIBILITY

Papuans and New Guineans were not the only victims of profit-seeking Europeans. In 1880, five hundred and seventy gullible Europeans sailed to New Ireland because they believed the claims of Charles Marie Bonaventure du Brei, Marquis de Rays (1832–93). There were no stone buildings and lush fields, as pictured in de Rays' newspaper *La Nouvelle France*; rather the immigrants arrived to find themselves on the shore of a mosquito-infested, dense jungle. Among the colonists were 340 Italians from Veneto who had paid a thousand gold francs each for a long sea voyage to a cannibal island. Happy European planters and friendly compliant islanders, pictured in the promotional literature, were nowhere to be seen.

When they arrived at what de Rays had labeled Port Breton, near present day Kavieng at New Ireland's northern tip, the would-be settlers were forced to trade clothing to islanders for food. Six Europeans escaped to Buka in the Solomons, where five were eaten. The sixth agreed to become a cannibal. Survivors were eventually rescued, 217 arriving in Sydney. Many settled in Australia. Before his scheme was halted, the swindling marquis sent four colonizing expeditions to New Ireland. De Rays, who was intelligent enough never to have gone to New Ireland himself, was arrested and tried in 1882. He was given a four-year sentence and fined 3,000 francs, though he had swindled as much as two million from his victims.[77]

DUTCH NEW GUINEA

New Guinea was the biggest prize in the island Pacific, rich in resources and ancient cultures. No nation claimed eastern New Guinea, but officials of the Dutch East Indies Company announced that they recognized the claim of the Sultan of Tidore to western New Guinea. Since the Dutch claimed suzerainty over Tidore, they were able to stake their claim indirectly and without expense. Only on August 24, 1828, did the Dutch East Indies Company establish a settlement. It was Fort du Bus on the Vogelkop, and it served to mark their claim. Because the settlement had been established in a malarial area, it was abandoned in 1836. The Dutch claim to western New Guinea was always tenuous and, because their profits were made from agriculture in the East Indies, the company did not establish permanent settlements in the mountainous island until 1898.[78] The Netherlands' colony was west of 141 east longitude.

THE GERMAN NEW GUINEA COMPANY

The Neu-Guinea Kompanie was formed by investors in Berlin on May 26, 1884. On November 3, 1884, the company claimed the northern part of the eastern half of New Guinea, as well as neighboring islands. Company agents signed treaties of cession with a few men from Bogadjim and Madang; the New Guineans who signed could not read or fully comprehend the documents. Negotiations were carried out under the direction of special envoy Dr. Friedrich Hermann Otto Finsch (1839–1917), after whom the first administrative center, Finschafen, was named. Dr. Finsch exercised nominal control over 249,500 square kilometers (97,300 square miles).

Company agents were never able to occupy much of their domain, but established plantations around Madang and at Finschafen. The Germans named their colony Kaiser-Wilhelmsland after Kaiser Wilhelm I (1797–1888; r. 1871–88). The largest neighboring islands, forming the shape of a gigantic hook, were named Bismarck Archipelago for Chancellor Otto von Bismarck.[79] New Britain was named Neu-Pommern; and New Ireland, Neu-Mecklenburg. In the northern Solomon Islands, Germany claimed Bougainville and Buka Islands. Germany was clearly taking the leftovers of the world. With its heat, humidity, dense jungles, mountains, ravines, and warring tribes separated by hundreds of languages, the best that can be said for German New Guinea in the late nineteenth century is that on a world map, it appeared to be a significant colonial acquisition.

Stewart's Handbook for 1923 states, "The early history of Germany's New Guinea Protectorate is a dismal record of ineptitude and failure.... To enumerate all the blunders, misfortunes, and miscalculations of the New Guinea Company would require too much space." Editor Allen wrote that the chief administrator was changed twelve times in thirteen years and that the administrative center was moved three times. Allen explained, "Malarial fever depleted the staff, ships were lost on uncharted reefs, and money recklessly spent in ill-conceived experiments." Only two of seven mainland settlements survived, and the planters moved on to New Britain.[80]

The first European to travel 50 kilometers (31 miles) up the Sepik River was German official Dr. Friedrich Hermann Otto Finsch, in 1885. He named the river after Kaiserin Augusta, consort of the German emperor Wilhelm II. Other German Sepik River expeditions in the following two years reached 600 kilometers (370 miles) inland.[81]

THE KAISER'S GOVERNMENT TAKES OVER

On April 1, 1899, Germany assumed control over German New Guinea from the New Guinea Company. The company had lost nine million marks and no longer wanted to administer the area.[82] After that the colony made "sustained progress." Herbertshoe on New Britain became the first administrative center, replaced by Rabaul on New Ireland. Prussian law was enforced in the few areas actually under German control. Regular steamer service and wire connections were established, and before World War I the colony was showing a profit.[83] By 1914, German New Guinea had 1,273 Europeans. Colonial authorities feared the indigenous population would die out, and Asians were brought in to replace them as workers. Chinese indentured workers outnumbered Europeans with 1,700 people. Pay was five marks a month and contracts ran for three years. New Guinean workers numbered approximately 18,000. They were coerced into labor by the imposition of a ten-mark head tax. To earn cash, they had to perform some work for Germans.[84]

BRITAIN LAYS CLAIM TO PAPUA

Unsettled by the German interest in eastern New Guinea, the Queensland government sent Henry Chester (1832–1914), resident magistrate at Thursday Island in the Torres Strait Islands, to take possession of all of New Guinea that had not been already claimed by the Netherlands. Chester claimed the vast territory on April 4, 1883. London quickly disavowed the action of their Queensland colony.[85]

German claims soon prompted Britain to change course. On November 3, 1884, the German New Guinea Company annexed their huge possession. Commodore James Elphinstone Erskine, R.N. (1838–1911), ran up the union jack at Port Moresby on November 6, 1884, claiming Papua, the southeastern portion of the island, for Britain. Erskine acted under orders from Sir Thomas McIllwraith (1835–1900), premier of Queensland. McIllwraith had urged Britain to take over Papua and thus protect Australia from the Germans. Every square mile of New Guinea and its islands were now claimed by the Netherlands, Germany, or Britain.

Erskine, commander of the Australian Station, had arrived November 2, aboard HMS *Nelson*; also in the harbor were HMSS *Espiegle, Raven, Swinger,* and *Harrier*. HMS *Nelson* then sailed on the south coast, picking up some fifty chiefs with the intention of offering lavish entertainment aboard and explaining that their territories had been taken over. Erskine promised that native lands would not be alienated; unlike New Caledonians and Hawaiians, Papuans did not lose much land to whites, although land could be leased.[86]

Boe Vagi, chief of the tribe living on the site of Port Moresby, was made chief of all of the Motu tribes. The *Sydney Morning Herald* told its readers that Chief Vagi "was dressed in a shirt, with a handkerchief around his loins, and a red felt hat on his head; and some green leaves through the lobe of his left ear," the other chiefs being "destitute of clothing."[87]

What Britain claimed was a California–sized area of jungles, swamps and mountains, with an uncounted number of preliterate people speaking several hundred languages. Queensland and New South Wales bore the cost of administration.[88]

On September 4, 1888, Sir William MacGregor (1846–1919) arrived in Port Moresby as British administrator for Papua. Sympathetic to the indigenous population, MacGregor sought to protect land and labor from exploitation, and he recruited Papuans into the constabulary. He sent constables into the near-hinterland to maintain order. The area patrolled was a fraction of the land area claimed under the protectorate, and had either Christian missions or plantations nearby. His instructions did not include what would amount to a nearly impossible task of bringing the entirety of Papua under British control.[89]

Administrative building, Samarai Island, located off the southern shore of New Guinea at Milne Bay. Samarai Islanders were converted by missionaries starting in 1878. After Papua became a British protectorate, Samarai was designated an administrative center. By 1902 three times the tonnage of goods were shipped from there as from Port Moresby. Today it is a provincial backwater. Photograph by Robert Kirk.

Horrendous Crime, Horrendous Punishment

British sovereignty over Papua did not bring immediate respect for His Britannic Majesty's authority; respect would come from an assertion of armed strength. On April 8, 1901, tribesmen perpetrated a celebrated crime that had to be punished. Reverend James Chalmers (1841–1901) of the London Missionary Society, his associate Oliver Tompkins, and eleven Papuan assistants were clubbed to death and eaten by Goaribari Islanders off the coast of Papua. Goaribari Island is in the Gulf of Papua at the mouth of the Kikori River, near the border of Dutch (now Indonesian) New Guinea. Chalmers had served in Rarotonga, 1866–76, and at several stations in Papua from 1877. Goaribari tribesmen invited Chalmers and his companions to their *dobus* (long houses) and killed them there. In retaliation, officials at Port Moresby sent troops aboard the *Merrie England*; they killed at least twenty-four tribesmen and burned twelve *dobus*. Again, in an expedition two years later to recover Tompkins's skull, more villagers were slaughtered.[90]

On September 1, 1906, authorities in London transferred Papua to Australian administration. Sir Hubert Plunkett Murray (1861–1940), the Australian administrator from 1907 to 1940, founded *kiaps* (the Papuan pronunciation of *cops*) to discourage cannibalism and tribal warfare, and to deter missionaries from disturbing village customs. Australian administration had little or no effect on hundreds of thousands of tribesmen in the Highlands, still unaware that Caucasians existed.[91] Indeed, until the 1930s whites would not know how heavily populated the Highlands were.

Chapter 19

Hawaii Subdued, 1874–1914

KALAKAUA, A VERY MERRY MONARCH

That Hawaii would become the colony of a foreign power was probably unavoidable. In the entire South Pacific only Tonga escaped an imperial chokehold; Tonga had few natural resources, and successfully played Germany and Great Britain against each other. Unlike Tonga, the Hawaiian Islands had Pearl Harbor on the route between American west coast ports and Asian ports. The archipelago's rich soil was ideal for growing sugar cane and pineapple. Americans came to dominate the missionary effort, economy and government.

Hawaii might have retained independence longer had her "merry" monarch Kalakaua been more prudent during his seventeen-year reign from 1874 to 1891. David Kalakaua (1836–91) took the oath as king of Hawaii on February 13, 1874. His predecessor, William C. Lunaliho (1835–74; r. 1873–74) had died on February 3, and with him the royal house of Kamehameha came to an end. The newly elected legislature chose Kalakaua with thirty-nine votes to six for his principal rival, the popular dowager Queen Emma (1836–85), widow of King Alexander Liholiho (Kamehameha IV, r. 1854–63). When the election result was announced, partisans of Queen Emma rioted in Honolulu. Minister of Foreign Affairs Charles Reed Bishop (1822–1915) and Governor of Oahu John Owen Dominis (1832–1891), both Americans, asked for help from commanders of warships in the harbor. The USS *Tuscarora* and USS *Portsmouth* sent 150 men, and HMS *Tenedos*, 80 British forces. By morning the rioting had been quelled.[1] It was neither the first nor last time that foreign ships in harbor would attempt to control Hawaiian affairs.

THE KING MEETS U.S. GRANT AND P.T. BARNUM

On November 17, 1874, the new monarch left on the steamer *Benecia* for the United States to meet President Ulysses S. Grant and complete negotiations for a treaty of reciprocity to admit Hawaiian sugar and rice duty free. Because an advanced party of Americans residents of the islands had been sent ahead in October to begin negotiations, Kalakaua's visit was largely ceremonial. The first reigning monarch of any nation to visit the American republic, the king met Grant on December 15 and was received by a joint session of Congress on December 18. That night he was feted at a state ball.

After eleven days in the capital Kalakaua went to New York City, where impresario Phineas T. Barnum (1810–91) invited him to the Hippodrome. At the Hippodrome the band played "The King of the Cannibal Isles." To the crowd, Kalakaua was an exotic exhibit much like caged animals and the bearded lady. Kalakaua returned to Honolulu February 15, 1875, to be greeted by an adulatory crowd of 10,000.[2]

SUGAR ACERAGE GROWS

The Hawaiian Kingdom and the United States concluded a reciprocity treaty on January 30, 1875. It came into force on September 9. According to the treaty, the U.S. guaranteed Hawaiian sugar an advantage over all other nations' sugar imports. The treaty was a financial triumph for planters but a disaster for the indigenous population. Sugar acreage in the islands increased tenfold and in the next twenty-five years increased twenty times, leading to loss of lands held by the indigenous people.[3] *Haoles* acquired land partly because Hawaii's Polynesian population had declined dramatically from an estimated 200,000 or more in 1778 to 53,900 by 1876. The decline was due in part to gonorrhea and syphilis, which caused sterility and stillbirths. The islands were visited by epidemics of cholera (1804), influenza (1820s), mumps (1839), measles and whooping cough (1848–9), and smallpox (1853). From about 1876 Hawaii saw a rapid growth of total population, principally due to the immigration of Asian workers for sugar plantations.[4]

In 1876 Samuel Alexander (1836–1904) and Henry P. Baldwin (1842–1911), sons of missionaries, irrigated 1,300 hectares (3,000 acres) of Maui's dry central plain of Wailuku by constructing the 27-kilometer (17-mile) Haleakale Ditch at a cost of eighty thousand dollars. The project brought 150 million liters (40 million gallons) of water a day to the formerly arid plain. Six years earlier the partners had begun growing sugar on Maui. Sugar was to become the main source of island income until tourism in the 1960s. In Hawaii it is said, "The missionaries came to do good, but their children did well."[5]

German–born Claus Spreckels (1828–1908) became Hawaii's biggest sugar plantation owner when he leased from the Hawaiian government 9,700 hectares (24,000 acres) on Maui on July 8, 1882. Born in Hamburg, he had already made a fortune as owner of a brewery in San Francisco. Spreckels produced a third of the island's sugar and purchased the rest. Spreckels built a 48-kilometer (30-mile) water course to divert 227 million liters (60 million gallons) a day to irrigate his dry lands. He built Spreckelsville on Maui, the working center of his plantations. Spreckels built a state-of-the-art sugar refinery in San Francisco. On August 11, 1882, King Kalakaua signed a royal patent confirming Spreckels' ownership of the 10,400 hectares (24,000 acres) that had been leased. Having bought a partnership in W.G. Irwin and Company in 1880, Spreckels enjoyed a virtual monopoly on Hawaiian sugar production. The economy became dependent on sugar sales to the United States.[6]

FOREIGN FIELD WORKERS ARRIVE

Hawaiians had little interest in working long hours for low wages, so plantation owners imported labor. Between 1877 and 1885 approximately 2,500 Pacific islanders came to work as field laborers. Some 400 arrived from the New Hebrides; more came from other Melanesian islands and from the Gilbert Islands. Few remained at the expiration of their labor contracts. On September 30, 1878, the first Portuguese workers arrived from Madeira aboard the *Priscilla*. They numbered 68 males, 16 females and 35 children. Within the decade, 12,000 would arrive. Portuguese cabinetmaker Manuel Nunes introduced the ukulele to Hawaii in the late 1870s, adopted from the Madeira Island guitar called the *cavaquinho*.[7] Between December 1, 1880, and April 2, 1881, Hawaii admitted 4,400 Chinese laborers. With the labor vessels arrived smallpox.[8]

His Majesty's Circumnavigation

King Kalakaua became the first reigning monarch to circumnavigate the globe. He returned to Honolulu on October 29, 1881. His costly tour was of little or no benefit to the Hawaiian people. The king had traveled to Japan, China, Siam, Burma, India, Egypt, Italy, Belgium, Germany, Austria-Hungary, France, Spain, Portugal, the United Kingdom and across the United States. His purpose was to gain recognition for his kingdom and to observe how other monarchs ruled. He attended audiences with the Japanese emperor, the Siamese king, the Egyptian khedive, Queen Victoria, and President Chester A. Arthur. In his absence, Kalakaua's sister, Liliuokalani, served as regent.[9]

The Disreputable Gibson

On May 29, 1882, Kalakaua appointed Walter Murray Gibson (1822–88) prime minister. A naturalized citizen, Gibson had served in the legislature since 1876. Between 1882 and 1887, while other ministers were dismissed, Gibson served as prime minister, often holding other portfolios simultaneously. Like the unlicensed physician Shirley Baker in Tonga and Albert Steinberger in Samoa, Gibson dazzled his island monarch and held inordinate influence over him. Born in England and raised in the American South, Gibson had been expelled from the Latter Day Saints in 1864 after being accused of malfeasance while leading a Mormon settlement in Lana'i. The Lana'i colony, known as City of Joseph, had been established by ten LDS missionaries who had arrived in 1851 from the northern California gold fields. Having translated the Book of Mormon into Hawaiian by 1855, they were able to claim 4,500 adherents within the first six years.[10] Gibson had found the Lana'i colony without strong leadership in 1861 when he arrived. Taking charge, Gibson inappropriately registered LDS lands in his own name. In April 1862, in response to complaints of residents, a delegation of Mormon elders was sent out to investigate. They discovered that Gibson sold church offices for amounts from fifty cents to a hundred and sixty dollars. He was accused of preaching heretical doctrines, embezzlement, and maladministration.[11]

Kalakaua's Imperial Dream

Gibson failed to restrain the Kalakaua's lavish spending. Moreover, the prime minister excited the king with dreams of a Polynesian empire with Kalakaua as grand monarch. Gibson and Kalakaua devised a plan for Hawaii to dominate much of Polynesia. Gibson convinced the legislature to purchase a "navy" in the form of a retired guano boat, the *Kaimiloa*. The boat was loaded with cannons, machine guns and a military band to impress the people of Samoa with Hawaiian naval might. On December 26, 1882, Kalakaua sent cabinet member John E. Bush (1842–1906) aboard the *Zealandia* to Samoa. Bush was to enroll Samoa as a province of Hawaii, and if that went well, to try to obtain similar concessions in Tonga, the Cook Islands and the Gilberts. Bush arrived at Apia on January 3, 1887, and by February 17 had Samoan king Malieatoa's signature on a Treaty of Political Alliance and Agreement. What appeared to be a Hawaiian takeover of Samoa so alarmed the Second Reich that Berlin dispatched four warships in August. Bush was recalled promptly. The comic-opera Samoa fiasco alarmed *haoles*.[12]

THE MERRY MONARCH'S EXTRAVAGANCE

Haoles were alarmed at Kalakaua's extravagant spending. The king's former palace was razed and the cornerstone of Honolulu's Iolani Palace was laid in a Masonic ceremony on December 21, 1879. Workmen completed the pretentious residence on December 27, 1882, and that same evening the king gave a grand banquet for members of the Masonic Lodge, in which he held the thirty-third degree. The new palace was a financial burden on a poor country. The legislature in 1878 had approved $50,000 for the project, but the king's additions and changes raised the final cost to $300,000. Paneled in Hawaiian woods as well as American walnut and Oregon cedar, it contains a grand entry, grand staircase, throne room, dining room, drawing room, bedrooms, library and music room. A billiard room and kitchen were in the basement.

Lavish spending continued. On February 12, 1883, although he had been on the throne nine years, Kalakaua was crowned in an elaborate ceremony at the palace. Kalakaua paid $10,000 for two jeweled crowns with gold taro leaves. The king had learned about coronations on his recent world tour, and he felt he needed his own ceremony. The great feather cloak of Kamehameha I was placed on him, and he wore a whale-tooth necklace. When, like Napoleon I, Kalakaua placed a great gold crown on his own head, every cannon in Honolulu and the guns on ships in port boomed approval. A choir sang "Cry Out O Isles, with Joy." A large statue of Kamehameha I was unveiled outside the palace. The festivities included a ball, parade, horse race, yacht regatta and fireworks display, and banquet. Banquet guests chose from four soups, eight fish dishes, six entrees, dessert and a variety of fine wines.[13] A major disappointment was the absence of any crowned heads from Europe and Asia, many of whom had been invited. Expenditures for the coronation were three times the amount allotted by the legislature.[14]

THE "BAYONET" CONSTITUTION

Kalakaua's imprudence alarmed haoles. In January 1887, Americans and other *haoles* formed the Hawaiian League, a secret political organization whose members were determined to bring about, as they stated, a "decent and honest government in Hawaii." By 1887 Americans owned two-thirds of all taxable real estate, and as taxpayers they accused the administration and palace of being wasteful of public funds. The subversive organization attracted as many as four hundred men and allied with the Honolulu Rifles, which had been formed in 1884.[15]

Haoles had pressured King Kalakaua to dismiss Gibson. *Haoles* blamed Gibson for corruption and the king's lavish spending. They pointed to Gibson as the author of the awkward attempt to annex Samoa. Gibson expressed his fears in his diary: "Threats of violence

... Rumors of armed mob, purpose to lynch me."[16] *Haole* businessmen wanted an efficient administration run by their representatives and, ultimately, annexation by the United States. Dismissed by King Kalakaua on June 12, 1887, former prime minister Walter Murray Gibson sailed to San Francisco, never to return. Gibson died in San Francisco in 1888.[17]

On July 6, 1887, members of the Hawaiian League forced King Kalakaua to sign the "Bayonet" Constitution. The league threatened force if the king refused. Under its terms, Kalakaua yielded his authority to a *haole* cabinet and became in effect a constitutional monarch. The document specified property qualifications that prevented most Hawaiians from voting. The legislature passed acts to ease naturalization for white foreigners and to limit Chinese immigration.[18] Without public announcement, two days later the king signed four other documents—notes for the loan of $40,000, far exceeding the royal annual income—from sugar monarch Claus Spreckels.[19]

The *haole* government was amenable to allowing the United States to take possession of land for a coaling station at Pearl Harbor, Oahu, on November 9, 1887. In the age of steam-driven vessels, a mid–Pacific coaling station was an invaluable asset to a naval power. The use of Pearl Harbor for large naval vessels required removing coral at the entrance. In 1892 Congress appropriated a quarter of a million dollars for excavation of the harbor mouth and for establishing a naval station. The United States made Pearl Harbor its major naval base in the Pacific.[20]

THE FAILURE OF THE WILCOX REBELLION

Some Hawaiians were outraged at the seizure of power by whites. Armed members of the Liberal Hawaiian Association, composed of indigenous and part Hawaiians, marched on Iolani Palace on July 30, 1889, to force King Kalakaua to scrap the "Bayonet" Constitution and to seize power. The revolt was led by half–Hawaiian Robert William Kalanihapo Wilcox (1855–1903). The revolt was doomed to failure partially because the king was aware that an attempt had been planned to force his hand, and he stayed away from the palace to avoid being placed in a dangerous position. The attempted coup led to fighting in which seven were killed, twelve wounded, and seventy arrested. Wilcox was tried for treason, but was acquitted by a jury vote of nine to three. He was elected to the legislature, serving from 1890 to 1894.[21]

LILIUOKALANI TRIES TO REGAIN POWER

Princess Liliuokalani (1838–1917) became queen of Hawaii on January 10, 1891, when her brother, David Kalakaua, died at the Palace Hotel in San Francisco, age fifty-four. Kalakaua had left Honolulu for San Francisco on November 25, 1890. The king had no children, and his sister was heir apparent. The new queen was well aware Hawaiians had lost control of their own country and that *haoles* wanted the United States to take over her kingdom.

By the time of Liliuokalani's accession, Hawaii had been essentially transformed from an advanced Stone Age culture to a modern kingdom. The editor of *Paradise of the Pacific* exulted, "The country enjoys all the advantages of modern civilization in a higher degree than most European countries. Postal services, telegraphs, telephones, railroads and lighting by electricity...."[22] The ruling class was no longer the monarch and indigenous nobles, but sugar barons. These barons controlled about eighty percent of the agricultural land. Sugar planters saw annexation as the solution to declining profits. The United States Tariff Act of 1890 put Hawaiian sugar on its free list, opening imports to all, but as of July 1, 1891, gave American producers a two cents per pound bounty for sugar produced from beets, sorghum, cane or maple sap — all within the United States. The bounty gave American sugar an immense advantage over imported sugar, and the islands suffered economic depression as a result.

Liliuokalani was fluent in English, a practicing Christian and married to an American. Her husband, John Owen Dominis, was governor of Oahu and Maui. Had she not been queen, she might have been remembered for writing the song "Oloha Oe" or any of approximately 150 other songs. Whatever skills and abilities the queen possessed, she could scarcely escape a clash with *haoles*.[23]

The queen herself precipitated the crisis that ended her reign. On Saturday January 14, 1893, she revealed details of a new constitution she proposed to replace the "Bayonet" Constitution. According to the proposed document, only Polynesian Hawaiians and naturalized citizens would vote for representatives, and the monarch would appoint nobles to sit with them. The sovereign would have power to act without the advice and consent of her cabinet, and cabinet members would serve at her pleasure.[24]

HAOLES DEPOSE THE QUEEN

Events moved swiftly. Liliuokalani's announcement prompted 1,500 *haoles* to meet at the Armory in Honolulu. United States Minister John L. Stevens (1820–95) agreed that because the queen was subverting the constitution of 1887, his nation would take no action to save her throne. On January 17, 1893, *haoles* overthrew the monarchy and took power into their own hands. The recently-formed *haole* Committee of Safety, all but one of whose thirteen members belonged to the revolutionary Hawaiian League, also called the Annexation Club, occupied government buildings and announced that Queen Liliuokalani had been deposed. The USS *Boston*, anchored in Pearl Harbor, sent 162 Marines into Honolulu to protect the revolutionaries. The revolutionaries named a provisional government headed by Supreme Court Justice Sanford B. Dole (1844–1926). The committee suspended the writ of habeas corpus that was part of the constitution.[25] The monarchy, founded less than a century before by Kamehameha the Great, ended, and with it any semblance of ethnic Hawaiian control of their own affairs.

CLEVELAND EXPRESSES HIS DOUBTS

The delegation from the provisional government, which consisted of Lorrin A. Thurston and four other commissioners, had sailed to San Francisco on January 19, aboard the steam ship *Claudine*. They arrived in Washington, DC, on February 3, met with President Benjamin Harrison (1833–1901; term 1889–93) and impressed him favorably with their offer. Republican Harrison sent a treaty of annexation to the Senate on February 15, 1893. The *haole* revolutionaries appeared to be getting exactly what they wanted.

Timing was bad for the annexationists. Before a Senate vote could take place, Harrison's term was over, and Grover Cleveland (1837–1908; terms 1885–89 and 1893–97), a Democrat, was inaugurated. On March 9, Cleveland withdrew the treaty from the Senate for further study. Cleveland appointed former congressman James Henderson Blount (1837–1903) of Georgia to go to Hawaii to investigate public sentiment concerning annexation.[26] On March 28, 1893, the Blount Commission arrived in Honolulu. The Royal Hawaiian Band struck up, quite inappropriately, "Marching through Georgia," evocative of the destruction of Atlanta during the Civil War. Blount demanded the provisional government restore the queen to power. President Sanford Dole refused. Blount left Hawaii August 9, and reported to Cleveland and Congress that his impression was that the majority of indigenous Hawaiians wanted the monarchy restored and for Hawaiians to govern their own nation.

Indigenous Hawaiians had also sent a delegation to Washington, DC. A member of the royalist lobby, Liliuokalani's niece and heir to the throne, young and attractive Princess Kaiulani (1875–99), met with Cleveland and appealed to his sense of fairness. Cleveland withdrew the treaty for reexamination. Secretary of State Walter Quintin Gresham (1832–95) called the queen's overthrow "discreditable to all who engaged in it."[27]

On December 18, 1893, President Cleveland sent a 6,000-word message to Congress stating reasons he would not submit a treaty for annexation. Cleveland cited the Blount Commission's finding that the indigenous population wanted sovereignty restored. Annexationists in the islands would not achieve their goals while Cleveland was in the White House. However, Cleveland recognized Hawaii's provisional government.[28]

THE HAWAIIAN REPUBLIC

A constitutional convention had been convened in Honolulu on May 30, 1894. Delegates prepared a document by which the republic was governed. Article 32 stated that the president was "expressly authorized and empowered to make a Treaty of Political and Commercial Union between the Republic of Hawaii and the United States of America, subject to the ratification of the Senate." With Sanford Dole (1844–1926; terms 1894–1900) as president, the republic was proclaimed on the fourth of July 1894. The principal goal of the republic was to wait for Grover Cleveland to leave the White House in hope his successor would approve annexation.[29] In 1894 the American Congress repealed the McKinley Tariff and eliminated the bounty on domestic sugar. Hawaiian sugar had been restored to a privileged position without the nation being annexed.[30]

ANOTHER FAILED REBELLION

Hawaiian independence leaders made one last attempt to restore the monarchy. They collected money from supporters and bought arms. Royalists planned to march into Honolulu at midnight on January 6, 1895, to take over key buildings. That morning "instead of drilling, they sat around eating poi, drinking gin, telling jokes, or instructing their comrades in the basic facts of firing a rifle." Spies who planted themselves in the royalist camp alerted republic authorities. After a gunfight on the slopes of Diamond Head and nearby Manoa Valley, the insurrection collapsed.

When an arms cache was found buried in Liliuokalani's garden, the new officials placed her under house arrest. On January 24, 1895, the last queen of Hawaii abdicated. Lili-uokalani was put on trial, found guilty of insurrection, fined $5,000, and sentenced to five years' hard labor. President Dole excused the queen from the humiliating sentence.[31]

McKinley Agrees to Annex Hawaii

Because Congress had ended the sugar bounty, annexation was no longer essential for planters to maintain sugar profits; rather, a handful of leading figures in Washington perceived annexation to be in the national interest. In 1897, Democrat Cleveland left office and William McKinley (1843–1901; terms 1897–1901) was inaugurated. On February 15, 1898, the U.S. battleship *Maine* blew up in Havana Harbor. Known now to have been caused internally, the explosion was blamed on Spaniards. The United States declared war on Spain. Because the Philippines were a Spanish possession, on May 1, 1898, Admiral George Dewey (1837–1917) destroyed the Spanish fleet in Manila Bay. If the United States were to complete its subjugation of the Philippines, it would rely increasingly on its coaling station at Pearl Harbor.

Imperialist Senator Henry Cabot Lodge (1850–1904) and Navy Assistant Secretary Theodore Roosevelt (1858–1919) saw Honolulu as an essential strategic base on the way to Manila. If all of Hawaii were American, Pearl Harbor would be secured from foreign encroachment. Moreover, Alfred T. Mahan (1840–1914), a major proponent of American sea power, saw Hawaii as the first line of defense against Japan, which gave indications of rising as a Pacific naval power following its defeat of China in 1894. It was useless for anti-imperialists to remind the imperialists that the U.S. could have used Pearl Harbor without annexing the Hawaiian Islands.[32]

On August 12, 1898, President McKinley signed the Resolution for Annexation, sponsored by Congressman Francis G. Newlands (1846–1917). In order to take effect, it had to be ratified by the Senate or passed by joint resolution of both houses. The astonishing naval victory at Manila Bay guaranteed the treaty would become law. The Senate voted for it 42 to 21, and the House 209 to 91.[33]

Pacific Bastion

Congress passed the Organic Act of April 30, 1900, which provided a framework for territorial government in Hawaii. Laws existing under the recent republic became territorial law. The act made specific rules regarding elections, courts, legislation, and citizenship.

According to the census of 1900, 154,000 people resided in the Hawaiian Islands. These included 30,000 ethnic Hawaiians, 10,000 part–Hawaiians, 18,000 Portuguese, 9,000 Caucasians of other ethnicity, 26,000 Chinese, and 61,000 Japanese. Less than ten percent of the land had been retained by people of Hawaiian or part–Hawaiian ethnicity. Landless Hawaiians drifted into city and town slums.[34]

In the first decade of the twentieth century, communication between the islands and the mainland were vastly improved. On December 14, 1902, the Commercial Pacific Cable Company connected an undersea telegraph cable from San Francisco to Honolulu. Telegraph stations operated at Ocean Beach in San Francisco and at Waikiki Beach in Oahu. Within one year the line was open from Honolulu to Midway Island, to Guam and to

Manila. As a result a telegraph message could be sent around the world.[35] In 1908 Matson Navigation Company began passenger service from California to Hawaii aboard the steamship *Lurline*. Named for Claus Spreckels' yacht on which William Matson (1850–1917) had served as skipper, the earliest *Lurline* carried 51 passengers and 61 crew. Two years later the *Wilhelmina*, which carried 146 passengers to and from Hawaii, joined the *Lurline*.[36]

The United States military established a major presence in the islands. Dredging of the channel leading to the harbor had begun in 1902; the channel was deepened to 10.5 meters (35 feet) and widened to 180 meters (600 feet). Within a few years of annexation, several military facilities had been erected to protect Pearl Harbor and Honolulu: Fort Armstrong at the harbor entrance in 1907, Fort De Russy at Waikiki in 1908, Fort Ruger at Diamond Head in 1909, and forts Kamehameha and Weaver at the harbor entrance in 1913. Schofield Barracks in the island's center opened in 1909 and became the largest army post in the United States. Luke Field, on Ford Island in Pearl Harbor, opened in 1919. A dry docking facility for the American navy was formally opened at Pearl Harbor on August 1, 1919. American military personnel and their dependents flooded into the territory.[37]

A Cultural Oasis

Hawaiian language and culture was better preserved on Ni'ihau than elsewhere. Aubrey Robinson (1853–1936), owner of Ni'ihau, closed the Hawaiian island from 1915 onward to nonresidents. As a result of being isolated from many Western influences, Ni'ihau is the only island in the chain on which Hawaiian remained the first language. In 1864, Robinson's grandmother Elizabeth Sinclair (1891–92), a Scot and former New Zealand settler, had bought the entire island for $10,000 from King Kamehameha V; she reportedly declined to purchase Waikiki beach at the same price. The Robinson family ran sheep, cattle and horses, and grew sugar. Ni'ihau is the smallest of Hawaii's inhabited islands, measuring 180 square kilometers, or 70 square miles.[38]

By 1914, the year the Panama Canal opened and World War I began, the transformation of Hawaii, including Ni'ihau, was ongoing and irreversible.

Chapter 20

The Imperial Impulse, 1883–1918

EMPIRE BUILDING

By the early 1870s all Pacific islands had been found, but numbers of them had been left to govern themselves. Then, a final and all-encompassing imperial frenzy took place from about the mid–1880s to 1918. German unification was followed within fifteen years by the Fatherland's acquisition of colonies; that was the catalyst that set off the late-nineteenth-century imperial scramble called the New Imperialism. When the scramble subsided, all South Pacific territories—including minuscule islands without economic value—were under jurisdiction of a colonial power. These powers were Britain, France, Germany, Chile, and the United States. In Micronesia Spain lost colonies to the United States and Germany, and in 1914 Japan seized Germany's North Pacific islands. In 1914 New Zealand and Australia joined the imperial club when they seized Germany's South Pacific islands, and in 1920 the League of Nations legitimized the new status of their spoils by declaring them "mandated territories." By 1920 only Tonga retained nominal independence.

Historian of modern empires Eric Hobsbawm pointed out that the entire period of modern imperialism took place within the lifetime of one man, of imperialist Winston Churchill, who lived from 1874–1965. During the Age of Imperialism all of Africa except Liberia and Abyssinia were taken by European nations. Much of Asia was taken, but Japan and Siam in southern and eastern Asia escaped being colonies, or being carved into spheres of influence like China. Russia colonized Siberia and lands on its southern periphery. In the entire world Britain held the lion's share of overseas possessions, with France second, while Portugal, the Netherlands, Belgium, the United States, and Japan contended for third place. Germany and Italy, each unified in 1870–71, were latecomers to the game and took what was left. Hobsbawm's statement is largely true for Africa and Asia, but not for the South Pacific. Although Churchill died in 1965, the United States, France, Britain, and Chile retain possessions there in the early twenty-first century.[1]

Much of the South Pacific had already been taken before Germany entered the scene. In 1788, the first colonies in the South Pacific were British convict communities at Sydney and on previously uninhabited Norfolk Island. In 1838, the captain of a British naval vessel accepted responsibility for Pitcairn Island, making the descendants of mutineers—at their request—wards of the British government, and Pitcairn became the first European possession in Polynesia. By the Treaty of Waitangi Britain established control in New Zealand in 1840. In 1842 France claimed the Marquesas and the next year Tahiti. In 1853 France annexed New Caledonia and then the Loyalty Islands. On October 10, 1874, after expressing reluctance for several years, Britain annexed the Fiji Islands at the request of King Cakobau.

Colonial powers shared several motives, some frivolous. The metropole wanted to protect missionaries. Naval powers were convinced they needed strategic bases, particularly those where deposits of coal and other supplies could be left for their vessels. The powers wanted to prevent rivals from taking colonies that they perceived to be located in strategic areas. Traders and planters wanted protection from native people. The great powers wanted to curb the excesses of their own nationals in enslaving or otherwise abusing Pacific peoples. Places at the opposite side of the globe made good prisons for offenders. Humanitarians were eager to suppress slavery, cannibalism, infanticide, human sacrifice and other abominations. When a substantial number of Americans or Europeans lived on an island, they could request annexation; the Hawaiian archipelago is an example. Some colonies had natural resources to be exploited; among the resources was rich farmland which Europeans arrived to till, some having had their voyages subsidized. Historians mention markets as a cause of imperialism, and some Pacific people became good customers for muskets, textiles, tools, and alcohol, for which they traded copra, sandalwood, or their labor. And national leaders liked to dazzle their constituents with maps indicating their burgeoning empires; national pride, it was hoped, would head off manifestations of civil unrest at home. Pink splotches all over the world map reinforced British feelings of national superiority and reportedly caused pride to swell in the bosoms of schoolboys.

How could modern, industrialized nations justify seizing colonies in Africa, Asia, and the Pacific, often against the express wishes of their inhabitants? Social Darwinism, accepted at the turn of the century, expressed the concept of racial superiority as scientific fact.

LURED BY BIRD DROPPINGS

From the mid-nineteenth century, American traders were eager to acquire islands so they could hire gangs of workers to mine bird excrement. In 1856, Congress passed the Guano Islands Act. American citizens were authorized to mine guano from unclaimed Pacific islands. The following year, the United States claimed uninhabited Jarvis, Baker and Howland, all in the Line Islands. The eleven atolls that constitute the Line Islands stretch south of the Hawaiian archipelago for a distance of 2,350 kilometers (1,410 miles). Guano mining took place on Jarvis Island between 1858 and 1879; on Howland from 1859 to 1878, and again from 1886–91; and on Baker between 1859–78 and 1886–91. The United States claimed forty-eight islands under the act.[2] Guano, or bird droppings, was first utilized as fertilizer by British landowner and agronomist J.B. Lawes in 1842 at his estate at Rothamsted, England. Soil depletion in Europe and America had been identified as a major problem of agriculture, and the phosphate in guano was used to improve soil.[3] Lawes' experiments led to serious exploitation of some people in the South Pacific. Peruvian offshore islands were major guano depositories worked in the early 1860s by Polynesian slaves abducted by blackbirders. Makatea in the Tuamotus, Ocean Island, and Nauru each had rich deposits that was mined, and the ecology of each of these islands was beyond repair.[4]

GERMANY CARVES OUT ITS PLACE IN THE SUN

A significant factor in competition for colonies, not only in the Pacific but in Africa and East Asia as well, was the unification of Germany as a nation on January 18, 1871. Germany became a great power and, therefore, felt the need to build an overseas empire.

On December 6, 1882, men who wanted to promote overseas colonies for the eleven-year-old Second Reich founded the Deutcher Kolonialverein in Frankfurt-am-Main. Imperial chancellor Prince Otto von Bismarck (1815–98; appointment 1871–90) had been content to see other colonial powers clashing over far-flung real estate and wanted to consolidate German power on the European continent. However, on June 23, 1884, Bismarck publicly accepted the Kolonialverein position; as historian A.J.P. Taylor argued, the "Iron Chancellor" saw it as a way to disturb but not unduly provoke Britain while improving relations with Britain's rival, France.[5] Most areas of the world worth taking had been swallowed, if not completely digested, and Germany had to satisfy herself with what was left. Within two years imperial Germany began to acquire colonies in Africa, in Micronesia, and in the South Pacific.

On November 3, 1884, the German New Guinea Company claimed the entire northeast of New Guinea, the Bismarck Archipelago and the northern Solomons. Traders and planters were able to occupy only minuscule coastal enclaves. Britain claimed Papua three days later when Commodore Elphinstone ran up the union jack at Port Moresby.

NAURU STRIPPED BARE

The German colony that underwent the most total transformation was Nauru. On April 14, 1887, Germany annexed the 21-square-kilometer (8.1-square-mile) island. Since it was charted in 1798, visiting captains had traded firearms and alcohol for food. Nauru's twelve Micronesian tribes had been at war since 1878. The gunboat *Eber* landed troops in October 1888 and disarmed the islanders. Bullets and disease helped reduce the population from an estimated 1,400 in 1843 to 900 people in 1888.[6]

Composed of coral and phosphate, the lagoon and ponds yielded ample seafood, and fresh water was adequate. Life in Nauru would remain relatively undisturbed until after rich phosphate deposits were identified in 1899. Nauru phosphate had a rich content, as high as eighty percent.[7] In 1905, a British firm, the Pacific Islands Company, bought the right to mine guano from a German company, Jaluit-Gesellschaft, for £2,000 and £12,500 in PIC shares. The Pacific Islands Company paid the German government 25,000 marks per annum as well as royalties for tonnage shipped. The inhabitants of the island, whose opinion had not been solicited, and whose insular world was being irreversibly stripped bare, were paid five pfennigs per ton and twenty marks for every copra-producing tree that was taken down. The compensation to Nauruans, assuming commoners received anything at all, could not begin to pay them for the loss of their island's surface.[8] Douglas L. Oliver wrote: "The old native culture of Nauru ... was only superficially described by early visitors and was so overwhelmingly transformed by events of the last five decades that the past cannot be recovered."[9]

THE SCATTERED COOKS

Captain Edmund Bourke of HMS *Hyacinthe* proclaimed a British protectorate over Rarotonga on October 26, 1888, and in the next few days over five more southern Cook Islands. These islands included Aitutaki, Mangaia, Atiu, Mauke, and Mitiaro.

On September 23, 1773, Captain James Cook charted Manuae, the first of the Cook

Island group he would find. He named Manuae Hervey Island in honor of a lord of the Admiralty, Augustus John Hervey (1724–79), third earl of Bristol. The name Hervey was given to the entire southern group, including Rarotonga and Aitutaki. It was Russian Admiral Adam von Krusenstern who, in 1824, changed the name to the Cook Islands in his work *Atlas de l'Ocean Pacifique* (1823–26). Krusenstern commanded the first Russian circumnavigation, August 1803 to August 1806.

On April 13, 1777, Cook's boat crews threaded their way through coral reefs to find sufficient scurvy grass and other food on uninhabited Palmerston Atoll. Cook named the 56-square-kilometer (22-square-mile) atoll for Henry Temple, second viscount Palmerston (1739–1802), a lord of the Admiralty from 1768 to 1777.[10] It consists of eight islets on the reef fringing the placid lagoon.

The Palmerston population speaks English rather than Cook Islands Maori. Like the Pitcairners, they are a hybrid people, the descendants of Polynesians and a British seaman. The founding father was William Marsters, born Richard Masters (1831–99), a sailor from Leicestershire. On July 8, 1863, aboard the schooner *Horai*, Marsters was landed on Palmerston Atoll, some 435 kilometers (270 miles) northwest of Rarotonga. He had left England at age twenty-two, a married man, shortly after the birth of his second child; his wife and children never saw him again. John Brander, a planter from Scotland, had employed Marsters to harvest coconuts and beche-de-mer on Palmerston. Marsters brought with him Akakingaro, a Polynesian woman, from Penrhyn Island. Then he brought to Palmerston her cousin, Toupou, and then a third woman, Matavia, from Penrhyn Island. He situated his three Polynesian wives on three corners of the atoll, which he designated Head, Middle and Tail. By these three women he had eight, six, and six children — eight girls and twelve boys in all. When they had grown, some of his children married half-brothers and sisters. By 1946 the New Zealand government counted over 5,000 descendants of the patriarch.[11]

Only in March 1835 were all fifteen Cook Islands— scattered in 230 square kilometers (88 square miles) of ocean — placed with accuracy on a map. Uninhabited Nassau was the last to be charted, by Captain John D. Sampson of the whaling ship *Nassau*.[12]

The London Missionary Society had converted the inhabitants, and now London wanted to secure the widespread islands from French or German intervention. The union jack was raised over each island, but it is uncertain if the *ariki* (chiefs) who agreed to a protectorate fully understood its full implications.[13]

New Zealand governor Uchter Knox, fifth earl of Ranfurly (1856–1933; term 1897–1904), annexed the island of Niue for Great Britain on April 20, 1900. In 1887 Niuans, through their last king, Fata-a-iki (r. 1887–96), had petitioned the British government to protect the island. Fourteen months later, on June 11, 1901, Great Britain transferred responsibility to New Zealand.[14]

On June 11, 1901, New Zealand claimed sovereignty over the Cook Islands. Prime Minister William Seddon of New Zealand wanted to annex the Cook Islands, but islanders knew about the Maori Wars and preferred to be administered by Great Britain. Britain failed to act. In 1901 the chiefs signed a treaty of annexation, and Wellington accepted a challenging administrative task in that between the northernmost island, Penrhyn, and the southernmost, Mangaia, are 1,433 kilometers (890 miles) of ocean travel. The first resident commissioner was Lieutenant Colonel W.E. Gudgeon (served 1901–09); Gudgeon took powers into his own hands, including some considered those of the *ariki*.[15] On September 29, 1903, the administration of Niue was separated from that of the Cook Islands, both New Zealand protectorates.

House, Palmerston Atoll, Cook Islands. In 1863 William Marsters from England arrived at Palmerston and married three women. Marsters' descendants continue to inhabit Palmerston. They speak English as their first language and live in Western style houses, thanks to shipwrecks. The approach to the island is treacherous and several ships have been destroyed by sharp coral. Islanders build their homes and their church from the wreckage. Photograph by Robert Kirk.

THE GILBERT AND ELLICE ISLANDS

An agreement made with Germany in 1886 allocated the Gilbert and Ellice Islands to Britain. Islanders were neither informed of the arrangement nor asked their agreement. By June 17, 1892, Captain Davis of HMS *Royalist* completed his journey through the Gilbert Islands (now Kiribati), declaring each a component of a British Protectorate.[16] Captain Gibson, R.N., of HMS *Curacao*, completed a voyage through the major islands that compose the Ellice (now Tuvalu) group by October 16, 1892, declaring British suzerainty over each Island. By Order in Council, the sixteen Gilbert Islands and nine Ellice Islands were consolidated on November 10, 1915, under a single administration. The two groups shared a British resident commissioner. Gilbert Islanders are primarily Micronesian, while Ellice Islanders are Polynesian.[17]

One of the Gilbert and Ellice group would prove far more valuable than all the others combined. On January 3, 1801, Captain Jared Gardner aboard the ship *Diana* discovered the 6.5-square-kilometer (4-square-mile) Island he named Ocean Island. A century later, on May 3, 1900, Albert F. Ellis (1869–1951), an Australian expert, identified the purest known phosphate of lime on Ocean Island, also called Banaba. Ellis obtained a 999-year lease from two Banabans who did not necessarily have the power to approve, in the name of all the people, the stripping away over time of the surface. Mining operations began August 28, 1900. Phosphates would bring large profits, but the profits did not go to Banabans. On September 26, 1901, Captain Reginald Godfrey Olway Tupper (b. 1859) aboard

HMS Pylades annexed Ocean Island for Britain. On November 28, 1901 Ocean Island was incorporated into the Gilbert and Ellice protectorate.[18]

On January 12, 1916, by Order in Council the Gilbert and Ellice Islands Protectorate (now Kiribati and Tuvalu) was declared a British crown colony. The administrative move had little effect on the lives of the islanders.[19]

Commander C.F. Oldham of HMS *Egeria* raised the union jack on three Union (now Tokelau) coral atolls, the first on June 21, 1889, declaring them a British protectorate. The small strings of *motus* surrounding lagoons had no rich resources to be exploited, nor did Britons want to settle there; rather, Britain was intent on keeping their combined 12.2 square kilometers (4.75 square miles) from Germany. The Polynesian population had been much decreased by blackbirders and disease. Known until 1946 as the Union Islands, on February 29, 1916, they were attached to the Gilbert and Ellice Islands for administrative purposes. The new possession consisted of Atafu, Nukunonu, and Fakaofo atolls.[20]

No Island Left Unclaimed

In the last two decades of the nineteenth century every place was taken. France tightened its grip by declaring Tahiti a colony on December 30, 1880, when the last king was pensioned off; the change of designation had little effect on the fewer than 6,000 remaining Tahitians.

On May 13, 1881, Britain annexed 36-square-kilometer (14-square-mile) Rotuma Island. Britain governed the Polynesian population as part of Melanesian Fiji. Tribal wars had been exacerbated by division between Protestants and Catholics, and the people had been victimized by escaped convicts. The chiefs asked for imperial protection.[21]

On November 2, 1881, France annexed the Gambiers and the Tuamotus. They were administered as part of French Oceania.[22]

On April 5, 1887, France signed a treaty with the local ruler that made Wallis (Uvea) Island a protectorate. On February 16, 1888, she claimed Futuna and Alofi, forming the Wallis and Futuna possession.[23]

On November 16, 1887, Britain and France agreed to govern the New Hebrides under a joint naval commission; on October 20, 1907, they would begin to rule the islands as a condominium. They preempted German annexation by doing so.[24]

On March 17, 1888, Captain Wiseman of HMS *Caroline* annexed 322 square-kilometer (124-square-mile) Christmas (now Kirimati) Island for Britain. Two days later he annexed Fanning (now called Tabuaeran), which is 11 kilometers (7 miles) in diameter. Both of these Line Islands had had copra plantations since the mid–1850s and populations of contract workers. Uninhabited Christmas Island had been discovered on December 25, 1777, by Captain James Cook. Christmas (or Kirimati) formed seventy percent of the entire land area of Britain's Gilbert Islands. The perimeter is 150 kilometers (93 miles), making it the atoll with the largest land area in the world.[25] In 1913 a coconut plantation was established on Christmas Island, which had been leased for 87 years by Father Petrics Emmanuel Rougier (1864–1932). Rougier had workers plant 400,000 trees. On January 27, 1916, Christmas Island (Kirimati) was joined to the Gilbert and Ellice Islands colony.[26]

On March 16, 1888, France claimed Raiatea, Tahaa, and Huahine as protectorates, and three days later added Bora Bora.[27] On February 16, 1897, France conquered Raiatea, the last holdout in the Society Islands.[28]

Chile became a colonial power when it claimed Easter Island on September 9, 1888. A decade before, the population had fallen to barely over a hundred.

On January 3, 1893, whites overthrew Queen Liliuokalani of Hawaii, and on April 12, 1898, the United States annexed the archipelago as a territory.[29] Hawaii became a state only in 1959.

On March 15, 1893, Britain claimed New Georgia, Guadalcanal, Makira, Santa Cruz, Rennel, and Malaita, constituting them as the Solomon Islands protectorate. Governing the fiercely independent population with minimal expenditure, British authorities exerted remarkably loose control over the vast majority.[30] Britain completed her protectorate on November 14, 1899, by claiming the Santa Cruz Islands, Rennel, Ontong, Java and the Bellona Islands.[31]

The Samoan Islands were partitioned on December 2, 1899. Germany took the major islands of Upolu and Savai'i, while the United States was assigned Tutuila and smaller islands east of longitude 171. Britain was compensated elsewhere.[32] On May 18, 1900, Tonga and Britain signed a Treaty of Friendship and Protection. Tonga kept its king and its customs but not its foreign policy, defense, currency, or banking functions.[33]

By 1900, virtually every South Pacific island, atoll, and rock had been claimed.

New Forms of Rule

Imperialism enabled and accelerated the transformation of the lives of South Pacific people. Some colonial powers were more benevolent than others. All had a positive effect by lessening the incidence of tribal wars, cannibalism, infanticide, murder, and other tribal customs, which were declared to be punishable. Colonial governments were better able to protect people from blackbirders, malevolent beachcombers and other Western intruders.

As South Pacific people became Westernized through education, religion, marriage, and living, working or studying abroad, a new form of tribal leader emerged — not through inherited place or through providing generous feasts, but by becoming a functionary or teacher or clergy member, military petty officer or policeman. Members of this new class replaced chiefs on some islands and interposed themselves between their home governments and chiefs or big men on others. They added a new layer of control and of tribute in the form of taxes.

The Great War and Pacific People

Although they could easily have remained out of the fight, Australia and New Zealand rushed to aid the mother country in colonial struggles elsewhere. On March 29, 1885, a contingent of volunteers from New South Wales arrived in the Sudan to assist British forces in fighting the Islamic leader, the Mahdi. From 1899 to 1902 New Zealand troops and Australian troops sailed to South Africa to aid Britain in its fight against the Boers.[34] In 1900, when the great powers sent troops to China to suppress the so-called Boxer Uprising, three Australian colonies contributed naval forces.[35] The two self-governing dominions would make their greatest contribution to Britain in World War I.

World War I left the South Pacific with minor physical scars, compared to pockmarked European battlefields. Except for those who went to fight at Gallipoli or in France, few lost their lives. The German fleet had dashing adventures in the Pacific, but their feats had no real effect on the war's outcome. During the first months of the struggle, Germany lost her Pacific colonies, but those losses did not impede her war effort. Australia and New Zealand justifiably took renewed pride in their fighting forces. Some indigenous islanders participated, but they received little more than thanks. In all, the First World War did not have as great an effect on the South Pacific as did the Second World War. Rather, it was influenza, a tragic aftershock of the Great War, that brought to a new level the transformation of the South Pacific that had begun four hundred years before when Balboa told Europe of an expanse of wonder and possibility beyond Darien.

AUSTRALIANS AND NEW ZEALANDERS GO TO WAR

When the war commenced at the beginning of August 1914, New Zealand had been a self-governing dominion for seven years, and Australia a federal commonwealth for fourteen. If they had declared neutrality, the Central Powers would probably not have taken the trouble to attack either. Britain could not compel either to assist her. Yet, both rushed to offer assistance to the mother country.

To relieve pressure on their own soldiers, the British government was eager to involve as many troops from the empire in the fight against Germany as possible. On August 5, 1914, Prime Minister Joseph Cook (1860–1947; term 1913–14) informed the Australian people that his cabinet had declared war on the Central Powers. Britain had declared war two days previously. Cook offered Britain the Australian fleet and 20,000 volunteers.[36]

For all of Prime Minister Cook's zealous loyalty to the United Kingdom, Australians saw themselves as a separate people whose men could enlist but were not to be compelled to join the fight. In a plebiscite held on October 28, 1916, the young nation narrowly defeated military conscription. Australian prime minister William M. Hughes (1862–1952; P.M. 1915–23) visited England in the summer of 1916 and returned to urge the conscription of additional men to be sent to war zones; yet, in a second plebiscite held January 10, 1918, a majority of voters again refused to sanction a call-up. Some voters may have been asserting a degree of independence from Great Britain. Others suffered from high inflation brought on by war and resented Australia's participation.[37]

New Zealand also declared war on August 5. The first 8,000 members of the Expeditionary Force sailed on October 16, 1914, delayed by caution for German raiders. General Sir Alexander Godley (1867–1957), nephew of Robert Godley, a founder of Canterbury, led the 8,500-man contingent. They sailed on ten troopships to Albany, Western Australia. The combined New Zealand and Australian forces— ANZACs— sailed together and arrived at Alexandria, Egypt, on December 3, 1914.[38] In early 1916, 111 Maori volunteers sailed with 213 volunteers from Rarotonga, Niue, and the Gilbert and Ellice Islands. Unlike Australia, New Zealand did enforce conscription, but only from 1916. Still smarting from land loss and their marginalization, Maoris from the Waikato region refused conscription; seventy-four were sent to prison camp and punished with a diet of bread and water.[39]

FIJI TROOPS

The first contingent of sixty Europeans resident in Fiji sailed from Suva to Europe aboard RMS *Makura* on the first day of 1915. British authorities at first barred ethnic Fijians from enlisting, but in 1917 a hundred were taken to Calais, France, to work as cargo handlers.[40]

Ethnic Fijian war hero Ratu Sukuna (1888–1958) at the outbreak of war was studying at Oxford. The young chief tried to enlist in the British army but was refused on racial grounds. Ratu Sukuna made his way to France and fought on the Western Front with the French Foreign Legion. On at least four occasions in 1915 he made heroic assaults on German positions. He did not leave the front until he was wounded. The hero returned to Suva on March 30, 1916, and was greeted by a cheering crowd, which carried him off on their shoulders. France awarded Ratu Sukuna the Medaille Militaire for supreme gallantry. Because he was an ethnic colonial subject, he was not permitted to wear the medal in Fiji; then, in 1931 the secretary of state for the colonies informed Suva officials that "this should be treated as a special case and that permission be given to Ratu Sukuna to wear the decoration."[41]

FRENCH PACIFIC TROOPS

On August 29, 1914, the first 165 Tahitian troops sailed for Europe. They formed Le Battalion des Tirailleurs du Pacific. All eligible French males living in Pacific colonies were conscripted and sailed from Papeete to New Caledonia for military training. They were sent from Nouméa to fight on the Western Front.[42] Between 1915 and 1918, 1,036 Europeans and 1,134 Kanaks served in France from New Caledonia. Those who died included 162 Europeans and 374 Kanaks. Kanaks, some 207 of whom died of disease, suffered twice the percentage of fatalities (32.9 percent) of whites (15.6 percent).[43]

KANAKS STRIKE FOR INDEPENDENCE

To High Chief Noel of Koné in New Caledonia, fighting for the French did nothing to free the island from foreign rule. "Fight for freedom instead of for France," Noel admonished. In April 1917, during what were clearly the darkest days of the First World War for France, Noel started an insurrection. Noel chose a time when he thought the French would least be able to put up a strong resistance; his revolt was the last real hope for the Kanaks of getting some or all of their island back from French settlers. Insurrectionists struck in the hill country between Koné and Hienghène. Kanaks raided settlers' farms, attacked military installations, and ambushed troop columns. Before the revolt was suppressed, fourteen French and well over a hundred Kanaks had been killed. When the revolt ended, some 250 were jailed, 78 tried, 61 convicted and two executed in October 1920.[44]

ADVENTURES OF THE GERMAN FLEET

The German fleet in the Pacific was noted for extraordinary accomplishments. On September 7, 1914, personnel from the cruiser *Nürnberg* destroyed the wireless station at Fanning (Tabuaeran) Island. A cable between Vancouver, British Columbia, and Southport, Queensland, was linked at Fanning; thus, communications were severed temporarily between North America and Australia. By diving for the cable ends and reconnecting them, technicians restored communications within two weeks.[45]

To defend Papeete from German guns, Governor William Maurice Fawtier (b. 1867; term August 1913–October 1915) mobilized all sixty troops and called for a hundred volunteers. He interned German citizens. On September 22, 1914, two German warships commanded by Vice Admiral Maximilian Graf von Spee (1861–1914) bombarded Papeete by firing more than a hundred shells into the town. Shelling caused fires in the central market and other structures. One Polynesian and one ethnic Chinese were killed. Damage estimated at £150,000 was the worst the Central Powers inflicted on an Allied colonial possession in the Pacific during the war. The French feared the town could be taken, so they lit their coal stocks on fire, dynamited the lighthouse, and destroyed documents. The French commander threatened to execute forty Germans recently captured aboard the freighter *Walküre* if von Spee did not leave. Von Spee took *Gneisenau* and *Scharnhorst* to the Marquesas. In the Marquesas they commandeered goods from stores at Taiohae on Nuku Hiva and on Hiva Oa.[46]

From October 12 to 18, 1914, the German Far East Fleet, intent on sinking Allied shipping, rendezvoused to replenish supplies at Easter Island, which was neutral territory because Chile had not entered the war. The ships were the armed cruisers *Scharnhorst* and *Gneisenau* and the light cruisers *Leipzig*, *Nürnberg*, and *Emden*. In December 1914, von Spee took his squadron to South America to prey on British ships. Off the Falkland Islands the British navy destroyed *Scharnhorst*, *Gneisenau*, *Leipzig*, and *Nürnberg*. Von Spee was killed.[47]

British naval guns sank the German commerce raider *Dresden* on March 14, 1915, while it was undergoing repairs in Cumberland Bay, Juan Fernandez Island, also a possession of neutral Chile. Shell holes can be seen on a cliff overlooking the bay. *Dresden* lies 54 meters (180 feet) below the surface. Before it was shelled by the British ships *Glasgow* and *Kent*, Lieutenant Wihelm Canaris (1887–1945), later head of Hitler's military intelligence (Abwher), negotiated with the British. As a result, most of his crew were saved and interned in neutral Chile. Three German sailors are buried in the local cemetery at San Juan Bautista.[48]

On April 6, 1917, the day the United States declared war on the German Empire, naval authorities interned crews of German merchant ships and gunboats in Honolulu Harbor. Several German ships had arrived during the course of the war to find safety from Allied warships in the commodious harbor of a neutral nation. Americans interned the crews on the mainland and transferred the ships to their own merchant and naval fleets.[49]

The German sea raider *Wolf* used Denham Bay, Raoul Island, in the Kermadecs as a base to capture the steamer *Wairauna* on June 3, 1917. On June 16, the *Wolf* crew captured the American schooner *Winslow*, unloaded its cargo and sank it on June 22. The Germans sunk the *Wairuna* June 17 after taking off its cargo. In all, Fregattenkapitan Karl August Nerger (1875–1947) was responsible for capturing fourteen ships and laying mines in the Tasman Sea, which destroyed thirteen other vessels. The *Wolf* had left Kiel, Germany, on December 16, 1916, and returned February 24, 1918, after 451 days at sea. Nerger brought back 467 prisoners of war and a cargo of valuable raw materials.[50]

LUCKNER, THE "SEA DEVIL"

On August 24, 1917, after slipping through the British North Sea blockade and sinking or commandeering fifteen Allied ships with minimal loss of life, the 1571-ton German commerce raider *Seeadler*, commanded by Count Felix von Luckner (1881–1966), was wrecked on Maupihaa, a small atoll in the Society Islands. Thus began what was the greatest sea adventure of the Great War. A tsunami had swept von Luckner's ship onto a reef, stranding the fifty-nine crew and forty-six Allied prisoners. Von Luckner, known as the "Sea Devil" for his exploits, took five men in a ship's launch 3,700 kilometers (2,300 miles) to Fiji. There, he planned to commandeer a ship, return for his crew, and carry on sea raiding. The six Germans arrived at Wakaya in Fiji's Lomaiviti Group. Instead of seizing a ship, the six found themselves incarcerated as prisoners of war in New Zealand.

When a French trading ship, *Lutece*, anchored off Maupihaa, the stranded Germans seized it at gunpoint and left the French crew on Maupihaa with the prisoners while they sailed the *Lutece* to South America. Four of the prisoners on Maupihaa, Americans, took the other available open boat and sailed 1,600 kilometers (990 miles) to Pago Pago, where they reported von Luckner's activities and arranged for the rescue of those stranded on Maupihaa. The *Lutece*, renamed *Fortuna* by its German captors, ran into rocks off Easter Island. The crew was incarcerated by Chilean authorities until the end of the war.

Von Luckner and his fellow prisoners, meanwhile, escaped from New Zealand by taking the prison commander's motorboat. They were captured in the Kermadec Islands, where they had sought provisions. They were repatriated to Germany only in 1919.[51]

GERMANY LOSES HER PACIFIC EMPIRE

New Zealand's governor general from 1917 to 1920, Arthur William de Brito Saville Fojambe, the second earl of Liverpool (1870–1941), received orders from London on August 6, 1914, to occupy German Samoa. On August 29, New Zealand troops took German Samoa without a battle. The Samoa Land Corporation, owned by the government in Wellington, took over German plantations and commercial interests.

The Samoan people managed to preserve their ancient customs and institutions during what would be forty-eight years of New Zealand rule, but not so the Chinese workers brought in by the Germans. The *Truth*, published in Auckland, complained, "It is a remarkable feature that New Zealand is being asked to take over the control not only of a captured German colony but the loving care of a horde of cheap and nasty Chinese coolies."[52]

New Zealand had erected daunting barriers against Chinese immigration to its own shores, and when Samoa was still under New Zealand military jurisdiction, Chinese workers were expelled. Germans had employed Chinese on plantations, and in October 1914, there were 2,184. By June 1919, only 876 remained. When they left Samoa, Chinese were dispossessed of most of their earnings by being forced to exchange their wages to pounds sterling.[53]

On November 11, 1914 Australian troops took German New Guinea. A few weeks earlier, on September 16, they had taken outposts in the Bismarck Archipelago. Six Australians were killed. The volunteer German militia consisted mainly of planters. Plantation owners were returned to Germany after the war and compensated through reparations for their losses. New Guinea remained under Australian military rule until 1920.[54]

Australia waited three and a half months after war was declared to take Nauru because it was of little strategic value and Australian taxpayers would have to assume responsibility for feeding the inhabitants. Australian troops took Nauru on November 6, 1914, and sent all Germans on the island as prisoners of war to Australia. Australia left a garrison of fifty-two men to guard a valuable prize — an island covered by guano.[55] That Australia finally took Nauru during the war was due to pressure on behalf of the Pacific Islands Company, which wanted to resume phosphate exports.[56]

With the loss of Samoa to New Zealand, New Guinea and Nauru to Australia, and the Marshall and Caroline islands to Japan, the three-decade German colonial presence in the Pacific was ended. Australia and New Zealand became colonial powers.

GALLIPOLI

On October 31, 1914, the Ottoman Empire entered the war on the side of the Central Powers—Germany, Austria-Hungary, and Bulgaria—an act that led to an invasion of Ottoman territory by Allied forces and a considerable loss of Australian and New Zealand lives.

On April 3, 1915, ANZACs embarked from Egypt en route to the Gallipoli Peninsula, which dominates the passage from the Mediterranean to the Black Sea. First Lord of the Admiralty Winston Churchill persuaded the high command to force an entrance through the narrow Bosporus and the Dardanelles. If successful, the campaign would have split a gaping hole in the Ottoman Empire, Constantinople would have fallen, and Britain would have sent supplies through the Black Sea to its ally, imperial Russia. Britain could have taken Ottoman possessions in the Near East. The Allies could have opened a southeastern front in the Balkans, drawing German troops, and possibly breaking the anguishing deadlock in northern France and Belgium. The bold maneuver in the Dardanelles could have brought Allied victory. The high command agreed to Churchill's gamble if vital troops were not withdrawn from the stalemated Western Front. As a result, troops from Australia and New Zealand played a prominent role.[57]

ANZAC troops went ashore on the Gallipoli Peninsula on April 25, 1914. They were part of an army of 400,000 imperial and 79,000 French troops. The fight at Gallipoli is the great epic of Australian and New Zealand military history, a baptism in blood that unites the two nations in sad sentiment.

The campaign got off to a terrible start. The Turks knew the troops were coming. Currents on April 25 would not allow landings at wide beaches, so men landed at narrow beaches shadowed by steep cliffs. Two thousand ANZACs were killed the first day. A survivor recalled that the landing was "indescribable.... Many were gunned down while still in the water.... Corpses lay in rows on the sand or half way up the cliffs, men lay about cut, bleeding and dying." The ANZACs held on for 238 days from April to December, during which 7,600 Australians died and 19,000 were wounded. New Zealand forces lost 2,721 dead and 4,752 wounded, from a total of 8,450 troops. New Zealand casualties amounted to eighty-eight percent.

Twenty thousand ANZACs were evacuated from the Gallipoli Peninsula on December 18, 1915. In all, 150,000 died on both sides before the Allies realized the campaign could not succeed and ordered forces back to Egypt. The evacuation was performed at night in stealth, without loss of life.[58]

PASSCHENDAELE

New Zealand armed forces suffered severe losses not only at Gallipoli, but at the Battle of Passchendaele. Passchendaele, also known as Third Battle of Ypres, was fought by

Allied forces in Flanders against imperial German troops and proved to be the most lethal battle of the Great War for New Zealanders. The twelfth of October was their single most lethal day. From June to November 1917, New Zealand forces lost 800 men killed, including 45 officers, and 2,700 wounded. A New Zealand participant recalled, "The shells came thick and fast, I was in the midst of a storm of spouting, belching mud and fire and flying fragments." ANZACs fought at the Somme, Messines and in other battles over two and a half years on the Western Front.[59]

ARMISTICE AND COUNTING THE DEAD

An exhausted and famished Germany agreed to an armistice on November 11, 1918, and the Great War ended. Australia had lost 54,000 dead out of 330,700 who went overseas; 155,000 were wounded. New Zealand sent 101,000 troops overseas. New Zealand counted 16,317 dead and 41,202 wounded, a devastating casualty rate of 56.3 percent. These casualties, which included Maoris, amounted to a third of New Zealand males between twenty and forty. Australian prime minister William M. Hughes arrived on opening day, January 18, 1919, to participate in the Paris Peace Conference. When the League of Nations was instituted to prevent war, Hughes was instrumental in having the recognition of race equality omitted from the League Covenant. Hughes demanded reparations from Germany for losses in the war, but failed to achieve that goal. In spite of a sixty-eight percent casualty rate inflicted on Australian volunteers, Hughes stated that the war "saved us from physical and moral degeneracy and decay."[60]

Chapter 21

An Ongoing
Transformation, 1918–20

DIRE PREDICTIONS

For over a century, by 1920, strangers from beyond the seas had come to the Pacific for anything profitable: fur from otters and seals, sandalwood, beche-de-mer, pearls, pork, whales, guano, turtle shell — even shrunken heads. They came to save souls and reform "savages." They came for sex and sunshine and adventure. The strangers took the land they said they needed and rearranged logic to justify displacing the inhabitants from it. They organized Pacific island people and Asian people for work on vast plantations to produce profitable sugar, cotton, pineapple, coconut oil and copra for export. They put others to work digging in mines. They claimed every last atoll in the name of their sovereign governments. They stayed to rule. The footprint they impressed was vast and deep.

In some South Pacific communities by 1920, older people hardly recognized a society and landscape that had been transformed since they were children. As I.C. Campbell stated: "Social structures were crumbling, chiefs abused their authority, and legitimate authority was undermined; men abandoned their families, houses lapsed into decay and gardens were neglected; the people became visibly indolent or decrepit; the cheerful buoyancy of spirits was superseded by listless demoralization." It seemed as if people impacted by contact with Europe and America had lost their desire to live.[1]

In 1920 the anthropologist Bronislaw Malinowski wrote: "Now once you make life unattractive for a man ... you can cut the taproot of his vitality. The rapid dying out of the native races is ... due more to wanton interference with their pleasures and normal occupation ... than to any other cause."[2]

Most communities did not die out, but were able to increase their often mixed-race populations in the twentieth century. Some isolated communities in Melanesia and New Guinea neither died out, nor were even aware that change had taken place. Many people did, however, become painfully aware of foreign penetration when their communities were devastated by the worldwide influenza pandemic.

INFLUENZA

In 1918, South Pacific people had suffered and died from introduced diseases for well over a century, but the worldwide influenza or "Spanish flu" pandemic came as a crushing blow. When the great European powers threw tens of thousands of their young male citi-

246

zens into the inglorious hell of the trenches on the Western Front, the leaders could not have foreseen that the new disease would kill more people than the war itself, in fact more than any single agent in all of recorded history. Influenza did its lethal work within two years, leaving anywhere from fifty to a hundred million dead. Most deaths occurred from September to December 1918, while the war ground to an agonizing halt.[3] Influenza killed through viral pneumonia that destroyed the lungs. It could come quickly or it could take its time, but the results were too often the same.[4]

The so-called Spanish flu, or influenza, was first reported in Haskell County, Kansas, in January and February 1918. Soon troops at Camp Funston, Kansas, were infected, infected men were shipped off to France, and the contagion spread to exhausted doughboys near Brest and Bordeaux. From there, the worldwide pandemic spread rapidly and infected tens of millions.[5]

The pandemic reached New Zealand in September 1918. An observer noted, "I stood in the middle of Wellington City at 2 P.M. on a weekday afternoon, and there was not a soul to be seen — no trams running, no shops open, and the only traffic was a van with a white sheet tied to the side with a big red cross painted on it, serving as an ambulance or hearse. It really was a City of the Dead."[6] An estimated 8,600 people died in New Zealand over a period of just two months out of a population of 1,160,000. Seven times more Maoris died than did Pakehas.[7]

In Australia ships arrived with as many as forty-three percent of passengers ill, but authorities quarantined the vessels and Australians remained safe — until December 1918. In that month ninety ill soldiers returned on a troop ship. They too were quarantined, but somehow the disease spread, probably through infected medical personnel who treated them and returned to shore. Australia lost fewer people than any other Westernized country, a third of the death toll per thousand of the United States.[8]

Influenza struck some Pacific island populations with lethal ferocity. Samoan deaths outpaced those of all other colonies or nations. The American SS *Talune*, sailing from Auckland, brought influenza to Western Samoa on November 7, 1918. The *Sydney Daily Telegraph*'s Apia correspondent wrote of the *Talune*, "Although she had many cases on board, she was permitted to land several sufferers, two of whom soon died. There were no restrictions and people went off and came ashore as they chose." New passengers, though, were asked not to board because the crew was too ill to welcome them. In about seven days the infection spread through Upolu and traveled to Savai'i. The first victim succumbed within two days.

Ninety percent of Samoans were infected, and twenty-two percent of men died from influenza. The *Daily Telegraph* correspondent disclosed that "many died from starvation [because] the survivors were too weak to prepare and apportion the food."[9] New Zealand administrators were blamed for allowing the ship to dock and for failing to take steps to quarantine victims. Dissatisfaction with official handling of the medical emergency would be cited as a cause for the *Mau* movement for Samoan independence in the 1920s.[10] When the disease abated, from a population of 38,302, the survivors numbered 29,802.[11]

Residents of American Samoa were fortunate to escape the pandemic. Authorities in Pago Pago proclaimed a quarantine on November 23, to last as long as influenza threatened. The colony lost no people to the pandemic.[12]

The *Navua*, a steamer from San Francisco carrying passengers ill with influenza, arrived in Papeete on November 17, 1918. When the disease had done its gruesome work, one seventh of Tahitians had succumbed. In France the death rate from influenza was five per thousand, but in the Society Islands it was 155 per thousand — 30 times greater, indicating the relative susceptibility of Polynesian populations. Males died at a rate of 150 per thousand and females age 35–39 at 220 per thousand. Deaths for those over sixty, ostensibly from flu, were between forty and fifty percent. In the Society Islands deaths were estimated at about four thousand.[13] Temporary restrictions on travel prevented the epidemic from spreading to the Marquesas, Tuamotus, and Austral Islands.[14]

Influenza was blamed for killing eight percent of Tongans in 1918, an estimated thousand people.

The first deaths to be reported from the influenza pandemic in Fiji were in the Suva area on November 17, where an estimated eighty-five to ninety percent of the population eventually had the flu, although not necessarily at the same time.[15] Fiji lost fourteen percent of its population from November 25 to December 10.[16] Many deaths were said to have been caused by Fijians dipping themselves into cooling water to assuage fevers. By December 28, 1918, the flu in Fiji had been halted, no further deaths being reported.[17]

MANDATES: DOMINATION BY ANOTHER NAME

The League of Nations established a mandate system ostensibly to monitor the management of former German and Ottoman possessions by victorious powers. Mandated

Native of New Ireland. This man from New Ireland in the Bismarck Archipelago of New Guinea was painted in 1843 and 1844 by Auguste Whalen. It appeared in the *Oceanie* volume of *Moeurs, Usages et Costumes de tous les Peuples du Monde* (Brussels: Librairie Historique-Artistique, 1844).

colonies were to achieve independence — eventually. New Guinea, Nauru, and Samoa were Class C mandates, indicating unreadiness for early sovereignty, as contrasted with Mesopotamia, Palestine, and Syria, which were Class A, viewed as approaching readiness in a matter of a few decades. Freedom of conscience and religion of the mandated populations were to be respected. In no mandated territory was the opinion of the people solicited concerning their change of colonial masters.

Australia and New Zealand, recently colonies themselves, became colonial masters. Because New Zealand had taken over Samoa in August 1914, the League mandated Samoa to its jurisdiction on December 17, 1920.[18] Nauru was mandated, on December 17, 1920, not only to Australia, which had taken it from Germans, but to the British Empire. The phosphate-rich island was to be administered jointly by the United Kingdom, Australia, and New Zealand. If Nauru had had no resources, only Australia would have assumed mandate responsibilities, but per acre, Nauru was one of the richest prizes on Earth. A phosphate consortium was established so that the three powers could share the profits from guano mining.[19]

New Guinea was mandated to Australia on December 17, 1920. As a Class C Mandate, its independence was not expected to occur in the foreseeable future. Although New Guineans had inhabited their island and governed their own affairs for 30,000 years and probably longer, they were judged to be pathetically unprepared for parliamentary democracy — or any other form of national self government. Cannibalism had been ended in settled areas, but warfare was ongoing, as it probably had been for millennia. In 1920, Australian Percy Allen wrote: "A belief in ghosts and spirits appears to be universal. In almost every village there is a sorcerer, who propitiates or exercises the evil spirits with incantations or offerings.... "Any kind of sudden, unaccountable, illness is immediately attributed to the black sorcerer."[20]

A Board of Expropriations, appointed by the Australian government, arranged the sale of German property consisting of 268 plantations, 20 large stores and workshops, and other facilities. The money paid by Australians for these properties was used to defray German reparations to Australia.[21] According to *Stewart's Handbook of the Pacific Islands*, the population of former German New Guinea in 1920 was thought to be declining due to "race suicide ... [and] various diseases, some of which have been brought to the islands by Europeans."[22] A proclamation in *pijn* summed up the transfer from the House of Hohonzollern to the House of Windsor: "No More um-Kaiser; God Save um-King."[23]

Ongoing change in other areas of the South Pacific was also characterized by the white man's dominance.

AUSTRALIA C. 1920

In the six decades from 1860 to 1920, over 600,000 immigrants were granted assisted passage to Australia.[24] These newcomers raised the population to five and a half million. When the convict colony was founded at Sydney in 1788, it was hoped and expected that Aborigine rights would be respected and that white impact on their lives would be minimal and perhaps beneficial. "It would be hard," wrote W.E.H. Stanner, "to sustain any such thesis for the 1820s and impossible from the 1830s onward." By the 1890s, continued Stanner, white settlement had reached deep into the interior of the continent and "dispossessed the Aborigines of all land of good pastoral potential and brought hundreds of tribes to ruin." Europeans justified their land aggrandizements by calling on "political authority, law, morals, religion, and rationality." It was not until the 1930s that Aborigine rights reemerged as a national consideration.

By 1901 Aborigines numbered 67,000, down from an estimated quarter million or more in 1788. The Australian anthropologist Walter Baldwin Spencer (1880–1929) wrote in the 1920s, "It is inevitable that the full-blooded Aboriginal must disappear."[25]

NEW ZEALAND C. 1920

By 1921 Maoris had reached a population nadir in terms of their percentage of New Zealand's total population. With 56,987 people, their population had fallen — not in total numbers—but from 48.6 percent in 1858 to about 4.5 percent. In 1921 Europeans numbered 1,214,677.[26] About ninety percent of Maoris lived in rural areas, mostly in Northland and on the east coast.[27]

As land-hungry *pakehas* entered the country, the Maoris lost more land. The Native Lands Acts passed in 1862 and 1865 allowed whites to purchase land from Maoris rather than from the crown. Like the Dawes Severalty Act passed in 1887 in the United States, the Native Lands Acts made the alienation of property easier and led to a significant loss of Maori lands. By 1900, North Island Maoris had lost three-quarters of their lands. Transactions and confiscations were "carried out in an often unscrupulous manner that left a legacy of bitterness."[28]

Between 1910 and 1921, Maoris lost a further 5,725,710 hectares (2,290,284 acres). Legislation was amended to make it even easier for Maoris to sell land. During the same decade Maori councils were allowed to lapse, and health services deteriorated.[29] It was not until 1926 that a commission was appointed to reexamine land transactions between Maoris and *pakehas*. The commission concluded that the transactions had been unjust and recommended compensation.[30]

TAHITI C. 1920

During the decade 1911 to 1921, those who analyzed population trends in French Polynesia had been "pessimistic about the chances of native inhabitants holding their own in the long battle with infant mortality rates, infertility and low resistance to imported diseases."[31]

That legendary Tahiti had been transformed in the century and a half since Wallis and his men anchored there is beyond dispute. An observer wrote in the *Herald* (Melbourne) in early 1923: "The truth is that the island is completely civilised from end to end. The only real houses are the one or two built by white men in imitation of the old. The only folks who wear *pareaus* are those same white men who sit half-naked in the midst of clothed native servants. The only roads are metaled, and the only walks really possible are along those same roads, for the native paths have long since been deserted and overgrown with largely imported and very rank weeds. The mountains are inaccessible, and the sea coast districts are not, solely because there is motor service twice a day and a bicycle shop and a garage full of taxis in Papeete." In the same article Robert Kreable described women bathing in the sea in "shapeless Mother Hubbards, with their chemises on underneath as an additional precaution.... The fair houris of romance are, on the whole, very distinctly plain prostitutes of the town ... and they will shuffle through the hula hula only if drunk and beyond the city limit, wherein the performance is forbidden by law."[32]

In addition to giving up polygamy, infanticide, human sacrifice and other barbaric practices forbidden by missionaries, Tahitian life was changed even more by French governance. No longer scattered, dwellings were concentrated in villages. Manufactured products became necessities, and economic competition became necessary for many, while work was more specialized and performed by individuals often away from home rather than at home by the family. Work expanded beyond what was essential to live, as did wants.[33]

In 1911 visitor Henri Lebeau had called Tahiti a "hospital island": "In this splendid place ... all is ruin, misery, human decrepitude." Observers predicted the Tahitians were "doomed to die out." Predictions of dying races provided a convenient apology for imperialism: The people were obviously unfit physically and morally and should be confined to reservations and have their lands appropriated.[34] After 1921, Tahiti's population would rise steadily.

The Tuamotus lost more than a thousand people since 1911, falling from 3,715 to 2,676.

RAPA-ITI C. 1920

Rapa-iti in the Austral Islands lost probably nine-tenths of its people between the time Vancouver and his crew had visited in 1791, and 1920. Missionaries in 1826 had estimated 2,000. The census of 1911 counted 183 and by 1920 the number had actually risen to 220. Epidemics, alcoholism, and blackbirders diminished the population steadily. More were lost, at least temporarily, when men shipped out as crew on European ships.[35]

THE MARQUESAS C. 1920

In 1919 writer John W. Church visited all six of the Marquesas that remained inhabited. He marveled at the Bay of Virgins, also known as Hanavave Bay, on Fatu Hiva. Framed by gigantic pillars, a section of collapsed volcanic crater wall reveals a verdant valley. The valley winds upward toward the island's center. The Bay of Virgins is one of the world's jaw-dropping sights that justifies using the word *awesome*. All around the valley and on the slopes above it Church noted thousands of *paepae*, stone slabs on which huts had once existed. By 1919 they had been abandoned, their inhabitants dead, mostly victims of decades of lethal disease.

Church estimated the entire population on the six inhabited islands at 1,950, down from the official French count four years earlier of 3,004. Summarizing his finding, Church prophesied, "There can be no doubt that this drunken, disease-ridden remnant of the Marquesan race is beyond redemption; and all the French colonial administration can do is ... let the nation die off as speedily as possible." He concluded, "It can be seen that the days of the Marquesan are numbered. I do not believe that there will be a single full-blooded Marquesan in ten years."[36] In the period 1911–25, life expectancy at birth was only seventeen.

The vocabulary of the ancient Marquesans had names for leprosy, bronchitis, abscesses and impetigo, but none for the diseases that would nearly wipe out their people: tuberculosis, venereal disease, typhoid, influenza, and smallpox. Anthropologist Robert Suggs wrote, probably underestimating the population, "Marquesan society died a horrible, wasting death. By the early 1920s, only 1500 confused, hostile, and apathetic survivors remained of the possible 100,000 to 120,000 that had inhabited the islands in 1767.... Christianity had triumphed, and so had France, but at what a price!"[37]

The survivors, a strikingly handsome people, had lost the memory of their collective past. As late as the 1870s, Church reported, some could recite their genealogy going back 135 generations. But by 1919, Church found nobody who could. It was no longer necessary because French authorities designated their leaders; furthermore, plenty of land lay vacant, ready for planting and gathering.

The death rate was substantially higher than the birth rate. An observer wrote in 1920, "The natives behold with dismay the approaching extinction of their race, and have grown

so despondent that they, never an industrious race, have now ceased altogether from production."[38]

Yet, all was not lost. Although missionaries and French troops could enforce outward
obedience, "the natives as a whole have clung with sullen desperation to the customs of the
past." Church wrote, "Not only does the Marquesan refuse to receive the white man's culture, but he has lost his own as well. His vices he has retained and added to them those of
the race which conquered him, but his own particular arts and virtues have disappeared."[39]

Mangareva c. 1920

An observer in the second decade of the twentieth century described the five hundred
inhabitants of Mangareva as "poor and decadent, diseases introduced by the white man and
insanitary modes of living having taken their vitality."[40] Laval and his fellow Picpusian
fathers had helped reduce the population from an estimated 9,000 by conscripting converts
to erect church architecture more suited for northern France than the tropics.

Easter Island c. 1920

In 1920 the people of Easter Island were counted as 283, having fallen from at least
two to three thousand when Roggeveen arrived in 1722. A visitor in 1922, Professor Macmillan Brown, reported in the *Christchurch Press*, "These were among the hungriest people in
the world. They lived on some fish and sweet potatoes and were allowed lamb a few times
a year by Williams and Balfour, the company that ran starving cattle and sheep over the
island."[41] Such was their state of destitution that Professor Brown later argued forcefully
that the Rapanui were not capable of having created the *moai* and that the great heads were
the achievement of a long vanished empire.[42]

In September 1916 the Republic of Chile designated three thousand hectares in the
vicinity of Hanga Roa as *parcelas*—small plots of land for the use of the indigenous population. The government maintained tight control and locked up islanders for insulting a
Chilean. By the end of the second decade of the twentieth century, as Steven Fischer stated,
"Easter Island was infamous as Pacific Islands' worst administered colony."[43]

The Cook Islands c. 1920

Missionaries in the 1830s estimated six to seven thousand people on Rarotonga, the
largest of the Cook Islands. By 1920 there were counted 3,287, less than half. Other islands
in the Cooks had fared even worse; Mangaia's population, at 1,200, was a third of 3,567
counted in 1845. Manihiki's population fell from about 1,200 in 1852 to 426, although some
may have relocated to Rarotonga.[44] Niue, formerly administered with the Cooks, had 4,576
people in 1900, and 3,750 two decades later. Infant mortality, neglect of the elderly, tuberculosis and filariasis were cited by the resident medical officer as probable causes for the
disturbing decline. *Stewart's Handbook* for 1923 cited as causes of population decline "severe
epidemics, immorality, intoxicating liquors, and careless use of European clothing." New
Zealand authorities had sought to stem alcoholism in the same way Americans did beginning in 1920, through prohibition.[45]

TONGA C. 1920

In 1920 the population of the Tongan kingdom was approximately 23,759, not including 571 Europeans. In legal theory, every Tongan male was to receive an allotment of 3.4 hectares (8.5 acres) when he reached age sixteen. For this he was to pay annual tax and plant his allotment with coconuts. No land could be sold. As a result, Tongans did not lose land to foreigners.[46] Tongans continued to be ruled by their statuesque queen, 1.91 meters (6' 3") tall, and by nobles in a feudal economy. Although they lost a thousand people to influenza in 1918, they did not suffer the wrenching transformation that some Pacific people did.[47]

HAWAII C. 1920

The Hawaiians lost their land and traditional culture. *Haoles* and Asians moved in to work and many stayed. Military bases and personnel became a permanent part of the new culture. Intermarriage of races created future generations with only part Hawaiian ancestry.

The United States census of 1920 showed the population had increased thirty-three percent since 1910, and stated Hawaii's population to be 255,881. The percentage of full and part Hawaiians had fallen from twenty-four in 1900 to sixteen percent in 1920. Asians played an increasing economic and later political role in the islands. By 1920 pineapple plantations flourished on Oahu, Molokai, Maui and Kaua'i, and canned pineapple became the second largest export product.[48] Tourism was only beginning to be important, with 9,700 visitors counted in 1922.[49] The proliferation of plantation agriculture, the growth of urban areas, particularly Honolulu, changed the landscape so it would be totally unrecognizable to a pre-contact Polynesian were he able to return.[50]

NEW CALEDONIA C. 1920

From 1878 to 1920 the Kanak population of New Caledonia fell more than two thirds, from an estimated 70,000 in 1853 to an estimated 20,000. In addition, some 17,000 Europeans and 30,000 Loyalty Islanders, New Hebrideans and Asians lived on Grand Terre. It seemed as if the Kanaks were rapidly shrinking in number, as were their land holdings.[51] Under the so-called *indignant* system, they lost a host of fundamental human rights.

FIJI C. 1920

Although uncounted numbers of Fijians had been sent prematurely to their graves by disease, Christianity and colonial rule had mitigated the terror with which commoners had lived in pre-contact times. No longer did chiefs launch canoes over live people, leaving broken bodies. Victims were no longer buried with supporting posts when dwellings were erected. The widows of chiefs were no longer hastened into death so they might join their late husbands. Men stopped roasting enemies and missionaries. Warfare ended.

Perhaps the greatest transformation that took place in Fiji was of the Fijians themselves. Writing in the *Sydney Mail* in 1921, a Mr. McMahon observed that the Fijians "are so tractable, of so kind a disposition, so hospitable and gentle, that it is difficult to believe that 50 years ago they were reputed to be the most truculent savages and cannibals of the South Pacific. The Fijians have taken to the white man's civilization, religions, and education with wonderful promptness, and yet without loss of individuality."[52]

British authorities disturbed the traditional lifestyle of the culturally conservative Fijians as little as possible. The Fijians lost comparatively little land. However, wants and needs for articles produced in Europe led numbers of them to seek work on plantations.[53]

As of January 1, 1920, all indentures in Fiji were canceled. Those most affected were Indians, the first of whom had arrived in 1879. No more indentured workers had been transported since November 1916. The reasons for the end of the practice were that Indians in Fiji were agitating for its termination, and at the same time Indian labor became a cause of leaders such as Mahatma Gandhi (1869–1948) in the sub-continent. Gandhi, who had arrived in India the previous year from South Africa and become the leader of the nonviolent independence movement, promised that ships carrying indentured laborers from Calcutta or Bombay en route abroad would be picketed; at the same time, women marched on the viceroy's office demanding an end to recruiting. Labor in Fiji was not worth the price Britain would have to pay during World War I if the issue were to contribute further to the already advanced unrest in its largest possession — the crown jewel — India.[54]

The growth of Indian influence in Fiji, particularly now that all were free of indentures, disturbed many ethnic Fijians. More than half of 60,000 Indians who were resident at the time decided to stay. The Indian population was growing and so was the wealth of these industrious people. The *Sydney Mail* reported in 1922: "Every Indian settlement increases its population by thousands every year; these settlements are crowded with children healthy and happy.... At times women and children can be met lavishly adorned with silver ornaments, their heads, noses, lips, feet, ears, breasts, arms, fingers, ankles, and toes literally hidden by native jewelry."[55] Many raised sugar for themselves or became servants, traders, craftsmen, taxi drivers, merchants or professionals. All provinces of India were represented, and visitors heard ten or more different languages and dialects spoken. They were of various religions: Hindus, Sikhs, Moslems and Christians. In Fiji, caste and religious differences were largely overlooked, and women were freed of many traditional restrictions weighing on their sisters in India. Indians produced most of the nation's sugar, on land leased from Fijians.[56]

Only 84,475 ethnic Fijians were counted in 1920–21, or 53.71 percent of Fiji's population. When Europeans began coming to Fiji around 1800 there had been an estimated 200,000. By 1921 Indians numbered 60,634, constituting 38.56 percent of the population. It was clear to Melanesian Fijians that Indians through their intellect, determination, hard work and growth in numbers were becoming a significant factor in their country.[57]

NAURU C. 1920

When Nauru was mandated to Britain, Australia, and New Zealand, phosphate mining continued. The *Sydney Mail* of February 22, 1919, published a description of the overwhelming sensorial experience the inhabitants underwent in their once idyllic home: "Day and night there are the crash and buzz of heavy machinery, the clangour and din of many workshops, the beats of the steam hammers, the roar of furnaces from smithies and foundries, the shrill of sirens of locomotives, the deafening rumble and rattle of phosphate-laden trucks."[58]

In July 1919, Nauruans sent a petition to Britain's King George V (1865–1936; r. 1910–36) asking an end to mining, a practice that destroyed their coconut trees, limited their cropland, and stripped away their landscape. The petition described their lands as "absolutely useless. Nothing remains except rocks and stones. It is so badly ruined that no tropical tree of any kind could grow on it."[59] They asked that their lands be returned to them and compensation be made for desecration caused by strip mining. They complained that under the three-power mandate, Nauruans were forbidden to leave a designated area between sunset and sunrise. The petition was ignored.[60] In 1920, 149,609 tons were taken from the island.[61]

Nauru's population had fallen from 1,310 in 1912 to 1,113 in 1920; the influenza that swept the island was chiefly responsible.[62]

New Hebrides c. 1920

In the New Hebrides Anglo-French condominium, as a result of alcoholism, communicable diseases and the labor trade, population had declined to an estimated 70,000, described as "uncivilized natives." Approximately 400 French and 300 British lived in the archipelago.[63]

In 1923, *Stewart's Handbook of the Pacific Islands* stated in regard to New Hebrides and the Solomon Islands in particular, that following the period of exploration, there "followed a sad period from which few islands in the Pacific escaped, in which the scum of the white race carried on their bloodstained trade in whaling products and sandalwood. The horrors of the labour traffic for the Queensland plantations were added, so that in a few decades the native race was so weakened that in many places its preservation seems hopeless."[64]

The Solomon Islands c. 1920

British administrators ran the Solomon Islands like a business, arranging or abetting land sales and leases to planters. Probably about five percent of the good agricultural land had been alienated by 1914. Planters had brought in a million pounds to invest in the lands. The independent and bellicose nature of the tribes made a census impossible, but authorities estimated the population at somewhere around 100,000 to 150,000.

The demand for labor exceeded willing workers, and administrator Charles Woodford feared the supply would continue to decline.[65] With the declining labor supply came declining beliefs in tradition. When whites violated sacred objects, customs, and even survived the most vehement curses of sorcerers, people had to question the validity of their own beliefs. Their sense of loss and bewilderment was so great that observers, "bemoaning the passing of the formerly vigorous and perhaps somewhat idealized culture, predicted the extinction of the Melanesian race."[66]

Transformed

Of course transformation continued after 1920 and will continue as long as people inhabit South Pacific lands. Four hundred years after the first European sailed from the

Boat and huts, Laughlin Islands. The Laughlin Islands, also called the Budi Budi Group, are seldom visited by other than traders from other parts of Papua New Guinea. The few inhabitants of these flat coral islands eat taro, coconuts, fish and occasionally pork. While the lives of Pacific islanders have been substantially transformed in the last few centuries, the lives of these Austronesians have not. Photograph by Robert Kirk.

Atlantic to the Pacific, lives of the indigenous people in most — but not all — places had changed substantially. By 1920, for those who survived the invasion of diseases, much transformation has been in the form of positive change. Metal implements of all kinds, particularly tools, made work faster and more efficient. Literacy opened the door to unprecedented levels of education and to the benefits that come with it. Laws and their enforcement lessened the terror of inhumane tribal practices and opened opportunities for individual advancement of status. The lives of many women were improved. Medical science improved health and extended life — much more so after 1920 than before. Religion promised eternity to the soul. Missionaries' strictures replaced pre–Christian taboos with new ones; some of the new ones were beneficial.

Other aspects of the transformation have been negative. Chief among them is communicable disease. Alcohol, to which the people were not accustomed, debilitated many, including chiefs and kings. Weapons revolutionized warfare and transformed traditional — almost ritualistic — combat into killing frenzies. "Biological imperialism" introduced rabbits, mice, mosquitoes, and hefty quadrupeds, all of which changed life for indigenous people. Tribesmen were struck by the stark and jarring realization that beliefs and practices handed down for hundreds or thousands of years were simply wrong. New layers of government control were imposed so that taxes or tribute and labor were due to the appointed government of a foreign power as well as to customary chiefs. Unfamiliar foods introduced inordinate amounts of fats and salt into what had been healthy diets. Indentured laborers were brought in, and in numerous areas the indigenous population became a minority.

Change of all kinds transformed lives: dress inappropriate to the climate; new ways of building; multi-storied structures in pulsating urban areas; racing traffic; the opportunity to travel great distances; environmental desecration; labor that was longer and more difficult than that necessary for traditional life needs; regulations and arcane laws to understand or circumvent; money as a medium of exchange; confinement for some to reservations; the rude intrusion of world wars on a grand global scale; bloody fights for autonomy in new encompassing states. All of these changes and more happened as the result of contact with the Western world. Transformation continues.

Appendix

Timeline of Significant Events

1513: Balboa sees the South Pacific from the Isthmus of Panama.
1521: Magellan sails across the ocean he names *Pacific*.
1568: Mendaña reaches the Solomon Islands.
1595: Mendaña arrives in the Marquesas and the Santa Cruz Group.
1542–43: Tasman finds Van Diemen's Land, New Zealand, Tonga and Fiji.
1709: Original "Robinson Crusoe," Selkirk, is rescued at Juan Fernandez Island.
1722: Roggeveen visits Easter Island, Bora Bora, and Samoa.
1754: Dr. James Lind identifies the cause of and cure for scurvy.
1762: John Harrison's marine chronometer measures longitude accurately.
1767: Wallis finds and visits Tahiti.
1769–70: Cook charts the Society Islands, New Zealand and New South Wales.
1773–74: Cook visits Polynesia and finds New Caledonia and New Hebrides.
1774: Cook proves that Terra Australis Incognita does not exist.
1778–79: Cook revisits Polynesian islands and finds Hawaii; he is murdered.
1788: The First Fleet (of prisoners) arrives at Botany Bay, Australia.
1789: Mutineers take the *Bounty*, set Capt. Bligh adrift, and go to Pitcairn Island.
1797: London Missionary Society arrives to convert Tahitians.
1810: Kamehameha becomes king of the Sandwich Islands (Hawaii).
1815: Pomare II consolidates his power in Tahiti.
1819: Whaling begins in the Pacific Ocean.
1829: Fremantle claims all of Australia for Great Britain.
1834: Catholic priests arrive to convert Mangarevans (Gambier Islanders).
1839: Rev. John Williams is murdered on Eromanga (New Hebrides).
1840: Chiefs sign Treaty of Waigangi, ceding New Zealand to Britain.
1841: Missionaries begin conversions in the Loyalty Islands.
1842: France annexes the Marquesas and Tahiti (1843) as protectorates.
1845: Maori chief Hone Heke burns *pakeha* town of Kororareka (Russell).
1845: Taufa'ahau proclaims himself Tupou I.
1851: Gold is discovered in Victoria; population swells.
1853: France annexes New Caledonia and the Isle of Pines.
1854: American whalers in the Pacific earn $10.7 million — an all-time high.
1856: Pitcairn Islanders are removed to Norfolk Island, a former prison.
1860: Anglo-Maori Wars resume on North Island, New Zealand — to 1872.
1862–63: Peruvian blackbirders enslave small-island inhabitants.
1864: French convicts arrive in New Caledonia.
1868: Last of 162,000 convicts over 81 years arrive in Australia.
1869: The Suez Canal brings the South Pacific closer to Europe.
1871: Cakobau of Bau is proclaimed king of Fiji.

1874: Britain annexes Fiji at the request of King Cakobau.

1875: A measles epidemic kills 40,000 in Fiji.

1876: Trucanini, the last Tasmanian, dies. She was born about 1812.

1878: New Caledonia Kanaks launch a guerrilla war to get land back.

1879: First indentured laborers from India arrive in Fiji.

1880: France declares Tahiti a colony; Pomare V abdicates.

1882: First refrigerated ship brings New Zealand meat and dairy products to Britain.

1884: German commercial interests claim part of New Guinea.

1884: Britain claims Papua to save it from German colonization.

1887: United States acquires rights to Pearl Harbor, Oahu, Hawaii.

1888: Chile annexes Easter Island.

1889: A hurricane wrecks U.S. and German ships at Apia, Samoa.

1893: *Haoles* overthrow Queen Liliuokalani of Hawaii, proclaiming a republic.

1893: Britain claims the southern Solomon Islands.

1893: New Zealand passes liberal laws, including women's suffrage.

1897: France conquers Raiatea and claims all the Society Islands.

1898: United States annexes Hawaii as a territory.

1899: U.S. and Germany divide Samoa. U.S. gets Pago Pago and Tutuila.

1900: Tonga becomes a British protectorate but keeps its king.

1900: Pacific islands populations fell by estimated half in 19th century.

1901: Australian states unite as a federal commonwealth.

1902: An undersea cable links Australia and Hawaii to the rest of the world.

1906: Last of 62,000 Melanesian laborers leave Queensland .

1907: Britain and France control New Hebrides as a condominium.

1911: Australian authorities take children from Aborigine families (to 1970).

1914: World War I: Allies seize German Samoa, New Guinea, and Nauru .

1914: ANZACs and Pacific islanders sail to Europe to fight in World War I.

1914: The Panama Canal brings Pacific islands closer to the U.S. and Europe.

1915: ANZACs suffer huge losses at Turkey's Gallipoli Peninsula.

1918: An influenza pandemic devastates Pacific island communities.

1920: Nauru, New Guinea, and Samoa become League of Nations mandates.

1920: Island populations are predicted to decline further and become extinct.

Chapter Notes

INTRODUCTION

1. Campbell, *History of the Pacific Islands*, p. 151.
2. Kunitz, "Historical and Contemporary Mortality."
3. Lucas, *Pitcairn Register Book*, p. 54.
4. Kirk, *Pitcairn Island*, p. 238.
5. Williams, *Narrative of Missionary Enterprises*, p. 201.

CHAPTER 1

1. Boxer, *Portuguese Seaborne Empire*, pp. 35–37.
2. Conrad, *Lord Jim*, p. 155.
3. Boxer, pp. 46–51.
4. Erlichman, *Conquest, Tribute and Trade*, p. 154.
5. Bergreen, *Over the Edge*, p. 200.
6. Sherry, *Pacific Passions*, pp. 37–53.
7. Bergreen, p. 114.
8. Sherry, pp. 53–55.
9. Bergreen, p. 227.
10. Sherry, pp. 54–59.
11. Bergreen, p. 391.
12. Francia, *History of the Philippines*, p. 53.
13. Oliver, *Pacific Islands*, pp. 3–13.
14. Howe, *Where the Waves Fall*, p. 17.
15. Stanley, *South Pacific Handbook*, pp. 34–37.
16. Lal and Fortune, *Pacific Islands*, p. 63.
17. Oliver, pp. 14–37.
18. Campbell, *History of the Pacific Islands*, pp. 28–39.
19. J.P. Thompson, "Islands of the Pacific," p. 553.
20. Fischer, *Island*, p. 16.
21. Campbell, *History of the Pacific Islands*, pp. 32–33.

CHAPTER 2

1. Erlichman, *Conquest, Tribute and Trade*, p. 161.
2. Sherry, *Pacific Passions*, pp. 69–73.
3. Francia, *History of the Philippines*, pp. 51–60.
4. Countries Quest, "Papua New Guinea, History."
5. Lightbody and Wheeler, *Papua New Guinea*, p. 8.
6. Vinayvalpo.com, "Valparaiso, Chile."
7. Parry, *Spanish Seaborne Empire*, pp. 130–31.
8. Craig and King, *Oceania*, p. 180; Sherry, pp. 104–18.
9. Woodward, *Robinson Crusoe's Island*, pp. 5–8.

10. Michener and Day, *Rascals in Paradise*, pp. 197–201.
11. Dodge, *Islands and Empires*, p. 20.
12. Michener and Day, pp. 190–224.
13. Sherry, pp. 156–59.
14. Sherry, p. 173.
15. Lansdown, *Strangers in the South Seas*, pp. 42–3.
16. Sherry, pp. 162–79; Harcombe, *Vanuatu*, p. 163.
17. Craig and King, *Oceania*, pp. 295–96.
18. Day, *Rogues*, p. 181.
19. Souhami, *Selkirk's Island*, p. 93.
20. Day, *Rogues*, pp. 190–92; Souhami, pp. 83ff.; Woodward, pp. 34ff.
21. Day, *Rogues*, pp. 193–98.
22. Sherry, p. 281.
23. Sherry, pp. 277–81.
24. Woodward, pp. 79–87.
25. Woodward, pp. 89–90; Sherry, pp. 298–301.
26. Corney et al., "Voyage," p. 120.
27. Carrington, ed., *Discovery of Tahiti*, p. xxvi.
28. Salmond, *Aphrodite's Island*, p. 355.
29. Levuka.wordpress.com, "1781."
30. Fletcher and Keller, *Tonga*, pp. 13–14.

CHAPTER 3

1. Boxer, *Dutch Seaborne Empire*, pp. 1–30.
2. Sherry, *Pacific Passions*, p. 192.
3. Mulvaney and Kamminga, *Prehistory of Australia*, p. 69.
4. Welsh, *Australia*, pp. 4–5.
5. Welsh, pp. 6, 10.
6. Feeken and Feeken, *Discovery and Exploration*, p. 37.
7. Welsh, p. 6; Sherry, pp. 206–08.
8. Sherry, pp. 197–201.
9. Sherry, pp. 202–05.
10. Hughes, *Fatal Shore*, p. 47; Manning Clark, *Short History*, p. 18.
11. Oliver, *Polynesia*, pp. 225–27.
12. Craig and King, *Oceania*, p. 283; Oliver, *Polynesia*, p. 227.
13. Craig and King, p. 283.
14. Stanley, *Fiji*, p. 16; Craig and King, p. 283.
15. Sherry, p. 228.
16. Craig and King, p. 283.
17. Sherry, p. 237.
18. Welsh, pp. 7–9; Craig and King, p. 283.

19. Day, *Rogues*, pp. 185–85; Sherry pp. 249–50; Manning Clark, *Short History*, p. 18.
20. Welsh, pp. 9–10; Day, pp. 186–89.
21. Sherry, p. 269.
22. Sherry, p. 270.
23. Fischer, *Island*, p. 53.

CHAPTER 4

1. Carrington, ed., *Discovery of Tahiti*, pp. xxii–xix.
2. Dousset and Tallemite, *Great Book of the Pacific*, p. 36.
3. Sherry, *Pacific Passions*, p. 347 n.
4. Sherry, pp. 304–06.
5. Carrington, pp. 137–40.
6. Carrington, p. 154.
7. Carrington, p. 167.
8. Dodd, *Rape of Tahiti*, p. 58.
9. Carrington, pp. 166–67.
10. Carrington, pp. 207–08.
11. Howarth, *Tahiti*, p. 32.
12. Salmond, *Aphrodite's Island*, pp. 45–85.
13. Howarth, p. 32.
14. Salmond, pp. 93–95.
15. Salmond, pp. 97–98.
16. Salmond, p. 102.
17. Aldrich, *France and the South Pacific*, p. 2.
18. Lansdown, *Strangers in the South Seas*, p. 82.
19. Salmond, pp. 103, 116–17.
20. Salmond, p. 104.
21. Salmond, pp. 118–23.
22. Gray, *Voyages to Paradise*, p. 41.
23. Withey, *Voyages*, pp. 75–90.
24. Dear and Kemp, *Oxford Companion*, pp. 497–98; Electric Scotland, "Significant Scots."
25. Edwards, ed., *Journals*, p. 40.
26. Howarth, pp. 72–73.
27. Edwards, p. 41.
28. Edwards, p. 41; Withey, pp. 107–08.
29. Moorhead, *Fatal Impact*, pp. 69–70.
30. Edwards, p. 48.
31. Edwards, pp. 55–56.
32. Thomas, *Cook*, pp. 62–83; Withey, pp. 61–76.
33. Salmond, p. 239.
34. Howarth, p. 11.
35. Salmond, pp. 237–55.
36. Withey, p. 220.
37. Thomas, pp. 147–50; 163–66; Salmond, pp. 258–260.
38. Howarth, p. 83.
39. Withey, p. 232; Salmond, pp. 263–79.
40. Howarth, p. 87.
41. Howarth, pp. 90–92.
42. Edwards, p. 287.
43. Edwards, p. 290.
44. Edwards, p. 295.
45. Salmond, pp. 312–18.
46. Howarth, p. 88.
47. Edwards, p. 350.
48. Salmond, pp. 301–312.
49. Salmond, p. 313.
50. Salmond, pp. 312–18.
51. Kirch and Rallu, eds., *Growth and Collapse*, p. 32.
52. Dodge, *Islands and Empires*, p. 43.
53. Thomas Blake Clark, *Omai*, p. 26.
54. Hibbert, *George III*, p. 80.
55. Salmond, pp. 389–402.
56. Howarth, pp. 120–31; Salmond, pp. 338–84.
57. Salmond, pp. 396–402.
58. Salmond, pp. 403–04.
59. Salmond, pp. 419–43.
60. Salmond, pp. 444, 446.
61. Howarth, p. 133.
62. Howarth, pp. 134–35.
63. Salmond, pp. 444–47.
64. Salmond, pp. 454–55.
65. Wahlroos, *Mutiny and Romance*, p. 291.
66. Howarth, p. 156.
67. Howe, *Where the Waves Fall*, pp. 117–18.
68. Dodd, pp. 34–36.
69. Landsdown, *Strangers*, p. 142.
70. Howarth, p. 187; Howe, pp. 135–36.
71. Howarth, p. 187; Craig, *Polynesian Mythology*, p. 209.
72. Howe, p. 92.
73. Newbury, *Tahiti Nui*, p. 9.
74. Howe, pp. 138–40.
75. Newbury, p. 29; Craig, *Polynesian Mythology*, pp. 243–44.
76. Howarth, p. 190; Garrett, *Stars*, pp. 20–21.
77. Howe, p. 147.
78. Dodge, *Islands and Empires*, p. 91; Virginia Thompson and Richard Adloff, *The French Pacific Islands*, p. 14.
79. Howarth, p. 199.
80. Howarth, 196–97.
81. Moorhead, *Fatal Impact*, pp. 92–93.
82. Howarth, p. 203.
83. Howarth, p. 198.
84. Moorhead, p. 96.
85. Howarth, pp. 200–01.
86. Newbury, pp. 59–60; Thompson and Adloff, p. 14.
87. Howe, p. 151; Furnas, *Anatomy of Paradise*, pp. 180–81; Linnekin, "New Political Orders," p. 213.
88. Howe, p. 151.
89. Frederick Debell Bennett, *Narrative*, p. 76.
90. Newbury, pp. 59–60.
91. Schmitt, "Urbanization," p. 71.
92. Moorhead, pp. 97–98.
93. Frederick Debell Bennett, p. 81.
94. Moorhead, p. 97.
95. Frederick Debell Bennett, pp. 148–49.
96. Howarth, pp. 197–98.
97. Dodd, pp. 90–91.
98. Kotzebue, *New Voyage*, p. 168.
99. Furnas, p. 273; Howe, pp. 145–46.
100. Craig, *Polynesian Mythology*, p. 209.
101. Newbury, pp. 82–102; Thompson and Adloff, pp. 14–15.

CHAPTER 5

1. Kirk, *Pitcairn Island*, pp. 25–27.
2. Kirk, pp. 19–24; Rodger, *Wooden World*, pp. 120–24.
3. Kirk, 23–27; Alexander, *Bounty*, pp. 105–25.
4. Howarth, *Tahiti*, p. 150.
5. Bligh, *Mutiny*, p. 134.
6. Rodger, p. 227.
7. Kirk, pp. 29–30.
8. Kirk, pp. 31–34; Alexander, pp. 142–57.
9. Kirk, p. 37.
10. Kirk, pp. 37–39.
11. Nicolson, *Pitcairners*, pp. 29–31.
12. Kirk, pp. 9–10.

13. Kirk, pp. 46–47; Nicolson, pp. 33–39.
14. Kirk, pp. 39–43; Nicolson, pp. 52–53.
15. Wahlroos, *Mutiny and Romance*, pp. 155–57.
16. Kirk, pp. 34–36; Michener and Day, *Rascals in Paradise*, pp. 173–74.
17. Kirk, pp. 43–44; Alexander, pp. 180 ff.
18. Wahlroos, p. 126.
19. Kirk, pp. 64–67.
20. Wahlroos, pp. 434–35.
21. Kirk, pp. 52–55; Nicolson, pp. 54–56.
22. Kirk, pp. 75–81.
23. Kirk, pp. 82–90; Nicolson, pp. 109–18.
24. Kirk, pp. 86–87.
25. Brodie, *Pitcairn's Island*, p. 82.
26. Kirk, pp. 87–89.
27. Kirk, pp. 111–17.
28. Clarke, *Hell and Paradise*, p. 107.
29. Kirk, pp. 111–18.
30. Kirk, p. 124.

CHAPTER 6

1. Edwards, ed., *Journals*, p. 123.
2. Edwards, p. 127; Hughes, *Fatal Shore*, pp. 53–57.
3. Edwards, p. 130.
4. Sherry, *Pacific Passions*, p. 333.
5. Edwards, pp. 138–41.
6. Mulvaney and Kamminga, *Prehistory of Australia*, p. 69.
7. Mulvaney, p. 81.
8. Edwards, p. 174.
9. Edwards, p. 155.
10. Mulvaney, p. 81.
11. Hughes, p. 55; Withey, *Voyages*, p. 160.
12. Edwards, pp. 170–71.
13. Edwards, p. 190.
14. Hughes, p. 55.
15. Hughes, pp. 28–42; 57.
16. Blainey, *Tyranny of Distance*, p. 29.
17. Welsh, *Australia*, pp. 35–46; Hughes, pp. 67–99.
18. Welsh, p. 43.
19. Blainey, pp. 46–47.
20. Stone, ed., *Aborigines*, p. 23.
21. Blainey, pp. 46–47.
22. Keneally, *Australians*, pp. 2–3.
23. Welsh, pp. 37–40.
24. Mulvaney and Kamminga, *Prehistory of Australia*, p. 67.
25. Stone, p. 24.
26. Mulvaney, pp. 67–68.
27. Clarke, *Hell and Paradise*, pp. 9–10.
28. Blainey, p. 32.
29. Welsh, pp. 44–46; Hughes, pp. 99–100.
30. Welsh, p. 46; Hughes, pp. 104–05.
31. Welsh, pp. 53–55; Manning Clark, *Short History*, pp. 29–31.
32. Welsh, pp. 48–49.
33. Keneally, p. 161.
34. Hughes, p. 108.
35. Welsh, pp. 63–64.
36. Hughes, p. 110.
37. Welsh, pp. 61–62.
38. Larkins, *101 Events*, pp. 18–19.
39. Mulvaney, pp. 407–09.
40. Larkins, pp. 22–23.
41. Welsh, p. 136.
42. Welsh, pp. 67–68.
43. Day, *Rogues*, p. 145.

44. Michener and Day, *Rascals in Paradise*, pp. 177–89; Day, *Rogues*, pp. 143–58; Welsh, pp. 67–69.
45. Welsh, p. 71.
46. Welsh, pp. 69–81.
47. Welsh, p. 75.
48. Blainey, pp. 131–33.
49. Hughes, p. 455.
50. Manning Clark, *Short History*, p. 105.
51. Manning Clark, p. 107.
52. Manning Clark, p. 143.
53. Welsh, pp. 148–49; Hughes, pp. 441–55.
54. Sherry, p. 233.
55. Hughes, pp. 354–55.
56. Welsh, p. 124.
57. Hughes, p. 162; Manning Clark, p. 135.
58. Manning Clark, p. 115.
59. Hughes, p. 580.
60. Welsh, pp. 95, 127; Grattan, *Pacific to 1900*, I, 87–91.
61. Welsh, pp. 125–26.
62. Dodge, *Islands and Empires*, p. 122.
63. Stone, p. 66.
64. Brands, *The Age of Gold*, pp. 55–61; 263–66.
65. Manning Clark, p. 119.
66. Denoon et al., *History*, p. 141.
67. Welsh, pp. 205–09; Manning Clark, pp. 119–139.
68. Denoon et al., p. 131.
69. Manning Clark, p. 131.
70. Denoon et al., p. 141.
71. Moorhead, *Fatal Impact*, p. 178.
72. Manning Clark, pp. 121–22.
73. Manning Clark, pp. 129–31; Welsh, pp. 211–14.
74. Denoon et al., p. 145.
75. Sherry, pp. 245–46.
76. Manning Clark, pp. 141–42.
77. Stone, p. 93.
78. Stone, p. 95.
79. Welsh, p. 249.
80. Manning Clark, pp. 186–91; Welsh, pp. 320–35; Denoon et al., p. 196.
81. Manning Clark, p. 198.
82. Manning Clark, pp. 196–99; Welsh, pp. 340–43.
83. Manning Clark, p. 164.
84. Manning Clark, p. 181.
85. Welsh, pp. 488; 491–92; Danielle Celermajer; "Stolen Generation"; Terry McCarthy, "Stolen Generation," p. 28.
86. Denoon et al., p. 203.

CHAPTER 7

1. *Old Hobart Town News,* "Trucanini's Story of Herself"; Keneally, *Australians*, p. 299.
2. Ryan, *Aboriginal Tasmanians*, pp. 175–76.
3. Ryan, p. 220.
4. Ryan, p. 9.
5. Ryan, pp. 50–51.
6. Edwards, ed., *Journals*, pp. 446–47.
7. Edwards, p. 450.
8. Mulvaney and Kamminga, *Prehistory of Australia*, p. 339.
9. Ryan, p. 14.
10. Mulvaney, p. 343.
11. Arrell Morgan Gibson, *Yankees in Paradise*, p. 113.
12. Welsh, *Australia*, pp. 58–59.
13. Blainey, *Tyranny of Distance*, p. 106.
14. Ryan, pp. 66–69.

15. Welsh, pp. 64–65.
16. Hughes, *Fatal Shore*, pp. 123–25.
17. Ryan, p. 77.
18. Welsh, pp. 106–09.
19. Ryan, p. 73.
20. Welsh, pp. 110, 112.
21. Welsh 110; Day, *Rogues*, pp. 246–52.
22. Hughes, pp. 219–26.
23. Hughes, p. 232.
24. Day, *Rogues*, pp. 239–46.
25. Ryan, p. 4.
26. Ryan, pp. 83–85.
27. Ryan, pp. 94–95.
28. Ryan, p. 107.
29. Hughes, pp. 419–21.
30. Hughes, p. 423.
31. James Blackhouse Walker, *Early Tasmanians: Papers Read Before the Royal Society of Tasmania during the Years 1888 to 1889* (Hobart: The Society, 1902), p. 239.
32. Stone, ed., *Aborigines*, pp. 39–40.
33. Hughes, p. 423.
34. Hughes, pp. 398–401.
35. Welsh, pp. 119–20.
36. Manning Clark, *Short History*, p. 124; Hughes, pp. 571–72.
37. About Australia, "Tasmania History."
38. Hughes, p. 601.
39. Hughes, p. 424.
40. Moorhead, *Fatal Impact*, p. 178.

CHAPTER 8

1. King, *New Zealanders*, p. 22–38.
2. Edwards, ed., *Journals*, pp. 70–77.
3. Withey, *Voyages*, pp. 145–50.
4. Oliver, *Polynesia*, pp. 248–50.
5. Thomas, *Cook*, pp. 86–110; Withey, pp. 129–46; Owens, "New Zealand Before Annexation," p. 30.
6. Sherry, *Pacific Passions*, pp. 379–81.
7. Estensen, *Discovery*, pp. 224–26; Owens, p. 30.
8. Thomas, pp. 169–80; Raeside.
9. Edwards, pp. 276–77.
10. J.C. Beaglehole, *Exploration*, pp. 284–86.
11. Edwards, p. 325.
12. Edwards, p. 331.
13. Edwards, pp. 452–53.
14. Okihiro, *Island World*, p. 147.
15. Dodge, *Islands and Empires*, p. 78.
16. Owens, pp. 31–32.
17. King, p. 46.
18. Dodge, p. 144.
19. Howe, *Where the Waves Fall*, p. 211.
20. Howe, p. 216.
21. *Dictionary of New Zealand Biography*, s.v. "Kendall, Thomas" (by Judith Binney), updated September 1, 2010, http://www.TeAra.govt.nz/en/biographies/1k9/1.
22. King, p. 39; Dodge, p. 146.
23. "Kendall, Thomas" (see note 21).
24. Owens, pp. 36–37, 47; *Dictionary of New Zealand Biography*, s.v. "Leigh, Samuel" (by W.A. Chambers), updated September 1, 2010, http://www.TeAra.govt.nz/en/biographies/1l6/1.
25. King, p. 39.
26. Howe, p. 214.
27. *New Zealand History Online*, "Musket Wars."
28. *Te Ara — The Encyclopedia of New Zealand*, s.v. "Colenso, William" (by George Conrad Peterson), updated April 23, 2009, http://www.teara.govt.nz/en/1966/colenso-william/1.
29. *Te Ara — The Encyclopedia of New Zealand*, s.v. "Pompallier, Jean Francis" (by Maurice Warwick Mulcahy), http://www.teara.govt.nz/en/1966/pompallier-john-baptist-francis/1; Owens, p. 37.
30. Howe, pp. 224–26.
31. Chambers, *Traveler's History*, pp. 140–41; Oliver, *Polynesia*, pp. 255–56.
32. S. Percy Smith, "Migration."
33. Whitmore, "The Moriori: Early Settlers of the Chatham Islands."
34. Oliver, p. 255.
35. *Te Ara — The Encyclopedia of New Zealand*, from *An Encyclopaedia of New Zealand, 1966*, s.v. "Thierry, Charles Philip Hippolytus, Baron de" (by Ruth Miriam Ross), www.teara.govt.nz/1966/thierry-charles-philip-hippolytus-baron de/1.
36. Grattan, *Pacific to 1900*, pp. 171–75; Gardner, "Colonial Economy," pp. 59–60.
37. Thorndon, "1839."
38. *Te Ara — The Encyclopedia of New Zealand*, from *An Encyclopaedia of New Zealand, 1966*, s.v. "Akaroa, French Settlement at" (by Bernard John Foster), http://www.teara.govt.nz/en/1966/akaroa-french-settlement-at/1.
39. Orange, "Maori People," pp. 38–43; Owens, pp. 42–43.
40. Owens, pp. 42–43.
41. "Akaroa, French Settlement at" (see note 38); *Te Ara — The Encyclopedia of New Zealand*, s.v. "Whaling" (by Jock Phillips), updated March 2, 2009, http://www.teara.govt.nz/en/whaling.
42. *Dictionary of New Zealand Biography*, s.v. "Langlois, Jean François" (by Peter B. Maling), updated September 1, 2010, http://www.TeAra.govt.nz/en/biographies/1l2/1; "Akaroa, French Settlement at" (see note 38).
43. King, p. 40; Orange, pp. 30–35.
44. Owens, p. 51.
45. Orange, pp. 42–48.
46. Orange, p. 43.

CHAPTER 9

1. Withey, *Voyages*, pp. 376–80.
2. Edwards, ed., *Journals*, p. 533.
3. Wisniewski, *Rise and Fall*, p. 7.
4. Edwards, p. 532.
5. Withey, pp. 359–64.
6. Wisniewski, p. 14.
7. Withey, pp. 376–96.
8. James, *Rise and Fall*, p. 140.
9. Withey, pp. 397–400.
10. Wisniewski, p. 15; Withey, pp. 397–400.
11. Joesting, *Uncommon*, pp. 45–46; Okihiro, *Island World*, pp. 138–42.
12. Wisniewski, p. 16.
13. Daws, *Shoal of Time*, p. 34.
14. Daws, p. 35.
15. Day, *People*, pp. 41–43.
16. Day, *People*, p. 27.
17. Wisniewski, p. 20; Craig and King, *Oceania*, pp. 141–42.
18. Joesting, pp. 89–91; Day, *People*, pp. 59–61; Shineberg, *Sandalwood*, pp. 1–5.
19. Day, *Rogues*, pp. 3–34.

20. Day, *People*, p. 66; Craig and King, *Oceania*, p. 150.
21. Fischer, *Island*, p. 27.
22. Day, *People*, p. 74–75; Wisniewski, pp. 25–26.
23. Conklin, "Henry Opukahaia (Obookiah)."
24. Daws, *Shoal of Time*, pp. 63–66.
25. Wisniewski, p. 27.
26. Dodge, *Islands and Empires*, p. 120.
27. Okihiro, p. 59; Wisniewski, pp. 27–28.
28. Dodge, p. 121.
29. Day, *Points South*, pp. 39–41.
30. Day, *Points South*, p. 47.
31. Day, *Points South*, pp. 44–45.
32. Day, *People*, p. 81.
33. Duhaut-Cilley, *Voyage to California*, p. 207.
34. Furnas, *Anatomy of Paradise*, p. 134.
35. Campbell, *History of the Pacific Islands*, p. 70; Day, *People*, pp. 82–83.
36. Day, *Shoal*, pp. 106–111; Daws, *Hawaii*, pp. 80–81.
37. Joesting, pp. 82–85.
38. Arrell Morgan Gibson, *Yankees in Paradise*, p. 252; Think Quest, "Parker Ranch."
39. Okihiro, p. 171.
40. Big Island Visitors Bureau, "History of Paniolos and Ranching on Hawaii's Big Island."
41. Daws, *Shoal of Time*, p. 79.
42. Furnas, p. 148.
43. Kuykendall, *Hawaiian Kingdom*, p. 90.
44. Daws, *Shoal of Time*, p. 78; Howe, *Where the Waves Fall*, p. 169.
45. Daws, pp. 94–96.
46. Joesting, pp. 84–85; Day, *Hawaii*, pp. 111–12.
47. Daws, pp. 133–34; Day, *People*, 111–12.
48. Daws, p. 97.
49. Frederick Debell Bennett, *Narrative*, pp. 219–20.
50. Day, *People*, pp. 104–05.
51. Garrett, *Stars*, p. 140.
52. Melville, *Typee, Omoo, Mardi*, p. 231.
53. Mawer, *Ahab's Trade*, pp. 79–80.
54. Wisniewski, p. 26.
55. Mawer, p. 179.
56. Campbell, *History of the Pacific Islands*, p. 64.
57. Day, *People*, pp. 131–32; *Economic Expert*, "Maui."
58. Okihiro, pp. 138–44.
59. Sunio, "Reverend William Richards."
60. Okihiro, p. 157.
61. Dodge, p. 82; Day, *Hawaii*, p. 93.
62. Daws, *Shoal of Time*, pp. 78–79.
63. Daws, *Shoal of Time*, pp. 80–81; Day, *People*, p. 92.
64. Apple, "Maui-Lahaina Crime Punishment."
65. Mawer, pp. 205–06.
66. Daws, *Shoal of Time*, pp. 138–39.
67. Schmitt and Nordyke, "Death in Hawaii."
68. Wisniewski, p. 49; Daws, *Shoal*, pp. 139–43.
69. Siler, *Lost Kingdom*, p. 22.
70. Mawer, pp. 267–74.
71. Wisniewski, p. 53; Morris, ed., *Encyclopedia of American History*, pp. 280–81.
72. Mawer, pp. 321–22.
73. Hawaii-Nation.org. "Kingdom of Hawai'i Constitution of 1840."
74. Clement, "From Cook to the 1840 Constitution."
75. Mawer, pp. 125–26.
76. Heffer, *United States*, p. 91.
77. Daws, *Shoal of Time*, p. 115.
78. Day, *People*, pp. 121–22.
79. Daws, *Shoal of Time*, p. 114.
80. Day, *People*, pp. 125–26; Campbell, pp. 86–87.

81. Siler, p. 20.
82. Wisniewski, p. 48; Day, *People*, pp. 126–127; Joesting, pp. 145–46.
83. Wisniewski, p. 50; Daws, *Shoal of Time*, pp. 52–53.
84. Horne, *White Pacific*, p. 92.
85. Campbell, p. 152.
86. Day, *People*, pp. 224–25; Wisniewski, p. 59.
87. Wisniewski, p. 71; Day, *People*, p. 226.
88. Dodge, *Islands and Empires*, p. 189; Wisniewski, p. 59.
89. Wisniewski, p. 63; Day, *People*, pp. 190–91.
90. Wisniewski, p. 58; Siler, p. 33.

CHAPTER 10

1. Daws, *Dream of Islands*, pp. 25–29.
2. Daws, pp. 30–34.
3. Campbell, *History of the Pacific Islands*, p. 76.
4. Frederick Debell Bennett, *Narrative*, p. 101.
5. Frederick Debell Bennett, p. 149.
6. Craig and King, *Oceania*, p. 60; Daws, *Dream of Islands*, pp. 39–40.
7. Kloosterman, "Discoverers of the Cook Islands."
8. Maretu, *Cannibals and Converts*, pp. 19, 42.
9. Daws, *Dream of Islands*, pp. 46–47.
10. Maretu, p. 19; "Cook Islands: What Is In Our Past?" http//:www.ck/history.htm.
11. Snow and Waine, *People from the Horizon*, p. 132.
12. Grattan, *Pacific to 1900*, p. 197.
13. Garrett, *Stars*, pp. 116–19; "Religion of the Cook Islands," http://www.ck/religion.htm.
14. Daws, *Dream of Islands*, pp. 48–50.
15. "John Williams," *Answers.com*, http://www.answers.com/topic/john-williams.
16. Daws, pp. 58–59.
17. Garrett, pp. 88–89; Stanley, *South Pacific Handbook*, p. 265; Furnas, *Anatomy of Paradise*, 286–89.
18. Furnas, pp. 286–89.
19. Murray, *Pitcairn*, p. 182.
20. Snow and Waine, p. 132.
21. Stanley, *South Pacific Handbook*, p. 265.
22. Furnas, p. 288.
23. Garrett, pp. 88–95; Family Search, "Gambier Islands."

CHAPTER 11

1. Suggs, *Hidden Worlds*, p. 32.
2. Suggs, p. 57.
3. Suggs, pp. 36–45.
4. Dening, ed., *Marquesan Journal*, p. 27.
5. Edwards, ed., *Journals*, p. 340; Sherry, *Pacific Passions*, p. 402.
6. Dening, p. viii; Suggs, p. 53.
7. Dening, pp. 22–24.
8. Howe, *Where the Waves Fall*, pp. 117–18.
9. Suggs, p. 48.
10. Craig, and King, p. 171.
11. Heflin, *Herman Melville's Whaling Years*, pp. 222–23.
12. Suggs, pp. 50–52.
13. Arrell Morgan Gibson, *Yankees in Paradise*, pp. 316–17.
14. Joesting, *Uncommon*, pp. 87–88.
15. Heflin, pp. 223–24; Suggs, p. 49.
16. Dening, p. 28.
17. Howe, p. 92.

18. Dening, p. 27.
19. Dening, p. 105.
20. Dening, p. viii.
21. Garrett, *Stars*, p. 267; Suggs, *Hidden Worlds*, p. 54.
22. "Vicarate Apostolic of Central Oceania," *Catholic Encyclopedia*, www.newadvent.org.cathen/11200b.htm; Howe, pp. 117–18.
23. Aldrich, *Greater France*, p. 21.
24. Suggs, p. 116.
25. Newbury, *Tahiti Nui*, pp. 104–05.
26. Newbury, pp. 111–113.
27. Melville, *Typee, Omoo, Mardi*, p. 13.
28. Daws, *Dream of Islands*, pp. 76–84; Day, *People*, pp. 241–53; Howarth, *Tahiti*, pp. 206–08.
29. Daws, pp. 257–66.
30. Campbell, *History of the Pacific Islands*, pp. 152–53; Suggs, p. 53.
31. Maude, *Slavers in Paradise*, pp. 31–37.
32. Maude, p. 159.
33. Suggs, p. 126.
34. "Paul Gauguin Biography," *Encyclopedia of World Biographies*, http://www.notablebiographies.com/Fi-Gi/Gauguin-Paul.html.
35. Dening, p. 18; Dodge, *Islands and Empires*, pp. 198–00.
36. Campbell, pp. 152–53.
37. Dening, p. viii.

CHAPTER 12

1. Fischer, *Island*, p. 18.
2. Diamond, *Collapse*, pp. 90–91.
3. Fischer, *Island*, p. 33.
4. Fischer, *Island*, p. 48.
5. Fischer, *Island*, p. 20.
6. Sherry, *Pacific Passions*, pp. 265–68; Craig and King, *Oceania*, pp. 76–77.
7. Flenley and Bahn, *Enigmas*, p. 192.
8. Fischer, *Island*, pp. 54–57.
9. Corney et al., "Voyage."
10. Sherry, p. 389.
11. Edwards, ed., *Journals*, p. 336.
12. Fischer, *Island*, p. 68.
13. Edwards, p. 338.
14. Fischer, *Island*, p. 65.
15. Fischer, *Island*, p. 69.
16. Edwards, p. 337.
17. Fischer, *Island*, p. 71.
18. Postnikov, "First Russian Voyage."
19. Nation Master, "Moai."
20. Fischer, *Island*, p. 60.
21. Fischer, *Island*, pp. 73–75.
22. Pelta, *Rediscovering Easter Island*, p. 34.
23. Fischer, *Island*, p. 86.
24. Fischer, *Island*, p. 89.
25. Okihiro, *Island World*, p. 168.
26. Maude, *Slavers in Paradise*, pp. 15–18.
27. Maude, pp. 6–10, 48–49.
28. Maude, pp. 63–73.
29. Maude, pp. 74–82.
30. Maude, pp. 83–87.
31. Fletcher and Keller, *Tonga*, p. 131.
32. Maude, pp. 40–41.
33. Maude, p. 164; Campbell, *History of the Pacific Islands*, p. 111.
34. Fischer, *Island*, pp. 99–101.
35. Fischer, "Rongorongo."

36. Fischer, *Island*, p. 101.
37. Fischer, *Island*, p. 110.
38. Maude, pp. 156–61.
39. Fischer, *Island*, p. 120.
40. Fischer, *Island*, pp. 113–14.
41. Maude, pp. 156–61.
42. Fischer, *Island*, p. 21.
43. Fischer, *Island*, pp. 125–27.
44. "The Other Mystery of Easter Island," http://www.scribd.com/doc/969/The-Other-Mystery-Of-Easter-Island.
45. Fischer, *Island*, pp. 141–42.
46. Fischer, *Island*, pp. 154–156.
47. "Katherine Routledge," Absoluteastronomy, http://www.absoluteastronomy.com/topics/Katherine_Routledge.
48. Fischer, *Island*, p. 163.

CHAPTER 13

1. Aldrich, *France and the South Pacific*, p. 18.
2. Aldrich, p. 35.
3. Dodd, *Rape of Tahiti*, pp. 81–82.
4. Dodd, p. 87.
5. Newbury, *Tahiti Nui*, pp. 92–98; Aldrich, *France and the South Pacific*, pp. 22–23; Dodd, pp. 86–87.
6. Dodd, p. 116.
7. Newbury, pp. 105–110.
8. David Howarth, *Tahiti: A Paradise Lost*, pp. 212–13.
9. Daws, *Dream of Islands*, pp. 77–79; Day, *People*, pp. 253–57.
10. Meville, *Typee, Omoo, Mardi*, p. 430.
11. Daws, pp. 78–79.
12. Murray, *Pitcairn*, p. 143.
13. O'Brien, "Think of Me as a Woman," p. 108.
14. Dodd, p. 126.
15. Newbury, p. 115.
16. Dodd, p. 122.
17. Melville, p. 451.
18. Dodd, p. 118.
19. Newbury pp. 115–117, pp. 120–22; "History," Tahiti 1, http://www.tahiti1.com/en/indentity/history.htm; Thompson and Adloff, *French Pacific Islands*, p. 15.
20. Melville, p. 453.
21. Newbury, p. 117.
22. Newbury, p. 121.
23. Dodd, p. 123.
24. Aldrich, *France and the South Pacific*, p. 188.
25. Dodd, p. 140.
26. Newbury, p. 126; Thompson and Adloff, p. 15.
27. Melville, p. 640.
28. Dodd, p. 166.
29. Dodd, pp. 191–92.
30. Newbury, p. 122.
31. Aldrich, *France and the South Pacific*, p. 63.
32. Lal and Fortune, *Pacific Islands*, p. 195; Aldrich, *France and the South Pacific*, p. 63.
33. Breward, *Churches*, p. 38.
34. Dodge, *Islands and Empires*, pp. 71–73.
35. Howarth, *Tahiti*, p. 206.
36. Dodge, p. 199.
37. Newbury, p. 128.
38. Dodge, p. 199.
39. Kirch and Rallu, eds., *Growth and Collapse*, p. 26.
40. Aldrich, *France and the South Pacific*, p. 141.
41. Dodd, p. 185.
42. Newbury, p. 170.

43. Yuan-chao, "Chinese in Tahiti," p. 742; Newbury, pp. 172–73; Thompson and Adloff, p. 91.

44. Dodd, p. 174.

45. Aldrich, *France and the South Pacific*, p. 181.

46. Newbury, pp. 200–01; Thompson and Adloff, p. 15.

47. Aldrich, p. 142.

48. Daws, *Dream of Islands*, p. 221.

49. Daws, pp. 233–35.

50. Daws, pp. 241–42.

51. *New York Times*, "Shelled by French Warships," February 21, 1897, p. 1.

52. *West Coast Times*, "Raiatea," March 17, 1897, p. 1.

53. Aikman, *Cyclopedia of Christian Missions*, pp. 75–76.

54. Richards, "Earliest Foreign Visitors," pp. 3–10.

55. Hanson, *Rapan Lifeways*, pp. 27–29.

56. Hanson, pp. 29, 31.

57. Maude, *Slavers in Paradise*, pp. 160–61.

58. Hanson, pp. 33–44, 50–51.

59. W.N. Gunson, "Journal of a Visit," pp. 199–203.

60. Stanley, *South Pacific Handbook*, p. 251.

61. Newbury, p. 202.

62. Niumy, ed., *South Pacific Islands Legal Systems*, p. 638; Thompson and Adloff, p. 23.

63. Aldrich, pp. 42–43.

64. Aldrich, pp. 112.

65. Campbell, *History of the Pacific Islands*, p. 166; Thompson, p. 19.

66. Sherry, *Pacific Passions*, p. 314.

67. Nation Master, "Wallis and Futuna."

68. Craig and King, p. 320.

CHAPTER 14

1. Edwards, ed., *Journals*, p. 390.

2. Moorhead, *Fatal Impact*, p. 69.

3. Withey, *Voyages*, pp. 287–94; Thompson and Adloff, *French Pacific*, p. 237.

4. William Stewart, *Admirals of the World*, pp. 88–89.

5. New Zealand Electronic Text Center, "Admiral Jules Sébastien César Dumont D'urville 1790–1842."

6. Shineberg, *Sandalwood*, pp. 52–53.

7. Shineberg, pp. 48–51.

8. Shineberg, p. 54.

9. Howe, *Where the Waves Fall*, p. 309.

10. Howe, p. 311; Thompson and Adloff, p. 238.

11. Stanley, *South Pacific Handbook*, p. 771.

12. Shineberg, pp. 32–33.

13. Hutton, *Missionary Life*, pp. 306–07.

14. Shineberg, pp. 29–30; Snow and Waine, *People from the Horizon*, p. 118.

15. Shineberg, pp. 35–39.

16. Couper, *Sailors and Traders*, p. 122.

17. Shineberg, pp. 44–45.

18. Wright, *France in Modern Times*, pp. 215–18.

19. Aldrich, *France and the South Pacific*, p. 145; Thompson and Adloff, p. 241.

20. Aldrich, p. 146.

21. Nouvelle Calédonie, "Isle of Pines."

22. Dodge, *Islands and Empires*, pp. 170–71; Thompson and Adloff, p. 239.

23. Percy S. Allen, *Stewart's Handbook*, 1923 edition, p. 117.

24. Howe, 327; Thompson and Adloff, p. 239.

25. Stanley, *South Pacific Handbook*, p. 731.

26. Craig and King, *Oceania*, p. 206.

27. Aldrich, *Greater France*, p. 206.

28. Aldrich, *France and the South Pacific*, p. 173.

29. Aldrich, p. 178.

30. Denoon, pp. 226–27; New Caledonia, "Penal Colony New Caledonia."

31. Thompson and Adloff, p. 261.

32. New Caledonia, "Penal Colony."

33. Aldrich, *France and the South Pacific*, pp. 178–79; Aldrich, *Greater France*, pp. 218–19.

34. Stanley, *South Pacific Handbook*, p. 716.

35. Denoon, p. 154; Thompson and Adloff, p. 244.

36. Thompson, p. 241.

37. J.C. Furnas, *Anatomy of Paradise* (New York: William Sloane Associates, 1947) pp. 368–69.

38. Aldrich, *France and the South Pacific*, pp. 106–07, 189; Grattan, *Pacific to 1900*, pp. 458–59; Howe, pp. 317–18; Rosenblum, *Mission to Civilize*, pp. 168–69; Dousset and Tallemite, *Great Book of the Pacific*, p. 220; Thompson, pp. 242–43.

39. Aldrich, *France and the South Pacific*, p. 147.

40. Aldrich, 163.

41. Dousset and Tallemite, p. 218.

42. New Caledonia, "Penal Colony."

43. Aldrich, *Greater France*, pp. 212–14.

44. Aldrich, *France and the South Pacific*, p. 183.

45. Aldrich, *France and the South Pacific*, p. 144.

46. New Caledonia, "Penal Colony"; Grattan, *Pacific to 1900*, p. 458; Stanley, *South Pacific Handbook*, p. 724.

47. Aldrich, *France and the South Pacific*, pp. 182–83.

48. Aldrich, *France and the South Pacific*, p. 50.

49. Thompson and Adloff, pp. 263–64.

50. Aldrich, *France and the South Pacific*, p. 150.

51. Grattan, *Pacific to 1900*, p. 459.

52. Denoon, p. 244.

CHAPTER 15

1. Howe, *Where the Waves Fall*, pp. 12–17.

2. Edwards, ed., *Journals*, pp. 306–07.

3. Withey, *Voyages*, p. 273; Salmond, *Aphrodite's Island*, pp. 408–09.

4. Edwards, 465.

5. Withey, pp. 328–37.

6. Rayment, "Antoine Raymond Joseph de Bruni D'Entrecasteaux."

7. Howe, *Where the Waves Fall*, p. 118.

8. Michener and Day, *Rascals in Paradise*, pp. 289–318.

9. Gunson, "Coming of Foreigners," pp. 99–101.

10. Finau et al., *Island Churches*, p. 147; Latukefu, "Wesleyan Mission," p. 115.

11. Garrett, *Stars*, p. 71; Gunson, pp. 110–111.

12. Urbanowicz, "John Thomas, Tongans and Tonga!"; Latukefu, p. 115.

13. Laracy, "Catholic Mission," p. 123.

14. Campbell, *History of the Pacific Islands*, p. 71; Lal and Fortune, *Pacific Islands*, p. 185.

15. Howe, pp. 187–90.

16. Craig and King, *Oceania*, p. 291; Laracy, pp. 142–43.

17. Howe, p. 191.

18. Rutherford, *Shirley Baker*, pp.156–71; Stanley, *South Pacific Handbook*, p. 386.

19. Rutherford, *Shirley Baker*, p. 32; Howe, p. 193.

20. Marcus, "Contemporary Tonga," pp. 225–26.

21. Stanley, *South Pacific Handbook*, p. 402; Rutherford, ed., *Friendly Islands*, pp. 28–31.

22. Fletcher and Keller, *Tonga*, pp. 97–98.
23. Rutherford, *Shirley Baker*, pp. 42–47.
24. WIPO, "Tonga: Act of Constitution."
25. Rutherford, *Shirley Baker*, pp. 161–62; Campbell, *History of the Pacific Islands*, pp. 88–89.
26. Howe, p. 194.
27. Rutherford, *Shirley Baker*, pp. 162–63.
28. Rutherford, *Shirley Baker*, pp. 167–69; Campbell, p. 90.
29. Rutherford, *Shirley Baker*, pp. 171–72.
30. Campbell, p. 190; Rutherford, *Shirley Baker*, pp. 180–89.
31. Burley, "Archaeological Demography"; Kirch and Rallu, eds., *Growth and Collapse*, p. 181.
32. Wood and Ellem, "Queen Salote Tupou III"; Rutherford, ed., *Friendly Islands*, pp. 192–93.
33. Howe, p. 195.
34. Howe, pp. 234–35.
35. Daws, *Dream of Islands*, p. 55.
36. Craig and King, p. 5.
37. Malua Theological College, "Malua Theological College History"; Davidson, *Samoa Mo Samoa*, p. 37.
38. Philbrick, *Sea of Glory*, pp. 134–35.
39. Davidson, pp. 38–40.
40. Campbell, pp. 95–96; Davidson, pp. 45–47.
41. Davidson, pp. 38–39; Campbell, pp. 96–97.
42. Howe, pp. 248–251.
43. Davidson, pp. 48–50.
44. Davidson, pp. 52–53; Linnekin, "New Political Orders," p. 192.
45. Davidson, pp. 54–55.
46. Campbell, p. 89.
47. Davidson, pp. 57–58; Campbell, p. 99; Linnekin, p. 192.
48. Dudden, *American Pacific*, p. 65; Arrell Morgan Gibson, *Yankees in Paradise*, p. 228; Bailey, *Diplomatic History*, pp. 422–23; Craig and King, pp. 201–02.
49. Howe, pp. 252–53.
50. Dudden, p. 65.
51. Bailey, p. 424; Howe, p. 252; Arrell Morgan Gibson, p. 338; Davidson p. 62.
52. Dodge, *Islands and Empires*, p. 177.
53. Davidson, pp. 63–65; Bailey, pp. 425–26; Linnekin, p. 208.
54. Daws, *Dream of Islands*, pp. 172–215.
55. U.S. Congressman Eni F.ZH. Faleomavaega, "American Samoa: Treaties," <www.house.gov/faleomavaega/treaties/shml>.
56. Ben Cahoon, "American Samoa."
57. Stanley, *South Pacific Handbook*, pp. 432–33; Heffer, *United States*, pp. 194–95.
58. Hiery, *Neglected War*, pp. 8–9.
59. Wendt, "Guardians and Wards," pp. 29–30.
60. Colbt, ed., "German Samoa," p. 255.

Chapter 16

1. D.R. Hainsworth, "Lord, Simeon," *Australian Dictionary of Biography,* http://adb.anu.edu.au/biography/lord-simeon-2371.
2. Dodge, *Islands and Empires*, p. 64.
3. Linnekin, "New Political Orders," p. 189.
4. Go-Fiji, "Fiji Myths and Legends," *Fiji Travel Guide*; Sal Lealea, "Fiji's Cannibal History," *Fijian Custom and Culture.*
5. Stanley, *Fiji*, p. 18.
6. Dodge, p. 65.

7. Dodge, pp. 65–67; Howe, *Where the Waves Fall*, pp. 97–100.
8. Ralston, *Grass Huts,* p. 14.
9. Campbell, *History of the Pacific Islands*, p. 91.
10. Howe, p. 260; Craig and King, *Oceania*, p. 86.
11. Howe, p. 256.
12. John Elphinstone Erskine, *Journal of a Cruise Among the Islands of the Western Pacific*, p. 465.
13. Scarr, *Fiji*, p. 19; Garrett, *Stars*, p. 102.
14. Scarr, pp. 13–14.
15. Garrett, p. 102.
16. Philbrick, *Sea of Glory*, pp. 59–66.
17. Philbrick, p. 196.
18. Philbrick, p. 226.
19. Dodge, p. 116.
20. Gravelle, *Fiji's Times*, pp. 61–65.
21. Philbrick, pp. 298–300; Heffer, *United States*, pp. 85–87; Craig and King, *Oceania*, pp. 336–37.
22. Campbell, p. 93; Stanley, *South Pacific Handbook*, p. 554.
23. Gravelle, pp. 96–97; Howe, pp. 268–71.
24. Howe, p. 271.
25. Gravelle, pp. 81–86; Campbell, 92–94; Grattan, *Pacific to 1900*, p. 463.
26. Scarr, p. 27; Gravelle, pp. 89–92.
27. Gravelle, p. 97.
28. Campbell, p. 93; Sweetman, *American Naval History*, pp. 55–56.
29. Howe, p. 273; Campbell, p. 93.
30. Campbell, p. 93; Timothy L. Francis, "Irregular Warfare and the Vandalia Expedition to Fiji, 1859," *Small Wars Journal* (posted February 3, 2009), www.smallwarsjournal.com.
31. Campbell, p. 94; Gravelle, p. 102; Howe, p. 274.
32. Snow and Waine, *People from the Horizon*, pp. 136–37.
33. Levuka.wordpress.com, "July 13, 1869{in}; Campbell, p. 94.
34. Scarr p. 45.
35. Gravelle, p. 120.
36. Horne, *White Pacific*, p. 77.
37. Scarr, p. 57.
38. Linnekin, pp. 193–94.
39. Snow and Waine, p. 181.
40. Gravelle, pp. 218–19.
41. Campbell, p. 95; Linnekin, pp. 193–94.
42. Scarr, p. 96.
43. Scarr, p. 75.
44. Craig and King, p. 87.
45. Gravelle, pp. 139–43; Denoon, "New Economic Order," p. 245.
46. Scarr, pp. 78–79.
47. Scarr, p. 78; Campbell, pp. 158–61.
48. Denoon, "Land, Labour and Independent Development," p. 159.
49. Scarr, p. 79.
50. Coulter, *Drama of Fiji*, p. 204; Scarr, pp. 79–83; Gravelle, pp. 150–54; Campbell, pp. 175–76; Denoon, "New Economic Order," p. 230.
51. Scarr, p. 98.
52. Gravelle, pp. 161–4.
53. Howe, p. 338; Dodge, p. 161.
54. Coulter, p. 294; Howe, p. 329; Scarr, p. 78–79.

Chapter 17

1. Olwyn Whitehouse, "Nelson — New Zealand Bound."

2. Reed, *Story of New Zealand*, pp. 193–96.

3. King, *New Zealanders*, pp. 48–49; Oliver, *Polynesia*, pp. 177–78.

4. *Te Ara—The Encyclopedia of New Zealand*, from *Encyclopaedia of New Zealand, 1966*, s.v. "Sheep Farming: General Management and Breeds," updated April 22, 2009, http://www.teara.govt.nz/en/1966/sheep-farming/1.

5. Dodge, *Islands and Empires*, p. 80; Ralston, *Grass Huts*, p. 61.

6. Grattan, *Pacific to 1900*, pp. 385–86; Sorrenson, "Maori and Pakeha," *Oxford History of New Zealand*, pp. 178–79.

7. King, pp. 50–54.

8. King, pp. 58–59.

9. Sorrenson, pp. 178–9.

10. *Te Ara—The Encyclopedia of New Zealand*, s.v. "Scots: The Otago Settlement" (by John Wilson), http://www.teara.govt.nz.en/scots/3.

11. The Prow, "New Zealand Company," http://www.theprow.org.nz/new-zealand-company/.

12. Gardner, "Colonial Economy," pp. 62–63.

13. Dalziel, "Politics of Settlement," pp. 92–93.

14. Belich, "Governors," pp. 87–88.

15. Parsonson, "Pursuit of Mana," pp. 154–56; King, 58–59; Donald Denoon, "Land, Labour, and Independent Development," p. 168.

16. Gardner, p. 66; Gold Mine Experience, "Thames Gold Field," http://www.goldmine_experience.co.nz-/edu-history.html; Denoon et al., *History*, p. 141.

17. Zuljan, "First Taranaki War," *Armed Conflicts Events Data*, http://www.onwar.com/aced/nation/nap/newz/ftaranaki1860.htm.

18. Sorrenson, pp. 183–84; Dodge, p. 153.

19. Sorrenson, pp. 182–83; King, p. 60; Belich, "Governors," pp. 91–94.

20. Gardner, p. 163.

21. Grant Morris, "Chief Justice Pendergast."

22. Dalziel, "Politics," pp. 96–97.

23. Dalziel, "Railways and Relief Centres," pp. 101–04.

24. Orange, "Maori People," pp. 43–44; *Te Ara—The Encyclopedia of New Zealand*, s.v. "Immigration Regulation, 1881–1914: Restrictions on Chinese and Others" (by Ann Beaglehole), http://www.teara.govt.nz/en-/immigration-regulation/2; Denoon et al., *History*, p. 193.

25. Denoon, "Land, Labour and Independent Development," p. 152.

26. Denoon, "Land," pp. 175–76; Denoon, "Immigration Regulation."

27. Bill Glover, "History of the Atlantic Cable and Undersea Communications: Pacific Cable 1902–26."

28. Gardner, p. 80.

29. Richardson, "Parties and Political Change," pp. 201–07; Hamer, "Centralization and Nationalism, 1891–1912," pp. 126–30.

30. Hamer, p. 149.

31. Richardson, 203; Hamer, pp. 135–36.

32. Hamer, pp. 142–43.

33. King, pp. 74–87.

34. New Zealand Government, "Maori Ethnicity in Households"; Dodge, p. 197.

Chapter 18

1. Headrick, *Tools of Empire*, pp. 58–76.

2. Howe, *Where the Waves Fall*, p. 482.

3. Sherry, *Pacific Passions*, p. 307.

4. Salmond, *Aphrodite's Island*, p. 110.

5. Salmond, p. 114.

6. Sherry, p. 335.

7. Edwards, ed., *Journals*, p. 380.

8. Craig and King, *Oceania*, p. 154.

9. Daws, *Shoal of Time*, p. 28; Fletcher and Keller, *Tonga*, p. 13.

10. Craig and King, p. 154.

11. Welsh, *Australia*, p. 43.

12. J.C. Beaglehole, *Exploration*, pp. 320–21.

13. Day, *Rogues*, pp. 221–34; Day, *People*, pp. 137–48.

14. Shineberg, *Sandalwood*, p. 13.

15. Harcombe, *Vanuatu*, pp. 145–46.

16. Shineberg, pp. 17–19.

17. Couper, *Sailors and Traders*, pp. 88–89; Joesting, *Uncommon*, pp. 109–10.

18. Shineberg, pp. 22–26.

19. Harcombe, p. 146.

20. Howe, p. 321.

21. Van Trease, *Politics of Land*, pp. 14–16; Harcombe, p. 157.

22. Howe, p. 323.

23. Howe, p. 326.

24. Daws, *Dream of Islands*, pp. 55–64.

25. Daws, pp. 55–56.

26. Dodge, *Islands and Empires*, p. 96.

27. Howe, pp. 293–95.

28. Lal and Fortune, *Pacific Islands*, p. 191.

29. Campbell, *History of the Pacific Islands*, pp. 118–19.

30. Howe, pp. 303–05.

31. Blaine, "Itinerary and Acts."

32. Howe, p. 297.

33. Howe, pp. 299–300.

34. English, "Geddie, John"; Campbell, p. 118; Linnekin, "New Political Orders," p.199.

35. Snow and Waine, *People from the Horizon*, p. 127; Howe, pp. 299, 301–03.

36. Harcombe, pp. 130–31.

37. Harrison, "John G. Paton."

38. Howe, p. 302; Robertson, *Erromango*, pp. 64–78.

39. Howe, pp. 300–01.

40. Robertson, pp. 148–56.

41. Resture, "Bishop Patteson."

42. Campbell, p. 120; Clarke, *Hell and Paradise*, pp. 151–52.

43. Resture, "Bishop Patteson."

44. Torres Strait Regional Authority, "History of Torres Strait to 1879."

45. Snow and Waine, *People from the Horizon*, p. 182; Ward, "Goodenough, James Graham."

46. Howe, pp. 303–07.

47. Howe, p. 327.

48. Howe, p. 329; Denoon "Land," p. 174.

49. Dodge, *Islands and Empires*, pp. 160–63; Welsh, *Australia*, pp. 255–57.

50. Resture, "Kanakas and the Cane Fields."

51. Howe, p. 331.

52. Donald Denoon, "Land," p. 179; Resture, "Kanaks and the Labor Trade"; Harcombe, pp. 261–62.

53. U.K. Parliament, "Pacific Islanders' Protection Act 1872{in}; Denoon, "Land," p. 180.

54. Corris, "Blackbirding," pp. 85–90.

55. Howe, p. 333.

56. Grattan, *Pacific to 1900*, pp. 469–70.

57. Howe, p. 338.

58. Judith A. Bennett, *Wealth of the Solomons*, pp. 21–30.

59. Judith A. Bennett, pp. 34–38.
60. Judith A. Bennett, p. 113.
61. Dodge, p. 178; Judith A. Bennett, p. 103.
62. Krieger, *Conversations with Cannibals*, p. 186.
63. Judith A. Bennett, pp. 128–29.
64. Denoon, "New Economic," 221; Judith A. Bennett, pp. 103–04.
65. Judith A. Bennett, p. 115.
66. Stanley, *South Pacific Handbook*, p. 854; Craig and King, p. 266.
67. Aldrich, *France and the South Pacific*, pp. 131–33.
68. Campbell, p. 123.
69. Dodge, p. 180.
70. Campbell, p. 145; Craig and King, pp. 316–17; Snow and Waine, pp. 179–81.
71. Stanley, *South Pacific Handbook*, p. 814.
72. West, "Stanley, Owen."
73. Turner, *Historical Dictionary*, p. 170.
74. Grattan, *Pacific to 1900*, p. 492.
75. Brown, *Notes*, pp. 137–39.
76. Turner, p. 8.
77. Furnas, *Anatomy of Paradise*, pp. 307–12, Michener and Day, *Rascals in Paradise*, pp. 52–81.
78. Ricklefs, *History of Modern Indonesia*, p. 137; Lightbody and Wheeler, *Papua New Guinea*, p. 141.
79. Turner, pp. 96–97; Campbell, pp. 162–63; Denoon, "New Economic," p. 220.
80. Percy S. Allen, *Stewart's Handbook* (1923), pp. 366–67.
81. Lightbody and Wheeler, p. 141.
82. Turner, pp. 96–97.
83. Percy S. Allen (1923), pp. 360–61.
84. Percy S. Allen (1923), pp. 366–67.
85. Millar, *Australia*, p. 304.
86. Denoon et al., *History*, p. 155.
87. Whittaker et al., *Documents and Readings*, pp. 460–61.
88. Turner, pp. 32–33.
89. Turner, p. 154.
90. Prendergast, "Chalmers, James."
91. Welsh, pp. 412–13; Turner, pp. 17–18; 173–74.

CHAPTER 19

1. Daws, *Shoal of Time*, pp. 187–99; Wisniewski, *Rise and Fall*, pp. 64–66; Day, *People*, pp. 199–200.
2. Daws, *Shoal of Time*, p. 202; Wisniewski, *Rise and Fall*, p. 67.
3. Daws, pp. 202–04; Day, *People*, p. 203; Wisniewski, p. 68.
4. Wisniewski, p. 63.
5. Dodge, *Islands and Empires*, p. 189; Day, *People*, pp. 167–68.
6. Daws, *Shoal of Time*, pp. 226–30; Wisniewski, pp. 69–70.
7. Daws, *Shoal of Time*, p. 211; Day, *Hawaii*, p. 225.
8. Siler, *Lost Kingdom*, p. 88; Wisniewski, 71.
9. Wisniewski, p. 74; Daws, *Shoal of Time*, pp. 216–19.
10. Daws, 220–25; Wisniewski, p. 73; Michener and Day, *Rascals in Paradise*, pp. 121–55; Day, *People*, p. 193.
11. Michener and Day, pp. 132–34.
12. Daws, *Shoal of Time*, pp. 235–39; Michener and Day, pp. 142–50.
13. Siler, p. 104.
14. Siler, p. 101; Wisniewski, p. 76; Day, *People*, pp. 204–05.
15. Daws, *Shoal of Time*, pp. 243–48; Day, *People*, p. 208; Wisniewski, pp. 82–83.
16. Siler, p. 142.
17. Michener and Day, pp. 152–53; Wisniewski, pp. 82–84.
18. Daws, *Shoal of Time*, pp. 247–50; Wisniewski, pp. 83–84.
19. Siler, p. 80.
20. Daws, *Shoal of Time*, pp. 252–53; Wisniewski, p. 85.
21. Wisniewski, pp. 87–88; Day, *People*, pp. 210–11.
22. Horne, *White Pacific*, p. 93.
23. Wisniewski, pp. 89–90; Daws, *Shoal of Time*, pp. 263–65; Day, *People*, pp. 212–14.
24. Siler, p. 201.
25. Wisniewski, pp. 95–98; Day, *People*, pp. 213–18; Daws, *Shoal of Time*, pp. 270–80; Tate, *United States*, pp. 155–93.
26. Daws, *Shoal of Time*, pp. 277–78; Wisniewski, pp. 98–99; Tate, pp. 192–212.
27. Daws, pp. 277–78; Tate, pp. 229–37; Day, *People*, pp. 216–17.
28. Daws, pp. 277–78; Day, *People*, pp. 216–17; Tate, pp. 246–47.
29. Tate, p. 258; Daws, pp. 275–77.
30. Wisniewski, p. 107.
31. Daws, p. 283; Wisniewski, pp. 104–06.
32. Tate, p. 298; Wisniewski, p. 107.
33. Tate, pp. 305–06; Daws, p. 290; Wisniewski, pp. 108–09.
34. Day, *People*, pp. 233; Wisniewski, *Hawaii*, pp. 10–12.
35. McAdie, "Trans-Pacific Cable"; Wisniewski, *Territorial*, p. 14.
36. Matson, "Matson's History."
37. Wisniewski, *Hawaii*, pp. 23–25.
38. Nation Master, "Niihau."

CHAPTER 20

1. Hobsbawm, *Age of Empire*, p. 79.
2. Rosenberg, "Guano Island Act"; Dudden, *American Pacific*, p. 65.
3. Bellamy-Foster and Magoff, "Leibieg, Marx," pp. 134–39.
4. Wiley-VCH, *Ullman's Agrochemicals*, vol. 1, pp. 4–6.
5. Taylor, *Germany's First Bid*, pp. 17–21.
6. Craig and King, *Oceania*, p. 202.
7. Dodge, *Islands and Empires*, p. 192.
8. Hiery, *Neglected War*, pp. 116–17; Denoon, "New Economic Orders," p. 236.
9. Oliver, *Pacific Islands*, p. 317.
10. Withey, *Voyages*, pp. 326–27; Thomas, *Cook*, p. 205.
11. Stanley, *South Pacific Handbook*, pp. 352–53.
12. Resture, "Nassau Island."
13. Craig and King, p. 61.
14. Grattan, *Pacific to 1900*, p. 509; Craig and King, pp. 207–08,.
15. Campbell, *History of the Pacific Islands*, p. 147; Grattan, p. 509.
16. Suarez, *Early Mapping*, p. 188.
17. Craig and King, pp. 301–02.
18. Craig and King, p. 214; Denoon et al., *History*, p. 155.
19. Craig and King, pp. 147–49.
20. Resture, "Fakaofu Island Tokelau."

21. Stanley, *South Pacific Handbook*, 709.
22. Newbury, *Tahiti Nui*, p. 202.
23. Craig and King, p. 320; Stanley, *South Pacific Handbook*, p. 520.
24. Campbell, *History*, p. 123.
25. Withey, p. 359.
26. Resture, "Micronesia: Christmas Island: History."
27. Thompson and Adloff, *French Pacific*, p. 15.
28. Cahoon, "French Polynesia."
29. Tate, *United States*, pp. 305–06.
30. Krieger, *Conversations with Cannibals*, p. 186.
31. Craig and King, p. 266.
32. Dudden, pp. 65–66; Bailey, *Diplomatic History*, p. 427.
33. Campbell, p. 89; Rutherford, *Shirley Baker*, p. 90.
34. King, *New Zealanders*, pp. 74–87; Millar, *Australia*, p. 62; Welsh, *Australia*, pp. 330–32.
35. Millar, pp. 63–64.
36. Welsh, pp. 364–77; Denoon, p. 269.
37. Welsh, pp. 372–75.
38. King, pp. 109–10; Denoon, p. 269.
39. New Zealand History Online, "Resistance to Conscription."
40. Gravelle, *Fiji's Times*, pp. 185–86.
41. Gravelle, p. 187; Scarr, *Fiji*, p. 120.
42. World at War, "French Polynesia"; Thompson, p. 17.
43. Thompson and Adloff, p. 251.
44. Muckle, "War of 1917," pp. 12–13; Thompson, pp. 249–50.
45. Glover, "History of the Atlantic Cable."
46. Newbury, pp. 265–66; Thompson, p. 17.
47. Glover.
48. Woodward, *Robinson Crusoe's Island*, pp. 219–22.
49. Wisniewski, *Hawaii*, pp. 17–18.
50. Enright, "Count Dohna and His *SeaGull*."
51. Gravelle, pp. 188–93.
52. Davidson, *Samoa Mo Samoa*, pp. 90–92; Hiery, 220; King, 105; World at War, "Samoa Timeline."
53. Hiery, p. 168.
54. Hiery, pp. 23–27; Millar, p. 305.
55. Hiery, pp. 117–18.
56. Hiery, p. 125.
57. Gilbert, *First World War*, pp. 104–06.
58. King, p. 116.
59. Denoon, pp. 272–80; King, pp. 117–32.
60. Millar, pp. 121–22; Denoon, 269–70; Welsh, 379–84.

Chapter 21

1. Campbell, *History of the Pacific Islands*, pp. 152–53.
2. Howe, *Where the Waves Fall*, p. 349.
3. Barry, *Great Influenza*, pp. 4–5.
4. Barry, p. 34.
5. U.S. National Center for Infectious Diseases, "Modeling the Impact."
6. Barry, p. 333.
7. New Zealand History Online, "Nineteen Eighteen Flu Pandemic."
8. Barry, p. 376.
9. Percy S. Allen, *Stewart's Handbook* (1923), p. 126.
10. Davidson, *Samoa Mo Samoa*, pp. 94–95; Denoon, "New Economic Orders," p. 247.
11. Barry, p. 364.

12. U.S. National Center for Infectious Diseases, "Modeling the Impact."
13. Percy S. Allen (1923), p. 230.
14. Newbury, *Tahiti Nui*, pp. 270–71; Thompson and Adloff, *French Pacific*, p. 18.
15. Denoon, "New Economic Orders," p. 247.
16. Barry, p. 364.
17. U.S. National Center for Infectious Diseases, "Modeling the Impact."
18. Hiery, *Neglected War*, pp. 195–98.
19. Hiery, pp. 120–25.
20. Percy S. Allen (1920), p. 180.
21. "Mandated Territory," *www.pngbual.com/300soci8al_sciences/_/EOLmadates.pdf*.
22. Percy S. Allen (1923), p. 366.
23. Denoon, "New Economic Orders," p. 223; Millar, *Australia*, p. 305; Percy S. Allen (1923), pp. 340–41.
24. Blainey, *Tyranny of Distance*, p. 167.
25. Stanner, "Australian Aborigines," pp. 150–52.
26. Sorrenson, "Maori and Pakeha," *Oxford History of New Zealand*, pp. 172–73.
27. New Zealand History Online, "Overview — NZ in the 1920s."
28. Sorrenson, 171–73.
29. Butterworth, "Rural Maori Renaisance?," p. 160.
30. Sorrenson, 171–73.
31. Newbury, pp. 271–72.
32. Robert Keable, "The Truth About Tahiti," *Melbourne Herald*, April 7, 1923; Percy S. Allen (1923), p. 424.
33. Aldrich, *France and the South Pacific*, p. 194.
34. Nicole, *The Word*, p. 144; Rosenblum, *Mission to Civilize*, p. 169.
35. Percy S. Allen (1920), p. 164.
36. Church, "Vanishing People," p. 306.
37. Suggs, *Hidden Worlds*, pp. 57–58.
38. Percy S. Allen (1920), p. 166.
39. Church, pp. 299–303.
40. Percy S. Allen (1920), p. 161.
41. Percy S. Allen (1923), p. 461.
42. Fischer, *Island*, p. 183.
43. Fischer, pp. 177–78.
44. Percy S. Allen (1923), pp. 65–67.
45. Percy S. Allen (1923), pp. 48–50.
46. Percy S. Allen (1923), pp. 191–93.
47. Percy S. Allen (1920), p. 96.
48. Wisniewski, *Hawaii*, p. 35.
49. Wisniewski, p. 39.
50. Budnick, *Hawaii's Forgotten History*, p. 47.
51. Percy S. Allen (1920), p. 17.
52. Percy S. Allen (1923), p. 495.
53. Percy S. Allen (1923), p. 467.
54. Gravelle, *Fiji's Times*, pp. 194–98; Scarr, *Fiji*, p. 125.
55. Percy S. Allen (1923), p. 500.
56. Campbell, pp. 175–76.
57. Coulter, *Drama of Fiji*, p. 204; Dodge, *Islands and Empires*, p. 200; Snow and Waine, *People from the Horizon*, p. 154.
58. Percy S. Allen (1920), 30.
59. Hiery, p. 126.
60. Hiery, pp. 125–26; Denoon, "New Economic Orders," p. 247.
61. Percy S. Allen (1923), p. 99.
62. Percy S. Allen (1923), p. 95.
63. Colby, ed., *New International Yearbook*, p. 458.
64. Percy S. Allen (1923), p. 505.
65. Judith A. Bennett, *Wealth of the Solomons*, pp. 148–51.
66. Judith A. Bennett, p. 115.

Bibliography

Abara Banaba. "Abara Banaba Information." http://www.banaban.com.

About Australia. "Tasmania History." http://www.aboutaustralia.com/facts/tasmania/history/1856.

Absolute Astronomy. "Katherine Routledge." http://www.absoluteastronomy.com/topics/Katherine_Routledge.

Aikman, Reverend John Logan. *Cyclopedia of Christian Missions*. London: British Society for Propagation of the Gospel among Jews, 1860.

Aldrich, Robert. *France and the South Pacific Since 1940*. Honolulu: University of Hawaii Press, 1993.

_____. *Greater France: A History of French Overseas Expansion*. European Studies Series. New York: Palgrave, 1996.

Alexander, Caroline. *The Bounty: The True Story of the Mutiny on the Bounty*. New York: Viking, 2003.

Allen, Helena G. *Kalakaua: Renaissance King*. Honolulu, 1995.

Allen, Percy S. *Stewart's Handbook of the Pacific Islands*. Sydney: McCarron, Stewart and Co., 1920.

_____. *Stewart's Handbook of the Pacific Islands*. Sydney: McCarron, Stewart and Co., 1923.

Anderson, Charles Robert. *Melville and the South Seas*. New York: Columbia University Press, 1939.

Anonymous. "Other Mystery of Easter Island." http://www.scribd.com/doc/969/The-Other-Mystery-Of-Easter-Island.

Apple, Russell. "Maui-Lahaina Crime Punishment." http://www.maui-lahaina-sun.com/lahaina-crime-punishment.html.

Australian Broadcasting Corporation. "Places: Solomon Islands." http://www.abc.net.au/ra/pacific/places/country/solomon_islands.htm

Australian Government. "Norfolk Island Historical Events." http://www.11sac.gov.au/Territories ofAustralia-NorfolkIsland.

Australian War Memorial. "Sudan (New South Wales Contingent) March–June 1885." www.awm.gov.au/atwar/sudan.asp.

Bahn, Paul, and John Flenley. *Easter Island, Earth Island*. New York: Thames and Hudson, 1992.

Bailey, Thomas A. *A Diplomatic History of the American People*. 6th ed. New York: Appleton Century Crofts, 1964.

Barry, John M. *The Great Influenza: The Epic Story of the Deadliest Plague in History*. New York: Viking, 2004.

Beaglehole, J.C. *The Exploration of the Pacific*. Stanford: Stanford University Press, 1966.

_____. *The Life of Captain James Cook*. Stanford: Stanford University Press, 1974.

Beechey, Frederick. *Narrative of a Voyage to the Pacific and Bering Strait*. London: H. Colburn and R. Bentley, 1831.

Belich, James. "The Governors and the Maori, 1840–1872." In *The Oxford Illustrated History of New Zealand*, edited by Keith Sinclair, pp. 75–98. Auckland: Oxford University Press, 1990.

Bellamy-Foster, John, and Fred Magdoff. "Leibieg, Marx and the Depletion of Soil Fertility." *Monthly Review* 50, no. 3 (July-August 1998): 134–39.

Bennett, Frederick Debell. *Narrative of a Whaling Voyage Round the Globe from the Year 1833 to 1836*. London: Richard Bentley, 1840.

Bennett, Judith A. *Wealth of the Solomons: A History of a Pacific Archipelago, 1800–1978*. Honolulu: University of Hawaii Press, 1987.

Bergreen, Laurence. *Over the Edge of the World: Magellan's Terrifying Circumnavigation of the Globe*. New York: Harper Perennial, 2004.

Big Island Visitors Bureau. "History of Paniolos and Ranching on Hawaii's Big Island." http://72.3.133.161/activities-cultural/464/history-of-paniolo-ranching-on-hawaiis-big-island.

Blaine, Michael, compiler. "Itinerary and Acts of George Augustus Selwyn." *Anglican History*. www.anglicanhistory.org/nz/selwyn/blain-acta.pdf.

Blainey, Geoffrey. *The Tyranny of Distance: How Distance Shaped Australia's History*. Rev. ed. Melbourne: Sun Books, 1983.

Bligh, William. *The Mutiny On Board H.M.S. Bounty*. New York: Signet Classic, 1961.

Boxer, C.R. *The Dutch Seaborne Empire, 1600–1800*. New York: Alfred A. Knopf, 1965.

_____. *The Portuguese Seaborne Empire 1415–1825*. Middlesex: Penguin Books, 1969.

Brands, H.W. *The Age of Gold: The California Gold Rush and the New American Dream*. New York: Doubleday, 2002.

Breward, Ian. *A History of the Churches in Australasia*. Oxford: Oxford University Press, 2001.

British Library. "EP/AF/001 Gilbert and Ellice Islands Colony: Administrative History." http://www.bl.uk/website_search/search?q=cache:L8kDTAmRZRUJ:www.collectbritain.co.uk/about/policies/endangeredarch/pdf/gande_islandscol.pdf+legislative&access=p&restrict=public&output=xml_no_dtd&ie=UTF-8&client=public&site=public&oe=UTF-8&proxystylesheet=public.

Broadway Musical Home. "South Pacific." www.broadwaymusicalhome.com/shows/south-pacific.htm.

Brodie, Walter. *Pitcairn's Island and the Islanders in 1850*. London: Whitaker, 1851.

Brown, George. *Notes on the Duke of York Group: New Britain and New Ireland*. Reprint, Whitefish, MT: Kessinger Publishing, 2006.

Buck, Peter Henry. *Explorers of the Pacific: European and American Discoveries in Polynesia*. 3rd ed. Stanford: Stanford University Press, 1966.

_____. "Louis Duperrey." *Explorers of the Pacific: European and American Discoveries in Polynesia*. Bernice P. Bishop Museum, James Burney. Digitized version at New Zealand Electronic Text Center. http://www.nzetc.org/tm/scholarly/tei-BucExpl-t1-body-d19-d6.html#n95.

_____. "Peter Dillon." *Explorers of the Pacific: European and American Discoveries in Polynesia*. Bernice P. Bishop Museum, James Burney. Digitized version at New Zealand Electronic Text Center. http://www.nzetc.org/tm/scholarly/tei-BucExpl-t1-body-d20-d6.html.

Budnick, Rich. *Hawaii's Forgotten History*. Honolulu: Aloha Press, 2005.

Burley, David V. "Archaeological Demography and Population Growth in the Kingdom of Tonga." In *The Growth and Collapse of Pacific Island Societies: Archaeological and Demographic Perspectives*, edited by Patrick V. Kirch and Jean-Louis Rallu, pp. 177–202. Honolulu: University of Hawaii Press, 2007.

Burns, Bill. "Bamfield Cable Station: British Columbia, Canada." *History of the Atlantic Cable and Undersea Communications from the First Submarine Cable of 1850 to the Worldwide Fiber Optic Network*. http://atlantic-cable.com/CableCos/Bamfield/index.htm.

Butterworth, G.V. "A Rural Maori Renaissance? Maori Society and Politics 1920–51." *Journal of the Polynesian Society* 81, no. 2 (June 1972): 160–95.

Cahoon, Ben. "American Samoa." World Statesmen. http://www.worldstatesmen.org/Am-Samoa.html.

_____. "French Polynesia." World Statesmen. http://www.worldstatesmen.org/Fr_Polynesia.html.

_____. "Kiribati." World Statesmen. http://www.worldstatesmen.org/Kiribati.htm.

_____. "New Zealand." World Statesmen. http://www.worldstatesmen.org/New_Zealand.htm.

_____. "Tokelau." World Statesmen. http://www.worldstatesmen.org/Tokelau.html.

_____. "U.S. Unincorporated Possessions." World Statesmen. http://www.worldstatesmen.org/US_minor.html.

Campbell, I.C. *Gone Native in Polynesia: Captivity Narratives and Experiences in the South Pacific*. Westport, CT: Greenwood Press, 1998.

_____. *A History of the Pacific Islands*. Berkeley: University of California Press, 1996.

Carrington, Hugh, ed. *The Discovery of Tahiti: A Journal of the Second Voyage of H.M.S. Dolphin Round the World under the Command of Captain Wallis, R.N., in the Years 1766, 1767, and 1768*. Wiesbaden: Ashgate, 2010.

Caslon Analytics. "Aust Telecoms: Beginnings." http://www.caslon.com.au/austelecomsprofile1.htm.

Catholic Encyclopedia. "Vicarate Apostolic of Central Oceania." www.newadvent.org.cathen/11200b.htm.

Celermajer, Danielle. "The Stolen Generation: Aboriginal Children in Australia." Carnegie Council. http://www.carnegiecouncil.org/resources/publications/dialogue/2_12/section_1/5142.html/:pf_printable?pagewanted=all.

Central Intelligence Agency. "New Zealand." *The World Factbook*. https://www.cia.gov/library/publications/the-world-factbook/geos/nz.html.

Chambers, John H. *A Traveler's History of New Zealand and the South Pacific Islands*. Northampton, MA: Interlink Books, 2004.

Chapman, Robert. "From Labour to National." In *The Oxford History of New Zealand*, 2nd ed., edited by Geoffrey W. Rice. Auckland: 1992.

Church, John W. "A Vanishing People of the South Seas: The Tragic Fate of the Marquesan Cannibals." *National Geographic* 36, no. 4 (October 1919): 275–306.

Clark, Manning. *A Short History of Australia*. 3rd rev. ed. New York: NAL Penguin, 1987.

Clark, Thomas Blake. *Omai: First Polynesian Am-*

bassador to England. Honolulu: University of Hawaii Press, 1969.

Clarke, Peter. *Hell and Paradise: The Norfolk-Bounty-Pitcairn Saga*. Ringwood, Victoria: Viking, Penguin Books Australia, 1986.

Clement, Russell. "From Cook to the 1840 Constitution: The Name Change from Sandwich to Hawaiian Islands." www.evols.library.manoa.hawaii.edu/bitstream/10524/495.

Colby, Frank Moore, ed. "German Samoa." *The New International Yearbook, 1917*. New York: Dodd, Mead, 1918.

_____. "New Hebrides." *The New International Yearbook*. New York: Charles Scribner's Sons, 1921.

_____. *The New International Yearbook, 1919*. New York: Charles Scribner's Sons, 1920.

Columbia Encyclopedia. "Alejandro Malaspina." Answers.com. http://www.answers.com/topic/malaspina-alejandro-italian-spanish-explorer.

_____. "John Williams." Answers.com. http://www.answers.com/topic/john-williams.

Commonwealth Secretariat. "New Zealand—Niue." http://www.thecommonwealth.org/YearbookInternal/140411/140413/niue/.

Conklin, Ken. "Henry Opukahaia (Obookiah)." Personal Web site. http://www.angelfire.com/hi5/bigfiles/opukahaia.html.

Conrad, Joseph. *Lord Jim*. A Pennsylvania State Electronic Classic Series Publication. pt.scribd.com/doc/714623/22-CHAPTER-22-Chapter-22/.

Convicts to Australia. "Hougoumont—Arrived in WA in 1868." http://members.iinet.net.au/~perthdps/convicts/con-wa42.html.

The Cook Islands Website. "Religion in the Cook Islands." http://www.ck/religion.htm.

Corney, Bolton Glanvill, ed., Felipe González de Haedo, and Jacob Roggeveen. "Voyage of Captain Don Felipe González in the Ship of the Line San Lorenzo with the Frigate Santa Rosalia in Company, to Easter Island in 1770–1." http://archive.org/details/voyagecaptaindoo00unkngoog.

Corris, Peter. "Blackbirding in New Guinea Waters, 1883–84." *Journal of Pacific History* 3 (1968): 85–105.

Cook, J., T. Furneaux, and W. Hodges. "Captain Furneaux's Narrative." In *A Voyage Towards the South Pole, and Round the World, Performed in His Majesty's Ships the Resolution and Adventure in the Years 1772, 1773, 1774, and 1775*. London, 1777. www.geocities.com/7557/massacre.html.

Coulter, John Wesley. *The Drama of Fiji: A Contemporary History*. Rutland, VT: Tuttle, 1967.

Countries Quest. "Papua New Guinea, History." http://www.countriesquest.com/oceania/papua_new_guinea/history.htm.

Couper, Alistair. *Sailors and Traders: A Maritime History of the Pacific Peoples*. Honolulu: University of Hawaii Press, 2009.

Cowan, James. "The Liberation of the Samoans." Extract from "Famous New Zealanders: No. 41: Michael Joseph Savage: The First Labour Prime Minister of New Zealand." *New Zealand Railways Magazine* 11, no. 5 (August 1, 1936). Digitized version at New Zealand Electronic Text Centre. http://www.nzetc/tm/scholarly/tel-Gov11-05Railti-body-d3d2.html

Craig, Robert D. *Dictionary of Polynesian Mythology*. Westport, CT: Greenwood Press, 1989.

Craig, Robert D., and Frank P. King. *Historical Dictionary of Oceania*. Westport, CT: Greenwood Press, 1981.

Crocombe, Ron. *The South Pacific: An Introduction*. Suva: Institute of Pacific Studies, University of the South Pacific, 2001.

Crook, William Pascoe. *An Account of the Marquesas Islands, 1797–99*. Forward by Greg Dening. Papeete: Haero, 2007.

Crystal, Ellie. "Easter Island—Rapa Nui." http://www.crystalinks.com/easterisland.html.

Dalziel, Raewyn. "The Politics of Settlement." In *The Oxford History of New Zealand*, 2nd ed., edited by Geoffrey W. Rice. Auckland: Oxford University Press, 1992.

_____. "Railways and Relief Centres." In *The Oxford Illustrated History of New Zealand*, edited by Keith Sinclair, pp. 99–124. Auckland: Oxford University Press, 1990.

David, Andrew. *The Voyage of HMS* Herald *to Australia and the South-west Pacific 1852–61 under the Command of Captain Henry Mangles Denham*. Melbourne: Miegunyah, 1995.

Davidson, J.W. *Samoa Mo Samoa: The Emergence of the Independent State of Western Samoa*. Melbourne: Oxford University Press, 1967.

Daws, Gavan. *A Dream of Islands*. New York: W.W. Norton and Co., 1980.

_____. *Shoal of Time: A History of the Hawaiian Islands*. Honolulu: University of Hawaii Press, 1968.

Day, A. Grove. *Hawaii and Its People*. Honolulu: Mutual, 1993.

_____. *Hawaii and Points South: True Island Tales*. Honolulu: Mutual, 1992.

_____. *Rogues of the South Seas*. Honolulu: Mutual, 1986.

Day, A. Grove, ed. *Mark Twain's Letters from Hawaii*. Honolulu: University Press of Hawaii, 1971.

Dear, I.C.B., and Peter Kemp. *Oxford Companion to Ships and the Sea*. Oxford and New York: Oxford University Press, 2006.

Dening, Greg, ed. *The Marquesan Journal of Edward Robarts, 1797–1824*. Honolulu: University of Hawaii Press, 1974.

Denoon, Donald. "Land, Labour and Independent Development." In *The Cambridge History of the Pacific Islanders,* edited by Donald Denoon. Cambridge: Cambridge University Press, 1997.

_____. "New Economic Orders." In *The Cambridge History of the Pacific Islanders,* edited by Donald Denoon. Cambridge: Cambridge University Press, 1997.

Denoon, Donald, and Philippa Mein-Smith with Marivic Wyndham. *A History of Australia, New Zealand and the Pacific.* Oxford: Oxford University Press, 2000.

Diamond, Jared. Collapse: How Societies Choose to Fail or Succeed. New York: Viking, 2005.

_____. "Easter's End." *Discover* 16, no. 8 (August 1995): 63–39.

Dodd, Edward. *The Rape of Tahiti.* New York: Dodd, Mead, 1983.

Dodge, Ernest S. *Islands and Empires: Western Impact on the Pacific and East Asia.* Minneapolis: University of Minnesota Press, 1976.

Doeherty, James C. *Historical Dictionary of Australia.* Metuchen, NJ, and London, 1992.

Dousset, Roselene, and Etienne Tallemite. *The Great Book of the Pacific.* Secaucus, NJ: Chartwell Books, 1979.

Dudden, Arthur Power. *The American Pacific: From the Old China Trade to the Present.* New York: Oxford University Press, 1992.

Duhaut-Cilly, Auguste. *A Voyage to California, the Sandwich Islands, and around the World in the Years 1826–29.* Translated and edited by August Fruge and Neal Harlow. Berkeley: University of California Press, 1999.

Dunstall, Graeme. "The Social Pattern." In *The Oxford History of New Zealand,* 2nd ed., edited by Geoffrey W. Rice. Auckland: Oxford University Press, 1992.

Economic Expert. "Maui." http://www.economic-expert.com/a/maui.htm.

Edison, Carol. "South Sea Islanders in Utah." *Utah History Encyclopedia.* http://www.media.utah.edu/UHE/s/SOUTHSEAILANDERS.html.

Edwards, Philip, ed. *The Journals of Captain Cook.* London: Penguin Books, 1999.

Elections New Zealand. "Maori and the Vote." http://www.elections.org.nz/democracy/history-/maori-vote.html.

Electric Scotland. "Significant Scots: Sir Gilbert Blane." http://www.electricscotland.com/history/other/blane_gilbert.htm.

Ellis, William. *History of the London Missionary Society.* London: John Snow, 1844.

Ellsworth, George S., and Kathleen Clayton Perrin. *Seasons of Faith and Courage: The Church of Jesus Christ of Latter Day Saints in French Polynesia.* Sandy, UT: Yves R. Perrin, 1994.

Encyclopedia of World Biographies. "Paul Gau-guin Biography." http://www.notablebiogra-phies.com/Fi-Gi/Gauguin-Paul.html.

English, John, ed. "Geddie, John." *Dictionary of Canadian Biography Online.* http://www.biographi.ca.

Enright, Saint-Patrick. "Count Dohna and His *SeaGull:* Ships—*Wolf II, Jupiter, Wachtfels.*" http://smsmoewe.com/ships/smsms84.htm.

Erlichman, Howard J. *Conquest, Tribute and Trade: The Quest for Precious Metals and the Birth of Globalization.* New York: Prometheus Books, 2010.

Erskine, John Elphinstone. *Journal of a Cruise Among the Islands of the Western Pacific.* London: John Murray, 1853.

Estensen, Miriam. *Discovery: The Quest for the Great South Land.* New York: St. Martin's Press, 1999.

Faleomavaega, U.S. Congressman Eni F.H. "American Samoa: Treaties." *www.house.gov/faleo-mavaega/treaties.shml.*

Family Search. "Gambier Islands." https://www.familysearch.org/learn/wiki/en/Gambier_Islands.

Feeken, Edwin H., and Gerda E. Feeken. *The Discovery and Exploration of Australia.* Melbourne: Thomas Nelson, 1970.

Ferguson, Niall. *Empire: How Britain Made the Modern World.* London: Penguin Books, 2003.

Feuer, Lewis S. "End of Coolie Labor in New Caledonia." *Far Eastern Survey* 15, no. 17 (August 28, 1946): 264–67.

Fiji Sugar Corporation. "History of Sugar in Fiji." http://www.fsc.com.fj/history_of_sugar_in_fiji.htm

Finau, Makisi, Teeruro Leuti, Jione Langi, and Charles W. Forman. *Island Churches: Challenge and Change.* Suva: Institute of Pacific Studies, University of the South Pacific, 1992.

Fischer, Steven Roger. *Island at the End of the World.* London: Reaction Books, 2005.

_____. "Easter Island's *Rongorongo* Script." http://www.netaxs.com/~trance/fischer.html.

Flenley, John, and Paul Bahn. *The Enigmas of Easter Island.* Oxford: Oxford University Press, 2002.

Fletcher, Matt, and Nancy Keller. *Tonga.* Melbourne: Lonely Planet, 2001.

Flude, Anthony G. "The New Zealand Company, 1837–1858." Personal Web page. http://home-pages.ihug.co.nz/tonyf/nzco/nzc0.html.

_____. "Ocean Island." Personal Web page. http://www.homepages.ihug.co.nz/tonyf/ocean/ocean.html.

Foley, Mairead. "Everything You Need to Know about Lord Howe Island." Ezine Articles. http://ezinearticles.com/?Everything-You-Need-to-Know-About-Lord-Howe-Island&id=180 56.

Francia, Luis H. *A History of the Philippines: From Indios Bravos to Filipinos*. New York: Overlook, 2010.

Francis, Timothy L. "Irregular Warfare and the Vandalia Expedition to Fiji, 1859." *Small Wars Journal*, February 3, 2009. www.smallwarsjournal.com.

Fullerton, Laurie. *New Caledonia: A Travel Survival Kit*. Hawthorn, Victoria: Lonely Planet, 1990.

Furnas, J.C. *Anatomy of Paradise*. New York: William Sloane Associates, 1948.

Gardner, W.J. "A Colonial Economy." In *The Oxford History of New Zealand*, edited by W.H. Oliver with B.R. Williams. Wellington: Oxford University Press, 1981.

Garrett, John. *To Live Among the Stars: Christian Origins in Oceania*. Geneva and Suva: World Council of Churches in association with the Institute of Pacific Studies, University of the South Pacific, 1982.

_____. "Wesleyans Enter Fiji." http://www.justpacific.com/fiji/engravings/williams/wesleyans.pdf.

Gibson, Arrell Morgan. *Yankees in Paradise: The Pacific Basin Frontier*. Albuquerque: University of New Mexico Press, 1993.

Gibson, Richard. *Cook Islands: 1820–1950*, edited by Ron Crocombe. Wellington: Victoria University Press, 1980.

Gilbert, Martin. *The First World War: A Complete History*. New York: Henry Holt, 1994.

Glover, Bill. "History of the Atlantic Cable and Undersea Communications: Pacific Cable 1902–26." http://atlantic-cable.com/Cables/1902Pacific GB/index.htm.

Go-Fiji. "Fiji Myths and Legends." *Fiji Travel Guide*. http://www.go-fiji.com/mythsandlegends.html.

Gold Mine Experience. "Thames Gold Field." http://www.goldmine_experience.co.nz/eduhistory.html.

Goretti. "Iñigo Ortiz de Retes: El ayalés que le puso nombre a Nueva Guinea." *Historias de Ayala: Historias, leyendas, cuentos y todo lo demás*. http://historiasdeayala.blogspot.com/2009/06-/inigo-ortiz-de-retes-el-ayales-que-le.html.

Graham, Jeanine. "Settler Society." *The Oxford History of New Zealand*, 2nd ed., edited by Geoffrey W. Rice. Auckland: Oxford University Press, 1995.

Grattan, C. Hartley. *The South-west Pacific since 1900*. Ann Arbor: University of Michigan Press, 1963.

_____. *The South-west Pacific to 1900*. Ann Arbor: University of Michigan Press, 1963.

Gravelle, Kim. *Fiji's Times: A History of Fiji*. Suva: Fiji Times, 1980.

Gray, William R. *Voyages to Paradise: Exploring in the Wake of Captain Cook*. Washington, DC: National Geographic Society 1981.

Green, Roger C. "Protohistoric Samoan Population." In *The Growth and Collapse of Pacific Island Societies: Archaeological and Demographic Perspectives*, edited by Patrick V. Kirch and Jean-Louis Rallu, pp. 203–31. Honolulu: University of Hawaii Press, 2007.

Gunson, Niel. "The Coming of Foreigners." In *Friendly Islands: A History of Tonga*, edited by Noel Rutherford. Melbourne: Oxford University Press, 1977.

_____. "Cover, James Fleet (1762–1834)." *Australian Dictionary of Biography*. http://adb.anu.edu.au/biography/cover-james-fleet-1927.

Gunson, W.N. "Journal of a Visit to Raivavae in October 1819 by Pomare II, King of Tahiti." *Journal of Pacific History* 1 (1966): 199–203.

Hainsworth, D.R. "Lord, Simeon." *Australian Dictionary of Biography*. http://adb.anu.edu.au/biography/lord-simeon-2371.

Hamer, David. "Centralization and Nationalism, 1891–1912." In *The Oxford Illustrated History of New Zealand*, edited by Keith Sinclair, pp. 125–52. Auckland: Oxford University Press, 1990.

Hanson, F. Allan. *Rapan Lifeways: Society and History on a Polynesian Island*. Boston: Little Brown, 1970.

Harcombe, David. *Vanuatu: A Travel Survival Kit*. Hawthorn, Victoria: Lonely Planet, 1991.

Harrington, Daniel. "Complete Timeline of Hawaiian History." *Hawaiian Encyclopeia*. http://www.hawaiianencyclopedia.com/part-1-complete-timeline-of-ha.asp.

Harrison, Eugene Myers. "John G. Paton: The Apostle of Christ to the Cannibals..." *Worldwide Missions: Missionary Biographies*. http://www.wholesomewords.org/missions/biopaton.html.

Hawai'i Forgiveness Project. "Law of the Splintered Paddle." http://www.hawaiiforgivenessproject.org/stories/Forgiveness-Stories-web-06.htm#paddle.

Hawaii-Nation.org. "Kingdom of Hawai'i Constitution of 1840." *Hawaii: Independent and Sovereign*. www.hawaii-nation.org/constitution-1840.html.

Headrick, Daniel R. *The Tools of Empire: Technology and European Imperialism in the Nineteenth Century*. New York: Oxford University Press, 1981.

Heffer, Jean. *The United States and the Pacific: History of a Frontier*. Translated by W. Donald Wilson. Notre Dame, IN: Notre Dame University Press, 2002.

Heflin, Wilson Lumpkin. *Herman Melville's Whaling Years*, edited by Mary K. Bercaw Edwards and Thomas Farel Heffernan. Nashville: Vanderbilt University Press, 2004.

Hibbert, Christopher. *George III: A Personal History*. New York: Basic Books, 1998.

Hiery, Hermann Joseph. *The Neglected War: The German South Pacific and the Influence of World War I*. Honolulu: University of Hawaii Press, 1995.

Hiney, Tom. *On the Missionary Trail: A Journey through Polynesia, Asia, and Africa with the London Missionary Society*. New York: Atlantic Monthly Press, 2000.

Hobsbawm, Eric. *The Age of Empire, 1875–1914*. New York: Pantheon, 1987.

Hooker, Brian. "The European Discovery of the Cook Islands." Finding New Zealand. http://findingnz.co.nz/av/gav22.htm.

Horne, Gerald. *The White Pacific: U.S. Imperialism and Black Slavery in the South Seas after the Civil War*. Honolulu: University of Hawaii Press, 2007.

Howarth, David. *Tahiti: A Paradise Lost*. New York: Penguin, 1983.

Howe, K.R. *Where the Waves Fall*. Honolulu: University of Hawaii Press, 1984.

Hughes, Robert. *The Fatal Shore: The Epic of Australia's Founding*. New York: Alfred A. Knopf, 1986.

Hutton, James. *Missionary Life in the South Seas*. London: Henry King, 1874.

James, Lawrence. *The Rise and Fall of the British Empire*. New York: St. Martin's Griffin, 1997.

Joesting, Edward. *Hawaii: An Uncommon History*. New York: W.W. Norton, 1972.

Jonassen, Jon Tikivanotau M. "Polynesia in Review: Issues and Events, 1 July 2007 to 30 June 2008." Scholar Space. http://scholarspace.manoa.hawaii.edu/v21n.

Keable, Robert. "The Truth about Tahiti." *Melbourne Herald*, April 7, 1923.

Kelley, Darlene E. "Hawaii Chronology and the U.S." USGenWeb Archives. http://files.usgwarchives.net/hi/statewide/newspapers/hawaiian2gnw.txt

Keneally, Thomas. *Australians, Origins to Eureka*. Crows Nest, NSW: Allen and Unwin, 2009.

King, Michael. *New Zealanders at War*. Auckland: Penguin Books, 2003.

Kirch, Patrick V., and Jean-Louis Rallu, eds. *The Growth and Collapse of Pacific Island Societies*. Honolulu: University of Hawaii Press, 2007.

Kirk, Robert W. *History of the South Pacific since 1513: Chronicle of Australia, new Zealand, New Guinea, Polynesia, Melanesia, and Robinson Crusoe Island*. Denver: Outskirts Press, 2011.

_____. *Pitcairn Island, the Bounty Mutineers and Their Descendants*. Jefferson, NC: McFarland, 2008.

Kloosterman, Alphons M.J. "Discoverers of the Cook Islands and the Names They Gave: 7. Mi-tiaro." Cook Islands Library and Museum, 1976. Digitized version at New Zealand Electronic Text Center. http://www.nzetc.org/tm/scholarly/tei-KloDisc-t1-body-d7.html.

_____. "Discoverers of the Cook Islands and the Names They Gave: 9. Palmerston." Cook Islands Library and Museum, 1976. Digitized version at New Zealand Electronic Text Center. http://www.nzetc.org/tm/scholarly/tei-KloDisc-t1-body-d9.html.

_____. "Discoverers of the Cook Islands and the Names They Gave: 10. Penrhyn." Cook Islands Library and Museum, 1976. Digitized version at New Zealand Electronic Text Center. www.nzetc.org/tm/scholarly/tei-KloDisc-t1-body-d10.html

Ko Wai? "Sailing with the Ancestors." http://www.ko.wai.com/Sailing_With_The_Ancestors.html.

Kotzebue, Otto von. *A New Voyage Round the World in the Years 1823, 24, 25 and 26*. London: Henry Colburn and Richard Bentley, 1830.

Krieger, Michael. *Conversations with the Cannibals: The End of the Old South Pacific*. Hopewell, NJ: Ecco, 1994.

Kunitz, Stephen J. "Historical and Contemporary Mortality Patterns in Polynesia." In *The Anthropology of Disease*, edited by C.G.N. Mascie-Taylor, pp. 124–66. Oxford: Oxford University Press, 1993.

Kuykendall, Ralph S. *The Hawaiian Kingdom, 1778–1854: Foundation and Transformation*. Honolulu: University of Hawaii Press, 1965.

Lal, Brij K., and Kate Fortune. *The Pacific Islands: An Encyclopedia*. Honolulu: University of Hawaii Press, 2000.

Lansdown, Richard. *Strangers in the South Seas: The Idea of the Pacific in Western Thought*. Honolulu: University of Hawaii Press, 2006.

Laracy, Hugh. "The Catholic Mission." In *Friendly Islands: A History of Tonga*, edited by Noel Rutherford. Melbourne: Oxford University Press, 1977.

Larkins, John. *101 Events that Shaped Australia*. Adelaide: Rigby, 1979.

Latukefu, S. "The Wesleyan Mission." In *Friendly Islands: A History of Tonga*, edited by Noel Rutherford. Melbourne: Oxford University Press, 1977.

Lealea, Sal. "Fiji's Cannibal History." *Fijian Custom and Culture*. http://www.fijiancustomculture.com/2009/10/fijis-cannibal-history.html.

Levuka.wordpress.com. "1781: Spanish frigate Nuestra Señora del Rosario, visited Vava'u, Tonga." *Levuka History and Timeline*. http:levuka.wordpress.com/1781-Spanish-frigate.

_____. "July 13, 1869: First Half of Cakobau Debt

Paid by Polynesia Company: 27,000 Acres Sold." *Leveuka History and Timeline.* http://levuka. wordpress.com/2008/10/08/july-13–1869-first-half-of-cakobau-debt-paid-by-polynesia-company-27000-acres-sold/.

Lightbody, Mark, and Tony Wheeler. *Papua New Guinea: A Travel Survival Kit.* South Yarra and Berkeley: Lonely Planet, 1985.

Linnekin, Jocelyn. "New Political Orders." In *The Cambridge History of the Pacific Islanders,* edited by Donald Denoon, 185–217. Cambridge: Cambridge University Press, 1997.

Lord Howe Island Board. "Early Settlers (1833–1880)." Exerpt from *Lord Howe Island: 1788–1988.* National Library of Australia, 1989. Digitized verion at http://www.lordhoweisland.nsw. au/library/early_settlers.pdf.

Lovett, Richard. *The History of the London Missionary Society, 1795–1895,* vol. 1. Oxford: Henry Frowde, 1899.

"Loyalty Islands," http://www.reference.com/br owse/Loyalty_Islands.

Lucas, Sir Charles, ed. *The Pitcairn Register Book, 1790–1854.* London: Society for the Promotion of Christian Knowledge, 1929.

Macdonald, Barrie. *Cinderellas of Empire: Towards a History of Kiribati and Tuvalu.* Canberra: Australian National University Press, 2001.

Mackay, Alexander. "A Compendium of Official Documents." New Zealand Electronic Text Center. http://www.nzetc.org/tm/scholarly/tei-Mac 01Comp.html.

Malua Theological College. "Malua Theological College History." http://www.malua.edu.ws/ History/tabid/4285/language/en-NZ/Default. aspx.

"Mandated Territory." *www.pngbual.com/300social_sciences/_/EOLmadates.pdf.*

Marcus, George E. "Contemporary Tonga." In *Friendly Islands: A History of Tonga,* edited by Noel Rutherford. Melbourne: Oxford University Press, 1977.

Maretu and Marjorie Tuainekure Crocombe. *Cannibals and Converts: Radical Change in the Cook Islands.* Suva: Institute of Pacific Studies in Association with the Ministry of Education, Rarotonga, 1983.

Masterman, Sylvia. *The Origins of International Rivalry in Samoa, 1845–1884.* London: Allen and Unwin, 1934.

Matson. "Matson's History." http://www.matson. com/corporate/about_us/history.html.

Mattsen, Elaine. "Norfolk Island Mutiny." http:// newsgroups.derkeiler.com/pdf/Archive/Soc/soc.g enealogy.ireland/2006–12/msg00012.pdf.

Maude, H.E. *Slavers in Paradise: The Peruvian Labour Trade in Polynesia, 1862–64.* Canberra: Australian National University Press, 1981.

Mawer, Granville Allen. *Ahab's Trade: The Saga of South Sea Whaling.* New York: St. Martin's, 1999.

McAdie, Alexander G. "The Laying of the American Trans-Pacific Cable," *History of the Atlantic Cable and Underseas Communications.* http:// www.atlantic-cable.com/Article/1902/jurnElec /index.htm.

McCarthy, John. "Smith, Sir Ross Macpherson (1892–1922)." *Australian Dictionary of Biography.* http://adbonline.anu.au/biogs.A110726.htm.

McCarthy, Terry. "The Stolen Generation." *Time,* October 2, 2000, p. 28.

McNab, Robert. *From Tasman to Marsden: A History of Northern New Zealand from 1642 to 1818.* Dunedin: J. Wilkie, 1914. New Zealand Electronic Text Center. http://www.nzetc.org/tm/ scholarly/tel-McNTasm.html.

_____. *Murihiku: A History of the South Island of New Zealand and the Islands Adjacent and Lying to the South, from 1642 to 1835.* Wellington: Whitcombe and Tombs, 1909. http://www.nzetc. org/tm/scholarly/tei-McNMuri.html.

McRobie, Alan. "The Politics of Volatility." In *The Oxford History of New Zealand,* 2nd ed., edited by Geoffrey W. Rice. Auckland: Oxford University Press, 1992.

Melville, Herman. *Typee, Omoo, Mardi.* New York: Library of America, 1982.

Michener, James A., and A. Grove Day. *Rascals in Paradise.* Greenwich, CT: Fawcett Crest, 1957.

Millar, T.B. *Australia in Peace and War: External Relations, 1788–1977.* New York: Palgrave MacMillan, 1978.

Moore, Clive. "Good-bye, Queensland: Australian South Sea Islander Community and Deportation, 1901–1908." *New Federalist* no. 4 (December 2000): 22–29.

Moorhead, Alan. *The Fatal Impact.* New York: A Dell Book, 1966.

Morris, Grant. "Chief Justice James Pendergast and the Treaty of Waitangi: Judicial Attitudes." www.legalhistorian.org/conferences/.

Morris, Richard B., ed. *Encyclopedia of American History.* New York: Harper and Row, 1965.

Mortensen, Reid. "Slaving in Australian Courts." *Journal of South Pacific Law* 4, 2000. http://www. paclii.org/journals/fJSPL/vol04/7.shtml.

Motteler, Lee S. *Pacific Island Names: A Map and Name Guide to the New Pacific.* 2nd ed. Honolulu: Bishop Museum Press, 2006.

Muckle, Adrian. "The War of 1917 in New Caledonia." *Quarterly Bulletin,* Australian National University Research School of Pacific and Asian Studies vol. 5, no. 1 (March 2004):12–13.

Multilingual Archive. "Overseas Departments and Territories of France." http://wally.worldlingo. com/ma/enwiki/en/Overseas_departments_and_ territories_of_France.

Mulvaney, John, and Johan Kamminga. *Prehistory of Australia*. Sydney: Allen and Unwin, 1999.

Mundus. "Council for World Mission Archive." Mundus: Gateway to Missionary Collections in the United Kingdom. http://www.mundus.ac.uk/cats/4/249.htm.

_____. "Melanesian Mission." http://www.mundus.ac.uk/cats/4/909.htm.

Murray, Reverend Thomas Boyles. *Pitcairn: The Island, the People, and the Pastor*. London: Society for Promoting Christian Knowledge, 1860.

Museum of Australian Democracy. "Constitution Act 1856." *Documenting a Democracy: Australia's Story*. http://foundingdocs.gov.au/item-did-6-aid-6-pid-6.html. http://www.everythingperu/com/constitutional-province-of-.

_____. "Pacific Island Labourers Act 1901." *Documenting a Democracy: Australia's Story*. http://foundingdocs.gov.au/item-did-15.html.

Mytinger, Caroline. *Headhunting in the Solomon Islands*. London: Macmillan, 1942.

Nation Master. "John Macarthur (Wool Pioneer)." http://www.nationmaster.com/encyclopedia/John-Macarthur-(wool-pioneer).

_____. "Moai." http://www.statemaster.com/encyclopedia/moai.

_____. "Niihau." http://www.nationmaster.com/encyclopedia/Niihau.

_____. "Robinson Crusoe Island." http://www.statemaster.com/encyclopedia/Robinson-Crusoe-Island.

_____. "Wallis and Futuna." http://www.statemaster.com/encyclopedia/wallis-and-futuna.

Neatorama. "Tattoo Timeline 1802." http://www.neatorama.com/2008/02/21/tattoo_timeline/.

New Caledonia. "1878: The Great Kanak Rebellion." CroixduSud.info. http://www.croixdusud.info/hist_eng/hist_1878_eng.php.

_____. "Penal Colony, New Caledonia." CroixduSud.info. http://www.croixdusud.info/hist_eng/hist_bagne_eng.php.

New History Online. "Takaroto Potatau Matutaera Tawhiao." http://www.nzhistory.net/people/takaroto-poatau-mautuera-tawhiao.

Newbury, Colin. *Tahiti Nui: Change and Survival in French Polynesia, 1767–1945*. Honolulu: University of Hawaii Press, 1980.

New Zealand Electronic Text Center. "Admiral Jules Sébastien César Dumont D'urville 1790–1842." http://www.nzetc.org/tm/scholarly/name-207864.html.

New Zealand Government. "Maori Ethnicity in Households." Statistics New Zealand. http://www.stats.govt.nz/browse_for_stats/people_and_communities/Households/housing-profiles-maori-ethnicity-in-households/household-composition.aspx.

New Zealand History Online. "Musket Wars." http://www.nzhistory.net.nz/war/new-zealands-19th-century-wars/the-musket-wars.

_____. "Nineteen Eighteen Flu Pandemic." http://www.nzhistory.net.nz/culture/influenza-pandemic-1918.

_____. "Obtaining Land — The Treaty in Practice." http://www.nzhistory.net.nz/politics/treaty/the-treaty-in-practice/obtaining-land.

_____. "Overview — NZ in the 1920s." http://www.nzhistory.net.nz/culture/1920s/overview.

_____. "Resistance to Conscription — Maori and the First World War." http://www.nzhistory.net.nz/war/maori-in-first-world-war/resistence-to-conscription.

_____. "Waikato-Tainui Claim." http://www.newzealandhistory.net/politics/treaty/the-treaty-in-practice-waikato-tainu.

New Zealand Ministry for Culture and Heritage. *Dictionary of New Zealand Biography*. http://www.teara.govt.nz.

New Zealand Ministry of Foreign Affairs and Trade. "French Polynesia." http://www.mfat.govt.nz/Countries/Pacific/French-Polynesia.php.

_____. "New Caledonia." http://www.mfat.govt.nz/Countries/Pacific/New-Caledonia.php.

New Zealand Ministry of Justice. "Supreme Courts of New Zealand." http://justice.govt.nz/courts/the_supreme_court.

New Zealand Register of Archives and Manuscripts. "Western Pacific High Commission." http://www.nram.org.nz.

New Zealand Tourism Guide. "Auckland, New Zealand — History." http://www.tourism.net.nz/new-zealand/about-new-zealand/regions/auckland/history.html.

Nicole, Robert. *The Word, the Pen, and the Pistol: Literature and Power in Tahiti*. Albany, NY: SUNY Press, 2001.

Nicolson, Robert B. *The Pitcairners*. Sydney: Angus and Robertson, 1965.

Niumy, Michael A., ed. *South Pacific Islands Legal Systems*. Honolulu: University of Hawaii Press, 1993.

Norfolk Island, the Website. "Bloodless Genocide: A Political History of the Pitcairn People in Norfolk Island from 1856 to 1996. http://www.pitcairners.org/bloodless_genocide2.html.

Nouvelle Calédonie. "Isle of Pines." http://www.nouvellecaledonietourisme-sud.com.

Novara-Expedition. *The World Circumnavigation of H.M. Frigate Novara 1857–1859*. http://www.novara-expedition.org/en/e_geschichte.html.

O'Brien, Patty. "Think of Me as a Woman: Queen Pomare of Tahiti and Anglo-French Imperial Contest in the 1840s Pacific." *Gender and History* 18, no. 1 (November 2006): 108–32.

Okihiro, Gary Y. *Island World: A History of Hawai'i and the United States*. Berkeley: University of California Press, 2008.

Old Hobart Town News. "Trucanini's Story of Herself." http://oldhobarttownnews.blogspot/2011/10/trucanini's-story-of-herself.

Oliver, Douglas, L. *Polynesia in Early Historic Times.* Honolulu: Bess Press, 2002.

_____. *The Pacific Islands.* Rev. ed. Honolulu: University of Hawaii Press, 1983.

Orange, Claudia. "The Maori People and the British Crown, 1769–1840." In *The Oxford Illustrated History of New Zealand,* edited by Keith Sinclair, pp. 21–48. Auckland: Oxford University Press, 1990.

Owens, J.M.R. "New Zealand Before Annexation." In *The Oxford History of New Zealand,* edited by W.H. Oliver and B.R. Williams. Wellington: Oxford University Press, 1981.

Pacific Union College. "Mangareva." *Pitcairn Island Encyclopedia.* Pitcairn Island Study Center. http://library.puc.edu/pitcairn/pitcairn/encyclopedia3.shtml

Pararas-Carayannis, George. "The Tsunami Page." http://www.drgeorgepc.com/Tsunami1998PNG.html

Parliament of Australia. *Parliamentary Handbook of the Commonwealth of Australia for the 42nd Parliament: Referendums and Plebiscites, 2003–06–10.* http://parlinfo.aph.gov.au/parlInfo/download/handbook/newhandbook/2008–12–19/toc_pdf_repeat/Part%205%20-%20Referendums%20and%20Plebiscites.pdf;fileType=application%2Fpdf.

Parliament of Samoa. http://www.parliament.gov.ws.

Parry, J.H. *The Spanish Seaborne Empire.* New York: Alfred A. Knopf, 1966.

Parsonson, Ann. "The Pursuit of Mana." In *The Oxford History of New Zealand,* edited by W.H. Oliver and B.R. Williams, pp. 140–67. Wellington: Oxford University Press, 1981.

Pelta, Kathy. *Rediscovering Easter Island.* Minneapolis: Lerner, 2001.

Philbrick, Nathaniel. *Sea of Glory: America's Voyage of Discovery: the U.S. Exploring Expedition 1838–1842.* New York: Viking, 2003.

"Pitcairn's Island," *Illustrated London News,* November 6, 1852m pp. 373–4.

Playford, Phillip E. "Hartog, Dirk (1580–1621)." *Australian Dictionary of Biography.* http://adb.anu.edu.au/biography/hartog-dirk-12968.

Postnikov, Alexey V. "The First Russian Voyage Around the World and Its Influence on the Exploration and Development of Russian America." http://www.sochistdisc.org/2005_articles/postnikov_article.htm.

Prendergast, Patricia A. "Chalmers, James (1841–1901)." *Australian Dictionary of Biography.* National Centre of Biography, Australian National University. http://adb.anu.edu.au/biography-/chalmers-james-3187/text4781.

The Prow. "New Zealand Company." http://www.theprow.org.nz/new-zealand-company/.

Quanchi, Max, and John Robson. *Historical Dictionary of the Discovery and Exploration of the Pacific Islands.* Lanham, MD: Scarecrow Press, 2005.

Raeside, J.D. "Thierry, Charles Philippe Hippolyte de," *Dictionary of New Zealand Biography www.dnzb.govt.nz.*

Ralston, Caroline. *Grass Huts and Warehouses: Pacific Beach Communities of the Nineteenth Century.* Honolulu: University Press of Hawaii, 1976.

Rayment, Leigh. "Antoine Raymond Joseph de Bruni D'Entrecasteaux." Discoverer's Web. http://www.win.tue.nl/~engels/discovery/entrecast.html.

Reed, A. H. *The Story of New Zealand.* New York: Roy Publishers, 1957.

Resture, Jane. "Bishop Patteson." http://www.janeresture.com/patteson/index.htm.

_____. "Fakaofu Island Tokelau." http://www.janeresture.com/tijekay_islands/fakaofo.htm.

_____. "Gardner Island, Phoenix Group." http://www.janeresture.com/kiribati-phoenix-group/gardner.htm.

_____. "Kanakas and the Cane Fields." http://www.janeresture.com/kanakas/index.htm.

_____. "Kanaks and the Labor Trade." http://www.janeresture.com/kanaks/index/htm.

_____. "Loyalty Islands." http://janeresture.com/loyalty/index.htm.

_____. "Micronesia: Christmas Island History." http://www.janeresture.com/kiribati_line/christmas_island.htm.

_____. "Midway Island History." http://www.janeresture.com/midway/.

_____. "Nassau Island." http://janeresture.com/nassau/.

_____. "Rose Atoll." http://www.janeresture.com/rose/.

_____. "Swains Island." http://www.janeresture.com/tokelauislands.swains.htm.

Richards, Rhys. "The Earliest Foreign Visitors and the Depopulation of Rapa Iti, 1824–30." *Journal de la Société des Océanistes* 118, no. 1 (2004): 3–10.

Richardson, Len. "Parties and Political Change." In *The Oxford History of New Zealand,* edited by W.H. Oliver and B.R. Williams, pp. 201–29. Wellington: Oxford University Press, 1981.

Ricklefs, M.C. *A History of Modern Indonesia since c. 1300.* Stanford: Stanford University Press, 1993.

Ridley, Matt. "Humans: Why They Triumphed." *Wall Street Journal,* May 22, 2010.

Robertson, H.A. *Erromango: The Martyr Isle.* London: Hodder and Stoughton, 1902.

Rodger, N.A.M. *The Wooden World: An Anatomy of the Georgian Navy.* New York: W.W. Norton, 1986.

Rosenberg, Matt. "Guano Island Act." About.Com: Geography. http://geography.about.com/od/politicalgeography/a/guanoisland.htm.

Rosenblum, Mort. *Mission to Civilize: The French Way*. New York: Anchor Press, Doubleday, 1988.

Rutherford, Noel. *Shirley Baker and the King of Tonga*. Wellington: Oxford University Press, 1971.

Rutherford, Noel, ed., as told to by Ve'ehala and Tupou Posesi Finua. *Friendly Islands: A History of Tonga*. Melbourne: Oxford University Press, 1977.

Rutledge, Martha. "Patteson, John Coleridge (1827–1871)." Australian Dictionary of Biography. http://adb.anu.edu.au/biography/patteson-john-coleridge-4376.

Ryan, Lyndall. *The Aboriginal Tasmanians*. Crows Nest, NSW: Allen and Unwin, 1996.

Sache, Ivan, and Pascal Vagnat. "New Caledonia." http://flagspot.net/flags.nc.html.

Salmond, Anne. *Aphrodite's Island: The European Discovery of Tahiti*. Berkeley: University of California Press, 2009.

Scarr, Deryck. *Fiji: A Short History*. Laie, Hawaii: Institute for Polynesian Studies, Brigham Young University, 1984.

Schmitt, Robert C. "Urbanization in French Polynesia." *Land Economics* 38, no. 1 (February 1962): 71–75.

Schmitt, Robert C., and Eleanor Nordyke. "Death in Hawaii: The Epidemic of 1848–1849." http://levols.library.manoa.hawaii.edu.

Search.com. "Rimatara." http://www.search.com/reference/Rimatara.

"Shelled by French Warships,"*New York Times*, February 21, 1897, p. 1.

Sherry, Frank. *Pacific Passions: The European Struggle for Power in the Great Ocean in the Age of Exploration*. New York: William Morrow, 1994.

Shineberg, Dorothy. *The People Trade: Pacific Island Laborers and New Caledonia, 1865–1900*. Honolulu: University of Hawaii Press, 1999.

_____. *They Came for Sandalwood: A Case Study in the Sandalwood Trade in the South-west Pacific, 1830–65*. Melbourne: Melbourne University Press, 1967.

Siler, Julia Flynn. *Lost Kingdom: Hawaii's Last Queen, the Sugar Kings, and America's First Imperial Adventure*. New York: Atlantic Monthly Press, 2012.

Smith, Philippa Mein. *A Concise History of New Zealand*. Cambridge: Cambridge Concise Histories, 2005.

Smith, S. Percy. "The Migration to the Chatham Islands." *History and Traditions of the Maoris of the West Coast, North Island of New Zealand, Prior to 1840*. New Plymouth: Polynesian Society, 1910. Digitized version at New Zealand Electronic Text Center. http://www.nzetc.org/tm/scholarly/tei-SmiHist-t1-body1-d21-d8.html.

Smith, Vanessa. *Literary Culture and the Pacific: Nineteenth Century Textual Encounters*. Cambridge: Cambridge University Press, 1998.

Snijders, Jan. "Marist Studies." *A Piety Able to Cope*. www.mariststudies.org/docs/APAC90.

Snow, Philip, and Stefanie Waine. *The People from the Horizon: An Illustrated History of the Europeans among the South Sea Islanders*. Oxford: Phaidon, 1979.

Sollier, J.P. "Pierre Chanel." New Advent. http://www.newadvent.org/cathen/11769a.htm.

Sorrenson, M.P.K. "Maori and Pakeha." In *The Oxford History of New Zealand*, edited by W.H. Oliver and B.R. Williams. Wellington: Oxford University Press, 1981.

_____. "Maori and Pakeha." In *Australia, New Zealand and the Pacific Islands since the First World War*, edited by William S. Livingston and Wm. Roger Louis. Austin and London: University of Texas, 1978.

Souhami, Diana. *Selkirk's Island: The True and Strange Adventures of the Real Robinson Crusoe*. San Diego: A Harvest Book, Harcourt, Inc., 2002.

South-Pole.com. "Jules-Sebastien-Cesar Dumont d'Urville, 1790–1842." www.south-pole.com/p0000077.htm.

Stanley, David. *Fiji*. 7th ed. Emeryville, CA: Moon, 2004.

_____. *South Pacific Handbook*. 7th ed. Emeryville, CA: Moon, 2000.

Stanner, W.E.H. "The Australian Aborigines." In *Australia, New Zealand and the Pacific Islands since the First World War*, edited by William S. Livingston and Wm Roger Louis. Austin and London: University of Texas, 1979.

Stevenson, Robert Louis. *A Footnote to History: Eight Years of Trouble in Samoa*. New York: Charles Scribner's Sons, 1900.

Stewart, Donald. "The Dayspring." Emalus Library Online Documents Collection — Vanuatu. http://www.vanuatu.usp.ac.fj/library/Online/Vanuatu.stewart.htm.

Stewart, William. *Admirals of the World: A Biographical Dictionary, 1500 to the Present*. Jefferson, NC: McFarland, 2009.

Stone, Sharman N., ed. *Aborigines in White Australia: A Documentary History of the Attitudes Affecting Official Policy and the Australian Aborigine, 1697–1973*. Melbourne: Heinemann Educational Australia, 1974.

Suarez, Thomas. *Early Mapping of the Pacific: The Epic Story of Seafarers*. Singapore: Periplus Editions, 2004.

Suggs, Robert C. *The Hidden Worlds of Polynesia: The Chronicle of an Archaeological Expedition to*

Nuku Hiva in the Marquesas Islands. New York: Harcourt, Brace and World, 1962.

Sunio, Sheena. "Reverend William Richards." *Hotspots Hawaii.* http://hotspothawaii.com/nalostuff/May96/RICHARDS/html.

Sweetman, Jack. *American Naval History: An Illustrated Chronology.* Annapolis: Naval Institute Press, 2002.

Sydney Gazette. "Death of Captain Croker." *Sydney Gazette,* 25 July 1840. http://members.iinet.net.au/~nickred/newspaper/walter_croker.htm.

Tahiti 1. "History." http://www.tahiti1.com/en/indentity/history.htm.

Tate, Merze. *The United States and the Hawaiian Kingdom: A Political History.* New Haven: Yale University Press, 1965.

Taylor, A.J.P. *Germany's First Bid for Colonies, 1884–1885.* New York: W.W. Norton, 1970.

Te Ara — The Encyclopedia of New Zealand. *Encyclopaedia of New Zealand, 1966.* Edited by A.H. McLintock, originally published in 1966. http://www.teara.govt.nz/en/1966/.

Think Quest. "Parker Ranch." http://library.thinkquest.org/J0111103/bigisland/parkerranch.html.

Thomas, Nicholas. *Cook: The Extraordinary Voyages of Captain James Cook.* New York: Walker, 2003.

Thompson, J.P. "The Islands of the Pacific." *National Geographic* 40, no. 6 (December 1921): 543–58.

Thompson, Virginia, and Richard Adloff. *The French Pacific Islands.* Berkeley: University of California Press, 1971.

Thorndon, Pipitea. "1839: The New Zealand Company Arrives in Wellington." National Library of New Zealand. www.natlib.govt.nz/collections/online-exhibitions/pipitea-thorndon.

Torres Strait Regional Authority. "History of Torres Strait to 1879." http://www.tsra.gov.au/the-torres-strait/general-history.aspx.

Turner, Ann. *Historical Dictionary of Papua New Guinea.* 2nd ed. Lanham, MD: Scarecrow, 2001.

U.K. Parliament. "Pacific Islanders' Protection Act 1872." *Hansard 1803–2005.* http://hansard.millbanksystems.com/acts/pacific-islanders-protection-act-1872.

U.S. Census Bureau. "Hawaii: ACS Demographics and Housing Estimate 2008." American Factfinder. http://factfinder2.census.gov/faces/tableservices/jsf/pages/productview.xhtml?pid=ACS_08_1YR_CP5&prodType=table.

U.S. Department of State. "Background Note: Samoa." http://www.state.gov/r/pa/ei/bgn/1842.htm.

_____. "Background Note: Solomon Islands." http://www.state.gov/r/pa/ei/bgn/2799.htm.

_____. "Papua New Guinea." http://www.state.gov/j/drl/rls/hrrpt/2006/78787.htm.

_____. "Background Note: Solomon Islands." http://www.state.gov/r/pa/ei/bgn/2799.htm.

U.S. National Center for Infectious Diseases. "Modeling the Impact of Pandemic Influenza on Pacific Islands." The Free Library. http://www.thefreelibrary.com/Modeling+the+impact+of+pandemic+influenza+on+pacific+islands.-a0129363014.

Urbanowicz, Charles F. "John Thomas, Tongans and Tonga!" http://www.csuchico.edu/~curbanowicz/Pub_Papers/John_Thomas.html.

Van Trease, Howard. *The Politics of Land in Vanuatu: From Colony to Independence.* Suva: Institute of Pacific Studies, University of the South Pacific, 1987.

Vinayvalpo.com. "Valparaiso, Chile." http://www.vinayvalpo.com/valparaiso/about.html.

Wahlroos, Sven. *Mutiny and Romance in the South Seas: A Companion to the Bounty Adventure.* Topsfield, MA: Salem House, 1989.

Waitangi Tribunal. "Chatham Islands." www.waitangitribunal.govt.nz.

Walker, James Blackhouse. *Early Tasmanians: Papers Read Before the Royal Society of Tasmania during the Years 1888 to 1889.* Hobart, Tasmania: The Society, 1902.

Walker, Ranganui. "Maori People Since 1950." In *The Oxford History of New Zealand,* edited by Geoffrey W. Rice. 2nd ed. Auckland: Oxford University Press, 1992.

Ward, John M. "Goodenough, James Graham (1830–1875)." *Australian Dictionary of Biography.* http://adb.anu.edu.au/biography/goodenough-james-graham-3630.

Ward, Paul. "Jules Sébastian César Dumont D'Urville: *L'Astrolabe* and *Zélée* 1837–1840." Cool Antarctica. http://www.coolantarctica.com/Antarctica%20fact%20file/History/antarctic_whos_who_dumont_durville_astrolabe_zele.htm.

Wayfaring Travel Guide. "Rotuma." http://www.wayfaring.info/2009/07/31/rotuma/.

Welsh, Frank. *Australia: A New History of the Great Southern Land.* Woodstock and New York: Overlook, 2006.

Wendt, Albert. "Guardians and Wards: A Study of the Origins, Causes and the First Two Years of the Mau in Western Samoa." New Zealand Electronic Text Center. http://www.nzetc.org/tm/scholarly/tei-WenGua.html.

West, Francis. "Stanley, Owen." *Australian Dictionary of Biography.* http://adb.anu.edu.au/biography/stanley-owen-2692.

Wheeler, Tony, Nancy Keller, Jeff Williams. *New Zealand: A Travel Survival Kit.* Hawthorn, Victoria: Lonely Planet, 1977.

Whitehouse, Olwyn. "Nelson — New Zealand Bound." Personal Web page at http://freepages.

genealogy.rootsweb.ancestry.com/~nzbound/nelson.htm.

Whitmore, Robbie. "The Colonisation of New Zealand: French Colonists in Akaroa, South Island." *New Zealand in History*. Personal Web page. http://history-nz.org/colonisation4.html.

_____. "The Moriori: Early Settlers of the Chatham Islands." *New Zealand in History*. Personal Web page. http://history-nz.org/moriori.html.

Whittaker, J.L., N.G. Nash, J.F. Hockey, and R.J. Lacey. *Documents and Readings in New Guinea History, Prehistory to 1889*. Gladesville, NSW: Jacaranda, 1975.

Wiley-VCH. *Ullman's Agrochemicals*. Wiesbaden: Wiley, John & Sons, 2007.

Williams, John A. *A Narrative of Missionary Enterprises in the South Sea Islands*. London: George Baxter, 1838.

WIPO. "Tonga: Act of Constitution." www.wipo.int.wipolex/en/details.jsp?d=5409.

Wisniewski, Richard A. *Hawaii: The Territorial Years, 1900–1959*. Honolulu: Pacific Basin Enterprises, 1984.

_____. *The Rise and Fall of the Hawaiian Kingdom*. Honolulu: Pacific Basin Enterprises, 1979.

Withey, Lynne. *Voyages of Discovery: Captain Cook and the Exploration of the Pacific*. New York: William Morrow, 1987.

World at War. "French Polynesia 1903–1948: French Polynesia Timeline." http://www.schudak.de/timelines/frenchpolynesia1903–1948.html.

_____. "New Hebrides 1606–1948: New Hebrides Timeline." http://www.schudak.de/timelines/newhebrides1606–1948.html.

_____. "Samoa 1898–1951: Samoa Timeline." http://www.schudak.de/timelines/samoa1898–1951.html.

_____. "Wallis and Futuna 1616–1961: Wallis and Futuna Timeline." http://www.schudak.de/timelines/wallis&futuna1616–1961.html.

Wood, A.H., and Elizabeth Wood Ellem. "Queen Salote Tupou III." In *Friendly Islands: A History of Tonga*, edited by Noel Rutherford. Melbourne: Oxford University Press, 1977.

Woodward, Ralph Lee, Jr. *Robinson Crusoe's Island: A History of the Juan Fernandez Islands*. Chapel Hill, NC: University of North Carolina Press, 1969.

Wright, Gordon. *France in Modern Times*. 4th ed. New York: W.W. Norton, 1987.

Yuan-chao, Tung. "Chinese in Tahiti." In *Encyclopedia of Diasporas*, edited by Melvin R. Ember, Carol R. Ember, and Ian Skoggard. Vol 2. New York: Springer Science and Business Media, 2003.

Zuljan, Ralph. "First Taranaki War, 1860–61." *Armed Conflict Events Data*. http://www.onwar.com/aced/nation/nap/newz/ftaranaki1860.htm.

Index

Numbers in **_bold italics_** indicate pages with photographs.